Sociological Theory

Sociological Theory

Volume 3

Development Since the 1960s

Richard Münch

Nelson-Hall Publishers
Chicago

Library of Congress Cataloging-in-Publication Data
(Revised for vol. 3)

Münch, Richard, 1945-
   Sociological theory.

   Includes bibliographical references and indexes.
   Contents: v. 3. Development since the 1960s.
   1. Sociology — Philosophy.   2. Sociology — History.
HM24.M838   1993   301'.01   92-39833
ISBN 0-8304-1342-1 (v. 3)
ISBN 0-8304-1394-4 (case contains three volumes)

Manufactured in the United States of America

10   9   8   7   6   5   4   3   2   1

™ The paper used in this book meets the minimum requirements of American National Standard for Information Sciences—Permanence of Paper for Printed Library Materials, ANSI Z39.48-1984.

Contents

PREFACE

THESE VOLUMES have been written for students, teachers, scholars, and researchers. They emerged from many years of lecturing and teaching courses in sociological theory. I am therefore very much indebted to the many students who joined my classes and served as critical examiners of my presentation of sociological theories. They forced me first of all to make the greatest effort to present the theories in a way that allows students to understand their message and to critically discuss them. The reluctance of many theorists to do this leaves the teacher of a course in sociological theory with an enormous task. The favorable response of my students over many years of preparing presentations of theories in a teachable form has encouraged me to compile the results of these years of teaching in a textbook, which I hope will receive the same favorable response from many students in many theory classes.

These volumes have been written with the intention of providing texts for teaching sociological theory that overcome the weaknesses of those available to date. I endeavor to be more comprehensive in covering the whole development of sociological theory, from classical origins to contemporary debates. I have attempted to be less biased toward certain national and paradigmatical traditions in order to allow sociological theory to be taught on an international and pluralistic level. I have tried to present theories in a more systematically structured way, by revealing their core and their distinctive statements in order to allow easier access to their message. The theories are presented much more in discourse, throwing light on their more obscure aspects and on their erroneous aspects. I hope teachers will find the book as helpful for teaching sociological theory as I did the materials that eventually constituted the book.

These volumes have also been written for scholars. This work is not simply a history of social thought, but a reconstruction and continuation of sociological discourse with the aim of advancing our theoretical knowledge to a new level: constructing networks of theories by way of interparadigmatical and intertheoretical discourse. I hope that many of my colleagues will join this enterprise.

These volumes have also been written for researchers. The state of theoretical knowledge is presented in a systematically structured way, which I hope invites researchers to work with that knowledge and to relate empirical research to theoretical questions more than has been usual up to now. Their reluctance to do so was caused to a not inconsiderable degree by the often very confusing writing style of many theorists. I have tried very hard to improve upon that style of writing theory.

This project has been written with the support of many people: students, assistants, colleagues, friends, and family. Without their help the book would not have come to light. Many thanks to all of them. Special thanks go to Neil Johnson for working on the English language of this book.

For their assistance with references, preparing name and subject indices, and with word processing work, I wish to thank Susanne Gabele, Renate Kolvenbach, Christian Lahusen, Karin Rhau, and Willy Viehöver. Special thanks also go to Michael Opielka for valuable comments in the final stage of working on the manuscript.

INTRODUCTION TO VOLUME 3

THE DEVELOPMENT of sociological theory since the 1960s is characterized by renewal through reworking its classical contributions and by new
attempts at synthesis by way of interlinking the various contributions of
a plurality of paradigms. Synthesizing work is, however, no longer done by
a dominating individual theorist in an attempt to build grand theory. It is
much more a collective enterprise of competition and cooperation within
a worldwide scientific community of interrelated scholars who meet regularly at conferences. Nevertheless, the various contributions of individual
scholars to this common undertaking normally start out from their own
characteristic cores, which can be seen as concentrating on a specific field
of social action from which the other parts of the world are explored. Mostly
only the core aspect of an approach is located in a specific field of social
action, whereas other aspects stretch out to cover other fields of social action
as well. Moreover, the field of sociological theory has differentiated so much
that we now find there is more differentiation in understanding the nature
of a specific field of action. Thus we have a vast array of different views
of specific fields of social action.

I have ordered the different contributions to sociological theory in its
development since the 1960s according to a framework that sees social action
proceeding within an action space differentiated into four basic fields: the
economics of social action, with the function of opening and adaptation
to varying situations; the *politics of social action,* with the function of specification and orientation toward goal attainment; the *structure of social action,*
with the function of closing and integration as an ordered system; and the
symbolics of social action, with the function of generalization and latent

pattern maintenance within a framework of meaning (see chapter 2, volume 1; Münch 1982, 1987b). Each one of these fields has been studied in various forms with varying emphasis on its aspects or subfields and with more or less ability to stretch out to other fields of the action space.

Looking at the structure of social action, we will start with an analysis of French structuralism and its development to post-structuralism, deconstructionism, and postmodernism in the works of Claude Lévi-Strauss, Michel Foucault, Jacques Derrida, Jean Baudrillard, and Jean-François Lyotard.

The economics of social action has come under new scrutiny by the renewal of the economic approach to the social world in terms of rational choice theory. We will study this approach in the work of James S. Coleman. The Marxist view of the economics of social action has undergone new revisions since the 1960s, which we will investigate in Claus Offe's work on late capitalism and in Immanuel Wallerstein's and Terence K. Hopkins's world systems analysis.

Our understanding of the politics of social action has been improved by a variety of contributions, too. The American view of the politics of conflict as bargaining will be outlined in the works of Randall Collins and Samuel B. Bacharach with Edward J. Lawler. The French structuralist view of the politics of conflict will be pointed out in the works of Pierre Bourdieu and Alain Touraine. The British understanding of politics as class conflict will be analyzed in the work of Anthony Giddens. The German historical-genetic understanding of societal development as conflict settlement by the state's monopolization of physical force that initiates the general process of civilizing human life will be demonstrated by examining the work of Norbert Elias.

The study of the symbolics of social action has also undergone renewal by a plurality of approaches. There is the continuation of investigating the symbolic dimension of social interaction by the so-called labeling approach to deviant behavior. We will look at this development in the works of Howard S. Becker, Edwin Lemert, Richard Quinney, and Edwin M. Schur. There is also the elaboration of understanding social order as an outcome of ongoing symbolic negotiations as elaborated particularly by Anselm Strauss. Quite another view of the symbolic dimension of social action has been contributed by Lawrence Kohlberg's continuation of Piaget's cognitive-structuralist approach to studying the development of moral consciousness. The legacy of German idealism with its development toward Marxism and critical theory has been taken up and renewed in Jürgen Habermas's theory of communicative action. Finally, Niklas Luhmann's new systems theory will be treated under the heading of social action's symbolic dimension, because it originated from the German phenomenological tradition. Communication and meaning are central terms in Luhmann's theory—in a unique way, though, because of their integration into the framework of the biological theory of autopoietic systems.

Though we see these approaches to the social world as concentrating on a specific field of social action in the first instance, we will also see how they approach this field in a unique way that is shaped by its relation to other fields, and beyond that we will see how they stretch out to other fields in a more or less biased or balanced way in the process of constructing a more comprehensive theory that covers the whole action space.

After the analysis of the individual contributions made by a variety of approaches to the development of sociological theory since the 1960s, we conclude with a chapter on the network of sociological theory that has developed through all the periods since the beginnings of sociology in the nineteenth century.

PART ONE

The Structure of Social Action

THE SOCIAL AND CULTURAL WORLD AS A STRUCTURE: CLAUDE LÉVI-STRAUSS AND THE DEVELOPMENT FROM STRUCTURALISM TO POST-STRUCTURALISM AND POSTMODERNISM

OF THE classical founding fathers, it was Emile Durkheim (1895/1973a, 1912/1968) who made the strongest claim for the *sui generis* objective reality of social structure with his teaching of the social fact. He laid down a basic idea that continued to guide French thought for the following decades, whether in the positive sense that other scholars sought to confirm it or in the negative sense that they rejected it or rebelled against it. Structure and rationality versus spontaneity and power is a basic theme in French discourse. The school of thought that emerged along the structure side of this battle is what we call "structuralism."

Toward Structuralism

A first move in this direction was made by the linguist Ferdinand de Saussure (1916; for translation, see 1966), who applied Durkheim's conception of the social fact to language. He distinguishes between "*langue*" and "*parole*": *langue* refers to the structure of language that is a firm social fact underlying any single act of speaking or writing and giving this act a regular form common to all acts of speaking and writing. The act of speaking and writing and its outcome in the form of sentences, its concrete actuality, is what he calls *parole*; it is what a speaker makes of the common form in everyday actions. These are the unique acts of speaking and writing carried out by each person at a singular place and time. *Langue* is universal and uniform within a language community; *parole* is variable, changing from one time to another, one place to another, and one person to another. *Langue* has a structure as a formal system of words and their interrelationships that doesn't change from situation to situation. That structure is revealed

3

in synchronic studies, whereas change on the level of *parole* is investigated in diachronic studies.

Marcel Mauss, a nephew, coauthored a study with Durkheim on primitive classification (Durkheim and Mauss, 1901–1902; for translation, see 1963). Taking up and following his uncle's program, Mauss pointed out the normative structure of social exchange in his study on *The Gift* (Mauss, 1923–1924; for translation, see 1967). He first identified a form of gift exchange that can be called "total prestation." Here we have firmly established ties between tribal clans where exchange is exclusively the exchange of gifts. One party brings a gift to another party, which implies an *obligation* to be reciprocated at a later time. This obligation is normative in character, rooted in the community. Its violation calls for unanimous disapproval and loss of reputation. On the other hand, giving and receiving gifts brings reputation within the community, as exemplified in the Melanesian *kula* ring. Giving and receiving the ceremonial shells fills giver and receiver with *mana,* which gives emotional energy, public attention, and thus reputation. In distinction to this completely normative gift exchange, the "two-level exchange" founds the utilitarian exchange of goods on the normative exchange of gifts. Parties first exchange gifts, thus establishing trust, and then go on to exchange goods in utilitarian terms. The "potlatch" is a type of exchange where parties accumulate reputation by making wasteful gifts, such as throwing lavish parties, which also obliges the others to reciprocate and may result in their ruin or inability to reciprocate and thus in their total submission to the rich gift giver. In the "utilitarian exchange," what is given and what is accepted is based on economic calculation; however, social ties establish a common ground for trustful exchange.

The Elementary Structures of Kinship

Structuralism as a distinctive approach to social reality was made prominent by the anthropological studies of Claude Lévi-Strauss (Leach, 1974; Lemert, 1979, 1981; Kurzweil, 1980). It began to dominate French thought in the 1960s. In his first major work, *The Elementary Structures of Kinship* (Lévi-Strauss, 1947; for translation, see 1969a), Lévi-Strauss pointed out that the basic structure of tribal societies is constituted by the ties of kinship. There are definite rules of intermarriage between families, rules for exchanging women. This can take place in short cycles of immediate intermarriage between two families or in long cycles that bind together a whole set of families indirectly. The rules may prescribe matrilateral cross-cousin marriage, patrilateral cross-cousin marriage, or intermarriage between certain tribal sections in general, or the rules may just close out certain types of marriage. What makes human society a distinct type ranking above animal proto-societies is the institutionalization of the incest taboo. This forces people to marry across the boundaries of their family, and thus marriage becomes the tie that binds together larger systems of tribal society in relationships of solidarity. By giving away women to other families, a family creates obligations of reciprocation. The more one can give away, the more obligations of reciprocation are created. Other families become dependent on it. In this way a first form of aristocracy emerges, leading up to the military state, which replaces the kinship-based tribal society.

The Elementary Structure of Mythologies

According to Lévi-Strauss's study on kinship, relationships of solidarity make up the core structure of society from which any other phenomenon can be derived. In his later studies on tribal mythologies, he maintained the structuralist position but switched to a more ideational view. In a series of studies from *The Savage Mind* (Lévi-Strauss, 1962; for translation, see 1966) via *The Raw and the Cooked* (Lévi-Strauss, 1964; for translation, see 1969b), *From Honey to Ashes* (Lévi-Strauss, 1967; for translation, see 1973), and *The Origin of Table Manners* (Lévi-Strauss, 1968; for translation, see 1978) to *The Naked Man* (Lévi-Strauss, 1971; for translation, see 1981), he worked out the basic structure of tribal mythologies, pointing out their common logic by comparison. His position in these studies was to explain everything else that happens in a society as a derivation from the basic structure of such mythologies. They represent a code that, as the deep structure, underlies any actual thought, speech, and action on the surface of societal life. The most fundamental code would take the form of binary oppositions that could be put into a computer in order to bring about those thoughts and actions that are possible within that code by computer simulation.

Lévi-Strauss's movement from the rules of intermarriage and the relationships of solidarity that are constituted by them to the code of mythologies has to be attributed to the following reasons: The rules of intermarriage are concrete prescriptions of actions. They establish a one-to-one relationship between norm and action, and they prescribe definitely which concrete obligation on the part of Alter results from which action by Ego. Thus, working out such rules of exchange provides us with an instrument for understanding and explaining what happens and for predicting what will happen. However, this remains confined to those actions that are indeed covered by rules of exchange. There are, however, other actions that occur in societies, show a greater variation, and are not regulated by the rules of exchange. Revealing the social structure of kinship ties does not help us to understand them.

It is here that knowledge about the social structure of social ties shows its limitations and where Lévi-Strauss moves toward studying a deeper and therefore wider ranging structure that covers a greater number of social activities: the code of mythologies.

Inevitably, this is also a step toward greater vagueness in what can be derived from the deep structure. The relationship between a symbolic code and any concrete thought, speech, or action is a one-to-many relationship, that is, a certain idea that makes up part of a code always covers a wide range of activities and gives them an identity. Whenever we want to advance knowledge by this method, it cannot occur by reading a simple causal model into the code-action relationship. It doesn't make sense to expect such studies to be able to explain and predict distinct actions in terms of codes in a causal sense. Indeed, the reverse is the case. Structuralist studies of codes allow us to derive a common identity from many different actions. They also allow analyses on the level of deep structures. A code provides identity only as long as it preserves consistency. As long as people are devoted to maintaining an identity in their action we will see them working on consistency by assimilating what has affinity and rejecting what appears too remote. Inasmuch as such a code has been firmly established it allows us to predict *forms* of thought, speech, and action by way of consistency with the *form* of the code but not their concrete substance. We can make derivations from one formal statement to another one because the one is accompanied by the other in the formal code. For example, we can predict how the member of a religious community will generally define and evaluate certain events according to his or her belief. Alternatively, we can predict how a Marxist would interpret improvements of social welfare within capitalism, namely, as activities designed to maintain the system, because of our knowledge of the code of Marxist thought. Or we can explain why racial discrimination could not be maintained *as legitimate* in the United States, though a great proportion of the white majority would still have an interest in maintaining it. It could not be maintained *as legitimate* because that is inconsistent with the code of the United States Constitution.

These examples show that there is nothing mystical about structuralism and that we can make good use of it as long as we have a clear understanding of its strong and its weak sides and don't make claims for it or demands upon it that cannot be satisfied. First, there is the social structuralism of Lévi-Strauss's kinship studies. This type of structuralism allows us to understand why certain concrete actions provoke other concrete actions. This is particularly appropriate for relatively closed, simple societies and closed social milieus where a great deal of behavior is indeed regulated by concrete rules. It is no longer adequate where behavior is much more guided by general codes, interests, and power. On the other hand, we have cultural structuralism that studies the structure of symbolic codes. This is adequate for understanding the common identity and meaning of a variety of thought, speech, and action and the process of derivation, consistency production, assimilation, and rejection occurring within that code on the level of deep structure. This type of structuralism fails, though, whenever we want to explain and understand action guided by concrete rules, power, and interest. Yet one must realize that it is completely inappropriate to assess the merits of such an approach according to the criteria of one-to-one causal relationships.

Summary

1. The form and meaning of any single act is determined by being a part of an underlying social structure or cultural code.
2. A social structure relates actions in one-to-one relationships to each other.
3. A cultural code relates cultural signs and activities in one-to-many relationships to each other.
4. A code determines what elements can be assimilated by each other and what elements reject each other.

Critical Assessment

Social structuralism allows us to understand and explain actions that occur within closed social communities or milieux. It does not allow us to explain activities outside these boundaries that are guided by cultural symbols, power, or interests. Nor does it allow us to explain the production, reproduction, and transformation of structures, because these are caused by the penetration of symbols, power, and interests into social communities.

Cultural structuralism helps us to understand the constitution of a common form and meaning in a variety of actions and the tendencies for consistency to be produced by way of assimilation and rejection in cultural systems. It does not help explain action determined by concrete norms, power, and interests. Accordingly, it does not help explain the production, reproduction, and transformation of cultural codes by their interpenetration with action guided by concrete norms, power, or interests.

Related Theory and Further Developments:
Transformational Grammar, Post-Structuralism, and Postmodernism

Lévi-Strauss's structuralism has influenced every stream of thought in French social, linguistic, and literary theory since the 1960s in the form of continuation, variation, transformation, and rejection. We call this development "post-structuralism," and this was followed by "postmodernism." However, before we turn to this development we first take a short look at a structuralist theory of language that was created independently of Lévi-Strauss within the Anglo-Saxon context of linguistics: Noam Chomsky's transformational grammar.

Transformational Grammar: Noam Chomsky

Chomsky (1957, 1964, 1965, 1968) developed his approach with reference to Saussure's differentiation between *langue* and *parole* and with reference to a certain structuralist behaviorism elaborated by Harris (1951/1960) and Bloomfield (1957).

Chomsky struck down empiricism in Anglo-Saxon linguistics and revolutionized the field. He pointed out that any act of speaking or writing is not simply occasioned by situational circumstances but by the deep structure of a language. It is a reflection of that deep structure on the level of the surface structure. The deep structure is composed of certain rules from which a variety of sentences on the surface level can be constructed. Chomsky came to the solution that this generation of actual sentences from the deep structure can best be explained by the application of transformational rules and morphonemic rules. By application of these rules a variety of different sentences on the surface structure is generated from the deep structure of basic elements of a language.

Yet Chomsky's transformational grammar is different from French structuralism, and the difference is rooted in his Anglo-Saxon view. In Saussure's perspective, *parole* is the execution of *langue*. Chomsky introduces instead, in parallel to his differentiation of the deep structure and the surface structure of language, a differentiation between competence and performance on the part of the idealized speaker of the language. Competence involves the syntactical generation of a sentence according to the transformational rules as an ideal speaker of the language. His or her performance, however, is a personal activity in a situation of talk. Thus, the performance of speaking a language introduces a creative element that is not perceivable in Saussure's structuralism (see Giddens, 1987).

Post-Structuralism

Louis Althusser developed a post-structuralist type of Marxism, taking the economic structure of capitalism and its laws of reproduction as the deep structure of society (Althusser, 1965; for translation, see 1972; Althusser and Balibar, 1968; for translation, see 1970; see Benton, 1984). This, however, means moving structure from normative rules and symbolic codes to the economic field, which is in itself the home of societal dynamics. Thus we get a shift toward studying the dynamic and diachronic aspects of capitalism's economic structure and its laws of reproduction and transformation.

With this structuralist type of Marxism, Althusser opposed the subjectivist types that referred more to the early philosophical writings of Marx and to the concept of "praxis." His Marx was the Marx of *Capital* with its outline of the unchangeable laws of capitalist development rooted in its basic structure. However, this approach cannot be as economic as Althusser proclaims it to be. Without basic legal institutions, like property rights, contract law, labor legislation, and monopoly acts, there is no economic structure but only dynamics. The true locus of the economic structure is the legal system and not the economic one. Studying the dynamic development of capitalism means analyzing the interpenetration of the legal structure of capitalism with the dynamics of capital accumulation and technological rationalization. Revealing the structure of capitalism means ascertaining the nature of its legal institutions. Yet, explaining the transformation of capitalism requires more than that, namely, studying the effects of economic dynamics, political struggle, and public discourse on the change of capitalism's legal structure. Althusser's preoccupation with the economic sphere prevents him from reaching a full explanation of capitalism's structural transformation. In this respect, Godelier (1972) went further in developing Marxist structuralism.

Another field where structuralism flourished in the 1960s and 1970s was semiotics, the study of signs. The French literary theorist Roland Barthes (1963, 1967, 1970a, 1970b; for translation, see 1964, 1974, 1982, 1983) formulated a structuralist theory of signs. In the view of this theory, everything that happens becomes a sign according to its relationship to the "text" that underlies social action. An action is part of a text. We understand its meaning inasmuch as we get to know the whole text. Thus a piece of clothing receives meaning when we discover the life-style of which it is a part. Fashion itself is understood in its meaning inasmuch as we learn the message of the underlying text of the fashion industry as part of the capitalist economy. Jean Baudrillard (1972, 1973, 1977, 1979, 1986; for translation, see 1975, 1981, 1983a, 1983b, 1988) has worked alongside this approach arguing that advertising has led us to forget the use value of objects and to see only their "sign value."

A further well-received contribution to semiotics came from Umberto Eco (1975; for translation, see 1976), who pointed out the multi-level character of signs. An automobile, for example, can be seen (1) as a physical object, (2) as an instrument for doing things, (3) as an economic value, (4) as an indicator of social status, and (5) as representing a certain idea of individual mobility.

Jacques Lacan (1966; for translation, see 1977) has formulated a structuralist psychoanalysis. He conceives of the conflicts within the person as linguistic conflicts contained in the texts of the symbolic order into which he or she has been socialized.

The 1970s brought about a shift from reconstructing structures of texts toward "deconstructing" by way of working out the processes of their production and reproduction. This introduced an element of action, though it did not grasp the full meaning of agency. Jacques Derrida (1967a, 1967b, 1972;

for translation, see 1976, 1978, 1981) introduced "deconstructionism." In his view the world is a text; its meaning is produced and reproduced in writing. The action of writing, however, is not in the hands of the subject of action in ordinary situations in everyday life, as has been conceptualized in the Anglo-Saxon ordinary language approach originating from Wittgenstein (1953). For Wittgenstein, language games are interrelated with forms of life and are produced and reproduced in the ongoing practice of everyday life. Ordinary language anchored in the practice of everyday life is the center around which the meaning of signs is produced and reproduced. As a speaker of ordinary language, I know the meaning of the terms. I know to which objects in the world they refer, and I share this knowledge with my fellows who speak the same ordinary language and share the same life form with me. In Derrida's view, the production and reproduction of meaning is an ongoing action but an action that is determined by the sequence of signs and their interrelation in the process of writing a text. Thus it is the sequencing of signs and the interrelation of signs that determines their meaning on the level of writing a text, not the interrelationship of signs with everyday common practices in practical talk. Thus, the dynamic turn from structuralism to deconstructionism remains on the level of texts and does not step down to that of the agency of subjects engaged in practical talk. Deconstructionism moves only halfway from structure to agency, as Giddens (1987) has pointed out.

Text, sequence of signs, and writing, and not talk, are the locus for the production and reproduction of meaning in the deconstructionist view. In this sense deconstructionism carries on the decentering of the subject as it was established as a research program by structuralism. The same holds true for Michel Foucault's movement from structure to power in his version of post-structuralism. In Foucault's perspective, the development of knowledge is a process of rationalization in which the power that is imposed by its structure on the human being reproduces itself in the direction of growing sophistication in its deployment. We will turn to Foucault in the next chapter.

Finally, a number of new developments in structural sociology have been made recently in the United States. This kind of structuralism is concerned with the dynamics and dialectics of structures of social action. One version has been promoted by Peter M. Blau (1977) and another by Ino Rossi (1982, 1983).

Postmodernism

A shift from structuralism to spontaneism has been brought about by the so-called New Philosophers such as Jean-Marie Benoist (1975), Bernard-Henri Lévy (1977), Maurice Clavel (1975), and André Glucksmann (1977).

Recently, theories of postmodernity have pointed out the breakdown of established structures and the emergence of a multiplicity of coexisting and partly conflicting worlds (Bauman, 1987; Berger, 1986; Featherstone, 1989). Jean Baudrillard (1983a, 1983b, 1986, 1988) has moved from Marxist structuralism and post-structuralism toward postmodernism in his later work on the hyperreality produced by the mass media. Jean-François Lyotard (1979, 1983; for translation, see 1984) has presented a highly influential theory of postmodernity. Michel Maffesoli (1988) has worked out such a theory by revitalizing Georg Simmel's (1908; 1914/1926) classical theory of modernity. Whereas Marx (1867/1962; for translation, see 1967) served in the 1960s and early 1970s as intellectual hero to the French intellectuals, his position was taken over by Nietzsche (1901/1961; for translation, see 1968) in the late 1970s. This was a shift of the game from structure and rationality to power and spontaneity. Originally the field of spontaneity in French thought playing against structure was grounded in the vitalism of Bergson's (1932/1959) later work and afterwards in Sartre's (1943; for translation, see 1966) existentialism. Let us now take a closer look at Baudrillard's and Lyotard's theories of postmodernity.

Media Hyperreality: Jean Baudrillard

In his earlier work, Baudrillard argued from the perspective of a Marxist structuralism, but he abandoned this in his later work on the postmodern society in which mass media construct a reality of their own, a hyperreality that no longer signifies any other reality. Rather, it is that very hyperreality that determines the orientations and lives of people and makes the other spheres of life dependent on them. People live in a virtual world. The mass media produce a complex plurality of models that are taken as real by the people. Television series and advertising produce models of life that then become life simply because viewers take them as real. The economic and political structures that have thus far determined social life are replaced by a complex plurality of competing life models produced by the media. Nothing remains solid in postmodern society, and there are no longer any structures, for these dissolve in the hyperreality of a plurality of "simulacra," that is, mere simulations of life. There is a complete loss of historical agency in this media world. No longer is there a historical subject like the labor movement working toward changing the world to create a better one.

We can clearly see a contemporary version of Marxian alienation theory in Baudrillard's theory of media hyperreality. Just as the worker alienated him- or herself by producing the capital that became established as an external power with complete control over the worker, the postmodern individual alienates him- or herself by producing and consuming a media world that becomes established as the new external power with complete control over the individual. However, Baudrillard tells us only half the story. The other half is the dynamic change of society that is initiated by the media and to which social movements as historical actors still contribute. The success of contemporary ecological movements and of movements campaigning for the civil rights of minorities and women and for the civil rights of the people as a whole in the countries of former real-world socialism, cannot be understood and explained without reference to the dynamic effects of media reporting and investigative journalism. The revolution of 1989 in Eastern Europe was as much prepared in its cultural thrust by the expansion of public discourse through global media reporting from and into those countries as the French Revolution of 1789 was prepared in that thrust by the Enlightenment and the expansion of public discourse through journals.

The Postmodern Condition — Heterogeneity of Discourses and Economic Hegemony: Jean François Lyotard

Jean François Lyotard's theory of the postmodern condition points out the breakdown of unity of reason as the guiding force of the development of modernity and the loss of any idea of progress in the current state of the development of Western societies, which he calls "postmodernity." The classical meta-narratives of modernity, he proposes, are no longer valid and effective. They have been refuted by the factual development of history. This holds true for the three great meta-narratives of modernity: the idea of the emancipation of humankind, the idea of the telos of the spirit reaching its self-realization in history, and the idea of the fulfillment of meaning in history.

In terms of Hegel's dialectics modernity has broken up the original unity of experience and reality and has established the contradiction between reason and reality that bears its resolution in itself and moves modern society toward a higher order reunion of reason and reality. Eventually, in this view, the real world will be identical with the reasonable. According to Lyotard, history does not in fact move in this direction, as historical facts like the Holocaust prove. There is no universal reason at work that would realize itself in history. Instead, the unity of reason has split up into a plurality of heterogeneous and contradictory discourses or language games, in the terms of Wittgenstein (1953). There is no common criterion or rule that could help us to decide about the contradictory validity claims of the different discourses or language games. There is also no way to rank such claims in a hierarchy. The development of modernity always produces its victims; however, they cannot speak up to claim their rights because there is no universal language that would help them to sustain their claims against refutations.

This destruction of reason under the postmodern condition finally leads to the triumph of the real over the reasonable: Inasmuch as there is no common truth, reason, or rule, it is power that decides on the enforcement of validity claims. In the eyes of Lyotard it is the discourse of the economics of saving time that tends to establish its hegemony over the various other heterogeneous discourses of politics, science, law, morality, religion, or aesthetics. In the postmodern world, saving time via economic rationalization establishes its hegemony, because nobody can escape its necessities, whereas the other discourses are relegated to the minor position of holding up the economic process of saving time for a moment. Thus, finally, Lyotard's theory of postmodernity presents itself as Marxism stripped of belief in the dialectical resolution of the contradiction between reason and reality in the reasonable world of communism. Lyotard's theory of postmodernity looks like Marxism discovering the reality of pluralist society in Marxist terms. It is the plurality of possible validity claims that weakens reason so that it can no longer function as a guiding force against the factual development of society, which is thus left to the power struggle. It is economic necessity that then establishes its unchallenged hegemony.

A critique of Lyotard has to point out that it is his Hegelian-Marxian view of modernity that leads him to resignation with regard to the possibility of guiding societal development in terms of reason. The Hegelian Marxist sees the historical facts that run counter to reason because of his or her search for the full realization of reason in history, for the final resolution of all contradictions in the true synthesis. Minor progress in reducing suffering, injustice, and inequality and in broadening the rights to freedom and equality is nothing in the light of the original hopes. Lyotard knows, however, that any attempt whatever to totally resolve modernity's contradictions has to lead to totalitarianism. Synthesis of reason and reality is possible only by restricting the potential of reason to the real, in claiming the real to be reasonable or at least to be a necessary step toward the reasonable, and in imposing that view of the world on the people by force and totalitarian control, as was established in the world of really existing socialism in the former Soviet empire.

The dynamics of modernity, however, lives from the unbridgeable gap between reason and reality. Only as long as the two are independent of each other can reason expand its claims and exert its pressure on societal institutions and societal development. The paradox is that reason can have effects on reality only as long as it isn't identical with reality. Social development according to claims of reason proceeds by criticizing what exists in the world, not by its legitimation. In order to advance society in terms of reason we don't need the positive legitimation of something existing as valid once and for all; we need only criticism in order to make some progress. Moreover, such criticism doesn't require complete consensus. It is the same as with the progress of science that doesn't result from any consensus on the truth but from dissensus, which makes the search for the truth a never-ending process. Only as long as this search goes on can we assume that we will be able to make progress by learning from our errors. It is no different with societal development. As long as there is criticism we can assume that we will make some progress in doing away with errors. This doesn't guarantee that we will not make further errors. However, the very process of endless criticism allows us to correct them again. We can make only little progress, if any. However, this has been the very nature of modernity from its beginning. Such a theory of pluralism that avoids the resignation of current theorists of postmodernity and points out the totalitarian nature of the Hegelian-Marxian search for synthesis was formulated long ago by Karl R. Popper (1944/1966) in his work *The Open Society and Its Enemies* (see also Albert, 1980).

Postmodernity is nothing but modernity faced by disappointed Hegelian Marxists. Modernity has been pluralistic in its values from its beginning. Hegelianism and Marxism tried to reduce this pluralism by synthesis. Pluralism itself is, however, a basic claim of the modern value system. Freedom of thought, freedom to find one's own way through life, freedom of association, freedom of religion, and equal rights of individuals and groups to such freedom are common and universal claims of modernity. These freedoms are the nonarbitrary and unchangeable foundations of pluralism in modern society. Thus it is the idea of modernity itself that is opposed to a resolution of contradictions in a synthesis that can only be a totalitarian dissolution of pluralism. This is a common and universal claim of modernity that has to be safeguarded against attacks. A pluralist society cannot be indifferent to attempts to destroy its pluralism. Therefore the pluralism of modernity is not as arbitrary in character as it would appear to be in the view of the theory of postmodernity. Indeed, this consensus on basic rights to freedom and equality is the only thing that can explain developments of modern societies that have worked against existing violations of claims to freedom and equality.

Major changes in history can be explained only by reference to the penetration of claims to freedom and equality into the various realms of society. Without a chance to refer to commonly shared ideas, social movements from the labor movement to the civil rights movement, women's movement, and ecological movement would not have had effects on societal development. What they claim is mostly undebated in itself. What is debated mostly is the extent to which their claims can be realized in the face of competing claims. This is the area of compromising according to the rules of the game within a pluralistic society. There really are such rules of the game that are the commonly shared basis of a pluralistic society. Otherwise, we would not have peaceful competition among claims; instead, we would have war. This is indeed the fate of developing societies that are trying to follow the lead of modern Western societies. They dissolve in conflict because they lack common rules of settling that conflict. This balance of diversity and unity is the basic matrix of modern societies and so difficult to develop that many societies that try to do so fail. The newly rising democracies on the soil of socialism in the East will face a tough future as they endeavor to develop such a balance of unity and diversity in a pluralist society.

Finally, we have to qualify Lyotard's explanation of the triumph of economic discourse in terms of the weakness of reason resulting from its self-destruction in pluralism. From the very beginning of modern society the development of the capitalist economy has resulted from the dynamic cooperation between the profit orientation of the capitalist enterprise and the claim by the labor movement to an appropriate share in the wealth produced. Without the moral claim of the labor movement to such an appropriate share and the resulting mass consumption by the masses of the people, capitalist mass production would not have been possible. In this process the capitalist economy and the rights of workers to equality expanded at the same time. The same is true for any expanding noneconomic realm in modern society; they expanded in correspondence and mutual dynamic penetration with the capitalist economy. The welfare system, the services of the state, the sciences, the educational system, the civil rights movement, the women's movement, and the ecological movement all expanded in dynamic mutual penetration and cooperation with the capitalist economy. Indeed, they are unthinkable without a growing economy. This, however, is a development that does not simply result in the hegemony of the economic discourse, because the noneconomic systems have also expanded in modern society. It is the dynamic growth of all realms of society through mutual penetration and cooperation that is most characteristic of modern society. We have not only an expanding economy but also an expanding welfare system, polity, science, education, arts, mass media, and public discourse as well. In this process the economy doesn't only penetrate every sphere of society but is itself penetrated by every other system of society.

Lyotard argues very much along the lines of French postwar social theory, for which power is the major force in social development and which relegates any other force to a secondary status. He shares this view with Foucault, Bourdieu, Touraine, and many others. However, the world is far too complex to allow us such a reduction of its processes to a power game. Power is indeed a major force in history but not the only one. It is sometimes more dominant and at other times less dominant. It is dominant particularly in revolutionary situations when old rules have broken down and new ones have not yet been established. The societies formerly governed by socialism are going through such a process. In fact it may be that the Western societies are also going through such a process, though in a less dramatic way. It is this process that motivates social theorists to generalize a temporary change in modern society to a permanent state called "postmodernity." However, the pluralistic credo of modernity is such a general common idea that it covers what is called postmodernity without any change in its identity.

Postmodernity is not a new state of development of modernity or a state of development succeeding it. It is a view of current modernity propagated by disappointed former Marxists who, for the first time, have had to face up to the pluralistic character of modernity not as a temporary state on the way to the true synthesis in communist society but as a permanent fate of humankind. The major failure of Hegelians and Marxists is their inability to appreciate pluralism and the formal procedures of decision making in a pluralistic society in their own right as what makes sense of modernity, rather than the substantial claims that rise and fall in the cyclical oscillations of public discourse. Once they longed to replace the contradictions of pluralist society by the synthesis of communism. The consequence was a disaster for humankind. Currently, ecologism is on the way to replacing the communist synthesis. However, it will have similar defects unless its proponents learn that it is only one value in a society devoted to a plurality of values, and that its realization can be no more than a compromise with other values worked out time and again in the procedures of decision making that are more important than the substantial value of ecologism. Modern society has a god: pluralism. It does not accept any other equally ranking god, but only the peaceful competition of the second-order gods of substantial values like liberalism, voluntarism, socialism, or ecologism.

Two

THE REPRODUCTION OF POWER STRUCTURES: THE POST-STRUCTURALISM OF MICHEL FOUCAULT

FRENCH SOCIETY has been organized as a centralized power system since the establishment of the ancien régime by Louis XIV in the seventeenth century. The revolution of 1789, the establishment of Napoleon's régime in 1799, the restoration of the monarchy in 1814 interrupted by Napoleon's hundred-day interregnum in 1815, the Second Republic of 1848 to 1851, Louis Napoleon's regime of 1851 to 1870, the Third Republic of 1870 to 1940, the Vichy régime of 1940 to 1944, the Fourth Republic of 1946 to 1958, and the Fifth Republic established in 1958 did not change the centralized power system in French society. It is therefore no surprise that French social thought circles around viewing society primarily as a power system.

Discourse and Power

One of the most provocative and influential approaches to studying this power system during the last twenty years was worked out by Michel Foucault (1961, 1969, 1971, 1975, 1976, 1984a, 1984b, 1988; for translation, see 1965, 1972a, 1972b, 1977, 1978, 1980–1986). He moved from the structuralism of Lévi-Strauss toward post-structuralism, thereby concentrating less on the static features of structures and more on the processes of their reproduction. His approach is based on the assumption that the development of power systems proceeds in close interconnection with the development of cultural discourses. In his view, power and discourse make up a unity. The reproduction of power progresses in close interconnection with the production of knowledge. Thus, the evolution of knowledge has to be studied as a central element of the reproduction of power systems.

There are two grounds on which it is possible to support this thesis. First, cultural discourse is organized as a part of the power system in terms of power. Therefore it immediately contributes to reproducing that power system. Second, cultural discourse that opposes it actually becomes incorporated into the power system in that its results are utilized for the reproduction of power. An example of the first type of discursive reproduction of power is the organization of therapeutic discourse as an authority relationship between psychiatrist and patient, with the psychiatrist acting as an agent of social control. An example of the second type of discursive reproduction of power is incorporating criticism of procedures for the execution of criminal sentences into those procedures by way of reform, thus reestablishing social control on a more sophisticated level. Reproduction in this way is also a process of self-transformation toward more rationalized levels of power organization. As the examples show, cultural discourse contributes to the self-reproduction and self-transformation of power systems inasmuch as it is a part of the system or inasmuch as the results of independent cultural discourse are incorporated into the power system. Foucault doesn't formulate what he says about the self-reproduction and self-transformation of power systems by cultural discourse in this qualified way. Instead, he postulates this development as a universal statement without any qualification to specific conditions that contribute to its establishment. He starts with the general assumption

> that in every society the production of discourse is at once controlled, selected, organized and redistributed according to a certain number of procedures, whose role is to avert its powers and its dangers, to cope with chance events, to evade its ponderous, awesome materiality. (1972b:8)

However, Foucault himself seeks to escape this very process with his own critical and genealogical studies on the evolution of power and knowledge systems. If his universal statement were true, there would be no chance for him to himself escape that process. Therefore, in order to solve this paradox, we have to qualify his statement about the interconnection of discourse and power reproduction to specific conditions. Such a qualification is in fact the only way in which his work can make sense and escape the postulation of power as the one single factor that guides the evolution of society. And only in that way can he escape the paradox of actually contributing to power reproduction with his critical analysis of such power reproduction. Thus, contrary to Foucault's universal statement of power reproduction by cultural discourse, we can formulate the following two qualified propositions, specifying the conditions under which this process takes place:

1. The more cultural discourse is organized as a part of the power system, the more it will contribute to the self-reproduction and self-transformation of that system toward higher levels of rational organization and exertion of power.
2. The more the results of independent cultural discourse become incorporated into the established power system, the more cultural discourse contributes to the self-reproduction and self-transformation of that system toward higher levels of rational organization and exertion of power.

The Order of Discourse

In his inaugural lecture on "The Order of Discourse," delivered at the Collège de France on December 2, 1970, Foucault points out in a programmatic form the mechanisms that make discourse a constraining force on the part of the overall power system in society (Foucault, 1971). In doing so he argues against the common view of discourse as a creative force that produces ideas reaching beyond everything established so far in society, thus acting as a moving force in society resulting in social change, even revolutionary change. According to this view, cultural discourse has liberating and revolutionary effects and is a permanent danger for any established power system. Foucault does not completely rule out the chance of such liberating and revolutionary effects occurring. However, he emphasizes that sophisticated power systems are capable of controlling these effects to their advantage. It is only by revealing the procedures by which cultural discourse is organized as part of the power system and/or supports its self-reproduction and self-transformation that critical analysis can contribute to reestablishing the liberating and revolutionary forces of cultural discourse. This is the critical task that Foucault sets for himself. It is complemented by working out genealogies of evolving systems of knowledge as part of power systems, for example, the evolution of thought on the execution of sentences or on sexuality.

Coming to a general analysis of the procedures that exert constraining effects on discourse, Foucault (1971) distinguishes three types: external procedures, internal procedures, and procedures regulating the access to discourse. Inasmuch as discourse is constrained by these procedures, discourse itself has constraining effects on societal life, for it becomes part of the societal power system.

There are three externally constraining procedures: prohibition, the demarcation between reason and insanity, and the demarcation between the true and the untrue (Foucault, 1971: 10–23). These are principles of exclusion. They preclude everything from accepted knowledge that contradicts established prohibitions, understandings of reason, and truth. Prohibitions close out objects, certain times, and people from discussion. We are not allowed to talk about everything, we cannot speak about anything at any time, and not everybody can speak about particular things. Take as an example a class at a French lycée. The teacher may react to a pupil's statement about French politics by saying: "This is not part of the object of our discussion in this class." In doing so, he or she exerts the power of prohibition, thus limiting what can come up in discussion. As the whole school system works according to the program prescribed by the central governmental department of education, discussion at school is uniformly controlled. Who can speak about what at what time is minutely determined in this system. This, however, is only one example of many forms in which discourse is constrained by prohibition.

Another form of constraint on discourse is provided by the demarcation between reason and insanity. What is sane and what is insane is not inherent in every expression of an individual; it is rather an expression's conformity to the norms established in society that determines whether the expression is judged to be sane or insane. Reason is what society conceives to be reason; unreason is what society sees as unreason. And this societal definition of reason and insanity is backed up by the societal power system. It is itself an element of that power system and is one means by which society exerts its control over the individual. What is reasonable in one society appears insane in another society. The man who hears hidden voices can be admired as a saint in one society and branded as insane in another. Anything that threatens the organized life within the power system is treated as insane. It therefore needs controlling. One can argue that modern society has gone far in taking seriously what the so-called insane have to say; however, Foucault argues that the special attention paid to the talk of the insane doesn't abolish the demarcation but rather reestablishes it on a new, more sophisticated level of control. Listening to the talk of the insane is a better means of control than ignoring that talk.

A third form of constraint on discourse is the demarcation between the true and the untrue. This demarcation is rooted in the will to seek out truth that was established in the victory of scientific enterprise in the sixteenth and seventeenth centuries in a particular way. What can be an object of knowledge, how this object is perceived, and how knowledge about that object can be proven are all defined in a particular way by the enterprise of science and its particular way of reaching the truth. What does not correspond to these requirements of establishing scientific truth is disregarded and closed out of authorized discourse. This type of knowledge production is closely connected with the emergence of a power system in modern society that rules not by blind punishment but by a comprehensive system of information and finely graded controls. Because of that interconnection the demarcation of the true and untrue by the established methods of science is part of the overall power system. What can be established as true and what is rejected as untrue are not inherent in knowledge. Nor is there any inherent correspondence or noncorrespondence between ideas and reality. This correspondence is heavily determined by the methods applied in order to prove truth and falsity. Therefore demarcating a line between the true and the untrue is a procedure that enforces the establishment of science for making just that demarcation. What appears true and what appears untrue depends to a large degree on the enforcement of specific methods for proving truth. The very procedure of confirmation and falsification of knowledge is an exercise of power.

Foucault postulates these three external constraints on discourse in a universal statement. However, how could his own contribution to discourse escape this universal constraint on discourse if there were no exceptions to his universal statement? There are certainly greater or lesser external constraining forces on discourse; thus, discourse also contributes more or less to the reproduction of an established power system. We would therefore do better to formulate the following qualified propositions:

3. The more cultural discourse is externally regulated by prohibitions and by demarcations between reason and insanity and between the true and the untrue, the more limited will be its results and the more these results will reproduce the established knowledge on a new level of rationality.
4. The more the external prohibitions and demarcations between reason and insanity and between the true and untrue are linked to an established power system, the more cultural discourse will produce knowledge that contributes to reproducing that power system, transforming that system toward a new level of rationality based on an increasingly complex and finely graded technological system of information and control.

Internal procedures also exert their constraint on discourse: the commentary, the author, and the organization of disciplines (Foucault, 1971: 23–38). The commentary is a form of continuing discourse in a way that does not produce anything that has not been said before. The commentary is a secondary interpretation of a primary text; it is expected to reveal what has been said in the primary text. It is a repetition of the primary text's message and cannot add anything new. Because a large proportion of cultural discussion consists of commenting on primary texts, the results of discourse are limited to the meaning of primary texts. A great deal of discourse goes on that does no more than reproduce preestablished knowledge. This is an internal constraint on discourse.

The second internal principle that exerts a constraining force on discourse is the author. The texts produced by an author cannot emerge completely by chance. What an author writes is guided by his or her identity established in interaction with his or her public. The attribution of texts to the identity of an author exerts pressures on internal consistency in that author's work. Therefore, the more a person has written, the more that person is constricted by his or her own words, because everything has to fit in with what has gone before. Inconsistencies at least call for explanations, which again contribute to producing consistency. Thus, what can be said in discourse is limited by the need to maintain an identity as an author.

A third internal procedure constraining discourse is the organization of disciplines like physics, chemistry, botany, medicine, literature, and so on. In order to be accepted in discourse, a sentence has to be phrased in the dominating language of a discipline. It has to correspond to the prevailing model of thought or at least to be meaningfully related to the established model of thought. Thus there is pressure for coherence and systematic interconnection with prevailing language and thought in order to gain attention in discourse. This requirement of disciplinary coherence sets limits on what can become an element of discourse.

Foucault states his argument in a universal way. However, we have to reformulate it in a qualified form in order to escape the paradox stated above:

5. The more cultural discourse is internally regulated by the principles of commentary, author, and discipline, the more limited will be its results and the more these results will reproduce the established knowledge on a new level of rationality.
6. The more the internal regulations of commentary, author, and discipline are linked to an established power system, the more cultural discourse will produce knowledge that contributes to reproducing that power system, transforming that system toward a new level of rationality based on an increasingly complex and finely graded technological system of information and control.

In addition to the above, there are constraints on discourse resulting from the regulation of access to discourse and of behaving in discourse: rituals, discourse societies, and doctrines (Foucault, 1971: 38–47). Rituals prescribe the qualification one has to have in order to be admitted to discourse; they define the right behaviors, attitudes, gestures, circumstances, and symbols involved in discourse. Before one can participate in discourse, one must undergo socialization and examination in order to be able to conform to its rules. This ritualization of discourse makes behavior predictable but also sets limits on what can become an object of discourse. Rituals constrain discourse.

Discourse societies are the carriers of discourse. One has to be accepted into such more or less strictly established societies in order to participate in discourse. Professional societies like the American Bar Association or the American Medical Association have monopolized discourse on law or on medicine to a great extent, so that virtually nobody is heard in these discourses unless he or she is a member of the corresponding society. Lawyers or physicians who have been excluded from these societies are made nobodies in legal and medical discourse. These societies also define ranks in discourse. Lower ranking people have no chance of being taken seriously in discourse. Thus discourse societies, too, exert a constraining function on discourse.

Doctrines become established in discourse, and once that has happened they control what can be said and what cannot be said to a considerable degree. Doctrines are backed up by discourse groups. Discourse groups set up doctrines and set limits on discourse, and these limits of discourse exert constraints on those who raise their voices. They have to relate their contributions to the doctrines and use their language. Doctrines exert a constraining force on discourse.

Though Foucault again states these constraints on discourse in universal terms, we have to qualify them in order to escape the paradox stated above:

7. The more cultural discourse is regulated by rules of entry in the form of rituals, discourse societies, and doctrines, the more limited will be its results and the more these results will reproduce the established knowledge on a new level of rationality.
8. The more the regulations by rituals, discourse societies, and doctrines are linked to an established power system, the more cultural discourse will produce knowledge that contributes to reproducing that power system, transforming that system toward a new level of rationality based on an increasingly complex and finely graded technological system of information and control.

Thus far we have outlined Foucault's basic assumptions about the reproduction and transformation of power systems in cultural discourse. Foucault himself seeks to break this vicious circle in his critical analysis by pointing out the constraining forces working on and from discourse and by working out genealogies of evolving systems of power and knowledge. Four methodical principles have to guide these studies (Foucault, 1971: 53–55):

1. The principle of reversion states that we have to point out the constraining effects on discourse rather than the creative effects of such figures as the author, the discipline, and the will to seek out truth.
2. According to the principle of discontinuity, critical analysis has to bring to light all the suppressed contributions to discourse that can start breaking up the established systems of knowledge and power.
3. According to the principle of specificity, critical analysis has to demonstrate how discourse in its regulated character exerts power on the world.

4. According to the principle of externality, critical analysis has to reveal the external conditions, for example, those located in the power system, that make a certain evolution of knowledge in discourse possible.

The Evolution of Punishment

Having now outlined Foucault's theoretical program, we can look at one of his studies in order to find out how his program works. We may take his study *Surveiller et punir: La naissance de la prison,* which appeared in French in 1975. In this study Foucault demonstrates with the example of penal law and the execution of sentences how the power system is reproduced and transformed from a simple system of repression and torment to a sophisticated system of economically and technologically organized information and control. The major force that pushes development in this direction is cultural discourse in its two features specified in the first two propositions of his theoretical program: discourse as an authoritatively organized part of the power system, as in judicial investigation and judicial decision making, and independent discourse that is ultimately incorporated into the power system via processes of reform.

The traditional penal system was characterized by punishment as cruel torment (Foucault, 1975: Part 1). The violation of law was an offense against the sovereign who reacted with all his or her revenge. The criminal was tormented to death in public places in front of a large crowd. The punishment was a cruel spectacle that demonstrated the sovereign's revenge, reestablished his or her power, and served as a deterrent to potential criminals among the people. Judicial investigation was a mixture of suspicion and subsequent torture in order to find out the whole truth. The final punishment was a torment where the criminal had to confess his or her criminal act publicly before being tormented to death. This was the penal system that was still well established into the eighteenth century.

However, by the end of the eighteenth century, things began to change. Torture and torment were abolished and replaced by a finely graded system of imprisonment for a specified period of time (Foucault, 1975: Part II). The punishment was removed from public places and was executed behind the walls of the prison without a public audience. There were two causes that initiated this process, according to Foucault. First, there were a growing number of cases in which the public spectacle of torment no longer ensured the frightened submission of the people but gave rise to acts of solidarity between the criminal and the people, leading to protest, uproar, and rebellion. Thus, the system of torment was no longer an effective means of social control.

On the other hand, the Enlightenment initiated critique of the torment system from the humanitarian point of view, arguing for a system of trial and penalties that respected basic human rights. Moderation of the enforcement of sovereign power was demanded.

In this demand for moderation both a rational organization of social control and a humanitarian concern for the criminal converged. Under conditions in which the people are rebellious and the intellectuals critical, it is no longer rational for the maintenance of the power system to continue with the system of torture and torment. The exercise of power is rationalized into an economically and technologically organized system of information and control. The established power no longer sees the people purely as an object of exploitation and suppression but as a population that has to be led and organized in the most effective way. Economic calculation and technological organization enters into the exercise of governmental power. Such an economically calculating and technologically organizing governmental power is now primarily oriented toward finding out the best way of increasing its information on society and the individual and of improving social control over both of these by way of a finely graded system of punishments. The aim of such governmental power is to rationally develop society. Achieving this demands the rational control of society, not suppression and vengeful punishment.

A further causal factor that contributes to initiating the change from repressive law to restitutive law—as Emile Durkheim characterized this change in his classical study on the division of labor—is the change in the source of the law from a sovereign power toward a society of the people as postulated in the Enlightenment's contract theories. Now any violation of the law is not an offense against a sovereign power but a violation of contract law. And contract law doesn't call for revenge but for restitution of the original state of affairs. Thus a rational handling of law enforcement is now also in the interest of the people themselves. In the background of this change lies the rise of the capitalist economy and the bourgeoisie. Now we have property owners who are interested in restoring violations of their property rights and in maintaining the order that bears the system of private property. Violations of law move away from cruel homicide toward sophisticated fraud, theft, receiving stolen goods, and the use of counterfeit money. Penal law becomes an extension of civil law. Here any violation of the law gives rise to an interest in restoring the original state of affairs. This can be done in three complementary ways: first, by having the violator restore the original state of affairs; second, by resocialization of the violator so that he or she again becomes a trustworthy member of society and partner in economic exchange; third, by setting the punishment in such a way that it doesn't provoke protest and rebellion but just makes conformity more useful than deviation.

Law enforcement thus moves away from simply punishing a violation of law and toward finding out the complex social and psychic causes that gave rise to a criminal act. Law enforcement becomes more and more interested in the personality and social milieu of the criminal. This is the birth of criminology as a science of crime that contributes to developing an ever more sophisticated system of law enforcement and to examining ever more minutely the personality of the individual. The rationalization of law enforcement by criminology leads to moderation of punishment practices in order to avoid rebellion and toward a deeper control of the individual by investigating his or her personality and social milieu.

We have a convergence of several factors that give rise to the transformation of law enforcement from repression to restitution, resocialization, a finely graded system of punishments making conformity just more useful than deviation and to an extension of the system of information and control that penetrates the whole society and individual personality by establishing criminology as the science of criminality. Those factors comprise the dangerous rebellion of the people, the humanitarian criticism of intellectuals, theories of social contract postulated by the Enlightenment philosophers, the emergence of a capitalist economy based on the order of private property, and the emergence of governmental power no longer aiming solely at the exploitation and suppression of people but now at the rational organization of society. Going beyond Foucault in formalizing his argument, we can formulate the following proposition:

9. The more a power system moves from an interest in exploitation and repression of the people toward an interest in rationally organizing society, and the more it is expected to do so via a rising rational economy run by an increasingly powerful social class (e.g., the capitalist economy based on private property run by the up-and-coming bourgeoisie), and the more its repressive measures are challenged by a rebellious people and critical intellectuals on humanitarian grounds, then the more it will transform its law enforcement from repression toward restitution, resocialization, finely graded punishments making conformity more useful than deviation, extending its system of information and control penetrating every corner of society and the human personality by establishing criminology as a rational science of criminality, and it will do this increasingly the more this transformation is legitimated in corresponding theories (such as the theory of social contract).

Foucault points out how cultural discourse supported this general transformation of law enforcement in several movements: the movement toward generalized punishment, the movement toward greater clemency in punishment, the movement toward establishing discipline throughout society, the movement toward panoptism as complete control of the societal periphery by the power center. These movements all contributed to the birth of the prison as a total and ascetic institution that turns the violation of law into self-reproductive but controlled delinquency and contributes to the establishment of the custodial system as a core structure of society, a society minutely controlled by a self-reproductive power system.

The movement toward generalized punishment is part of the rational reorganization of the power system itself and is led by sophisticated conservative reformers who expect a better functioning system of social control from the following improvements:

* Minimal quantity of punishment: not too much to give rise to rebellion, but not too little to provoke deviation.
* Sufficient ideality, which means law enforcement has to aim at the mental calculations of the individual, presenting conformity as more useful than deviation.
* Punishment has to evoke in *potential* criminals the expectation that conformity is more useful than deviation.
* Complete certainty: the individual has to know clearly what is law and what results from its violation.
* Ordinary truth: judicial decision making has to find out the truth in an understandable way.
* Optimal specification: any special violation calls for a special treatment.

The movement toward clemency in punishment originating in Enlightenment thought complements the internal rationalization of law enforcement by the following criteria:

* No arbitrary punishment.
* Punishment primarily has to revitalize conformity.
* Punishment needs to be temporally graded.
* Punishment should address potential criminals and withhold them from criminal acts.
* Punishment should re-educate the criminal and needs pedagogic assistance.
* Punishment should recodify the law.

The movement toward establishing discipline in the personality becomes established throughout society (Foucault, 1975: Part 3). It begins at schools, goes on in the armed forces, industry, and bureaucracy, and becomes a major element in organizing orphanages, mental homes, and prisons. Discipline is based on a thorough education of the body, on the use of drill, and on panoptic inspection. The body is educated by measures like enclosure, parellation, attribution of functional positions, and rank. It is educated by control of activities like exact time schedules, temporally scheduled activities, the strict connection of body and gesture with symbolic control of the body, the systematic connection of body and object by use of instruments, and exhaustive utilization of the body. The body is also educated by the organization of developments like the combination of powers, placing the body, establishing chronological series, and imposing a system of commands.

Discipline is further established by means of drill involving hierarchical supervision, norm-producing sanction, and examination. Hierarchical supervision is established at a very early stage in the schools. Sanctioning produces norm continuity by way of exemplary court decisions and disciplinary punishment that evokes respect for the law, corrects deviation, is an element of a system of rewards and punishments, and attributes ranks and levels of achievement. Examinations are a society-wide control of conformity to societal norms; they are an invisible power and a documentation of every individual member of society, subjecting each one to social control. In French society, one has to know that the centralized examination system is indeed the means of social control *par excellence.*

These movements toward establishing a finely graded and thoroughly penetrating system of social control are finally completed by the movement toward the panopticon as a model for social control. The panopticon was designed by Jeremy Bentham as a model for a closed house where inspection is of primary importance: penitentiaries, prisons, houses of industry, workhouses, poorhouses, manufactories, asylums, lazarettos, hospitals, and schools. It is controlled by a tower in the center surrounded by a building constructed in the form of a ring. Every part of the surrounding building can be inspected from the central tower. Foucault conceives of this panopticon as a model for the power system in society. From its central position it penetrates every corner and each individual. This system is characterized by the following traits: (1) it makes use of discipline no longer simply to ban disorder but to organize society in an active way; (2) it extends disciplinary mechanisms throughout society into every institution; and (3) it brings every disciplinary institution under the control of the state. Thus, a centralized power system emerges that makes use of its power in the most economic way, intensifies and extends its power throughout society, and turns this power into overall societal production in every field of society from the economy to science, education, the armed forces, medicine, and so on.

We can summarize Foucault's analysis of movements resulting in the centralized, economically, and technologically organized power system in the following proposition:

10. The more movements aiming at generalized punishment, clemency in punishment, the establishment of discipline, and panoptical control converge, the more they give rise to a centralized power system that makes use of its power in the most economic, intensive, extensive, and productive way.

Finally, the birth of the prison is a result of the movement toward rationalization of social control described above (Foucault, 1975: Part 4). The prison is a total and ascetic institution. It is an institution aiming at controlling deviation and re-educating the criminal. The following features are designed to realize this goal: (1) change of the criminal's behavior; (2) dividing criminals into groups according to the character of their criminality; (3) flexible punishment; (4) labor as a means of re-education; (5) education of personality and resocialization; (6) control by specialized personnel; and (7) continued control and support of the criminal after imprisonment.

However, this sophisticated system of social control never succeeds in abolishing criminality, as Foucault points out; rather, it succeeds in systematically keeping criminality under control. Violation of the law becomes transformed into delinquency, a characteristic located in the personality and the social milieu of the criminal, which therefore becomes the main object of control and investigation by sentencing bodies, criminology, and psychiatry. In this process, however, the prison itself becomes a first-rate social milieu for producing delinquency for the very reason that delinquency is defined and controlled within a total institution. The prison paradoxically becomes the main source for reproducing delinquency. The high rate of recidivism is an apparent confirmation of this thesis.

The prison as such is not all that emerges in the manner that has been described, for there is also the penetration of society by a finely graded system of information and control resulting from that development. The whole of society becomes a custodial system based on the following traits: fine gradation of punishment, control of delinquents, regularization of punishment power, giving established law a natural status, and controlling the body in an interconnected complex of power and knowledge. It is a rationalized system of power.

We can summarize Foucault's final analysis of the birth of the prison in the following propositions:

11. The more social control is rationalized, the more it establishes the prison as a model of social control that turns the violation of law into delinquency but controls and reproduces delinquency at the same time.
12. The more the prison becomes established as a model of social control, the more society will be penetrated by a centralized and finely graded system of information and control and will be organized as a custodial system.

The Control of Sexuality

In the first volume of his *Histoire de la sexualité,* entitled *La volonté de savoir,* published in 1976, Foucault applies an explanatory strategy similar to his *Surveiller et punir.* He starts with a critique of the common thesis of repression that states that sexuality has been repressed since the Puritanism of bourgeois society emerged in the seventeenth century (Foucault, 1976: Part 2). This repression is supposed to have lasted up to the twentieth century, when the first attempts at liberating sexuality from its authoritative constraints became effective with psychoanalysis leading the way.

Foucault argues that this repression thesis is wrong, because it fails to reveal the true relationship between sexuality and the established power system of bourgeois society. Foucault conceives of repression particularly in the sense of prohibiting talk about sexuality. It is true, Foucault admits, that seventeenth-century Puritanism strongly established the legitimacy of only marital sexuality; however, at the same time, the Counter-Reformation strengthened the importance of confession, which particularly included confessing everything about one's sexual activity. This marked the beginning of extensive and intensive talk about sexuality. Discourse on sexuality became established as a common practice. Beyond the church, other institutions participated more and more in this discourse: literature, medicine, psychiatry, and psychoanalysis.

The development from the seventeenth century to the twentieth century is characterized by a growing number of institutions and disciplines that take part in the discourse on human sexuality. However, contrary to the repression thesis, Foucault doesn't accept that this growing discourse resulted in an eventual liberation of sexuality from repression in our own time. Foucault argues that there is no change from repression to liberation from the seventeenth to the twentieth century, but from the beginning of establishing discourse on sexuality in the seventeenth century the sexuality of the human individual has become the object of an increasingly deeper going, more penetrating system of knowledge that at the same time imposes a more finely graded and closer control on the sexuality of the human individual. The establishment of a science of sexuality is part of a power system that becomes increasingly more effective and penetrating as a result of the growth of knowledge about the sexuality of the human individual. The couch of the psychoanalyst is the modern confessional. The difference between the two is only that the psychoanalyst's couch is part of a much more sophisticated and finely graded form of social control (Foucault, 1976: Part 3).

What Foucault argues, however, can hold true only inasmuch as his propositions 1 and 2 can be applied, only inasmuch as discourse on sexuality is part of the power system and/or the results of independent discourse have been incorporated by the power system. This is certainly true for many of the forms of discourse he describes. The church confession, medicine, psychiatry, and psychoanalysis have exerted social control as part of the established power system in many forms. However, there have also been heretical forms of discourse on sexuality—including Foucault's own discourse—that have not been completely incorporated into the established power system, and thus they have been able to partly break the system. There have been not only cumulative extensions of power knowledge but also breaks in the power system involving qualitative changes in the nature of sexuality. That is, what appears as a rationalization of the power system in Foucault's view has very often been a break in that system initiated by heretical discourse. Thus we have to qualify Foucault's argument with the following specifications of propositions 1 and 2:

13. The more discourse on sexuality is organized as a part of the power system, the more it will contribute to the self-reproduction and self-transformation of that system toward higher levels of rational organization and exertion of power in the control of sexuality.
14. The more the results of independent discourse on sexuality become incorporated into the established power system, the more discourse on sexuality contributes to the self-reproduction and self-transformation of that system toward higher levels of rational organization and exertion of power.

Contrary to Foucault, but taking into account his own intention to initiate discourse that doesn't reproduce the established power system, we can formulate another proposition:

15. The more discourse (on sexuality) is independent of an established power system, the less its results can be incorporated by that system, and the more it is backed up by oppositional groups, then the more this discourse will contribute to breaking the established power system and to breaking its social control (of sexuality).

Foucault goes on from his central thesis of extension and intensification of the power system via discourse on sexuality and illustrates his thesis in the following steps: how discourse on sexuality is initiated, how the forms of social perversion become the object of minute documentation, and how a science of sexuality becomes established. He shows how this science of sexuality organizes discourse in an authoritative way as part of the power system: Discourse is authoritatively structured as confession, even in psychoanalysis. In the clinical codification of making the patient speak, the procedure becomes an examination. The postulate of general and diffuse causality forces the patient to speak about everything. The principle of inherent latency of sexuality requires the revelation of all hidden aspects of the patient's body and soul. The method of interpretation attributes the analyst a position of authority. The medicinization of the effects of the confession turns sexuality into pathology. The patient becomes an object of medical treatment. We can summarize this argument in the following proposition:

16. The more discourse on sexuality is organized as a confession, the more it will establish an increasingly penetrating control of the individual's sexuality.

Foucault goes on to describe the motive, methods, region, and periodization of his historical analysis of the establishment of the discourse on sexuality thus far characterized (Foucault, 1976: Part 4). The motive is his discovery of a growing will to attain knowledge, which is part of the established power's will to extend and intensify its control on society, to increase its capability of organizing society:

17. The more an established power system aims at extending and intensifying its control on society and its capability of organizing society, the more it will push forward the growth of knowledge about everything that happens in society, including knowledge about human sexuality.

Four rules apply to the intimate relationship between power extension and power intensification and the growth of knowledge on sexuality: (1) the rule of immanence states that the will to increase knowledge about sexuality is not autonomous but part of the power system itself. (2) The rule of permanent variation states that many different and varying power relationships are connected with the will to extend knowledge on sexuality. (3) The rule of the twofold conditioning relationship states that macro-power on the societal level and micro-power on the level of controlling individual sexuality (e.g., in the family) mutually condition each other. (4) The rule of the tactical polyvalence of discourse states that discourse supports the power system on the one hand but also can have the ability to undermine that system on the other. This fourth rule signifies that Foucault does indeed admit that discourse reproduces power only inasmuch as it is a part of that system or can be incorporated in its results by that system as stated in propositions 1, 2, 13, and 14. And we have here a formulation that supports proposition 15, though Foucault in his overall perspective tends to universalize falsely the supportive power-discourse interrelationship.

There are four regions in which the establishment of discourse on sexuality has taken place: (1) the hysterization of the female body; (2) the pedagogization of the child's sexuality; (3) the socialization of human reproduction; and (4) the psychiatrization of perversive lust.

In a chapter on periodization Foucault states that in the seventeenth century sexuality was closely regulated, but nevertheless one can detect the beginnings of investigation via confession. In the nineteenth century there was on the one hand a growing critique of sexual regulations and on the other hand a growing interest in scientific investigation. This was the time when the power interest in extending and intensifying knowledge on sexuality for improving social control converged with the intellectual interest in sexual liberation. Both gave rise to the control of sexuality by a science of sexuality, an increasingly sophisticated system of sexual control:

18. The more power interest in sexual control by way of improving knowledge on sexuality and intellectual interest in liberating sexuality converge, the more they will finally establish an all-embracing scientific system of controlling human sexuality.

Foucault closes with a chapter that describes the character of the thus established rationalized power system. It is a system that, in addition to the legal control of death, has developed an all-embracing power to make and organize life (Foucault, 1976: Part 5). It is an active power based on huge systems of information and control:

19. The more the power system resides in systems of knowledge, the more it will not only maintain order but actively make and organize life, and the more total in character it will become.

Critical Assessment

Coming to a final evaluation of Foucault's theory of discursive power reproduction, we can state that it provides good insights into the power-knowledge link. Foucault demonstrates how a power system is reproduced and transformed to a higher level of rationality by way of discourse and the production of knowledge. However, contrary to Foucault's own tendency, we have to qualify his statements to take account of the conditions that discourse is part of the power system and/or its results become incorporated into the power system. Furthermore, by doing this, we can make good use of Foucault's insights into the constraining effects of discourse, contrary to the common view of discourse as a liberating force. However, this holds true only inasmuch as discourse is indeed part of the power system and/or is authoritatively structured. This is not discourse where everybody can raise questions and make statements about anything on equal terms. Discourse of this kind, which is independent of power, has very different effects: It is always a challenge to power by virtue of its criticism. Foucault himself has to admit this critical power of discourse in order to extract himself from the hold of the power-knowledge machinery. How power systems depend on discourse in order to be considered legitimate is much less elaborated by Foucault. In fact, it is a residual category of his theory of the power-knowledge complex. Where he addresses this theme he cannot do so in terms of his theory of power-knowledge reproduction.

Another dimension of social reality that is not covered by Foucault's theory of power-knowledge reproduction is the situational change of power relations resulting from the dynamics of markets—economic, political, reputational, and cultural competition. He takes into account this dynamic dimension only as a dependent part of the self-reproduction of an established power system. That is, the working of this dimension is guided by the maintenance of the power system. However, a theory that gives markets and competition an independent status would point out how power relations changed against the interests of power holders because of changing constellations of competition.

Finally, Foucault doesn't pay attention to the fact that a power system in many cases cannot do everything, because it depends on the support of the people. It cannot change the traditionally prevailing world-views and norms rooted in society from one day to the next without losing so much support that its stability becomes seriously endangered. It also depends on relations of solidarity with the leading groups in society. Thus, it has to conform to this solidarity. If it did not, it would lose support and endanger its position. The effects of power are limited by the effects of solidarity, support, and traditional belief prevailing in society. These effects of solidarity, support, and life-world belief are outside the explanatory power of Foucault's theory of power-knowledge reproduction.

Summing up, we can say that Foucault points out how power is reproduced by discourse when power dominates everything in society including discourse. However, he doesn't show how power is reproduced and transformed when other forces of society exert their influence independently. He doesn't show how discourse, competition, and solidarity reproduce power in their own ways when they are not dominated by the power system. The more these procedures are independent, the more power is subject to the pressure of legitimation, competition, and solidarity demands.

Foucault's post-structuralism carried on the structuralist obsession with the self-reproduction of structures, and he doesn't address the dynamics rooted in human agency exercised in processes of legitimation, competition, and solidarity demands. This is why we have dealt with his approach as a continuation of structuralism, though the centrality of power moves him toward the politics of social action and social structure.

PART TWO

The Economics of
Social Action

THREE

HUMAN ACTION AS RATIONAL CHOICE: JAMES S. COLEMAN

THE ECONOMIC approach to sociological theory has flourished over the past twenty years, particularly in the United States. Continuing along the lines established by Homans and Blau, the new economic thought draws more explicitly on formal economic models and applies such models to explaining almost the entire range of social phenomena in terms of economic transactions: family behavior, socialization, social exchange, authority, trust, norms, sanctions, institutions, revolutions, social order, legitimacy, panic, and so on. Social phenomena of this kind always imply the involvement of actors who make a rational choice between alternatives in order to maximize their utility. Economic thought looks at social phenomena from this perspective. For this reason sociological theory viewed in such economic terms is called *rational choice theory.* One of the most successful theorists who has contributed to this new movement of economic thought is James S. Coleman (1971, 1974, 1986, 1990). We shall therefore examine his approach as a means of discussing rational choice theory.

The Principle of Rational Choice

The basic principle of rational choice theory states that the probability that an action will be carried out is a function of the gain in utility an actor expects from that action's outcome multiplied by the probability he or she attributes to the action's capacity to bring about the outcome (Coleman, 1990: 13–19). In a situation of choice, an actor carries out that action for which the value of its utility multiplied by the probability of such an outcome is highest. If I expect high utility from passing an exam in mathematics but have very little confidence that I will be able to pass it, whereas I expect only medium utility from passing an exam in psychology but expect to pass it with great confidence, I will take the exam in psychology.

A basic law of utility maximization is the law of diminishing marginal utility. It states that any unit of satisfying one of my needs or interests decreases the utility of any further unit of the same kind for me, simply because I become increasingly satiated with each new unit. For example, once I have eaten one ice cream cone, each extra cone has less and less utility for me down to the point at which I will refuse to eat any more ice cream at all. The same law holds true for anything that could become an object of my desire: food, clothing, housing, furniture, TV programs, conversations, parties, books, philosophy, physics, religion, prayer, dancing, walking, music, love, hate, and so on.

The Micro-Macro Link

Rational choice theory concerns the individual's choice of action among a set of alternative ways of acting. For applications to social phenomena that reach beyond the micro level of individual action and face-to-face interactions between a small number of actors, their choice situation has to be related to social and cultural structures on the macro level. Coleman (1990: 1–23) conceives of this relationship as a three-stage flow from the macro level to the micro level causing a certain behavior on the micro level that results in a certain effect on the macro level. For example, he interprets Max Weber's thesis on the relationship between ascetic Protestantism and the spirit of capitalism in the following way: the Protestant religious doctrine is a macro-level phenomenon, because it is a doctrine common to whole religious communities. That doctrine implies that the individual Protestant holds certain values like praise of hard work, trustworthiness, and reliability. This is the micro-level instance of the macro-level phenomenon of the religious doctrine of a whole community. The values of the individual lead him or her to adopt a certain economic behavior: working hard and being trustworthy and reliable in economic relations. In terms of rational choice, the individual's values and the religious community's values mean that behavior that is true to the values is positively sanctioned whereas behavior that violates the values is negatively sanctioned. Therefore, the individual maximizes utility by remaining true to his or her values. Inasmuch as a greater number of individuals act in that way and succeed in sanctioning their own and other people's behavior, then hard work, trustworthiness, and reliability become institutionalized as features of modern rational capitalism, which is finally a phenomenon on the macro level.

Carrying out his program, Coleman first investigates elementary actions and relations, then continues his analysis with an investigation of larger structures of action before turning to an analysis of corporate actors that leads to a specific perspective in pointing out basic structures and processes in modern society. This is all complemented by an outline of some basic processes using mathematical formalization.

Elementary Actions and Relations

The first level of analysis is concerned with elementary actions and relations.

Actors and Resources, Interest, and Control

According to Coleman's (1990: 27–44) economic view of the social world, the most basic elements of any action are the following: There is an actor who has an interest in different kinds of things and who controls resources in order to satisfy his or her interests. Inasmuch as the actor is in control of all resources needed to satisfy his or her interests, the actor will act to satisfy them in a straightforward way. However, in most cases, an actor does not control all the resources that he or she needs in order to satisfy his or her interests. In most cases, others are in control of a variety of such resources. This is why an actor develops an interest in resources that are controlled by others. Mostly, too, there are at least some others who are interested in the resources of the first actor in the same way. Here is the point where interaction between actors begins. That is to say, actors engage in interaction inasmuch as they are interested in resources that are controlled by someone else. Conceived in this way, interaction is always a transaction of resources for satisfying interests. Insofar as actors are interested in each others' resources, they engage in interaction.

There are two ways leading to the resources of another actor: power and incentives. If I control many more resources that another actor needs than he or she does of the resources I need but don't possess yet, it will be much easier for me to get his or her resources without paying an equivalent price in terms of resources I transfer to that actor than it is for him or her to obtain my resources in that way. In this case I can make use of my power in order to arrive at a transaction of resources that serves my interests. The second way of transacting resources has to be chosen if I don't have power of this kind over others. In this situation I have to attract others to the transaction by offering resources of my own that might be of interest to the others. Here the transaction comes much closer to an exchange of resources that are equivalent to each other. Such an exchange of equivalents occurs under the condition that the two actors who are engaged in the transaction possess resources in which they are mutually interested to an equal extent and under the further condition that both actors have access to alternative sources of interest satisfaction to the same degree.

Rights to Act

Since actors can interfere in each others' actions that are directed toward the satisfaction of interests, they are interested in setting limitations on such interference. This is done by defining *rights to act* (Coleman, 1990: 45–64). Insofar as I can rely on such a right to act I can start and go on with an action aiming at the satisfaction of my interests without having to fear the interference of others' actions that would prevent me from being successful in satisfying them.

Looked at in economic terms, the determination of rights to act is itself the outcome of transactions. By definition I have a right to carry out an action when those who are affected accept my action without dispute (Coleman, 1990: 50). These are the "relevant others." Such a right to act will be recognized by others insofar as they have no interest in the outcome of the action or insofar as I have enough power to be able to enforce the action. In both cases I can rely on a "general consensus" that I am entitled to carry out a certain action or a certain kind of action (Coleman, 1990: 67).

Authority Relations

Rights to control one's own actions can be given up at least partly and can be transferred to another actor (Coleman, 1990: 65–90). This is the way in which authority relationships become established. There are two ways of establishing authority. One is that the subordinate actor transfers rights to control his or her action to a superordinate actor, because the subordinate expects intrinsically to be better off by submitting to leadership in that way. This is conjoint authority. The other alternative is that the subordinate complies with such a transaction because of some compensation in terms of benefits that do not immediately flow from subordination itself but are paid because of that subordination. This is disjoint authority. In both cases, authority is a relationship that comes into being and continues to exist because both parties to the relationship draw some benefits from the interaction and are better off with it than with alternative forms of action. Both types of authority have peculiar defects relating to the subordinate's action. Conjoint authority might suffer from the subordinate actor's tendency to leave too much control of action in the hands of the superordinate actor. Disjoint authority might suffer from the subordinate's tendency to keep his or her cooperation at a minimal level.

Relations of Trust

The involvement of others in my action raises the question of whether or not I can trust them in the sense that they won't act in a way that is to my disadvantage. Much of my action must rely on such trust, because otherwise most of my action would be preoccupied with safeguarding against the possible detrimental acts of other people. I wouldn't be able to carry out what I really wanted to do. In Coleman's (1990: 91–116) economic view, it is a question of the rational allocation of my resources, whether I trust or do not trust other people. It is a kind of risk taking that is involved in such behavior. My choice is whether I trust someone else and take the chance of carrying out some action that promises the satisfaction of some of my interests or whether I don't trust that person and thus don't carry out that promising action and do engage in safeguarding against his or her possibly detrimental actions. The likelihood that I trust another person increases with the amount of gain I expect from an action that presupposes such trust and with the probability with which I expect trusting that person to achieve the effect I want.

Structures of Action

Thus far, we have outlined Coleman's view of elementary actions and relations. More complex systems and structures of action reach beyond the level of individual actions and relations and entail more durable and widespread relationships between actors: systems of exchange, authority systems, systems of trust, collective behavior, norms, and social capital. These more durable systems and structures of action rely on the same basic processes outlined for elementary action and relations, but these now work in more complex ways and form more complex interrelationships.

Systems of Social Exchange

Systems of social exchange depend on the expectation of a great number of actors that they will make some gains when they engage in processes of exchange (Coleman, 1990: 119–44). There must be enough demand and supply. The establishment of generalized media of exchange, like money, for economic transactions makes exchange independent of finding another person who wants what I can offer and who has what I am looking for. However, actors have to trust in the worth of the money received in transactions when it comes to purchasing other demanded goods or services. Otherwise they will not accept the money, and exchange on this basis will break down. A central bank can function as a guarantor of the money's value. The exchanging parties therefore have to trust in the monetary policy of the central bank. In noncash exchange using, say, credit cards, both buyer and seller have to trust in the proper execution of the money transactions by a third party that functions as a clearing house. Engaging in such transactions always implies the risk of trust. The more I expect success and the higher the gain I expect, the more likely it is that I will engage in exchange activities. This is also true for exchange beyond economic transactions using money, namely, social exchange for which the transaction of social approval and the attribution of status serves as a substitute for money.

Exchange doesn't always proceed on equal terms. There is always power involved. Unless both parties are equal in power, the exchange will proceed in favor of the more powerful party in exchange. Nevertheless, the exchange would not take place unless the less powerful party expects some gain from the exchange.

Authority Systems

Systems of authority become established when a number of actors realize that they would be better off in the long run transferring some of their rights to act to an authority that acts in order to provide public goods for them (Coleman, 1990: 145–74). The establishment of a whole system of authority also involves agents (administrators) of the principal authority having to be engaged in running the system. In this case the principal delegates some of his or her authority to the agents. This will occur as long as the principal expects to be better off even though he or she gives some power away to agents who might act against his or her interest. The principal has to take the risk of trusting that the agents will work in his or her interest.

However, another aspect of this is that the whole system works only as long as the agent who works primarily in the principal's interest and not in his or her own interest nevertheless also expects to be better off by engaging in this relationship. Identification with the other party has a strengthening effect on the relationship. However, that will come about only if each actor believes in the other party's willingness and ability to serve his or her interests. Making the agents working on different levels in the authority system responsible in the sense of relating their self-interest to the outcome of their work is a major problem of modern organizations and leads beyond Max Weber's ideal type of the hierarchical bureaucracy of disinterested bureaucrats. Decentralization involving self-interest in doing the job and surveillance by those who are affected by the agents' decision making is the device for building workable systems of authority.

Systems of Trust

Trust is involved in any complex system of action, because actors always have to take a lot of risk in order to proceed with their action in such systems. Otherwise actors would be paralyzed and avoid all involvement in such systems. Intermediaries play a major role in establishing trust within such far-reaching systems of action (Coleman, 1990: 175–96). Advisors tell many people how to act when they don't know for themselves what is the right way to act. We trust in their greater knowledge of the interdependencies of actions that we do not ourselves foresee. Guarantors take the responsibility for the outcome of an action and free other people from having to pay for possible damages resulting from participating in a certain action. Entrepreneurs take the risk of a new enterprise that involves the cooperation of many people who wouldn't take the risk themselves. In each one of these cases many people put trust in an intermediary person in order to keep their own risk within a certain limit. However, they take a risk when they trust such intermediaries.

Collective Behavior

Much of collective behavior, such as panics, riots, and mass movements, has been treated as emotional behavior that *cannot* be addressed in terms of rationality. According to Coleman (1990: 197–240), the opposite is true. Much of this behavior *can* be explained in terms of rational choice. For example, if I am in an escape panic situation, I expect that everybody will run to the exit; thus, I have to do the same and try to be one of the first at the exit. Otherwise, I would have no chance of getting out. The result is that everybody runs, with the effect of many people being hurt and much more time being needed to vacate the room. A bank panic works in a similar way and also inflicts the most damage on those who come late. The run on a bank by depositors wanting to withdraw their money accelerates the process that leads toward the bank's insolvency. Behavior in hostile crowds can be quite rational for the average person, because he or she receives support from those in the crowd and might be hurt by the same people if he or she did not cooperate in the hostile acts.

The Demand for Effective Norms

Large systems of action cannot operate on the basis of the immediate mutual sanctioning of actors, because the external effects of actions are much more widely scattered. They affect a wide range of people, not only those who are immediate to the originator of the action and who could react in order to restore the existing equilibrium of costs and benefits. This situation of widely scattered external effects by which people are affected without having a chance of making the originator responsible creates a "demand for effective norms" in order to regulate the action between people (Coleman, 1990: 241–65). There is, however, a demand for norms that help not only to avoid negative external effects (externalities) but also to bring about positive external effects (externalities), that is, benefits. Norms of etiquette and standards of speech, for example, help the members of status groups to preserve and enhance social esteem.

The Realization of Effective Norms

The demand for effective norms will not bring about the actual establishment of norms and their enforcement unless additional preconditions are met (Coleman, 1990: 266–92). A norm is a prescription or a proscription of certain actions held consensually within a social system. It is a public good, and as such it suffers from the corresponding dilemmas including the free rider and the commons dilemma (see below). Everybody derives advantage from existing norms and feels the disadvantage of the absence of norms, but each person's part in establishing and enforcing norms diminishes to nearly zero the larger the group grows. Doing something oneself toward establishing and enforcing norms brings about more costs than gains. Thus there is a permanent lack of norms in large systems of action.

According to Coleman, this problem can be solved to the extent that those people who are affected by behavior that is conforming or nonconforming to norms are able to share the costs of sanctioning the behavior or to impose second-order sanctions on the beneficiaries of norm-conforming behavior in return for themselves engaging in the sanctioning of behavior regulated by a norm. This can be achieved only if the beneficiaries are linked by social relationships. The closed network fulfills this condition most completely. In a closed network there is complete communication about conforming or nonconforming behavior and each actor is completely dependent on others so that an actor's application of sanctions will be honored immediately by the others. In this case motivation to engage in sanctioning behavior increases the extent that such behavior will be zealously pursued. Sanctions can be applied in such a context incrementally when many members participate in the sanctioning act, for example, by way of participating in gossip. They can also be applied heroically when one sanctioner carries out the sanction for all the others representatively.

The Internalization of Norms and the Self

The internalization of norms by way of socialization reduces the required amount of external sanctioning (Coleman, 1990: 292–99). Actors are interested in bringing about the internalization of norms in others, because it keeps down the costs of external sanctioning. Internalization itself is a process that proceeds with the establishment of the individual's self. The basis for establishing a self in the process of socialization is identification with the socializing agent. This identification comes about inasmuch as the socializee receives benefits from trusting the socializing agent and therefore sees his or her interests as being identical to those of the agent.

According to Coleman (1990: 503–28), the self can be broken down into two parts: the object self, which is the locus of interests and the motive to

maximize utility, and the acting self, which administers the resources necessary to satisfy one's interests and which carries out the action. The relationship between the two can be thought of as similar to that between a principal
and his or her agent. The one commands, the other carries out the commands. However, both need each other and perform economic transactions.
The object self is pleased by the acting self's successful satisfaction of its
interests; the acting self receives approval for doing so from the object self.
The core of the object self is based upon the most elementary organic needs
of the individual and expands through reinforcement of his or her activities
by the socializing agents in the environment with whom the individual identifies. What is reinforced positively by such socializing agents becomes part
of the individual's interests. For example, a boy whose achievements at school
are rewarded by parents and teachers with whom he identifies develops an
interest in achievement.

In the process of socialization, the number of people with whom one
comes into contact and with whom one identifies grows continually, so that
the interests that constitute the object self also grow in number. The basis
for identification in this process is always one's perception of benefiting from
taking the view of the socializing agent. In this way the internalization of
norms from the environment via socializing agents turns norms into interests
of the object self, which controls the acting self in carrying out the corresponding actions. External control is transformed into internal control.

Establishment of Norms by Authorities

There are social conditions under which neither closure of social relationships nor internalization help to motivate the individual to conform to
norms in his or her action. When social systems outgrow small communities, norms can be established only as positive law by an authority to which
the actors have transferred some of their rights to act. This occurs to the
extent that such a transaction seems more beneficial to them in the long
run than retaining the rights concerned (Coleman, 1990: 325–41).

Social Capital

Thus far, we have seen how much we rely on social relationships in order
to further our interests. We need parents, friends, teachers, fellows, colleagues,
trustees, advisers, and agents in order to get along in social life. This is what
Coleman (1990: 300–321) calls social capital. It is a system of mutual obligations that helps us in our everyday undertakings to get what we want.
And it is quite rational to commit ourselves to such obligations in as much
as we can expect a corresponding obligation to provide support on the part
of those other people to whom we have committed ourselves. What makes

such support available are close relationships, stability in our relationships, and a common ideology that unites us with others. It is therefore rational from the point of view of preserving social capital to stay in our relationships and not to change them all the time.

Corporate Action

Next, we come to the level of analyzing corporate action.

Constitutions and the Construction of Corporate Actors

With the growth of systems of action as regards the number of actors involved and matters covered or affected by them, the problems of organizing social life become ever more complex in character. Large systems of action are then organized as corporate actors inasmuch as the people form a constitution of basic norms that define rights and obligations and an authority structure that allocates responsibilities (Coleman, 1990: 325–70). In this way a corporate actor becomes established that is able to act like an individual actor in relation to other individual corporate actors. Families, clubs, religious communities, business corporations, voluntary associations, political parties, administrations, schools, and universities are examples of such corporate actors. For the legal system, they are "legal persons" that can be made responsible for their actions. For example, an individual can sue a business corporation for the harm he or she has suffered in using one of its products.

From the point of view of rational choice theory, people will create a constitution and authority structure for a corporate actor according to the benefits they expect and according to their starting positions of controlling more or less resources. They will accept a constitution and authority structure as legitimate as long as they see themselves as beneficiaries of the system. This doesn't presuppose an equal distribution of rights and obligations. It presupposes nothing but everybody's expectation that they will be better off with the system, even if some individuals make much less gain than others. According to Coleman such an authority system has "internal morality" as long as the members stay with the system, though they could withdraw the rights vested in the authority.

Dilemmas of Rational Action in Large Systems of Action

Applied to the analysis of large systems of action and corporate actors, rational choice theory points to a set of dilemmas that arise for the organization of social life in such systems. In large systems of action, the interdependence of choices that are rational in the situation of each individual leads to effects that make such choices less rational than the other choices that were rejected by the individuals. There are at least two basic dilemmas: the prisoner's dilemma and the public goods dilemma, of which the commons dilemma and the free rider dilemma are special cases.

The Prisoner's Dilemma

According to the prisoner's dilemma, lack of communication results in miscoordination of individual choices (Coleman, 1990: 203-4). Two prisoners who are accused of having both committed the same crime have to decide whether to confess or not without knowing the other's decision. If only one prisoner confesses, that prisoner will get one year in jail and the other will get ten years; if both confess, they will each get five years; if neither confesses, both will remain free. Because neither one knows what the other will do, each one has to fear that the other will confess so that he or she will be sentenced to ten years in jail. Therefore, each is likely to confess so that the result is five years each. This is a much worse result than would have been possible if they had been able to communicate and coordinate their action and had both held out.

The Public Goods Dilemma

The public goods dilemma is common to large groups when there is a question of the individual's contribution to the provision of such a public good or to the avoidance of a public evil (Coleman, 1990: 270–71, 341–44, 451–65, 937–38). Such goods or evils are indivisible and have to be consumed or avoided jointly. Examples of public goods are clean water, clean air, clean streets, clean beaches, safe neighborhoods, well-stocked libraries, rich museums, and wonderful parks. Public evils are dirty water, dirty air, littered streets and beaches, unsafe neighborhoods with high crime rates, poor libraries and museums, and ugly parks. The problem here is that the individual's part in providing for such public goods or in avoiding public evils becomes smaller and smaller the larger the group grows in membership. The effect of my contribution to clean air in a group of ten is one out of ten; in a group of seven million people in a metropolitan area it is one out of seven million. The effect of one person's action on clean air approaches zero. Therefore, I will contribute to such a public good or will contribute to doing away with air pollution less the more costly such an action is for me in terms of money, time, and suppressing my air-polluting habits. Because the probability that my action will have any noticeable effect on clean air is so small, even very small costs of contributing to clean air make such behavior individually less rational than behavior that maintains my polluting habits. I face losses but cannot expect gains. Thus, as a rationally calculating actor, I won't contribute to clean air.

The Commons Dilemma

The commons dilemma is a special case of the public goods dilemma. It occurs when farmers make joint use of a common pasture. In this case, there is a tendency toward overgrazing, so that the pasture finally is destroyed. Because each farmer contributes little to the overgrazing of the pasture but would lose a lot if he or she didn't make full use of it, there is no motivation for the rationally calculating farmer to refrain from overgrazing.

The Free Rider Dilemma

The free rider dilemma is also a special case of the public goods dilemma (Coleman, 1990: 273–76, 490). It presupposes the existence of a public good, like rich museums, libraries, wonderful parks, and clean air. The larger the group that shares such a public good, the more likely it is that there will be people who make use of the good without paying for it, because it is provided anyway. These are the so-called free riders. However, as the number of free riders grows, so does the probability of the public good no longer being provided.

The Organization of Large Systems of Action

From the point of view of a rational choice theory, the organization of behavior in large groups, like neighborhoods, organizations, cities, states, nations, and world society, has to take into account the basic dilemmas of individual rational action. One has always to be aware of the fact that the individually rational actor will do or avoid doing nothing unless that maximizes his or her utility, and will not refrain from doing something unless the costs of such action outgrow the expected gains. A first implication of this premise is organizing behavior in larger systems in such a way that as many goods as possible become divided, provisioned, and consumed individually, so that each actor has to pay individually for what he or she wants and does. Any action a person carries out has to be paid for individually. This also means paying for the costs that are effected by the person's action for other people. This is the problem of the external effects of my action on others. A rational organization of society needs structures that allow for the so-called internalization of any external effects of a person's actions. The effects of the actions of any actor, whether it is an individual actor or a so-called corporate actor such as a business firm, have to be translated into gains and losses to that actor before the actor will take such effects into account.

The ideal type of such a rational organization of a society of rational individuals has always been the market with its decentralized decision making according to Adam Smith's (1776/1937) famous principle of public wealth emerging from the interdependence of private vices (furthering self-interest).

Decentralization is the device for organizing many more social activities than economic behavior alone. Decentralization means breaking down social activity into small units, within which the external effects of an individual's action are much more likely to reflect back upon the individual than they would in large communities. There are fewer chances for the basic dilemmas of individually rational behavior to arise in small units than in large units.

With regard to the external effects of the small units on each other, the next stage of social organization would be making the small units responsible for their actions on the next level. That means the smaller communities have to treat themselves mutually as corporate actors and interrelate so that the external effects of one corporate actor's actions on the others will reflect back upon that actor in order to make the actor aware of the real costs of the action. The next level would be the organization of the larger community of corporate actors to form an even larger corporate actor that is made responsible for its action in relation to other individual and corporate actors by way of internalizing the external effects of action.

Modern Society

Finally, there is the level of analyzing basic problems of modern society.

The Responsibility of Corporate Actors

Coleman (1990: 421–50, 531–664) is very much concerned with the growing organization and determination of social life by corporate actors in modern societies. Corporate actors are artificial creations compared to "natural persons." The major question for modern societies in Coleman's view is how corporate actors can be held responsible for what they do, for the many internal effects they exert on their members and for the many external effects they have on the lives of people outside the corporation. His major proposal is very much in accordance with the liberal tradition: complementing or even replacing global viability as much as possible by independent viability.

What does Coleman's proposal mean? Viability exists inasmuch as an actor has whatever costs or benefits he or she creates for others translated into a corresponding amount of costs or benefits to him- or herself. That is, one simply has to pay individually for what one does to others, and one is honored individually for what one does to others.

Corporate actors, however, have become increasingly organized according to the principle of global viability (Coleman, 1990: 426–30). This means that the individual agent does not have to pay for whatever evil he or she produces; the corporation pays. For example, the corporation pays for the water pollution caused by one of its agents. The question here is, How can agents of corporations be monitored or controlled and made responsible for what they do (Coleman, 1990: 430–34)? First, the corporation is broken down into a number of smaller divisions that are responsible for their part of the whole product. This is divisional viability. Then a classical solution is forward policing, that is, control from top to bottom in a hierarchical system. This type of bureaucratic control, however, is less and less effective in complex systems. Backward policing is a new type of control that originated in Japan; one example is the work practice at Honda in automobile production. There, any production unit is allowed to send back any product that does not meet the standards of quality desired to the unit that supplied it.

Toward Restructuring Responsibility

Coleman sees this type of control as a step toward reintroducing decentralized independent viability that makes every agent on any level of a corporate actor responsible for what he or she does. The corporate actor has to be restructured internally and externally as a system of paired exchanges in which the exchanging parties can keep a mutual check on each other. Internally, this means decentralization, responsibility of small units, and the participation of employees in corporate decision making; externally, it means the surveillance of corporate action by those who are affected in the immediate and broader environment (Coleman, 1990: 553–78). That implies, for example, establishing regular negotiation between business corporations and customers' representatives or neighborhood representatives with regard to the safety of products for customers and the impact of the corporations' activities on the environment.

Summary

Premises of Rational Choice Theory

1. In a situation of choice an actor carries out that action for which the value of its utility multiplied by the probability of such an outcome is highest.
2. Any unit that satisfies one of an actor's interests decreases the utility of any further unit of the same kind.
3. Macro structures like a prevailing religious doctrine result in the community-wide positive sanctioning of behavior that conforms to the doctrine, thus causing individuals to adhere to the doctrine and to behave accordingly, which in turn contributes to the aggregation of such behavior in the community to make it an aggregated macro phenomenon.

Elementary Actions and Relations

4. Actors will engage in transactions with others involving resources the more they see other actors in the possession of resources in which they are interested and the more the other actors are interested in the resources they possess.

5. The more the parties in an economic transaction are equal/unequal in terms of power, the more they will draw equal/unequal benefits from the transaction.

6. The more others interfere negatively in actors' actions, the more actors will be interested in defining rights to act that are accepted by any affected others without dispute.

7. The less others are interested in my action and the more power I have, the more others will recognize my rights to act in a general consensus.

8. If actors expect the transfer of rights to an authority to be more beneficial than holding those rights themselves, they will make that transfer, because of either direct benefits (conjoint authority) or compensatory benefits (disjoint authority).

9. Under conditions of conjoint authority, the subordinate tends to leave too much control with the superordinate.

10. Under conditions of disjoint authority, the subordinate tends to minimize cooperation.

11. The greater the gain and the greater the probability of such a gain that I expect from joining another person's action, the greater will be my trust in that person.

Structures of Action

12. The greater the number of people who expect benefits from engaging in exchange, the broader the trust in others, and the broader the use of a generalized medium of exchange, the greater will be the extension of a system of exchange.

13. The more equally/unequally the power in a system of exchange is distributed, the more equal/unequal will be the outcomes of exchange.

14. The greater the number of actors who expect more benefits from transferring rights to act to the same authority than from holding the rights themselves, the more likely it is that a system of authority will be established.

15. The larger a system of authority grows, the more those in authority (principals) will be interested in delegating part of their authority to agents.

16. Principals and agents will identify with each other, trust each other, and cooperate more, the more both parts draw benefits from their cooperation.

17. The more systems of authority delegate responsibility to small units interacting directly with affected people and the more small units are directly accountable, the more effectively the system of authority will work, which is contrary to a hierarchically organized bureaucracy.

18. The greater the number of people who expect greater benefits by following the advice, action, and lead of intermediaries (advisors, guarantors, entrepreneurs), the greater will be the extent of trust in a system of action that might be used for the mobilization of cooperation.

19. The smaller the number of alternative actions for avoiding high costs, the more likely it is that actors will all do the same and hinder each other, for example, in panics that result from a fire in a room or a "run" on a bank.

20. The more a person is enclosed in a hostile crowd, the more beneficial it will be to participate in the crowd's action and the more costly it will be to refrain from such action.

21. The greater the number of external effects in a system of action, the greater will be the demand for norms.

22. The more the beneficiaries of norms are linked by social relationships, the more likely it is that norms will be established and upheld by zeal in sanctioning deviations either incrementally or heroically.

23. The more norms are internalized by actors, the less external sanctions have to be applied.

24. The more the socializee identifies with the socializing agent, the more likely it is that he or she will internalize the norms represented by the socializing agent.

25. The greater the benefits experienced by the socializee as coming from the socializing agent, the greater will be his or her identification with the agent, based on identical interests.

26. The greater the number of socializing agents a person identifies with, the greater will be the number of interests the person develops.

27. The more the individual's self grows, the more the object self, which sets the interests, and the acting self, which administers resources and carries out the actions, will engage in an economic transaction between principal and agent.

28. The larger systems of action grow, the more there will be an interest in regulating action by positive law set by an authority to which rights to act have been transferred.

29. The greater the benefits an individual draws from established social relationships (social capital), the more likely it is that he or she will uphold these relationships.

Corporate Action

30. The larger systems of action grow, the greater will be the interest in creating corporate actors by transferring rights to some acting bodies.

31. The more people draw benefits from the constitution and the authority structure of a corporate actor, the more they will accept them as legitimate.
32. The less chances people have to communicate in (large) systems of action, the more likely they are to engage in individually rational actions that turn out to be much less beneficial for them because of their interdependence than if they had coordinated their action (prisoner's dilemma).
33. The greater the number of people who have to contribute to and benefit from a public good, the smaller will be the part of each one's contribution and the less likely it is that each one will contribute to its provision (public goods dilemma, including the commons and free rider dilemmas as special cases).

Modern Society

34. The more social life is determined by large corporate actors with global viability (responsibility based on self-interest), the greater will be the number of external effects on people who have no chance of controlling such effects.
35. The more corporate actors are restructured by decentralization and the establishment of independent viability of small units in paired exchange, the smaller will be the number of uncontrolled external effects and the more such effects will be internalized by corporate actors.
36. The more corporate actors are controlled by the internal and external participation of affected people in decision making, the more they will internalize external effects.
37. The more global viability is replaced by independent paired viability, the more the qualities of a liberal society will be revitalized.

Critical Assessment

Let us now turn to a detailed examination and critical assessment of Coleman's rational choice approach.

Between Liberalism and Authoritarian Control

The ideal type of a liberal society results from the application of rational choice theory to answering the question, How should a society composed of free individuals who rationally maximize their utility be organized so that the individuals do not mutually hinder themselves as they do so? However, there are problems in organizing social life that cannot be solved by decentralization. This is always the case when people cannot coordinate their actions because of lack of communication, which brings about the prisoner's dilemma, and when goods demanded and used by individuals cannot be divided but have to remain public goods.

The borderline between public and private goods can be moved back and forth to a large degree. What in one society is a public good is a private good in another society. For example, in a centralized society like France, having a safe neighborhood depends on the relatively equally distributed control of national police, whereas in the United States, a safe neighborhood depends very much on how much private security the neighborhood itself can afford. Therefore, in a decentralized system like the United States the chance of being a victim of a criminal act varies much more according to the neighborhood in which one lives than it does in a centralized system like France. Societies vary in how broadly they define the realm of private or public goods. The United States is surely the society that has gone the farthest in expanding the realm of private goods and in restricting the realm of public goods to a minimum. Therefore, it is no surprise that rational choice theory flourishes best in this country. One could say the approach reflects the common sense of everyday life in American society in theoretical terms.

However, it can no longer be denied that there are things on earth that cannot be divided and consumed individually. They either turn out to be public goods or public evils, depending on people's ability, or lack of ability, to provide or preserve them. Clean air, clean water, public libraries, museums, parks, and safe streets exist inasmuch as they are preserved or provided collectively. However, how can they be preserved or provided in large societies where the public goods dilemma operates? This is the point at which liberalism becomes restricted by the establishment of authority in the perspective of rational choice theory. Establishing a government that is responsible for providing and preserving public goods including the regulation of behavior by norms that guarantee that social order is the common rational choice solution of the public goods problem. But what are the conditions under which such an authority is to be established?

The typical rational choice solution to this problem depends on individuals' ability to invest in long-term interests rather than only short-term ones. Inasmuch as individuals realize that they will be better off when they transfer some of their rights to act to an established authority (government) they will overcome the public goods dilemma. This solution might be chosen by actors and groups whether there is a balance of power between them or not. In the case of a balance of power, all actors and groups might draw the same benefits from the establishment of authority. In the case of an imbalance of power, the benefits might be unequal. Nevertheless, the less powerful actors or groups will still join the transaction if they expect more benefits from having an authority than from being without authority. The proposals in terms of rational choice range from arguing for a weak state empowered with a minimum of rights, with narrow limits and close control by the subordinates, to a strong state empowered with a maximum of rights, with less narrow limits and less close control by the subordinates, and even sometimes to an authoritarian state which escapes any control as long as it guarantees social order.

The history of utilitarian thought has brought forth solutions to the problem at both extremes of this continuum. Thomas Hobbes (1651/1966), Jeremy Bentham (1789/1970), and James Buchanan (1975) represent the strong state argument; John Locke (1698/1967), John Stuart Mill (1861/1974), and Robert Nozick (1974) represent the weak state argument. James Coleman's (1990: 531–78) concern with the growing determination of human life by corporate actors and with the problem of reintroducing some control over the actions of corporate actors by those who are affected points in the direction of saving liberalism from destruction by corporations that have outgrown any control by affected individuals. However, how should large corporations be controlled if their effects are very different for different actors and if their effects have such far-reaching ramifications worldwide that they cannot be foreseen and monitored by the actors immediately affected? This calls for control by government and laws that cover ever larger areas of the world. Thus the very search for control of large multinational corporations must result in the establishment of governmental and legal bodies that outgrow the nation state and are even larger corporate actors that impose their authority on the individual and reproduce the problem of how to control them on an even larger scale. Coleman's attempt at re-creating liberalism would end up in the foundation of new authority structures that destroy liberal society.

When it comes to the problem of controlling the negative effects of self-interested action on a large scale, utilitarian thought, which started with a liberal view of society, has very often ended up by establishing authoritarian state control, as seen in Hobbes to Bentham and Buchanan. This has been shown for utilitarian thought in classical studies by Halévy (1900) and by Parsons (1937/1968), who built his argument on Halévy's work. The original statement of the problem was formulated by Hobbes (1651/1966). According to Hobbes, individuals transfer rights to act to an established authority because of their long-term interest in maintaining social order. However, having once made that decision, they have no right to revoke it. They remain subjected to the authority as long as the ruler provides for social order, whatever the substance of that order might be. Thus, Hobbes switches from liberalism to authoritarianism when it comes to the problem of guaranteeing social order after the initial contract to transfer the rights of control over people's relations among themselves to an established authority. In the perspective of rational choice theory, the outcome of the search for social order has to be the same. There is nothing beyond the liberalism of self-interested people and authoritarian control of these people when their self-interested behavior produces self-destructive effects.

The World of Power and Conflict

The real social world, however, is more complicated than is envisioned by rational choice theory, so things do not always happen as we expect. One needs, for example, to take account of the world of power relationships.

Power in Economic Transactions

In rational choice theory's perspective there is an inclination to see any social interaction as a transaction of resources in which actors engage because they expect to be better off by making it. Applied to the power relationship of two actors, this would imply that both draw benefits from their transaction though the benefits might be unequal because of unequal power. Coleman (1990: 58-59, 63, 132-34, 139, 214-15, 689, 701, 728-29, 780-82, 799-800, 933-37) is well aware of this influence of unequal power on the outcomes of transactions for the two parties. He moves one step beyond the pure rational choice theory of economic transactions, because he conceives of power as an independent factor that shapes the outcome of transactions. Outside the economic paradigm, Coleman overlaps most with theories of power and conflict, though he nevertheless sees power and conflict primarily as factors that influence the utility calculations and outcomes of economic transactions. For example, in addressing the question of when revolutions occur he points out the conditions under which it is more beneficial for individual actors to engage in revolutionary activities than to avoid them (Coleman, 1990: 489-99). He does not come to a complete and thorough assessment of the unique nature of the power relationship and correspondingly of conflict, as a particular theory of power and conflict would do. Therefore, we have to take further steps in the direction of a true understanding of the nature and laws of power and conflict in order to reach a more comprehensive theory of human action.

The Power Relationship

We have to distinguish between making a choice of a transaction from many alternatives on a market from being forced into a transaction where an individual has nothing but the simple choice between subjugation to the decisions of another actor or incurring severe costs, because the other actor is in control of certain resources needed for the satisfaction of the individual's interests, for example, simply by possessing more physical force. In this case a person still makes a choice between submission to another and possibly losing everything. Nevertheless, the interaction is very different from one in which the person's opponent does not have complete control over resources and therefore has to set much more positive incentives in order to get the person's contribution, which might than take the form of a specified service for some remuneration and not simply of submission to the actor. This difference between the power relationship and the exchange of goods and services becomes confused by the rational choice theorist's inclination to reduce any social interaction to an economic transaction.

The Conflict Relationship
The same is true of any conflict that is settled by the application of power. In an economic transaction, both parties will be better off in the end. In conflict, the two parties have mutually exclusive ends, for example, both may want to win a tennis match, or to occupy and use a certain piece of land, or to occupy an office; or one party may want to expand governmental control of the economy while the other wants to reduce such governmental control. Here, power decides which party will succeed, and there is no room for both parties to benefit. Only inasmuch as the two parties give up part of their goals and are satisfied with less than complete goal attainment will there be room for negotiation and compromise. Here we leave the field of strict conflict between mutually exclusive goals and enter the field of economic transaction, because the goals involved no longer are mutually exclusive or because a whole set of goals is involved and the actors aren't committed to realizing certain goals totally.

This, however, by no means proves that any conflict can be transformed into negotiation. There remains a core of conflict in which actions move in the direction in which they are led by the goals set by the more powerful actors. Furthermore, there are unique laws governing this field of conflict and power. Whereas in situations of exchange, where many competing sources of interest satisfaction exist, relationships and commitments vary rapidly and actions move in many directions, in situations of conflict, relationships, commitments, and actions are focused upon the object and parties of conflict. In exchange situations, changes in relationships happen day by day; in power relationships, such changes are limited and occur only in longer waves of submission to power and the overthrow of those in power by new power aspirants, according to Pareto's theory of the rise and fall of elites. It is this dimension of power in social life with its specific laws that is out of the field of view of rational choice theory, because it tends to reduce social interaction to the economic transaction of resources.

Power in Collective Decision Making
The establishment of authority is therefore, in the first instance, dependent on the successful usurpation of power positions by actors or a group of actors, which then can be used to maintain authority at least as long as others don't succeed in usurping the very same positions. This might occur according to pure power politics in the Machiavellian sense or it might occur according to certain rules that determine the means that can be used to attain the power positions. These rules might be established by powerful actors

themselves, they might be the result of negotiations, they might be rooted in a traditional consensus or justified in a cultural discourse, or they might be the result of an interplay of these factors. Nevertheless, there remains a certain underlying logic of establishing and exercising authority by occupying power positions, even in the most pluralistic and democratic societies of contemporary modernity. The impact a government has on societal development is, for example, very much determined by how much its power position is confirmed by support from the population and how it makes use of that power in order to lead discussions and to make and enforce collectively binding decisions.

Great differences exist between weak and strong governments in pluralistic and democratic societies resulting from unsuccessful and successful mobilization and application of power. We have to make use of theories of conflict and power in order to understand and explain these processes. Rational choice theory's leveling out of power politics by economic transactions does not give us access to this dimension of social life and even leads to wrong views, explanations, and predictions in this area. For example, a powerful government might impose decisions that produce losses for many affected individuals and groups. As an agent of the collectivity and not of individual groups, it very often has to do so in order to serve the collectivity's long-term interests, for example, by way of imposing tax laws that make pollution of the environment very costly for the individual actor. Here, a powerful government might even make use of its position in order to lead the change of interests from the short-term individual level to the long-term collective level with positive effects experienced only by later generations. A weak government could not do that.

The World of Solidarity Relationships and Trust

There is the world of solidarity relationships. People live within limited solidarity communities of class, race, ethnicity, religion, or region that limit the self-interested individualism of their members from birth and their ability to associate and trust beyond their boundaries. This hinders the establishment and maintenance of a common authority system simply on the basis of long-term self-interest. A long time is needed to overcome the widespread mistrust by establishing associations beyond in-group boundaries. There is a basic associational problem of order that cannot be solved on the simple basis of placing long-term self-interest above short-term self-interest. The language of rational choice theory simply has no words for dealing with this problem appropriately. It does not make sense to reduce the problem of solidarity simply to a problem of the rational calculation of self-interest, because solidarity structures themselves determine what the individual might see as his or her self-interest.

Trust

Trust does not emerge simply from risk taking in economic terms as Coleman (1990: 91–116) wants to make us believe. It is exactly the opposite. Whether I engage in a joint action with other people and take that risk depends on how much I trust those people. This trust depends very much on familiarity and established ties, on overcoming the boundaries of primordial bonds and on breaking down barriers between aliens and enemies.

Trust residing on these preconditions enters the risk calculation as an independent variable that cannot itself be explained in economic terms. Familiarity or unfamiliarity, close ties or loose ties, friendship or hostility are there before I begin to calculate risk in specific situations. They reside in my feelings and emotional relationships and very often persist contrary to rational calculation. The fact that I trust someone I know and don't trust someone I don't know might be reasonable in terms of economic risk taking, but how do I deal with the fact that I normally don't get to know people whom I am not familiar with and whom I don't trust? My fellows and I might be hostile to other people because we have never gotten to know them because of mutual mistrust. This might have caused harmful conflict for a long time. Is this rationally calculated action in economic terms? I don't think so, yet it occurs all over the world every day.

The world is full of hostile outbreaks of minorities against majorities, of majorities against minorities, and of minorities against other minorities. Very often this results from the fact that one group doesn't allow the other group to enjoy the same rights. There is a rational economic aspect in hostile outbreaks between the groups, as Coleman points out, because participating in the actions of my own group brings benefits of support whereas refusing to participate results in harmful withdrawal of support or even punishment. However, is this a full account of what happens in such hostile outbreaks and of what causes them? Surely not. The very fact that the groups *see* and *feel* themselves to be enemies and engage in mutually harmful action when mutually beneficial action would also be possible exists before the group members begin to calculate the costs and benefits of participating in group action.

Why have some groups and nations succeeded in establishing friendly and mutually beneficial relationships while others have not, when entering into such positive relationships would be beneficial for all? Why have some nations been able to overcome group particularism and to establish common democratic decision making while others have not? Why are some more able to do so and others less, though such a process would be more beneficial for them all? There must be something that is not completely affected by or even resists rational learning of this kind. This is the resistance of the emotional against the rational, and no sociological theory that is based entirely on principles of rationality can have appropriate access to this dimension of social life. It would be absurd to reduce the emotional and nonrational to the rational, making the human being a thoroughly rational person. Telling hostile groups about the benefits resulting from turning hostility into friendship would not help very much. They would probably refuse to listen to such advice or they would at least refuse to receive such benefits. Emotions have to be redirected in this case.

Though there is an economics of emotions, it is not all that can be said about emotions. There is a core of emotions that cannot be redirected by new information; it can be redirected only by the creation of new emotions and by permitting old emotions to disappear. This is a process that takes a great deal of time. It requires the establishment of new ties. We can reduce discrimination of minorities by law, but we cannot legislate the emotions of people and that part of behavior that is directed by emotions. We cannot make whites and blacks like each other by law and cannot therefore change those aspects of their behavior which are based on liking or not liking each other. The fact that it might be harmful for a white person to marry a black person because both might lose emotional support from their fellows comes *after* the fact that whites and blacks do not feel as comfortable living with each other as they do living with their own group, because any negative view taken of a marriage between a white person and a black person is itself partly determined by the history of emotions involved in the relationship.

The redirection of emotions of whole groups requires the exemplary redirection of emotions by charismatic leaders. White leaders like John F. Kennedy and Lyndon B. Johnson who made the abolition of racial discrimination a common concern were important redirectors of emotions. Michael Gorbachev's historical success in turning the relationship between East and West from confrontation to cooperation was very much based on his ability to gather emotional support and trust from both parts of the world and to turn this emotional support into a redirection of emotions. Feelings of mistrust were increasingly replaced by feelings of trust. The process works like this: The leader of one of two hostile groups receives emotional support from both groups and serves as mediator in the sense of transmitting the support from one group to the other group. In order to do so, the leader must be someone who has appeal for both sides, so that people begin to trust him or her without exactly knowing whether he or she will turn that trust into economic gains.

Redirecting emotions also depends on bringing together people who have been kept apart, on the sharing of the rites of associating in common activities that have been kept separate before, on the development of common membership in voluntary associations and groups; it depends on the shared worship of what is sacred, and calls for sharing that part of life that is explicitly directed to association with one's fellows: spending time together at the workplace, at parties, at home, at a restaurant. This is how emotions and ties of solidarity are produced and permanently reproduced. It is different in nature from the market place of economically calculated exchange.

To reduce social interaction to the transaction of resources is, therefore, wrong. Economic exchange is something that is based on rational calculation and changes from situation to situation very quickly. Emotional ties of solidarity or emotional relationships of hostility change much more slowly. They are guided by different laws. Economically calculated exchange behavior moves toward that end which promises to bring about the highest achievement in utility maximization. Emotional association moves in the direction of mobilizing those ties that have existed before, while tending to avoid encounters in which people feel uncomfortable because of unfamiliarity.

A little observation might illustrate how this law of emotional association works: People who are used to living with their own group will stay with their group at a party for the whole evening and will not make an effort to get to know new people. However, people who are much more used to associating with a greater variety of people will also do so at that party. There are national differences in this type of associational behavior, by the way. Keeping with one's own is a behavior that is much more common at a party where the guests are mainly Germans than at a party with American guests. The German pattern is an outcome of imposing the American party on the German tradition of association with one's own (*Geselligkeit*).

Solidarity, Trust, and the Commitment to Norms

Relationships of solidarity and trust form the very network on which the normative regulation of behavior resides; otherwise, the whole of social life would be as short-lived as the fashions of the market. However, because social life often has some stable elements that do not change as rapidly as calculations of marginal utility do, we have to account for these elements in terms other than utility maximization. It is misleading to reduce ties of mutual support to nothing but social capital, because we do not gain access to the unique laws that guide the production and reproduction of such linkages if we conceive of them only in economic terms. Ties of support have an emotional basis, that of sharing a common life and a feeling of mutual belongingness. These are the features of life that make it probable that we will share a common view of the world, of what is true or untrue, right or wrong, beautiful or ugly, meaningful or meaningless with our fellows and will be negatively affected by deviations from expectations based on that common world-view and by any harm done to our fellows. This is the very locus of shared norms and a uniform sanctioning reaction to norm violations within groups.

People who live together confirm each other's views of what is right and wrong from day to day. Whether or not the norms they follow in doing so are to their advantage in maximizing their utility may be unknown to them or they believe so because it is their mutually confirmed view of the world. The utility calculation of the individual who lives in a community with other people cannot be carried out independently of what he or she has confirmed as useful for him or her by fellow community members. In the normative world in which a person believes, what is useful is very much shaped by what is considered right and proper. Different groups have very different views of what is right and proper and therefore also of what is useful or useless. For most middle-class youth it is rightful and useful to do his or her best in educational achievement; for the underclass gang member, it is right and useful to achieve as a drug dealer.

Inasmuch as the scope of norms outgrows groups who feel an immediate sense of belonging, more complex relationships of trust and support are necessary in order to have social life regulated by norms. However, these relationships too are not simply economic transactions, as Coleman would like us to believe. Common norms become replaced by positive law. Parliaments make law, courts ensure the persistence of the law, governments initiate and carry out the law, and the police enforce the law. However, how much behavior is indeed regulated by the law depends on relationships of support and trust.

I would not be able to decide whether the lawmaking of the legislature, the law guardianship of the courts, the law enactment of the government, and the law enforcement of the police were to my advantage if I had to try to make a rational economic calculation. If anything, the relationship functions the other way around. I believe in such an advantage because I trust their words. But why do I trust their words? There is something else that has an influence on my trust or mistrust. Parliaments, courts, governments, and police could not work without the support of people who trust them, because much of what they decide cannot be directly monitored, either in itself or its effects on the people, by the people themselves. The production and reproduction of trust is, therefore, the foremost task of any decision making. Otherwise, resistance and thus the breakdown of social order would abound.

This production and reproduction of trust, however, is a process that cannot be accounted for in purely rational economic terms, because the trust needed cannot be completely confirmed by utility outcomes. If political or judicial decision making had to prove any of its proceedings in terms of the maximization of utility, no decisions would ever be made. It is the very nature of political or judicial decision making that different parties draw different gains or losses from the process. There are always a great many losers in the process, those who don't get what they want. And people look not only at their own utility maximization but also at the utility maximization of others. They compare outcomes. In this situation, it is very likely that every individual and group would feel at a disadvantage compared to an alternative decision if they were able to monitor the decision making independently.

Why, then, are there not outbursts of radical opposition to such decision making? Why do such outbursts happen more often at some places than they do at others? The reason is that individuals' and groups' accounts of the advantages or disadvantages do not occur independently of the political and judicial bodies' ability to shape their view of the things and even their ability to decide without being monitored by everybody in every aspect of a decision. Political and judicial bodies work more or less on the basis of trust and support and thus are more or less capable of making people believe that what they do is right and to the advantage of the people. In open democratic systems this is only possible by way of succeeding against opposing definitions of the situation that are brought forth in public discussion and disseminated by the media. The production and reproduction of trust is an arduous but indispensable task in such systems.

Because of the many different possibilities and risks involved in decision making and the limited time available for the process, citizens become increasingly uncertain about the advantages and disadvantages of the decisions made. This is one reason why the citizens' own decision making becomes increasingly governed by their feeling of trust in public figures the more complex those decisions become. Politicians and judges then have to serve as mediators who gather and allocate support and trust. How much trust they can mobilize depends on their ability to establish a positive emotional relationship with the people. However, this need not go on completely unreflected. The trusted politician or judge has to live up to the highest standards of the culture prevailing in a society. The leader cannot be everybody's darling; that is, he or she cannot serve any particular interest. Otherwise he or she would too often cause disappointment, because others would be seen as getting something they don't deserve. The trustworthy leader succeeds in being accepted as he or she tells the people how they have to see things, what they should see as right or wrong, and what they should perceive as advantageous or disadvantageous. It is not the impossible convergence of independent interests in the leader's action that makes him or her trustworthy but an ability to establish supportive ties, to create a common view of things based on living up to the standards of the culture to an exemplary degree.

The World of Culture, Communication, and Legitimacy

This is the point where culture enters the field, another dimension of social life that does not exist in substance in the world of rational choice theory. Just as this theory fails to deal appropriately with the nonrational elements of social life when it comes to revealing the roots of trust, common norms, and binding decisions, it also fails to deal appropriately with the concept of rationality itself. It reduces rationality to the narrow concept of instrumental, economic rationality. Yet that leaves out of account the world of ideas, values, cognitions, norms, and expressions that is the object of communications between people. Both ideas and communications relate to each other according to laws that cannot be understood in terms of rational choice. People do live in such a world. What they believe and see and what they communicate to each other determine very much what they conceive of as the *legitimate* self-interests of themselves and of other people and whether they will respect the self-interests of these people. Whether I ultimately respect the rights of another ethnic group to have the same access to any public good as my group has depends largely on the culture within which I live. This culture entails the values, norms, and cognitions that serve as grounds for the legitimation or delegitimation of rights. Whether a right can be claimed successfully or not in the sense that it is accepted as legitimate or illegitimate can be explained not in terms of rational choice but only in terms of what are the relevant values, norms, and cognitions that can be mobilized in order to sustain a specific right. This is a meaning relationship of the logical derivation of rights froms values, norms, and cognitions and of consistency or inconsistency between rights on the one hand and values or norms on the other. There is no language in rational choice theory for dealing with this aspect of the world.

With regard to the establishment and maintenance of authority, we can say that ideas, values, norms, and cognitions are also always involved in this process. Whether a particular authority system will be accepted by the people as *legitimate* depends on how far it can be sustained by values, norms, and cognitions in which the people believe. And whether people believe in certain values, norms, and cognitions depends in the first instance on establishing consistency with what they have believed up to now and on initiating processes of cognitive learning by delivering new information. This discursive rationality cannot be reduced to instrumental rationality. Answering the question of whether a statement is meaningful or meaningless, right or wrong, elegant or inelegant, true or untrue is not the same as calculating whether it might maximize my utility to make such a statement. It might be meaningless, wrong, inelegant, or untrue but nevertheless useful in strategic terms to win the applause of a certain public.

This dimension of the social world is involved in the establishment, maintenance, control, limitation, and substantive determination of any authority system and social order and is completely outside the language of rational choice theory. A short statement by Karl R. Popper, who is well respected by rational choice theorists, might explain what I mean. Popper (1962/1969: 109–13) reports on a statement made by an anthropologist after having observed the discussion at a conference. The anthropologist talked about how the discussion was shaped by elementary processes of group dynamics. Popper asked the anthropologist whether he was at all interested in the substance of the discussion and how the discussion developed, because of the more or less convincing arguments brought forth by the participants. Popper was emphasizing the fact that there is something in the discussion that reaches beyond group dynamics, namely, the meaning relationship between words and sentences and their internal dynamics according to the rules of excluding contradictions, establishing internal consistency, and external corroboration with regard to the relationship of sentences to the real world. This cultural and communicative dimension in social interaction and social systems cannot be assessed purely in terms of rational choice theory. Any explanation of why people accept a certain system of authority as legitimate or not has to refer to such processes of communication. Given that the interests of individuals and groups are as diverse as they are in modern societies, it would be impossible to have any legitimate authority if an existing authority system had to rely on a convergence of interests alone. The attribution of legitimacy is much more a process of public communication in which certain definitions of legitimacy win precedence over others and shape the view of things very broadly. In this process, concepts of the legitimacy of rights to rule and of interests that may be privately pursued are defined for a broad variety of people. This definition of legitimacy doesn't occur in a cultural vacuum but in relation to ideas, values, norms, and cognitions that prevail in that culture. The attribution of legitimacy, then, depends on successfully sustaining rights to rule and to pursue interests with the backing of such prevailing values and on the unchallenged rule of such values.

Conflict about legitimacy is not simply a conflict of interests; in the first instance, it is a conflict concerning the proper relationship between concrete institutions and rights on the one hand and more abstract ideas and values on the other hand or even a conflict over what the right ideas and values are. This is a debate that has its own logic and proceeds independently of the multitude of interests. There is a great variety of interests within a society but only a limited set of key values, whether in harmony or disharmony with each other. Therefore, the attribution of legitimacy or illegitimacy to certain institutions or rights has to be decided without a chance to trace it back to the whole variety of interests articulated in society. The relationship has to be seen the other way around: The debate on legitimacy and illegitimacy shapes the view of interests themselves, setting limits for their acceptance as legitimate.

This is not to say that there is no relationship in the other direction. Discussants in a debate on legitimacy may try to further their own interests and derive advantage from the discussion's outcome. Nevertheless, the success of their attempt to do so depends on their ability to sustain their claims and proposals not only in terms of their own interests but also in terms of ideas and values that have a more general acceptance. Appealing to everybody's interests will also have only limited success, because of the sheer variety of interests. Thus, the laws that guide the attribution of legitimacy are different from those of economic transactions, which take place when both parties expect to be better off with the transactions than without them. A claim to legitimacy by one actor is accepted by the other when the first one succeeds in sustaining his or her claim by grounds for which he or she would get support by any third party. Attributing legitimacy is an act that involves more than two actors, refers directly to a collectivity, and proceeds according to laws that are different from the laws of economic transactions.

The World of the Self

The same limits of rational choice theory that have been pointed out thus far on the level of social systems also narrow down the view of the self. In Coleman's (1990: 503–28) view, the self consists of nothing but interests and resources at the disposal of an agent who carries out what is demanded by the interests according to the principle of maximizing utility. Purposive action is reduced to resource mobilization. What cannot be addressed appropriately in this perspective is the fact that an agent needs the personal willpower to pursue ends in the face of resistance. The individual will develop such a capacity only inasmuch as he or she is given the opportunity to fight for his or her goals against such resistance. In order to explain this, we need a conflict theory of personality development.

Learning processes are reduced to processes of reinforcing behavior by way of reward and punishment. What remains out of sight of such an approach is cognitive learning by recording and processing information according to the principles of external corroboration and internal consistency of information.

Identification is reduced to an identity of interests. What remains untouched by this perspective is the fact that, first and foremost, identification has an emotional basis in the establishment of a sense of mutual belonging or a sense of admiration and devotion. People are drawn together because they spend a lot of time together or because they experience the same dangers, the same distress, and the same joy, or because they are brought together by outside forces. In all cases, they tend to *see and feel* themselves as a unit. They will indeed *feel* joy and sadness together. In cases of admiration or devotion, the admiring or devoted party in the relationship attributes some extraordinary or even extraterrestrial qualities to the other person and therefore has a basic *feeling* of admiration and devotion without being able to prove, in terms of concrete benefits, what he or she draws from that relationship. It is rather the opposite: Because of the feelings of belonging, admiration, and devotion the individual sees his or her interests as being furthered by the admired person whatever he or she really does. The true devotee still feels benefited even by the worst harm done to him or her by the person he or she is devoted to. What is interesting to try to explain is why the devotee's perception of benefits becomes so distorted by devotion, rather than attempting to explain devotion as resulting from benefits received. This might have occurred at one time but no longer plays a part once devotion has emotionally blocked off cost-benefit analysis. This latter form of relationship in fact constitutes the core of identification, and it is thus outside the range of rational choice theory.

A final factor is the self's ability to reflect. In terms of rational choice, however, reflection is narrowed down to the terms of cost-benefit analysis. What about the self's ability to reflect about matters of fact, aesthetics, morality, and meaning? Are such matters reducable to cost-benefit analysis? Surely not. Whether a cognitive statement is true or untrue, a moral norm right or wrong, a work of art beautiful or ugly, or a text—including the text of life—meaningful or meaningless are questions that are raised and answered by the self constantly in very different ways, dependent on the culture in which the individual has grown up.

Reducing such questions to cost-benefit analysis might be possible in a culture that does indeed have such a narrowing effect on the human individual. The final triumph of the economic paradigm in Western culture with the help of many rational choice theorists who teach their students exactly the principles of such a culture might lead to such an identity between reflection and cost-benefit analysis. Fortunately, the world has still preserved at least some cultural pluralism so that we can still protest and work against the movement of establishing the cultural dominance of economic thought by propagating a particular and very American view of rationality as the universally valid one. This is group particularism in the guise of cultural universalism. If we want to preserve the full variety of human reflection, we have to turn to theories that trace the self's ability to reflect on its exposure to discourse and argumentation, to making statements that are then disproved, and to being permanently forced to revise disproved statements in the light of the principles of external corroboration and internal consistency of ideas. In paying attention to this core dimension of human reflection we will attain a much more complex view of the self's ability to reflect than a rational choice approach would make us believe.

The World of the Micro-Macro Link

A further problematic aspect concerns the micro-macro link (see Blalock and Wilken, 1979; Knorr-Cetina and Cicourel, 1981; Alexander, Giesen,

Münch, and Smelser, 1987). In Coleman's rational choice view the macro is an external condition for the human individual that sets positive or negative sanctions for individual behavior, but this in turn in aggregated form has aggregated effects on many other people to again form a macro condition for their behavior.

However, what does this have to say about the meaning relationship between texts that form part of a prevailing culture, such as the Bible in Christianity, and the interpretations of that text by particular religious communities and particular individuals? Here the text might open or close people's eyes depending on the meaning constructed in processes of discursive reasoning. And that very reasoning process might result in a change of the prevailing meaning of the text within the whole culture. The way from the macro to the micro and back to the macro is always dependent on establishing internal consistency and external corroboration in interpretations of a text. Whether certain interpretations will be rewarded or punished is an aspect that might play a role but only in a secondary way, without being able to replace the question of meaning completely.

There are also further types of macro-micro links that do not correspond to the rational choice model. A community or an individual who joins a wider community by way of identification on an emotional basis of devotion is guided by the macro community only because of that identification, which is a precondition for sanctions to work. On the other hand, their particular identification as a micro phenomenon results in strengthening the wider community's sense of belonging as a macro phenomenon. This is association as a link between the macro and the micro that cannot be completely understood in terms of rational choice because of the emotional core of the association.

Finally, the rational choice preoccupation with economic transactions leads to the dimension of pure power being overlooked in the macro-micro relationship. Where the greater community has enough power it can impose any command on the smaller units and individuals without a reciprocal effect being exerted by the smaller units and individuals in changing the larger system. On the other hand, where conflict between the macro and the micro prevails, there might be waves of the macro system's domination of the micro units, but these could be interspersed with periodical upheavals in which those micro units overturn that dominant relationship, leading to the establishment of new macro power over micro units. This power-and-conflict view of the macro-micro link cannot be appropriately addressed in terms of economic transactions.

The World of Norms

Another area where the limits of rational choice theory are immediately apparent is that of norms. Coleman (1990: 31–32, 241–42) claims, in a discussion of Parsons, to explain how norms emerge in social life rather than presupposing their existence. Yet this is an erroneous representation of what Parsons said about norms. Parsons's (1937/1968) problem was how to explain social order in terms of mutually predictable actions. This implies that not every part of social life changes from situation to situation or with a change of interests. His answer, like that of Kant, is that there must be something that is more stable than interests and that doesn't vary from individual to individual and from situation to situation, something they have in common and that they guard as sacred against the appetites of the profane world. This is the core of sacred norms that are rooted in people's sharing everyday life and building up a common feeling of belonging, a common view of the true and untrue, right and wrong, beautiful and ugly, meaningful and meaningless. Norms are part of this common life-world, for they are concepts of right and wrong. These norms emerge from sharing life as a unit, are reproduced in rituals of gathering and of punishing deviations, and are upheld by mutual support against violators. This is the locus of norms as the most stable parts of social life.

This, however, is not the whole story about norms, for it deals only with their *binding, obligatory,* and *stable* character. There are other aspects of norms that result from the penetration of other fields of human life into the very realm of norms. Situational change, learning processes, and economic transactions contribute to the *change* of norms according to interests. Communication, discourse, justification, and criticism contribute to attributing *legitimacy* or *illegitimacy* to norms. Authority and power contribute to the *enforcement* of norms. Whatever change occurs in such processes, however, new norms will still need to be anchored in the same way as others in a common life-world, in solidarity and rituals of affirmation, in order to be made stable cornerstones of social life. Inasmuch as norms become part of an individual's self, they are rooted in the same processes: anchored by identification with a community, changed by information recording and processing, legitimized by reflection, and enforced by willpower. Rational choice theory covers only a limited and distinctive part of the story of norms. A close look at the meaning of Parsons's message from 1937 warns us against premature conclusions in matters of norms.

The World of Liberal Society

Coleman's concern with preserving or reestablishing a liberal society against the all-embracing expansion of corporate action needs the same qualification as his whole approach. Liberty in terms of rational choice is a limited and one-sided concept. It is true that one element of liberty is decentralization, with individual responsibility and independent viability. However, as we have demonstrated, there is always the danger that the liberal call for guarding liberties purely in terms of controlling the external effects of instrumental action instrumentally will finally culminate in even greater governmental power.

The determination of the scope and limits of rights is a matter not only of negotiation, but also of discursive argumentation and validation of claims with *generally* acceptable grounds. Otherwise, the distribution of rights would never escape the power struggle based on catch-as-catch-can. We assume that modern societies have succeeded in developing an element of rational discourse in the definition of legitimate rights.

Liberal society would never work, however, without an element of trust and establishing a sense of citizenship that reaches beyond the boundaries of primordial ties. This will not continue to develop without rituals for celebrating common rights to citizenship explicitly on that level, thereby bridging the gap between classes, strata, and groups.

Finally, a liberal society needs power to be detached from everyday disputes by way of governmental centralization of power and its control by the legal system. A society in which each person believes he or she can police other's actions on his or her own behalf by relying on the firepower of his or her own weapons is in danger of destroying its liberties, because everybody has to fear everybody else. Such a society is close to Hobbes's state of nature. The monopolization of physical force by the government, though, needs close control by checks and balances, common norms, and legitimating discourse. A liberal society is a much more complex system than portrayed by rational choice theory.

The Merits and Limits of Rational Choice Theory

The advertisement for Coleman's book *Foundations of Social Theory* (Coleman: 1990) claims that it is the most important contribution to sociological theory since the publication of Parsons's *Structure of Social Action* (Parsons, 1937/1968). It is indeed a very important book for rational choice theory. However, if it were taken as a comprehensive statement of sociological theory in general, sociology would envision a much poorer future compared to its past, because *Foundations of Social Theory* is much less informed by the whole variety of social thought than was Parsons's *Structure of Social Action*. Almost nothing is preserved of the contributions to sociological theory from sources outside the rational choice paradigm itself. Those sources of sociological theorybuilding are treated as virtually nonexistent throughout the book. The theory attains comprehensiveness only by reduction; that is, by reducing whatever exists outside the sphere of economics to the laws of economics, rather than building a really comprehensive theory that would preserve the truth content of the great variety of contributions to sociological theory from its beginning to the present debates. This strategy of achieving comprehensiveness by reduction is common to the whole movement of rational choice theory, because its proponents seem to live a self-referential life in which they are backed up by other rational choice theorists and by the commonsense view of an overly economized culture.

There is no doubt that rational choice theory has its merits in explaining the economic aspects that occur throughout social life and beyond the realm of the economy itself, and we are indebted to Coleman for having contributed so much to that project. There is an economics of family life, love, friendship, authority, conflict, education, discourse, association, reading, the arts, and so on. However, this does not imply that those realms are nothing but economics. They have their own character and laws that have to be studied in themselves by a more differentiated and comprehensive approach to sociological theory. If rational choice theory took over sociology with its claim to universality, as it tries to do wherever it flourishes, this would be another triumph of the economic ideology in Western culture, a further expansion of the imperialism of economic culture. The future of sociological theory would be a bleak one. Therefore, we need to train young sociologists in the whole of social thought in order to keep open the variety of our culture for future generations.

An Application: Collective Decision Making

How incomplete rational choice theory is can be demonstrated with an application of the theory to explaining social processes. Let me take an application by Coleman (1971) to analyzing the conditions under which collective decisions will be made even though the members of a political system have different interests in outcomes.

Coleman starts with the central question of sociological theory as it was stated in classical terms by Thomas Hobbes: How is social order possible? Hobbes's answer was for people to conclude a contract to transfer all their power to a centralized authority that was obliged to guarantee civil order. As Coleman states, the predominant solution to the problem in modern sociology has been one formulated by Talcott Parsons: the commitment of people to a community and the socialization of younger people into that community, which has a tradition of commonly shared values and norms. To counter this sociological preoccupation with the normative solution of the problem of order, Coleman proposes that there are many situations in which societies, communities, organizations, or groups are in need of regulations that are binding for everybody without having common norms from which these decisions could be derived or without having common norms at all. This is where collective decisions instead of collective norms would solve the problem. It is a situation that is characterized by conflicting interests among the different parties involved. Coleman's question then is: Which are the conditions allowing for collective decisions to be realized when there are no common norms? In answering this question, he explicitly begins by making "an opposite error" compared to the common conception of man as a socialized member of a community with commonly shared norms:

> I will start with an image of man as wholly free: unsocialized, entirely self-interested, not constrained by norms of a system, but only rationally calculating to further his own self-interest. (1971: 273)

Exchanging Power

According to Coleman's economic approach, actors strive to maximize utility in choosing certain actions to perform. Every action brings about different outcomes with regard to the different preferences the actor has. What is important for the actor is the net utility generated by the action, that is, the final result after the costs of foregone utilities have been subtracted. Coleman calls this net utility of an action the "interest" of an actor in an action. In Homans's terms it is the profit consisting of reward minus costs. Now, inasmuch as the actions of people have effects, an actor's utility maximization depends on what kind of actions other people perform. If the actor lacks power over the actions of other people that have effects on his or her utility maximization, and if the actor has power over actions that have no effects on his or her maximization of utility and therefore don't interest him or her, the actor as a rational being, says Coleman, will be interested in exchanging power:

> Faced with a situation of a lack of power over actions which interest him, together with a surplus of power over actions which interest him little or not at all, the rational man will make an exchange of power. Thus he will engage in a special kind of economic transaction. (1971: 276).

Coleman starts with the same assumption as Hobbes — people's actions having effects on others — but he does not accept Hobbes's conclusion that a war of all against all results from this situation, which in its turn gives people the insight to conclude a contract obliging them to transfer all their power to a centralized authority that watches over the compliance of people with civil order. Coleman sees a chance for peaceful exchange emerging from this situation instead of civil war. The difference between the two is that according to Hobbes people use power and deceit to increase their power, while according to Coleman they exchange power over actions they are not interested in for power over actions they are interested in. However, Coleman also sees that the emergence of this peaceful exchange is bound to a very specific set of conditions.

Power Exchange in a Legislative Game

Coleman specifies these conditions using the example of a legislative game designed for purposes of studying collective decision making. This game is played by a number of legislators; each one represents a certain constituency and has to decide on eight political issues—either for or against legislative proposals in the following areas: civil rights, aid to education, defense appropriation, medical care for the aged, offshore oil to states, a federal seashore park, retaining a military base, and a federal dam. Each player is given cards representing the votes of his or her constituency on the issues by giving distributions per 100 voters: for example, a civil rights card might say 100 pro and 0 con, or 75 pro and 25 con, or 30 pro and 70 con, and so on. The legislators are interested in being reelected by their constituency and therefore try to see that bills are passed or turned down in such a way as to satisfy as many of their own voters as they can. In the game each legislator has the power of one vote for or against each bill, the rotating power to raise an issue on the floor, and some other prerogatives according to parliamentary procedure. This "internal" legislative power of the player has to be distinguished from "external" power (for example, physical force) he or she could use in order to enforce certain decisions. Inasmuch as the players are interested in a smaller number of issues than the eight mentioned above, they have power they don't need over some actions. This opens up the opportunity to exchange votes, that is, power. The rational legislator interested in only three issues will try to exchange his or her remaining five votes with legislators who are not interested in the same issues. Legislator A may be interested in civil rights, aid to education, and defense appropriation; Legislator B may be interested in medical care, offshore oil to states, and the federal seashore park. Because of their complementary interests, they are likely to exchange votes, so that B votes with A on the first three issues, and A votes with B on the second three. By exchanging votes in this way the legislators increase their power on the issues they are interested in. And that enables them to help decide their issues in a way that gives them a better chance of reelection than they would have had without exchanging votes. They maximize individual utility by exchanging votes, and they reach collective decisions. This is apparently a situation where the maximization of individual utilities goes hand-in-hand with the attainment of collective decisions, and no normative restrictions are given, as Coleman puts it.

Preconditions of Power Exchange

For individual maximization of utility and the making of collective decisions to coincide in the manner outlined, specific preconditions have to be met, as Coleman (1971: 282–85) explicitly states:

1. There must be several issues that have to be decided upon. Otherwise there is no opportunity for any exchange of power between different actors. If there is only one issue, the legislators will be either completely divided into "pro" and "con" factions or there may be people who have no opinion on the issue, and they may become the objects of attempts to influence them by the pro or con factions. In any case, contrary to the legislative game with a number of issues that allowed for there to be several winners, what we have here is a division between winners and losers. Conflict will be much more severe in this case, with the result that the losers put up enormous resistance to the decision, often making it difficult to enforce. As Coleman says, it is the dilemma of many small communities that they are plagued with controversies over a very limited set of issues, sometimes not more than school issues or water fluoridation (or today: environmental pollution and nuclear plants). On the other hand, larger cities have a much greater list of issues to decide on. Therefore, it is very often easier in the large communities to come to collective decisions, whereas the decisions of smaller, suburban communities may be subjected to unrelenting resistance.

2. A second condition for the working of exchange in collective decision making is that not all legislators are interested in all of the issues; otherwise, there would again be no exchange of power over different actions. A very heated political system where everybody is involved in everything and has an interest in every single issue is no place for the peaceful exchange of power. Severe conflict and resistance against decisions on the part of the losers is to be expected here.

3. A third condition for the working of exchange in collective decision making is that the legislators' interests in certain issues is distributed in such a way that legislators do not all share an interest in the same combination of issues. There must be a sufficient number of people who are interested in different issues. Otherwise, the interests would combine into one conflict running through a number of issues. There would be no chance of exchanging votes. A cumulation of conflict over several issues that always range the same people against one another is common in political systems that are characterized by group division across a number of qualities; religion, region, language, and class tend to associate and divide the same people in this case. Coleman mentions the division of Canada into French-speaking, Catholic, Quebec—which is economically depressed—and English-speaking, Protestant, non-Quebec—which is prosperous. Northern Ireland suffers from the division of Catholic, economically depressed, and politically powerless people versus Protestant, economically more prosperous, and politically powerful people. This cumulation of conflict dividing society into two parts makes it very difficult to reach collective decisions without facing enormous and often violent resistance.

These are the three conditions for the working of exchange as a device of collective decision making as specified by Coleman. However, the next question is, Are there further preconditions without which exchange of power would not work?

4. One such precondition is made up by the rules of the game. Why do actors enter into the peaceful exchange of votes, why do they abide by the agreements concluded, and why do they not make use of power external to the game like threatening to quit the game, holding up the process of decision making, or using physical force? Coleman (1971: 285–86) gives us the answer that actors learned in the process of exchanging power that it is more profitable for them in the long run to abide by the rules. Cases of breaching contracts occurred, but the longer the actors participated in the game, the more they became reliable partners of exchange. They learned their lesson. All we have to presuppose here, according to Coleman, is that these people are capable of acting rationally and act in a situation where the three above-mentioned conditions exist. However, Coleman played the legislative game with people who are used to the rules of parliamentary decision making. The number of players was limited so that deviations from the rules of the game were easy to communicate to other people. These were conditions that make conformity to the rules of the game very likely. However, the many breakdowns of parliamentary systems outside the small group of highly developed Western societies indicate a problem. Many systems in developing societies fulfill the three conditions specified by Coleman but never succeed in establishing democratic procedures of decision making. The use of external power, breaching of rules, mistrust, and refusal to exchange power are common features of these societies. The reason for their failure to establish a game like Coleman's must be sought in their inability to fulfill preconditions not treated as relevant by Coleman.

5. Another condition is that people trust each other enough to be willing to enter exchange. This trust can evolve only inasmuch as people perceive one another as fellow members of a community. It definitely cannot evolve between people who perceive themselves as members of separate communities who have nothing in common and are even mutual enemies. And it is a very common feature of political systems that different groups, parties, and movements see each other as enemies. Yet, between enemies there will be no trust and no exchange. At least a minimal feeling of fellowship must have developed beyond the borderlines of the individual groups in order to make trust and exchanges possible. Only the existence of such a minimal democratic community can turn the breaching of rules of the game from being a justifiable act against one's enemies into a violation of common rules that provokes the sanctions of the whole community against the

violator. It is this unified reaction of the whole community that brings violators back into line with the rules of the game. Only the working of this condition brought forth the results observed by Coleman: the fact that violators learned to abide by the rules in the long run. In a system without a dominating consensus of the democratic community, an actor would experience not unified sanctions bringing him or her back into line but conflict between different groups reacting aggressively and one group supporting him or her because they join in the unfriendly attitude toward the objects of his or her violation. Learning to abide by the rules of the game presupposes the unified reaction of the community that holds these rules in common.

6. The decisions made by the legislative body will be ineffective if there is no agency that provides for the enforcement of a decision in the case of resistance. Coming to a decision by way of exchanging votes in the legislative body does not have worth if some of the many people and groups within and outside the legislative body try to resist its realization by applying physical force. If there is no centralized authority with a monopoly on the means of physical force bound to any results of the legislative game, the decisions resulting from this game will not have effective power. There are many cases of underdeveloped democracies with a parliament deciding many things, but the judiciary and police force do not work for their enforcement. Thus, centralized authority with monopolized means of physical force is a further precondition for power exchange leading to collectively binding decisions.

7. Finally, Coleman's game was made up of rules the players apparently accepted as just. However, what would have happened if Coleman had introduced rules considered to be unjust by at least some of the players? They would not have played the game, but they would have argued about rules; and they would not have started playing the game until they had established a generally accepted set of rules. The experimenter may have tried to use his or her power to impose rules and some of the players may have subjected themselves to his or her authority, but this authority would not have created a generally assigned *legitimacy* of the rules. In order for the rules to attain that legitimacy, they need to be discursively justified in terms of generally accepted democratic values. Only such a discourse mediating between democratic values and rules of decision making actually provides for the legitimacy of the rules. This is a further precondition of decision making by way of power exchange that Coleman does not take into account.

Exchange of power on a political market allows for high flexibility and rapidity of exchange of decisions. But in order to overcome resistance, the decisions need to be enforced by a centralized authority with monopolized means of physical force; in order to have trustful exchange and conformity to the rules of the game, the game has to be anchored in a democratic community that includes every group; in order to be considered just and legitimate, the rules have to be discursively justified with regard to general democratic values. Economic theory illuminates one aspect of collective decision making — that political markets provide for flexibility and change in decision making; but it doesn't illuminate those aspects of decision making that are insoluably connected with this process: enforcement of decisions through authority, conformity to the rules of the game through consensual backing for applying sanctions against violations of the rules, and legitimacy of the rules through justification in discursive procedures. In order to throw light on these aspects we need theories of conflict, solidarity, and discourse that cannot be replaced by economic theory.

Related Theory and Research: Rational Choice Theory and Network Analysis

With Coleman's rational choice theory of collective decisions we have just one example of a growing movement of sociological theorizing. An ambitious attempt at explaining a variety of social facts in terms of rational choice, for example, has been made by Gary S. Becker in *The Economics of Discrimination* (1971) and *A Treatise on the Family* (1981). He says, for example, that it is inefficient for enterprises to discriminate but that it is most efficient for families; that is, one parent specializes in housework whereas the other specializes in outside work. However, one would like to know how Becker would explain why enterprises nevertheless discriminate and why families are increasingly abandoning the division of labor between home and business.

In distinction to economic "hardliners" like Gary S. Becker, a new branch of the economic approach has laid more emphasis on the importance of the normative framework within which economic transactions take place, the contractual framework of a liberal society. This is the approach of the so-called new contractarians like James M. Buchanan (1975) and Robert Nozick (1974). The emergence and persistence of the contractual framework is explained by Buchanan in utilitarian terms. The contractual framework and its backing up by the state frees individuals from providing for their security for themselves and allows them to concentrate on making profits within that framework. This utilitarian explanation of order in economic transactions is only a modern version of Hobbes's (1651/1966) classical solution of that problem. According to this view, a strong state has to guarantee social order in economic transactions. Just as Hobbes's argument for a strong state was opposed by Locke's (1690/1967) argument for a weak state, also based on utilitarian calculations, Buchanan's modern argument for a strong state is opposed by Robert Nozick's (1974) modern argument for a weak state. In Hobbes's and Buchanan's view, the people are in need of a strong state to control their appetites for breaking the rules; in Locke's and Nozick's view, the people need a weak state only to help them in making their contracts. Such a weak state evolves gradually from the converging interests of people in securing their freedom, life, and property. An element of Kant's (1793/1964d) universalism has been introduced by John Rawls (1972). According to Rawls, people will consent to basic contractual agreements insofar as they would be concluded in an original state of equality between people who don't know their societal position, who are reasonable, who have no interests in each other, and who have a moral sense of commitment to the principles they agree upon.

Thus, we have three diverging explanations of how the contractual order is guaranteed after it has originated from the state of nature: Buchanan's strong state, Nozick's convergence of interests in a minimal state, and Rawls's discursive justification by imagining an original state of consensus between equals.

Rational choice theory now interrelates increasingly with an approach that has become prominent under the name "network analysis" (Willer and Anderson, 1981; Wellman, 1983). An early example of such network analysis is Richard Emerson's (1972) extension of Homans's exchange theory. He put social exchange into different social networks and then formulated specific propositions on what would happen to the behavior of the exchanging parties. In *unilateral monopolies,* the actor in the monopoly position will hold constant or will decrease his or her resources, while the subordinate actors will try to mobilize outside resources in order to reach a balance. The resources provided by the monopoly actor become less valuable for the subordinate actors. A nonuniform distribution of resources in a unilateral monopoly will lead to a *specialization of exchanges* according to the specific resources of subordinates. A *closed circle* becomes established the more actors exchange the same goods, for example, love for love. Equal valuation but unequal distribution of resources leads to *stratification* and to the establishment of closed circles between actors on the same level of resources. Continuing Emerson's work, Karen S. Cook, together with Richard M. Emerson, Mary R. Gilmore, and Toshio Yamagishi (1983), demonstrated that complex networks tend to *decentralize* around those actors who have the best access to the greatest number of other actors' resources.

Network analysis of this kind has become a growing branch of sociological work in the United States in recent years. It is, first of all, a methodological innovation as demonstrated, for example, in the work of Laumann and Pappi (1976). One of the most prominent theoretical contributions to this development is Ronald Burt's *Toward a Structural Theory of Action,* published in 1982. Burt extends the network beyond immediate exchanges and tries to point out how the position of an actor in a greater network shapes his or her interests and potential actions (see also Burt, 1983). Along this line go Michael Hechter's (1987) studies that explain solidarity as the outcome of utility calculations of actors who are interrelated in a network. For example, party-voting loyalty of members of legislative bodies will exist as long as the group is capable of mediating individual goals, monitoring compliance, and providing selective incentives. Robert Axelrod (1984) explains the evolution of cooperation in terms of the rational calculation of egoistic actors. The chance that we might encounter someone with whom we have dealings in the present again in the future makes us assume that whatever we do to that person, positive or negative, will be repaid by him or her in equal terms. Therefore, a strategy of positive incentives and cooperation is most useful for rational actors. In this way they overcome the prisoner's dilemma. However, the problem that cannot be solved by Axelrod is that people do not act as farsightedly and rationally as assumed by rational choice theory.

All the objections elaborated in this chapter against Coleman's approach also hold true for the attempts formulated by Hechter, Axelrod, and others. Hartmut Esser (1990), for example, tries to show that rational choice theory is comprehensive enough to explain the guidance of behavior by habits, frames, or traditions. As long as it is more costly to change one's habits, frames, or traditions than to stick with them, it is the better choice for the rational actor to maintain them. This, however, is a pseudosuccess on the part of rational choice theory that results from simply changing the meaning of terms like "habit," "frame," or "tradition." Habits, frames, or traditions that are calculated rationally are no longer habits, frames, or traditions. They are turned from being unnoticed, unquestioned, and nondisposable determinants of action, including rational calculation, into calculated means applied to that action. However, inasmuch as habits, frames, or traditions exist, they determine what appears useful to us. They set the conditions under which rational calculation proceeds. As soon as we begin to look rationally at certain habits, frames, and traditions they are no longer effective and have been replaced by other habits, frames, and traditions that guide our view of those habits, frames, and traditions. Thus we need theories other than rational choice theory in order to explain the nonrational conditions under which rational action takes place.

Network analysis will prove useful the more it surpasses the limits of economic theory to take into account association and solidarity, communication and values, conflict and power, and processes and structures as features of social reality which cannot be reduced to economic utility calculations plus external conditions. Advances in this direction have been made by Reinhard Wippler and Siegwart Lindenberg in dealing with the micro-macro link (Wippler and Lindenberg, 1987; Lindenberg, 1989) and by Mark Granovetter (1985) in his work on economic action's embeddedness in social structures.

Finally, a growing branch of the literature explores the paradoxical aspects of rational choice, the limits of rationality, and the place of irrationality in human action. Raymond Boudon (1977, 1981) and Jon Elster (1979/1984, 1983, 1985, 1989a, 1989b) have particularly contributed to illuminating these aspects of human action. The limits of rationality are increasingly addressed under the heading "bounded rationality," particularly with reference to the work of Herbert Simon (1957). A theoretical branch that can be located in this context is expectation states theory as advanced by Berger, Wagner, and Zelditch (1985).

FOUR

THE CONTRADICTIONS OF LATE
CAPITALISM: CLAUS OFFE

IN A Marxist perspective, society and its development have to be conceived of primarily in terms of capitalism's logic of development. Marx assumed that the contradictory feature of this development would inevitably result in the breakdown of the social formation of capitalism. However, it was the successful survival of capitalism in the West and, at the same time, the failure of socialism and its deterioration into a totalitarian system of domination in the Soviet-bloc countries that created new problems for Western Marxist theory. There have been many attempts to explain these new developments in Marxist terms that have attributed the survival of capitalism to its capacity to cope with its own contradictions. The failure of socialism, on the other hand, has been attributed to historical circumstances and not to an inherent flaw in the program resulting from Marxist theory.

Claus Offe (1972, 1984a, 1984b, 1984c, 1985, 1987) has contributed one of the most interesting revisions of Marxist theory for explaining the survival of capitalism and the contradictions and conflicts accompanying its development. It is a neo-Marxist theory of "late" capitalism. Though Offe is not explicitly concerned with the reasons behind the failure of real-world socialism, he worked for a time on the assumption that it was due to historical circumstances and not to inherent faults of the program. Although he was not explicit about this assumption, he believed for some time that socialism is a solution for the contradictions inherent in capitalism. Like many Marxists, however, he lost confidence in the truth of this message in recent years. His skepticism on the chances of successfully establishing a movement that would lead to the replacement of late capitalism by socialism seems to derive from a skepticism he also feels about the feasibility of the program of socialism itself (Offe, 1984b: 323–58). In the meantime, he concentrates more on how the dangerous effects of modernity's dynamism can be kept under control rather than searching for a completely new society under the flag of socialism (Offe, 1989).

Capitalism: Structural Contradictions and Class Struggle

Offe's earlier work (Offe, 1972) is a great deal more Marxist in its perspective than his later work (Offe, 1984a, 1984b, 1984c, 1985, 1986, 1989, 1990; Offe and Heinze, 1986). However, even in his earlier work, Offe was a Marxist revisionist, because he gave organized markets, the state, science, and technology more importance in shaping the capitalist development than is usual from more orthodox Marxist positions.

Let us look at his earlier theory of capitalist development more closely, because it is a paradigmatic revision of Marxism that deals with the features of late capitalism, although it is in Marxist terms. After dealing with this earlier theory I will give some hints to Offe's later amendments of his revisionist Marxism that aim at a more balanced theory of modern society.

In a paradigmatic statement of his earlier work, Offe (1972: 7–25) starts with the definition of capitalism as a mode of economic production that is founded on private ownership of the means of production. The development of capitalism proceeds according to the logic of capital accumulation that is based on the self-realization of capital. Thus, contrary to traditional modes of production, the criterion of production is no longer the satisfaction of concrete needs, that is, the use value of its products, but rather the growth of capital itself, that is, the exchange value of products. Self-realization of capital means that invested capital, in the form of material resources and mechanical equipment (constant capital) on the one hand and labor (variable capital) on the other, has to provide surplus (excess value) realized in product sales so that the production process produces more capital than has been invested. This, in turn, can be reused in order to expand investment after the costs for resources, technology, and labor have been subtracted. In this way, invested capital produces more wealth, which can be reinvested on an increased level. This self-realization of capital leads to an increasing accumulation of assets, thus raising the total wealth of society in general to ever higher levels (disregarding at this stage the question of who profits from this accumulated wealth).

As Marx pointed out, the emancipation of the worker from his master, that is, from feudal relationships of domination and mutual duty, and thus his alienation from the means of production, provided the basis for establishing free labor as a commodity that could be purchased by the capitalist on the labor market. According to Marx's labor theory of value, the capitalist buys labor according to its real value, namely, the price that has to be paid for all the means of its reproduction: food, clothing, housing, and the education of children as the labor force of the future. Yet, because he can utilize labor beyond the time necessary to cover the cost of its reproduction, the capitalist has a source for producing surplus beyond the value of capital invested by him. Thus, in Marx's view, labor is the one and only source of capital accumulation.

The capitalist process of accumulation, however, is characterized by a fundamental contradiction: the form of production is increasingly societal, but the products (the surplus produced by labor) are privately appropriated by the capitalists. This is the capitalist version of the basic contradiction in the industrial economy: on the one hand, there is a growth in productive forces and, on the other hand, a change in the relationships of production, which first work to *promote* but then, in the course of time, *fetter* the development of these forces of production. Marx parallels this structural contradiction with the antagonism between the classes: the working class produces surplus and the capitalist class appropriates that surplus. The contradictory development of capitalism is immediately transmitted to the class struggle, with the proletariat acting as the moving force bringing about the replacement of capitalism by communism. Communism represents a higher mode of production able to resolve the contradictions of capitalism.

Late Capitalism: Structural Contradictions without Class Struggle

Offe argues that the parallels between structural contradiction, class antagonism, and class struggle have dissolved in the course of capitalism's development and have been replaced by a much more complex interrelationship of structural contradiction and conflicts between groups. The increasing complexity of such interrelationships is accompanied by the increasing complexity of the structural contradiction itself. This is what concerns Offe: the manifestations of the structural contradiction and its effects on conflicts in society.

It is not just the simple fact that the capitalist appropriates the surplus produced by the worker that characterizes the contradiction between increasing societal production and private appropriation. This is only one feature that gave rise to class struggle as the major conflict. The contradiction is much sharper than that. It means that, on the one hand, production is organized collectively, for example, using large-scale collective planning in big companies with a rationally organized division of labor. On the other hand, decisions on realizing the produced capital by way of further investments are made by single capitalists (or their representatives) on the basis of their particular interest in competition with other capitalists. There is no body that is responsible for making these decisions from the standpoint of the overall advancement of the economy, let alone the overall advancement of society.

Thus, according to the Marxist view, the collective planning of production in large enterprises is more rational than the organization of investment from the point of the whole economy or even society: this method is anarchical and has irrational effects, such as periodic overproduction resulting in nonrealization and thus destruction of capital, recession, inflation, and unemployment. The increasing replacement of the labor force (variable capital) by technology (constant capital) lowers the rate of profit, because labor, as the only source of surplus, decreases to an ever smaller portion of capital. This leads to a reduction in investment, because it becomes less profitable, with the consequence of stagnation.

These are the immediate irrational consequences of the private organization of economic decision making for the pure accumulation of capital. There are further consequences: single capitalists are unable to provide for infrastructure like transportation, schools, scientific research, hospitals, and jurisdiction (all necessary for orderly capitalist production), because investment in these public goods is not profitable. Other consequences are political unrest and protest resulting from repression and irrationalities in the capitalist appropriation of surplus, which cannot be kept under control by the decision of single capitalists.

A further expression of the contradiction between collective production and private appropriation is shown by the fact that economic production involves, directly or indirectly, the whole population, and economic decision making affects the whole of society. However, both are carried out in private without taking into account the effects of decisions on the whole of society from the standpoint of society itself. Only an organization for economic decision making from the viewpoint of society could solve this contradiction: the whole of society is affected, but the decision making is executed in an anarchical way by single companies.

Due to its inherent contradiction, the development of capitalism has self-negating effects. Its inability to make rational decisions from the standpoint of the whole economy, or even society, has effects that can result in its self-destruction: single capitalist enterprises are always in danger of being pushed out of the market; crises of realization due to excess production endanger capital accumulation in general; and the class struggle emerging from exploitation and repression endangers the persistence of capitalism as a social form. Marx assumes that these self-negating effects of the basic contradiction between collective production and individual private appropriation will eventuate in the breakdown of capitalism and its replacement by socialism. This is the point at which Offe breaks with Marx, pointing to the ability of the system of capitalism to establish institutions that compensate for its self-negating effects and seeing no movement that could be able to establish socialism successfully.

Mechanisms Compensating for the Self-Negating Effects of Capitalism: Organized Markets, Science and Technology, and State Regulation

According to Offe, the development of organized markets with the establishment of oligopolies, monopolies, cartels, and multinational corporations, and the elimination of price competition, self-financing, managerial planning, and long-term stabilization for profit have enhanced the capacity of the single capitalist enterprise to survive. This is because they abolish or reduce competition endangering the continued existence of an enterprise, penetrate both input and output markets by power, and liberate the single enterprise from cost pressure and problems of capital realization. The corresponding ideology is that of the replacement of the capitalist by the managerial class and the corporation "with a soul."

The capacity of the total capitalist economy for survival has been enhanced by two things: the institutionalization of technological progress, with science and technology as a prime production force; and the institutional linking of research and development with production and its subsequent reorganization. This has occurred thanks to the long-term profitable realization of capital by way of systematic innovation, overcoming stagnation, developing new investment outlets, and institutionalizing capital destruction. The corresponding ideology is that of technological, postindustrial society.

The regulation of the whole capitalist system by the state has enhanced capitalism's capacity for survival, because problems of realization are coped with by state intervention and because class compromise is actively organized by the state. The corresponding ideology is that of technocracy, the mixed economy, planification, the new industrial state, the active society, the pluralistic society, and the welfare state.

The Contradictory Effects of the Compensating Mechanisms

This institutionalization of mechanisms compensating for the self-negating effects of capitalist development has itself a double, contradictory face: on the one hand, it is a necessary precondition for capitalism's survival; on the other hand, it establishes counterstructures that work in noncapitalist terms (Offe, 1972: 27–63). These do not work according to the criterion of capital realization, which is only indirectly linked to the satisfaction of needs via markets, but according to the criterion of producing use value by immediately serving concrete needs. In this process, an increasing number of people are separated from immediate productive labor guided by capital realization, and an increasing amount of capital is drawn away from reinvestment and transmitted to nonproductive areas of consumption, for example, in health, welfare, and other services. The proportion of the population not working at all continues to increase, and the same is true for the work force not immediately involved in the production of surplus but in the provision of services.

Investment in nonproductive sectors also continues to grow. This development brings about an "erosion" of the traditional liberal legitimation of income distribution by the idea of the just exchange of equivalents. Income is increasingly based on criteria not located in market exchange. For a growing part of the population, the idea of legitimizing the system of capitalism has no meaning. This is the potential reserve of people who can be mobilized in protest movements against capitalism. These are people used to counting achievements in terms of their immediate use value, which then can become a measure for evaluating economic decision making itself. Anarchic economic decision making loses part of its legitimacy. After so many areas linked to economic investment have become socialized and have been brought under collective decision making, why should this not be the case for decisions on economic investment itself?

This is Offe's version of an assumption by Marx—that the growing socialization of production contains the building blocks for the replacement of capitalism by socialism. The collective organization of late capitalism's production has developed sufficiently far that only one farther step may be needed to extend the same treatment to economic investment. As the population living and working in the collectively organized noncapitalist institutions are most attuned to raising such questions, it is they, rather than the workers, who form the basis of a movement against capitalism and toward socialism, since the workers themselves immediately participate in capitalism's progress. This is Offe's explanation for the phenomenon that the new social movements are mostly made up of pastors, teachers, and students.

The state plays an increasingly central role in capitalist development (Offe, 1972: 65–105). The securing of capital accumulation needs overall guidance, which cannot be provided by the anarchic decision making of the single capitalist enterprises. This guidance becomes the function of the state, which has to decide like an "ideal total capitalist," providing for those conditions that further the capitalist process of accumulation as a whole. In doing so, the state has to make decisions against the particularistic interests of single capitalist enterprises, which place their short-term particular interest over the long-term interest of maintaining the system itself. On the other hand, the state has to absorb the protest and unrest arising from exploitation and repression in the economic sphere. The democratic state is most able to absorb such protest and unrest and to transform it into binding decisions, because it combines an openness to environmental complexity with the ability to enact decisions. However, linking the democratic state with capitalism also gives rise to a fundamental contradiction. On the one hand, the state has to provide for the conditions of capital accumulation even against the interests of single capitalist enterprises; on the other hand, the state has to be open to a growing number of people who think in terms of noncapitalist production of use values because they are not involved in capitalist production. In order to solve this problem, the state has to decide in the interest of furthering the accumulation process and, at the same time, has to conceal this alliance with capitalism in order to receive mass support for its decisions and for the total social formation of capitalism itself. However, there is no guarantee that the democratic state will be able to solve this problem indefinitely. There is always a chance that the state can be forced by democratic participation to intervene in the capitalist process to a degree that works contrary to the accumulation of capital. Capitalism needs the democratic state in order to guarantee the conditions of its continuation, but it is less able to live with that state the more the state is mobilized against the capitalist process itself.

This contradiction becomes particularly apparent in the modern welfare state (Offe, 1984a: 323–39). It is a necessary compensation for capitalist exploitation and in the interests of both total capital and labor. However, conservative critiques argue that the welfare state has undermined the productivity of the economy and thus its own sources of development. Labor costs have risen so far that capitalist enterprises have begun to stop investing when it involves expanding the labor force employed. Welfare payments have become good enough to be more attractive than boring work. The result is decreasing investment and increasing unemployment. The critique from the left, however, argues that the welfare state does not change the exploitation of wage labor but redistributes income within the work force rather than between capital and labor; its organization has become a bureaucratic instrument of social control, because it demands norm conformity for welfare payments; and it gives rise to the illusion that class antagonism between capital and labor has been overcome.

Offe says that both views are right and express the fundamental contradiction of the welfare state. Capitalist enterprises are indeed free to reduce investment inasmuch as they expect labor costs to be too high, and workers are free to escape from badly paid work in favor of welfare payments. On the other hand, the Leftists argue, the welfare state perpetuates the fundamental contradiction between collective production and individual appropriation inherent in capitalism. According to Offe, there is, however, no hope for the conservative or for the leftist to escape from the welfare state. The neoconservative critique cannot count on a movement broad enough to reach beyond the old middle class. The left critique cannot rely on a movement broad enough to go beyond the new middle class. However, whereas Offe denies the feasibility of the neoconservative model of reducing the welfare state, because capitalism cannot persist without welfare compensation, he sees in socialism, at least in theory, the means of escaping from the contradiction outlined above. Finding an optimal point between welfare state and capitalism is nearly impossible, even in theory, and is counteracted, in Offe's eyes, by the irrationalities of political compromising. The only way out is socialism, which means the collective organization of the whole society. However, there is no movement in sight to bring this about. Therefore, we have to live with the contradictions between welfare state and capitalism.

In his later work, Offe (1989) even gives up the search for socialism. The only thing now possible, in his eyes, is to keep the capitalist system in check by state regulation, welfare arrangements, and associations of solidarity. The main subject of his research now is the institutionalization of solidarity structures in a societal community within capitalist society. The market, the state, and societal community are the three basic institutions that must interrelate and keep each other in check in modern society.

Summary

1. The farther capitalism develops, the more the contradiction between collective production and individual (private) appropriation of products sharpens.
2. The sharper the contradiction between collective production and individual appropriation of products in capitalist development, the more difficult the survival of single capitalists, thus the more crises of capital realization will be intensified by lack of innovation, overproduction, and lack of investment, and the more class struggles will be aggravated.
3. The more difficult the survival of single capitalists, the more the system of capitalism will develop an organized market via oligopolies, monopolies, and cartels.
4. The more crises of capital realization endanger capital accumulation, the more the system of capitalism will create a close relationship with the development of science and technology and turn them into the foremost productive forces.
5. The more crises of capital realization and class struggles emerge, the more the system of capitalism will produce the state's intervention and regulation of class compromise.
6. The more the system of capitalism produces noncapitalist institutions compensating for its self-negating effects, such as organized markets, science and technology, and state control, the more the number of people not immediately involved in capitalist production of surplus value will grow and the more the amount of capital consumed in nonproductive areas for satisfying concrete needs will grow.

7. The greater the number of people not immediately involved in the capitalist production of surplus value and the greater the amount of capital consumed in nonproductive areas, the more the potential for doubts in the legitimacy of the capitalist mode of appropriation and also the idea of the collective organization of appropriation will grow.

8. The more noncapitalist institutions grow, the more society will be prepared to replace private appropriation of products by their collective appropriation, that is, to replace private, anarchic economic decision making by collective, rationally planned decision making.

9. The more the state tries to absorb unrest and protest resulting from capitalist accumulation, the more it will expand democratic participation and social welfare.

10. The more the state expands democratic participation, the more it will be under pressure to intervene contrary to the requirements of capitalist accumulation.

11. The more the state works as an ideal total capitalist in furthering conditions of capital accumulation and simultaneously expanding democratic participation, the more it will have to conceal its working for capital accumulation in order to receive mass support.

12. The more the state expands social welfare, the more the danger of growing labor costs increases, so that investment involving further employment is reduced. Thus, the worker will find welfare payments more attractive than badly paid work. Both of these result in recession and unemployment, and undermine the welfare system itself.

13. However much the state expands social welfare, it will not change the contradiction between collective production and private appropriation but will build up an apparatus of social control and repression and will establish the illusion of reconciliation of classes.

14. Insofar as the appropriation of products becomes collectively organized in socialism, the irrationalities of economic development pertaining to capitalism will dissolve.

15. Insofar as the socialist program turns out to be infeasible, modern capitalist society will keep its dangerous dynamism under control only if the market, the state, and the solidarity structures of the societal community interrelate and control each other.

Critical Assessment

In evaluating Offe's (1972) earlier theory of late capitalism, we can say that it points out the effects on societal development of the contradiction between collective production and private appropriation in capitalism, providing that this is the primary determining force in society. The effects are, namely, competition endangering the persistence of single capitalist enterprises, crises of capital realization, and class struggle. Then the theory predicts that this contradictory system will create its own mechanisms in order to compensate for its self-negating effects. The danger of single capitalist enterprises being pushed out of the market produces the organization of the market. The danger for total capital of suffering from a lack of innovation produces science and technology. The danger of the breakdown of the social formation of capitalism resulting from crises of capital realization and class struggle will produce state intervention.

Can we assume that capitalism produces these institutions simply because they are requirements for its own survival? Capitalism is not a self-organizing system capable of producing the conditions for its own persistence. The direction in which it develops depends on the actions of different groups of actors who act on the basis of very different ideas and goals and shape in very different ways the institutions directly or indirectly related to capitalism. What reason is there to assume that the above multitude of actions will bring about precisely those institutions that are needed to secure capitalism's survival? The situation is rather the opposite. In the meantime, capitalist accumulation has disseminated all over the world and has to live with very different surrounding institutions, which have supportive, intervening, or even destructive effects on capitalist accumulation in varying degrees. In historical terms, every kind of combination of capitalism with other institutions seems to be possible, certainly with very different effects on capitalist accumulation.

Oligopolies and monopolies developed in later phases in Britain but were there from the beginning when industrial capitalism took off in Germany in the second half of the nineteenth century. Oligopolies and monopolies develop because some enterprises have enough power to drive competitors from the market. There are many more single capitalists who suffer from this development than capitalists who profit from it. We cannot generalize that the establishment of oligopolies and monopolies results from the requirement of single capital's survival. It is a very conflictual process within the capitalist class, which is determined by the mobilization of power by some capitalists against others.

The institutionalization of science and technology and their close connection with economic production are features that have played major roles in the rise of capitalism from its beginning. It is a unique historical convergence and not a process conditioned by the systemic requirements of late capitalism. Without the cooperation of scientists, artisans, and entrepreneurs in eighteenth-century Britain, there would have been no rise of industrial capitalism at all. The prominent example is James Watt's cooperation with the entrepreneur Boulton in building the steam engine and applying it to production. Without the cooperation of science and industry, there would have been no rise of the chemical industry in Germany a hundred years later.

It is the same with the state. Capitalism developed with state aid from the beginning. Even in Britain, capitalist developments were furthered by the state's laws, which guaranteed economic expansion by way of free trade. In Germany, the capitalist development was furthered by a state that supported the establishment of large industrial corporations. Here, in particular, the state provided simultaneously for social welfare and social repression from the beginning of capitalist development and not as a result of later requirements of capitalism's persistence. Thus, capitalism and the welfare state were born at the same time. It is less the case that the requirements of developed capitalism give rise to state support, but rather that state support gives rise to capitalist development.

We can deduce from this discussion that Offe's earlier attempt at explaining the rise of the institutions of organized markets, science and technology, and state intervention in terms of the contradiction inherent in capitalism is insufficient functionalism. Whether and when these institutions emerge does not result so much from the systemic requirements of capitalism but from historical constellations, namely, the power of certain capitalist enterprises, the cooperation of science and industry, and the activity of the state.

Offe is right in pointing to the fact that capitalist accumulation is accompanied by the emergence of noncapitalist institutions. However, it is wrong to explain the emergence of such noncapitalist institutions solely in economic terms, that is, the functional requirements of capitalism's continued existence. Offe's (1972) earlier theory is not completely free from such functionalist assumptions, though his later theory moves well beyond such limitations.

Capitalism also coexists with other institutions. Which institutions develop along with capitalism therefore depends on factors other than the systemic needs of capitalism alone. Here we have to call upon processes reaching beyond economic requirements. In order to explain the development of capitalism and the shape it takes by combining with other institutions, we have to take into account not only the requirements of capitalism's survival but also the noneconomic processes involved in this development. What shape capitalism takes in a certain society and how it develops is determined by several factors: the chances for certain sectors of industry to advance economically; the state's political standpoint and its relationship to capitalist development; the ability of the working class to acquire the rights of citizenship; and the ability of the capitalist class to compromise with the working class. This leads to the inclusion, to a certain extent, of the working class in society, and proceeds in terms of legitimizing and criticizing the institutions as a result of public debates on organizing the economy and society in general. The success of institutional change also depends on the chances of receiving legitimation by the prevailing ideas and theories of society.

We need more than a theory that is entirely based on the contradictions of capitalism if we wish to explain these developments. We would have to expand Offe's earlier neo-Marxist theory of late capitalism by including theories of power, influence, and discursive argumentation. Indeed, this is the direction in which Offe himself increasingly revised his approach in his later works.

Finally, Offe's earlier analysis gives rise to the belief that a resolution of the basic contradiction of capitalism would also resolve the irrationalities of economic development, if capitalism were replaced by socialism where production *and* investment are collectively organized. This however, is nothing but a belief in the "great solution" typical of German thought since Hegel's idea of synthesis (1964–1971; for translation, see 1972, 1974) resulting from the dialectical contradiction of thesis and antithesis. There is no reason why socialism would not have to face similar or new problems arising from the application of collective (political) decision making to economic investment. This application would replace the economic rationality of making profits by the political rationality of gaining votes.

All existing socialist systems have had to struggle with a greater number of irrationalities in economic production and investment than the established capitalist economies. It is naive to believe that the failure of real-world socialism has been primarily caused by historical accidents and not by inherent faults of the program of socialism itself. The belief that collective, *political* decision making is an adequate device for solving *economic* problems is unfounded. We have good reason to be skeptical about such an overloading of political decision making.

The above criticism refers to Offe's (1972) earlier theory of late capitalism on which we have concentrated in this chapter because it has retained basic features of Marxism. Nevertheless, even in his early work Offe moves well beyond pure economic determination in that he introduces organized markets, the state, and science and technology as subsystems that not only are functionally required by the capitalist economy but also work on their own conditions and function for the society in general and shape the capitalist economy in its character. In particular, the state, the corresponding relationships of power and authority, and the preconditions of legitimacy are of special importance for understanding the system of late capitalism in Offe's perspective. Offe is very much a *political* economist who places special emphasis on the politics of the capitalist economy; and he has complemented this neo-Marxist *political* economy with elements of functional analysis even in his earlier work.

In his later work, Offe tries to surpass the limits of Marxism even further by complementing his perspective with elements of rational choice theory, Habermas's discourse ethics, and a theory of the societal community that relates to Parsons. In his present view, modern society can keep its dynamism under control only if it can find ways of interrelating and keeping in mutual check the market, the state, and the societal community as basic institutions. In the process, Offe has extended his earlier revisionist Marxism so much that we can assume he would subscribe to all criticism we have directed against his earlier theory and would make the revisions and extensions such criticism demands. His earlier work is a reflection of the renewal and interlinking of paradigms that have been in motion since the 1960s; his present work goes even further in this direction.

Related Theory and Research

Neo-Marxist theories of late capitalism flourished in the late sixties and early seventies, but declined as rapidly as they had risen in the late seventies and early eighties. An influential revision of Marxism in economic terms, which deals with monopoly capital, was formulated by Paul A. Baran and Paul M. Sweezy (1966). James O'Connor (1973) contributed a Marxist theory of the capitalist state's tendency to fiscal crisis, whereas Nicos Poulantzas (1968a; for translation, see 1968b) gave the state relative autonomy in Marxist analyses. In his view, the state is, on the one hand, the site of class struggles between factions of the capitalist class, and, on the other, it intervenes in the economy according to its own logic of maintaining political power.

FIVE

THE WORLD AS A SYSTEM: IMMANUEL WALLERSTEIN'S AND TERENCE K. HOPKINS'S WORLD SYSTEMS ANALYSIS

NOWADAYS, THERE is virtually no part of the globe where one can live a life independent of what is going on elsewhere. The world has become a global system of interdependent parts. This emergence and further development of the world system is the object domain of an approach advanced in the seventies and eighties by Immanuel Wallerstein, Terence K. Hopkins, and their colleagues at the Fernand Braudel Center for the Study of Economies, Historical Systems, and Civilizations at the State University of New York in Binghamton, New York. This approach is called world systems analysis (Wallerstein, 1974, 1979, 1980, 1983, 1984, 1989; Hopkins and Wallerstein, 1982). It is an approach formulated in Marxist terms that looks at the world economy, capital accumulation, including the capital-labor relationship, and worldwide interstate relations as driving forces of historical development. It is an economic approach centering on the macro level of the world economy and the interstate system. Compared to the original Marxian treatment of capital accumulation, world systems analysis approaches that development much more in terms of an economic development that incorporates every part of the world, and it includes interstate relations in the analysis much more, thus expanding the macroeconomic approach toward incorporating the elements of power and conflict. These, however, emerge from an economic basis: military dominance presupposes productive superiority.

Thus, the general thrust of the approach is an economic one, particularly because capital accumulation is seen as the center of historical development. Whereas the microeconomic approaches of rational choice and exchange theory place the individual's utility calculations at the core of their explanation of individual actions and their intended and unintended effects under given external conditions, the Marxist macroeconomic world systems analysis conceives of the world economy's capital accumulation as the major force that determines the world's, states', and societies' development on the macro level. The second force that exerts its influence on that development is the establishment of domination between states. But it is a force that is dependent on capital accumulation.

Another accompanying force is the relationship of association and dissociation between the different cultural communities of the world. Though Wallerstein and Hopkins (1982: 43) refer to this aspect of the world system, they do not deal with its influence on world development. What they completely miss is the effect of worldwide cultural and scientific discourse on the development of societies. Their approach is couched in economic terms with an incorporated secondary political element, and it centers on macroeconomic capital accumulation as the driving force of historical development.

The World System

World systems analysis starts with three basic assumptions: (1) there is one expanding world economy; (2) there are multiple expanding states; and (3) production interrelations, intra- and interstate politics are framed by the capital-labor relationship (Hopkins and Wallerstein, 1982: 11–13). This worldwide system originated in Europe in the sixteenth century and has progressively expanded over the entire globe from then on. The central feature of the world system is its differentiation into an economically more advanced core and an economically less advanced periphery. The core has shifted geographically over time from Central Europe to the North Atlantic area and is now tending toward the Pacific area. The system will progressively expand until it ultimately incorporates every part of the world. Formerly external areas have become part of the system and add to the periphery of the less advanced areas. This is the process of peripheralization of areas that formerly lived an independent life outside the system. "Core" and "periphery" designate complementary parts of the world economy that give rise to the differentiation of strong and weak states in a derivative way. The origin of the core-periphery differentiation is economic. The states expand within this system in the double sense that particular states in the core try to expand their domination over other states and over external peoples and areas in the process of peripheralization. The latter process results in an increased number of states within the overall system, which again increases the number of interstate relations. The extension of the dominion of core states and the firm establishment of their reign corresponds politically to the economic processes of peripheralization. As the world economy and the interstate system expand, interrelations of production and intra- and interstate relations are framed according to the capital-labor relationship that determines the course of action taken by individuals, households, communities, organizations, and states. In interstate terms, the peripheral states progressively provide the cheap labor force for the economically advanced core states.

That there is one world economy but multiple states is seen as contradictory (Hopkins and Wallerstein, 1982: 12). In terms of the world economy and in terms of worldwide capital accumulation there should be no barriers to trade, to exporting and importing capital, or against establishing production units in foreign countries. The expansion of the world economy interferes with the sovereignty of the states. On the other hand, the tendency of the states to establish sovereign power interferes with the expansion of the world economy, because it implies barriers for importing capital and commodities in favor of domestic industry. The convergence of the economic and political differentiation of core and periphery tends to reduce this contradiction, because in this case the expansion of capital in the world economy coincides with the expansion of the core states' dominion over the rest of the world.

The expansion of the world economy establishes a basic division of labor between the core and the periphery (Hopkins and Wallerstein, 1982: 44–50). The periphery works on a low level of technological development and provides simple agricultural products and mineral resources for industrial production. The core works on a high level of technological development and provides complex manufactured products. The trend that then arises is for low-cost labor to be recruited in the periphery by the industries of the core in the process of establishing industrial plants in the periphery. The exchange of these goods between core and periphery takes place on unequal terms. The periphery has to sell its simple products at low prices, whereas the complex manufactured products of the core are sold at high prices. In the periphery, low labor costs allow for low prices and do not exert much pressure toward technological innovation to save labor costs. In the core, higher labor costs resulting from the pressure of a strong labor movement and from the educational qualification of the work force demand higher prices for commodities and exert much more pressure for technological innovation. Technological innovation in the periphery mostly simplifies manual labor, whereas it is accompanied by higher demands for educational qualification in the core. Therefore, the gap between low labor costs and low prices of commodities in the periphery and high labor costs and high commodity prices in the core does not diminish; it may even widen as the world economy expands. Exchange remains unequal. The periphery has to sell many more low-priced products involving much low-cost labor in order to receive few highly priced manufactured goods from the core produced at high labor costs.

Capital accumulation is a global process, not a process that occurs only in the core involving only pure wage labor (Hopkins and Wallerstein, 1982: 14–23). According to Marx, capital accumulation results from the exploitation of the wage laborer who sells his or her labor power at the price of its reproduction costs. However, the worker produces more commodities than necessary for providing the reproduction of his or her labor power. The worker produces excess value, which is the source of the capitalist's profit extracted from the production process. This excess value is created by the worker but appropriated by the capitalist enterprise to expand its capital, thus leading to the process of capital accumulation. However, according to Wallerstein and Hopkins, the worldwide expansion of the capitalist economy of the core into the periphery always incorporates forms of exploitation of labor other than wage labor in the peripheral areas, for example, the exploitation of laborers who are not fully paid for reproducing their labor force, necessitating the production of some agricultural products on their own or by other members of their family. Peasants who on the one hand work for a company but on the other need to produce some of their own food in order to maintain their family fit into this category (Hopkins and Wallerstein, 1982: 48–50).

Between the center and the periphery, a semiperipheral area emerges as formerly peripheral areas progress toward a position between the core and still undeveloped areas or newly incorporated peripheral areas. However, areas formerly located in the core can shift toward the lower status of a semiperipheral area because they have lost their positions in the competition between core areas. The semiperipheral areas mediate between the core and the periphery, functioning as a core for the peripheral areas and as a periphery for the core areas, thus incorporating core and peripheral features (Hopkins and Wallerstein, 1982: 47).

The state system develops toward establishing the dominion of the core states over the peripheral states, because the core states draw much more power from their advanced economic development and can use this power to sustain unequal exchange between core and peripheral states. This is commonly called imperialism, which can be established in terms of formal political rule of the core over the periphery via colonialism or informal rule via economic suppression and exploitation (Hopkins and Wallerstein, 1982: 51–52).

The interstate relationship within the core can take on two forms. There may be several rival core states with no single one able to establish supremacy, thus involving a relative balance of power between rival states. The other possible form of the core state system is the establishment of the supremacy of one state, which can be called hegemony. In distinction to the reign of core states over peripheral states, hegemony does not primarily imply political domination of one state over the others but economic superiority (Hopkins and Wallerstein, 1982: 52–53).

The development of capitalism brought forth the conflict between the bourgeoisie and the proletariat as the major conflict in capitalist societies. The more this conflict has diminished in the core states, the more it has emerged as a conflict between the rich "bourgeois" populations of the core states and the poor "proletarian" populations of the peripheral states.

The global system develops in cyclical rhythms of differing lengths, of upswing, stagnation, and decline (Hopkins and Wallerstein, 1982: 53–54). On the one hand, there is a short-term trade cycle. On the other hand, Wallerstein and Hopkins state, the world economy overall has developed in long-term rhythms of upswing, stagnation, and decline embracing periods as long as 150 to 300 years in each phase. They assume that this is an unavoidable feature of capitalist development that, however, tends toward ever shorter waves. The crucial reason for these waves is the time lag in adjustments between production and consumption in the world economy.

There are three major secular trends in the development of the world economy (Hopkins and Wallerstein, 1982: 54–57). First, there is continual expansion of the capitalist world system involving the invasion of every corner of the world and the growing expansion of capital itself in volume. Second, the development of the capitalist world system leads to the commodification of nearly everything. Land, labor, and natural resources become transformed into commodities evaluated according to their value in exchange and no longer evaluated according to their value in use. Third, the development involves the permanent mechanization of production in the form of permanent technological innovation. Every enterprise is forced to go along with this in order to keep up with competitors. The industrial and the scientific-technological revolutions have been major events of this development. But overall mechanization is a permanent process. In this process, capital shifts in the core areas away from its labor basis (variable capital) toward its mechanical basis (fixed capital) and also involves repeated new incorporations of labor-based (variable) capital by employing low-cost labor in peripheral areas.

Basic Assumptions

We can summarize the basic assumptions of world systems analysis thus far:

1. The more the economic system of capitalism develops, the more it will expand throughout the world.
2. The more the economic system of capitalism develops, the more it will give rise to the development and incorporation of states and interstate relations.
3. The more the economic system of capitalism develops, the more production interrelations and intra- and interstate relations will be framed according to the capital-labor relationship.
4. The more the economic system of capitalism expands throughout the world and the more states become established in that process, the more the contradiction between the expansion of the economy and the sover-

eign jurisdiction of the states grows and results in conflicts between states and the world economy.

5. The more the economic system of capitalism develops, the more it will be differentiated into an economically advanced core and an economically backward periphery, and also into politically strong core states and politically weak peripheral states.

6. The more the world economy differentiates into an advanced core and a backward periphery, the more economic exchange between them involves the exchange of highly priced manufactured goods based on higher wages for low-priced agricultural and mineral products based on low wages and thus takes place on unequal terms.

7. The more the economic system of capitalism expands throughout the world, the more the process of capital accumulation involves the exploitation not only of pure wage labor of lifetime workers in the core but also of part lifetime workers also living by means of production of agricultural goods on their own in the peripheral areas.

8. The more the economic system of capitalism develops, the more semiperipheral areas will emerge between the core and the periphery and will mediate between them.

9. The more the state system develops, the more the core states will establish dominion over the peripheral states.

10. The more the state system develops, the more the core states will be balanced in rivalry, or one state will establish an economically based hegemony.

11. The more the economic system of capitalism expands throughout the world, the more the original internal conflict between bourgeoisie and proletariat will be replaced by the external conflict between rich core populations and poor peripheral populations.

12. The more the economic system of capitalism develops, the more it will do so in cyclical rhythms of upswing, stagnation, and decline, with a tendency toward shorter phases of ups and downs.

13. The more the economic system of capitalism expands throughout the world, the more it will incorporate formerly external areas as peripheral zones of the system.

14. The more the economic system of capitalism develops, the more it will turn land, labor, natural resources, and any products into commodities, leading to the commodification of everything.

15. The more the economic system of capitalism develops, the more it involves a permanent mechanization of the production process.

Specific Hypotheses

These basic assumptions of world systems analysis can be complemented by a set of more specific hypotheses grouped around three "antinomies": (1) economy/polity; (2) supply/demand; and (3) capital/labor.

Economy and Polity

The economy/polity antinomy results from the tendency of the expanding economy to break down barriers between states and the tendency of the states to maintain such barriers in order to preserve their sovereignty. The following hypotheses can be grouped around this antinomy (Hopkins and Wallerstein, 1982: 58–64):

1. As soon as the world system becomes established, there will be at least as many (if not more) commodity chains that cross state boundaries as remain within state boundaries.

This hypothesis states that international trade was established at the very beginning of the European economic system in the sixteenth century and has remained ever since. Only phases of economic decline have displayed a temporary reduction of international trade. The hypothesis means that international trade was a fundamental precondition for the development of capitalism and is not just a later outcome of that development.

2. The more the differentiation between core, semiperiphery, and periphery has been established, the more this stratification will be maintained in the further development of the system.

This hypothesis states the perpetuation of the established stratification in the system.

3. The closer a state is to the economically advanced core, the stronger its state machinery will be.

This hypothesis states the dependence of political strength on economic advancement. On the other hand, incorporation of formerly external states into the system's periphery weakens their political strength:

4. As soon as formerly independent states become incorporated into the peripheral zone of the world system, the strength of their state machinery will decline.

The origin of any superiority is productive advantage:

5. The greater the productive advantage of an area or state, the greater will be its commercial advantage after a time lag.

Commercial advantage, on the other hand, promotes financial advantage:

6. The greater the commercial advantage of an area or state, the greater will be its financial advantage.

Military advantage is seen as dependent on productive advantage and concomitant with commercial advantage. This demonstrates clearly that Wallerstein and Hopkins give the economic basis priority over the political basis:

7. The greater the productive advantage of a state, the greater will be its military strength, developing with a time lag and alongside commercial advantage.

The hegemonic power propagates freedom of trade in order to expand its hegemony:

8. The more a hegemonic power tries to expand its hegemony, the more it will propagate freedom of trade.

For a state that is moving toward hegemony, it is easier to expand dominion over peripheral states by way of informal rule than by colonization. On the other hand, declining hegemony calls for attempts to maintain power over peripheral states by way of colonization:

9. The more a power moves toward hegemony, the more it will expand its power over peripheral states by way of informal rule and less by way of colonization.

The decline of a hegemony coupled with world economic downturn calls for attempts to erect mercantilist barriers with other strong states in order to escape the downturn:

10. The more a hegemony declines along with the world economy, the more other strong states will try to escape that downturn by erecting mercantilist barriers.

The hegemonic power that faces economic weakness and has control over colonies will resist decolonization in order to be able to draw resources from the colonies:

11. The weaker a hegemonic power is economically, the more it will resist decolonization.

The peripheral zones draw their ability to achieve decolonization from growing economic strength:

12. The more a peripheral state advances economically, the better it will be able to achieve decolonization.

Trade proceeds along the following lines:

13. The more rivalry there is between states, the more they will tend to establish tariff barriers.
14. The more a hegemony becomes established, the more freedom of trade will be enforced.
15. The more the world economy grows, the more the core states will concentrate on certain products and exchange them; the more it declines, the more each state will diversify its production and will reduce external trade.
16. The more the world economy grows, the more semiperipheral states import from core states; the more it declines, the more they reduce those imports.
17. The more a hegemonic power becomes established, the more the peripheral states will turn to exchange with that power; the more a rivalry situation prevails in the core, the more individual peripheral states will be linked to specific core states in particular zones of influence or tariff zones.

Supply and Demand

Around supply/demand, the following hypotheses can be grouped (Hopkins and Wallerstein, 1982: 64–67):

1. Inasmuch as structural transformation occurs, it will be increasingly linked to clear patterns with a cyclical rhythm.
2. The more the world economy develops, the more cyclical rhythms will be shortened in their sequence.
3. The more the world economy develops and forms one system, the more cyclical rhythms will be synchronized between core, semiperipheral, and peripheral areas.
4. The more the world economy develops, the more it will do so in a steplike manner.
5. Inasmuch as stagnation occurs, it will affect different areas of the economy from earlier bouts of stagnation.
6. Whenever capital goods are produced on a world scale, they will regularly outstrip the demand from the consumer goods industry and thus lead to crises of overproduction and contraction.
7. The more the world economy expands, the more it will lead to the reallocation of effective demand resulting from increasing proletarization of the world labor force.

8. Inasmuch as the world economy expands, investment will flow from the core to the periphery, and work-force migration from the periphery to the core will increase.
9. Whenever expansion is followed by stagnation and vice versa, a period of transition in between will involve a particular pattern of increased rate of capital accumulation.
10. Whenver a period of transition occurs, ecological exhaustion, primarily of land and labor, will take place, especially in certain peripheral areas.
11. Whenever a period of transition occurs, class conflict and repression, particularly in peripheral areas, will intensify.
12. Whenever a period of contraction occurs, particular productive activities will be transferred from peripheral to core and semiperipheral areas.
13. Whenever a period of contraction occurs, real employment will be transferred from core to semiperipheral areas but not usually to peripheral areas.

Capital and Labor

Around capital/labor, the following hypotheses can be grouped (Hopkins and Wallerstein, 1982: 68–72):

1. The more the world economy expands, the more subsistence redoubt households will shift to become part lifetime proletarian households, and part lifetime proletarian households will become lifetime proletarian households.

However, up to now part lifetime proletarian households have constituted the majority. Core countries have more lifetime proletarian households than the other zones.

2. The more labor achieves lifetime status, the better it will be organized and the higher will be the costs of its reproduction borne by the employer. Therefore, real wage levels are higher in core countries than in peripheral countries.
3. Whenever a period of contraction occurs, part lifetime proletarian households will be exhausted and consequently will die earlier, and some lifetime proletarian households will shift to part lifetime status.
4. When and only when duress occurs, subsistence households will be moved into the wage-labor force, becoming part lifetime proletarian households.
5. Inasmuch as subsistence households move to become part lifetime proletarian households, their well-being will decrease overall; when part lifetime proletarian households move toward lifetime status, their well-being will increase overall.

Because the expansion of the world economy has moved a larger population of the periphery into becoming part lifetime proletarian households, the overall well-being of the world labor force has been declining. An increase in well-being is a phenomenon of only a few core countries.

6. The more real income increases as a result of the economic system's expansion, the beneficiaries will be the capitalists, professionals, technicians, higher civil servants, and bureaucrats.
7. The more the world economy develops, the more capital will be accumulated, reflected in the growing extent and worth of means of production, concentrated in terms of a growing scale of operation, and centralized in terms of a growing scale of ownership/control among a smaller number of owners/controllers of capital.
8. The more the ratio of nonhuman to human means of production increases, the more concentration of capital will increase.
9. The more the rate of accumulation (the rate of profit) declines, the more capital will be centralized.

The latter processes are valid only for the core areas where populations are fully proletarianized, and all means of production are capital. The exploitation of part lifetime proletarian labor in peripheral areas provides much better conditions for capital accumulation than could be expected if the process relied solely on the core countries:

10. The more the accumulation process involves part lifetime proletarian labor in peripheral areas, the higher will be the magnitude of accumulation, concentration, and in the long run centralization.

Critical Assessment

In evaluating world systems analysis, we recognize its concentration on the economic and, in a secondary way, the political dimensions of the world system. Capital accumulation is the basic feature of the development of that world system. Its laws are the primary forces that guide this development. Thus, we can learn from world systems analysis how the world would develop if capital accumulation were the primary force in this development. All special hypotheses are based on this basic assumption. However, we do not learn anything about the specific contribution of noneconomic forces to the development of the world system as a system that reaches well beyond the economic dimension, including the political dimension as an independent one and also the dimensions of community formation and culture. On the other hand, we can assume that even the world economy would not have developed in the way it did without having been pushed forward by the noneconomic factors of political domination, community formation, and cultural universalization.

The formation of the European state system in the epoch of absolutism was not simply an outcome of a developing economy and was not based simply on productive advantage. The emergence of Britain and France as the leading states in that development was very much a result of their establishment as unified, strong political units, in Britain based on the power of the national parliament and in France based on the power of the king. Because Germany did not become unified as a strong political power until 1870, it was not able to play an equal role in this system. The establishment of British and French imperialism was clearly based on political superiority in the European core. Without such political superiority economic advantage would not have been turned into the expansion of the economy into the periphery outside Europe to the same extent. The economically well-advanced Netherlands were able to play only a secondary part in that concert, because this was a small state lacking the political power that could compete with that of Britain and France. Thus we have to consider political power as an important force exerting its influence on the formation of the world system much more than Wallerstein's and Hopkins's world systems analysis allows. Political power primarily explains the formation of the core-state system and its political expansion over the world, and it contributes secondarily to the development of the world economy. This is the topic of geopolitical theory (Collins, 1988: 135–37).

That development cannot be fully explained without taking into account the formation of communities. Britain was well ahead of the other countries in forming national citizenship, which broke down barriers between estates and therefore included every stratum of society into an all-embracing process of economic production and political decision making. On the other hand, Britain was most able to establish its reign over the peripheral zones of the world by way of forming communal ties between the parts of its empire. This was Britain's advantage over France and the other powers attempting to establish imperial dominions—clearly a force of community formation, effective independently of any economic and political forces. The British Empire created a communal unity that served as an important basis for political dominion and economic expansion. Trade within one community is much easier to accomplish than trade between nonunified populations, even if they submit to one political authority. The British Empire was, however, more than political rule; it had its rituals and symbols of community. Its later transformation into the Commonwealth of Nations gives expression to the historically evolved communal ties. Looking beyond the case of Britain we have to recognize that the development of the European system was very much influenced by the formation and division of religious communities, first its foundation on one Christian church, then its division into Catholic and Protestant countries and communities after the Reformation. The religious wars and their outcomes very much determined the formation of the European state system, a force that clearly resides in community formation.

Today we are witnesssing the awakening of national groups all over the world that are fighting for the formation of independent communities. This is a force entering the world system and influencing its development that cannot simply be reduced to economic or political processes. In general, community formation and its preconditions explain primarily the development of the world system in its dimension of association and dissociation of people. In a secondary way, they contribute to the expansion or contraction of the world economy and the world state system.

Finally, no complete explanation of the development of the world system is possible without recourse to the fundamental contribution of European culture to that development. In Wallerstein's perspective, culture is no more than the ideological battleground of the economic world system (Boyne, 1990; Wallerstein, 1990a, 1990b). We would have to forget Max Weber's (1920–1921a/1972a, 1920–1921b/1972b, 1920–1921c/1971a) comparative studies of the relationship between the world religions and the development of the spirit of modern capitalism if we were to follow Wallerstein and Hopkins. As Weber demonstrated, there were economically and politically well-equipped powers in Asia, namely China and India, but they did not become the core of the world system developing from the sixteenth century on. As Weber discovered, the major force that explained that difference was the difference of the cultures. Whereas China and India relied on religious systems that had conservative effects, legitimating the existing order as the best possible order, the European culture centering in ascetic Protestantism introduced a revolutionary force: Mastery of an evil world on universal grounds became the dominating cultural attitude. Privileged intellectuals in Asia, Confucian literati in China and the Brahmins in India, were the carriers of a conservative ideology. In Europe, the nonprivileged bourgeois Puritans became the carriers of a revolutionary ideology that claimed the transformation of the whole world according to its values: the values of methodical rational action in economic and political enterprise aiming at dominating the world. This was the origin of the expansion of European culture all over the world, a culture that claimed universal validity for every corner of the world and that was not contemplative in character but aimed at the transformation of the world according to its basic principles. This culture was secularized in the Enlightenment but did not change its revolutionary thrust. It served as the cultural source of expansion not only of the capitalist economy all over the world but also of the notions of democracy, civil rights, and human rights, though with less success because of their much more complicated preconditions. When authoritarian and dictatorial powers all over the world are increasingly exposed to worldwide intellectual criticism, this is also a necessary consequence of the cultural development of the world system, as in earlier times was the economic expansion of that system.

In this perspective, what has originated from Europe since the sixteenth century is not simply the expansion of a world economy but, as Roland Robertson (1978, 1980, 1990) has put it, a process of globalization that has given rise to a world system that includes processes of economic, political, communal, and cultural expansion. It is also much easier to take into account in this perspective the major role of the Soviet Union and its dependent allies in the development of that world system. The Soviet bloc gained its position in the world much more from political (particularly military) power, from ideological commitment, and from strong hierarchical organization than from productive advantage, which is clearly contrary to Wallerstein's and Hopkins's (1982: 63) hypothesis of the dependence of military strength on productive advantage. On the other hand, the Communist ideology was one version of the European cultural claim to universal validity that attempted world domination and was rooted in ascetic Protestantism. Wallerstein's and Hopkins's world systems analysis is much too poor in its theoretical apparatus to be able to contribute anything to this cultural aspect of the world system's development. It also doesn't tell us anything about the system's development of communal associations and dissociations, and it doesn't take into account political power as a force that is effective independently of productive advantage or before productive advantage occurs. Thus, all in all, world systems analysis is an interesting opening of discussion of the world system's development, but much too limited in its theoretical sophistication. It needs enormous expansion to be able to give more complete answers to the questions it raises.

PART THREE

The Politics of Social Action

Six

CONFLICT AS NEGOTIATION RITUAL: RANDALL COLLINS

ECONOMIC THOUGHT looks at social interaction in terms of exchange, negotiation, and bargaining. Its predominance in American culture has also had its effects on sociological conflict theory. Conflict is not understood as an uncompromising fight between two individual or collective actors, each one committed to a specific goal and each trying to realize this goal against the resistance of the opposing party without any willingness to give up even a part of his or her intent. In contradistinction to such a radical view of conflict, the amalgamation of conflict theory with economic thought leads to conflict being conceived of as an ongoing process of bargaining. Randall Collins (1975, 1988: 208-25) has formulated a theory of conflict that concentrates on analyzing it as such a bargaining process. This is an approach to conflict that, on the one hand, fits in with the overall economic perspective in American thought while, at the same time, applying the conflict theory perspective to economic transactions. We can see this amalgamation from two viewpoints: The conflict perspective points to the processes of conflict settlement in economic transactions. The economic perspective points to the processes of economic transaction in the settlement of conflicts. Here we are particularly concerned with the first perspective.

Conflict, Ritual, Language, and Negotiation

Collins (1975: 56-61) starts with an image of a person as a sociable but conflict prone animal. People seek emotional gratification. In order to attain such a state in which their needs are satisfied, they require resources. A crucial resource that can be used to achieve gratification of needs is violent coercion, or in other words coercive power (Collins, 1975: 59). Using such coercive power, people can force other people to do certain things, overcome their resistance, and extract more specifically needed resources from the physical and social environment, particularly from other people, in order to attain their goals. However, it is an unpleasant experience for anyone to be subjected to the coercive power of other people; in particular, it prevents one from achieving the gratification of one's own needs. Inasmuch as people seek need gratification, they have to fight back against coercion from other people. Thus, they come into conflict with each other. All of them have to gain coercive power over each other, at least in order to overcome the coercive power of their opponents.

Viewing society in this way, Collins comes very close to Thomas Hobbes's (1651/1966) famous account of the state of nature where each person is somebody's wolf, and everybody lives in fear of all others. Hobbes lets his subjects in this disastrous state of nature come to the realization that it would be more useful for them to conclude a contract that obliges them to transfer their coercive power to a centralized authority that would then have to make use of this power only to maintain the rules of conduct, that is, order, and to punish any violation of this order. Though Collins relates to Hobbes as well as to Machiavelli and Marx in order to establish his conflict theory, he does not follow Hobbes along this line beyond his description of the state of nature. In Collins's view, civilized society features elements of the state of nature everywhere. Therefore, ongoing interaction has to be analyzed primarily in terms of conflict.

However, interaction cannot be fully described without referring to elements that reach beyond conflict. Collins (1975: 90–111) is well aware of this complex nature of social interaction, though he tends to relate these other elements to conflict in an instrumental way, as we shall see. First, social interaction brings people together, and we have to ask what holds them together. Speaking of groups as collective actors in conflict, we can ask, What holds the opposing parties together in order to continue with conflict settlement? And what holds the parties together internally? Collins's answers to these questions come from a reading of Durkheim's sociology and his preoccupation with the production of moral order. It is rituals in various forms that bind people together in a common solidarity. Religious and political ceremonies have this effect, but any everyday encounter involves some sort of ritual that exerts a binding effect on the individuals taking part in the interaction. A ritual concentrates people both physically and mentally on the group performing that ritual. It so concentrates "their attention as to generate a common mood and a common object of thought" (1975: 94).

Rituals bind people to common group ideas, images, and norms and generate common thought, common goals, and common interests in this way. Rituals provide for the stable elements people can share in processes of thinking and conversation, need gratification and exchange, and goal attainment and conflict. Being formally introduced to a person by another person establishes a link between the persons who had been strangers before. After having established that link, conversation becomes possible, and insecurity about how to talk to each other has been reduced. Signing a contract and shaking hands ceremonially underscore the binding effects of the contract for both parties. Settling a conflict with a formal agreement signed by both parties to that conflict ceremonially makes the agreement binding for both parties. Thus, social interaction not only consists to a large extent of processes of conflict settlement but also always includes elements of rituals that bind the parties of interaction together.

A further major aspect involved in social interaction is the use of language. Interaction implies conversation. In order to emphasize this element of social interaction, Collins refers to the phenomenological school in sociology, particularly to ethnomethodology and conversational analysis. The question here is one of how people can talk to each other and understand each other. As Collins puts it, there are two opposite poles in addressing this question. On the far "right," we have Parsons's position of an underlying common language, the terms of which are universally understood throughout a society. People of the same society have undergone the same processes of socialization and share the same language. They can rely on these preconditions whenever they encounter one another, so that they can converse and understand each other. On the far "left" is Garfinkel's emphasis on the indexicality of every expression used in conversation. First of all, there are expressions like "here," "now," and "there," which can be understood only in the situation in which they are being used. However, as Garfinkel points out, every word of language has indexical aspects to it and can be understood correctly only in the situation in which it is expressed. There are no universal expressions but only particular expressions. Thus, the coordination of action and mutual understanding have to be accomplished in practical action in concrete situations. Studies in ethnomethodology examine the rational procedures by which actors in a situation come to accomplish that task of understanding each other and coordinating their actions. Social interaction always involves the construction of meaning by both interacting parties. Only inasmuch as the two parties come to a common construction of meaning will they actually understand each other. Likewise, only inasmuch as they understand each other will they be able to coordinate their actions, to rationally pursue goals, and to attain the gratification of their needs. Thus, conversation and its major characteristic of seeking mutual understanding are major parts of social interaction; and we have to take into account the processes of constructing common meaning in order to fully understand social interaction.

However, arriving at a common understanding does not depend solely on the processes of communication itself. Collins is less concerned with the internal logic of communication and more concerned with the nonconversational determinants of communication. At this point he turns to a fourth basic feature of social interaction, the fact that it involves negotiations between parties who are oriented toward deriving advantages (rewards, utility) from social interaction:

> Life can be seen as a series of ongoing negotiations, and explanation is solidly rooted in the reality of little moments in time. (Collins, 1975: 114)

In doing so, Collins (1975: 133–52) introduces an economic element into the analysis of social interaction. According to this view, actors choose partners of interaction, begin and terminate interaction, or choose the content of their conversations according to expected advantages and disadvantages. The more advantages and the fewer disadvantages they expect from engaging in an interaction, the more they will enter and stay with that interaction. This economic calculation of advantages and disadvantages introduces a dynamic element into the process of interaction. Advantages and disadvantages drawn from a certain interaction change as time elapses during the interaction: alternatives may become available, the exchange may be accomplished so that the parties cannot offer any more to each other, or the points of reference may be changed. Life seen in this perspective is like an American cocktail party where one moves relatively rapidly from one guest to another, exchanging a few words but never committing oneself to talking to one or a few persons for a period of time. The rapid change of partners of interaction is a consequence of conceiving interaction in terms of economic exchange. As soon as the goods have been exchanged, the interaction is terminated, because continuing would not yield any further advantages.

Summarizing Collins's view of social interaction, we can say that he conceives of interaction primarily as something that involves conflict of interests, because people seek need gratification, and the gratification of one person's needs frequently implies preventing the gratification of another person's needs. Thus, in order to accomplish need gratification, they have to make use of coercive power to overcome the resistance of people who would be deprived of gratification by their action. The use of coercive power thus becomes a major element in social interaction aimed at achieving need gratification. However, this process of conflict is embedded in a wider world of social interaction. It is intermingled with rituals binding people together, conversation aiming at the common construction of meaning and negotiation oriented toward mutually drawing advantages from interaction, thus turning goal attainment, in its straightforward, uncompromising sense, into compromising, bargaining behavior.

Rituals, conversation, and negotiation have their specific effects on the process of conflict settlement. Ritual provides for order and predictability, conversation for rational understanding and rational planning, and negotiation for flexibility and change in conflict settlement. On the other hand, conflict settlement via the use of coercive power exerts its own effects on rituals, conversation, and negotiation. These elements of interaction themselves become instrumentalized as resources of domination. The powerful actor can make use of rituals in order to bind his subordinates to his or her command; this actor can set the terms of conversation and also the terms of negotiation. As a result, rituals, conversation, and negotiation support and enhance the actor's power position. Determining the effects of rituals, conversations, and negotiations on social interaction by way of instrumentalizing them for the advantage of the more powerful actors because of the application of their power to set the terms of these procedures is the direction that interests Collins most. The reason is that he sees social interaction primarily as a process of ongoing conflict. People with more power than other people can more easily turn rituals, conversations, and negotiations in the direction of serving their interests and increasing their advantages. This is the very essence of applying the conflict perspective to these aspects of social interaction. We can demonstrate how this works with Collins's analysis of conversation.

Conversation

Conversation consists primarily of communication and involves seeking to arrive at a common understanding of reality. But it also implies rituals, conflict, and negotiation. Rituals of conversation determine how to open, continue, and terminate a conversation. Conflict arises with regard to the terms, topics, and outcomes of conversation. Negotiation is oriented toward the advantages people can draw from a conversation. In addressing conversation in the conflict perspective, we have to emphasize those elements in it where conflict is involved. This is so to the extent that both parties do not want to talk in the same language and about the same topics, have contradictory opinions, and want to come to opposing results. In the case of contradictory opinions, if one person succeeds during the conversation in being proved right, the other person is automatically wrong. This is a conflict. In the conflict perspective, it will be settled according to the power resources the conflicting parties can command.

Collins (1975: 135–39) distinguishes between nonconversational and conversational resources. A nonconversational resource is the coercive power an actor has. The inquisitors of the Catholic church have the power to excommunicate, to close out of the church community those people who contradict the dominant opinion within it. Being in a position to prevent someone's promotion, mobilize social support against the opinion of another person, or withhold any gratification a person needs are positions that provide one with resources, which one may use to force another to give up the conversational dispute and to comply with one's own opinions. Conversational resources that can be used in the conversational struggle are the arguments one has at hand in order to support one's position and to question that of the opponent. We can formulate the following proposition:

1. The more nonconversational and conversational resources a participant in a conversation can mobilize, the more the conversation moves in the direction of his or her own language, topics, and opinions.

Though Collins does not formulate explicitly such a proposition in the list of his collected hypotheses, which is not systematic and more perplexing than enlightening in character, we can nevertheless derive such a proposition from his application of the conflict perspective to the analysis of conversation. However, we would have to formulate the conflict in conversation more precisely than he does himself in order to keep it separate from the other elements involved in conversation and in order to fully understand its unique character. Collins himself intermingles the conflict in conversation directly with conversational exchange and thus does not come to analyze precisely the specific nature of conversational conflict. It is always couched in terms of negotiation and bargaining, which implicitly introduces an economic element into the analysis of conversational conflict. He starts his analysis with the following statement:

Generally speaking, all talk is negotiation. (1975: 114)

People who negotiate in order to achieve need gratification are not in a position to rely solely on power resources, on the basis of which they can make other people comply with their demands. They do not have complete power over other people, and they face opposing power from them. A formal two-actor model where "Ego" interacts with "Alter" may aid the analysis. Ego's power over Alter increases the more Alter needs things that Ego can provide and the less alternative means of obtaining those things Alter has, and vice versa. According to this model, Ego can have power over Alter, but Alter can have power over Ego at the same time. The two relationships vary independently of each other. Ego may need Alter's love and may have no alternative, and Alter may need Ego's love and may have no alternative. This is a situation in which both partners have a great deal of power over each other and are completely at the mercy of each other's commands. Where both parties understand each other very well and act respectfully and gently, this may work very well. But if such respect and gentleness are lacking, this may be the basis for permanent war.

When we come to an analysis of bargaining processes, the question is: How do conflict and power enter the process of negotiation? The conflict in negotiation lies in the fact that Ego wants more from Alter than Alter is prepared to give in exchange for the incentives offered by Ego. Both start out in an exchange situation: for example, they might exchange work for wages, service for reputation, information for other information, a new academic paper for some advice on how to improve the arguments in it, entertainment for applause, and so on. Scientist Ego may tell colleague Alter about his or her recent research and seek some advice from Alter on how to improve that research. Ego may tell Alter only about the specific aspect of his or her work about which he or she seeks advice. However, Alter may wish to know more about Ego's work before giving an opinion or advice. Here, both are in an exchange and a conflict at the same time. The exchange is research information for advice, but they are not in agreement about the terms of the exchange. This is where the process of negotation begins. Ego has to find out how much interest Alter has in Ego's work and how many alternative means Alter has of obtaining the same research information. The less interested Alter is and the more alternatives he or she has, the more attractively Ego will have to present his or her research in order to get Alter's advice. Ego will have to disclose his or her most interesting ideas. On the other hand, the less interested Ego is in Alter's advice and the more alternatives Ego has, the more attractively Alter has to present his or her advice to Ego. If Ego has a lot of power over Alter, and Alter has little power over Ego in this sense, Ego can get Alter's advice in return for a poor presentation of the research. If Alter has a lot of power over Ego, and Ego has little power over Alter, Alter can get an attractive presentation of the best ideas in return for mediocre advice. If both have little power, they will exchange poor presentations for mediocre advice. If both have a lot of power, they will exchange attractive presentations for good advice. Thus, the terms of exchange in negotiation are determined by the power of the exchanging parties with regard to each other. Those with more power receive more than those with less power.

Collins does not formulate precisely how the outcome of negotiations depends on the power of the parties involved. Instead of "power," he includes only "resources" in his formulation of hypotheses:

2. The more conversational and nonconversational resources one has, the more conversational and nonconversational resources can be demanded in return and the more one can choose with whom to converse and about what to converse.

In this proposition we have combined the three major hypotheses Collins (1975: 158) formulates about resources and negotiations that build up the core of a theory of conversational negotiation. However, a closer look at this proposition shows that it is incomplete. Someone may have a lot of resources, but if the other person doesn't need these resources in a conver-

sation and/or has alternative sources of reward, he or she cannot be forced
by the first person to make any input to the conversational exchange. Ego's
resources do not in themselves establish his or her power over Alter, since
Alter's need for Ego's resources and Alter's alternatives also play their part.
Thus, we have to qualify Collins's resource proposition to become a power
proposition:

3. The more Alter needs the conversational and nonconversational
   resources that Ego can supply and the fewer alternatives Alter has, the
   more power Ego has over Alter; likewise, the more conversational and
   nonconversational services Ego can demand from Alter, the more Ego
   can choose whether to talk to Alter and on what topic.

The sequence of conversation in light of this power proposition depends
on how Ego and Alter can demonstrate their power to the opponent, using
particular strategies and situational tactics. Ego may impress Alter by mentioning the names of attractive conversational partners Ego purports to know
and by citing interesting ideas in order to gain Alter's attention, because
he or she knows that Alter is a very worthwhile partner in discussion and
because he or she sees no alternative. Ego provides Alter with the prospect
that Ego will also be a worthwhile partner in discussion and will be better
than alternative partners. In this way, Ego may motivate Alter to enter conversation. But Ego will be able to continue this conversation only as long
as he or she can live up to the initial promise. As soon as Ego falls short
of the expectations generated, he or she loses power on the market, because
competing conversational partners now become more attractive to Alter, and
Alter may make a move toward entering conversation with someone else.

Thus, inasmuch as conversation takes place in a marketplace, the partners in conversation are always confronted with the power of competitors
who can attract the attention of those people they would themselves choose
as partners of conversation. A market involves both exchange and conflict
by way of competition. The market influences the conflict between sellers
and buyers in terms of the prices of goods exchanged. If there is much competition between sellers, prices will go down. This is a so-called buyers' market. The power of sellers is small, and the power of buyers is great. If there
is much competition between buyers, prices will go up. This is known as
a sellers' market. The power of sellers is great, and the power of buyers is
small. The competition, that is, conflict between sellers and between buyers,
increases with the number of sellers and their need to sell something, or
with the number of buyers and their need to buy something.

We see in the market the dynamic force that introduces change into
conversational conflict. In the ideal sense, a market is a forum everybody
can enter in order to sell or buy something. A conversational market is always

open to the chance of a new supply of or demand for resources, and these change the terms of exchange between the conversational partners. In a closed relationship there is no escape from the verbal assaults of the one and only partner of conversation. In a marketplace we can quickly move to a more favorable conversation as soon as the present conversation becomes uncomfortable. It is also only in a market that presents alternatives that we may grow bored with a certain conversation and seek new ones. Only under this condition does the principle of marginal utility begin to work. In a closed relationship with no alternatives people may continue to talk endlessly about the same things. They never become satiated, because there is no alternative source of conversation. Collins intermingles economic considerations like these with the conflict perspective, so he fails to grasp precisely the specific effects of markets on conversation. He overgeneralizes when he says:

> Conversational relationships must be continually renegotiated, and it is not surprising that there is always a certain amount of change. Conversational resources get used up; interests and concerns change as new life circumstances open up new opportunities and narrow down [others]. Multiple sociable bonds (or networks of practical alliances) continually introduce strains to balance different conversational realities. All of these things result in a gradual tearing down and building up of relationships, keeping the conversational markets open, to a degree. (1975: 143)

Conversation is not a market per se. It can take place in very closed circles without any choice of conversational partners, terms, topics, and outcomes. A closed religious community, or any total institution, is not a conversational marketplace at all, but a place where one has no choice of language, partners, terms, topics, and outcomes in conversation. However, inasmuch as conversation does take place in a market, it occurs in a certain way, and this is what we want to know. We do not want to know whether conversation is a market or not, because this is an empirical question and has to be answered differently from case to case. However, we do want to know which effects a conversational market exerts on conversation. The effects are such that conversation involves a high rate of change of partners, language, topics, and outcomes resulting from the dynamics of the market that permanently offer a new supply and a new demand, and involve satiation with one good yet growing need for other goods. The more the market offers new goods, the more one becomes satiated with old ones. However, the increased quality of new products serving the same needs (e.g., TV, video, stereo, CD players or, in conversation, the complexity of theories) overcomes satiation and the working of the principle of marginal utility. Someone who has all these goods needs them again, as fast as improvements in quality enter the market. Taking these effects of the market of conversation into account, we can formulate a proposition of market dynamics:

4. The more conversation takes place in a market, the more rapidly the partners, languages, topics, and outcomes of conversation will change.

The principle of marginal utility is:

5. The more conversation takes place in a market, the more the following will hold true: The more one person has been talking to another person in a certain kind of language, on certain topics with certain outcomes, the less this person will continue to do so as time progresses.

The faster the market is supplied with product improvements, the less prone a person will be to discontinue consumption. Though Collins does not formulate such a principle, we can state it thus:

6. The more conversation takes place in a market, the more the following will hold true: The faster partners in conversation, languages, topics, and outcomes change their character, the more people will continue conversation.

A lively conversation can continue even in the face of alternatives, but a boring one will not continue. However, a boring conversation can continue where no market and therefore no alternatives exist.

These are the effects of market negotiation on conversation that can be pointed out on the basis of Collins's analysis. But we can be more precise if we differentiate the conversational market from conversation in general and conversational conflict in particular.

Thus far, we have looked at conflict and negotiation in conversational encounters. Continuing with the dimensions involved in social interaction, we can add further thoughts on the effects of rituals on conversation and on the internal process of conversation as such. From what we have said about rituals, we can infer that these are procedures that have an ordering effect on conversation, making its beginning, continuation, termination, language, topics, and outcomes predictable for the participants. Rituals are rooted in relatively closed and firm communities of people who feel close to each other and who re-create this closeness by associating periodically and performing rituals. People who are close to one another and who share such rituals have enough trust and feel enough security to enter conversations with one another. People who are physically and socially distant from one another do not feel secure and comfortable enough to enter and continue a conversation. Collins (1975: 132–33, 152–60) refers to this effect of closeness on conversation in the text and in several hypotheses addressing propinquity and closeness in the physical and social sense in various forms. We can summarize these hypotheses in a proposition of closeness:

7. The closer people are to one another socially, the more they will share
   rituals of solidarity confirmation; the more they do that, the more their
   closeness will be re-created; the more it is re-created, the more they will
   feel secure and comfortable enough to enter into and continue
   conversation.

People who live close to one another and share rituals also have rituals
of conversation in common that give their conversation and its language,
topics, and outcomes an ordered and predictable character. Pointing out this
effect of rituals on conversation more precisely than Collins does we can
formulate:

8. The more people share rituals of conversation, the more their conversation will proceed in an ordered and predictable way with an ordered
   and predictable language, topic, and outcome.

Collins (1975: 114–31) introduces several types of conversation that can
be understood as differently ordered by different rituals prescribing procedure, language, topic, and outcome. The following types of talk are based
on such different rituals: practical talk, shop talk, ideological or legitimizing talk, intellectual discussion, entertaining conversation, gossip, and personal conversation. All of these types of talk proceed according to their own
rules, which establish a specific ritual for each type of talk.

Finally, we have to distinguish more precisely than Collins does between
the internal processes of conversation as such and the effects of conflict,
negotiation, and ritual on conversation. Collins (1975: 103–11) says that common outlooks make the continuation of conversation easier. He also formulates hypotheses that address this process. We can say that people looking
for meaning in their actions will continue a conversation as long as they
see a chance of coming to a mutually shared sense and of coming to understand each other. However, the less they see such a chance, the less likely
they are to go on with a conversation that seemingly does not make sense.
Then they will change partners, language, and/or topic of conversation. We
can formulate a proposition of meaning:

9. The more participants in a conversation share a common language, the
   more they will arrive at a shared meaning and mutual understanding.

We can also add a proposition of continuity:

10. The more people come to mutual understanding in a conversation, the
    more they will continue to talk along the established lines.

Critical Assessment

Summarizing our discussion of Collins's conflict analysis of conversation at this point, we can say that this analysis would gain more precision if Collins disentangled the four basic dimensions of social interaction. He himself mentions, in a rather unsystematic way, the internal processes of conversation and the effects of conflict, negotiation, and rituals on conversation. A common language allows for mutual understanding and by way of this for the continuation of a conversation on the established lines. Conflict introduces a dynamic force into conversation, making its outcome dependent on the power the partners of conversation can mobilize. Negotiation on a conversational market makes changes in partners, language, topics, and outcomes in conversation very rapid. Closeness and rituals provide for order and predictability in conversation.

We can surely take a conflict perspective and see the effects of rituals, negotiations, and conversations mediated through their conscious use by powerful actors. The more power a participant in conversation has, the more he or she will be able to make use of rituals, language, and negotiations to further his or her goals. However, this holds true only inasmuch as there are power holders who are stronger than the binding effects of traditional rituals, the formalizing effects of language, and the changing effects of markets with many competing opponents. Thus, the conflict perspective is a useful one inasmuch as social life is a power game, but it is less useful and has to be complemented by other theories the more social life involves different characteristics, namely, the characteristics of rituals, conversation, and negotiation.

SEVEN

A THEORY OF BARGAINING: SAMUEL B. BACHARACH AND EDWARD J. LAWLER

AN INTERESTING theory of the bargaining process in terms of power was formulated by Samuel B. Bacharach and Edward J. Lawler in 1981. Compared to Collins's conflict approach, which understands the conflict process primarily as a process of bargaining, Bacharach and Lawler's theory concentrates in a more systematically formalized way on the internal aspects of bargaining – the aspects of power, context, tactical action, concessions, toughness, agreement, and termination – and much less on the embeddedness of bargaining in ritual and conversation.

Bargaining is a process in which two parties with conflicting interests engage in mutual compromising, including tactical impression management with regard to their power, and make concessions in order to motivate each other to come to an agreement with which the parties are better off than they would be under conditions of continued nonagreement, struggle, or withdrawal. Motivating the other party by means of both power and inducements characterizes the mixture of conflictual and economic elements in the process of bargaining. Neither party has enough power to motivate the opposing party to reach an agreement without making some concessions in order to provide incentives or, in other words, without giving something away to gain something in return. The two parties have goals that are in conflict. They cannot attain these goals at the same time to the same degree. Inasmuch as each makes use of power in order to overcome the resistance of the other party and to attain goals, both act as a political actor. Inasmuch as both calculate the costs of continuing this power game in terms of forgone benefits from alternative actions, for example, the power, resources, time, and energy saved or the rewards received from alternative sources, and both make concessions, they act as economic actors. Making a concession is an incentive for one's opponent to come to an agreement at a certain point where neither party attains its goals completely but both are better off from the economic point of view than by continuing the conflict or by withdrawing from the relationship. Thus, we have a conflict that is settled by both parties making tactical use of power *and* incentives. In a labor-management conflict, the two parties have goals that contradict each other: for example, raising wages 5 percent versus keeping wages at the existing level. Labor may emphasize its power by threatening a strike, while management may emphasize its power by threatening the exclusion of employees from working (firings or a lockout). On the other hand, management may signal that it is willing to raise wages 3 percent if labor agrees and gives up the intended strike. This concession by management is an incentive for labor, which now has to calculate whether it is better off with a guaranteed 3 percent wage increase and no strike costs than with an uncertain 5 percent and the strike costs. Management makes its concession on the economic calculation of being better off with 3 percent higher wages and no loss of production than with lower wages and disrupted production. The two will meet at the point where both calculate the benefits from an agreement as being higher than those that would ensue if they continued the struggle or withdrew from the relationship.

Basic Elements of Bargaining

Bacharach and Lawler (1981: 43–52) start their analysis of the bargaining process by making three assumptions: first, power is the essence of bargaining; second, bargaining is a process of tactical action; and third, bargaining power is subjective power. It is the power both parties can mobilize that determines their success in the bargaining process. This is the message of the first assumption. Power has to be introduced into the bargaining process so as to motivate the parties to make concessions, thus overcoming at least part of the opponent's resistance. This is the message of the second assumption. And it is the impression each opponent has of the other's power that motivates both to make concessions. The subjective view a party has of another party's power gives the latter power over the former in the bargaining process. Impression management, therefore, is a major part of bargaining. However, this does not imply that real possession of power does not play a role. Inasmuch as the power impressions one party conveys to another are tested in real action, an impression will break down if it cannot be backed up by real power. Bluffing works only as long as uncertainty prevails and tests of power can be avoided. Nevertheless, because bargaining frequently involves uncertainty about real power and tests can be avoided it is important for the actors to make power impressions on each other in order to be successful. This is the message of the third assumption.

Power

As to the meaning of the concept of power, Bacharach and Lawler (1981: 45–46) discuss three variants: (1) power as an outcome; (2) power as potential; and (3) power as tactical action. The first concept means that party A has power over party B when A's attempt to motivate B to an action is successful. But this is an unsatisfactory definition of power, because there may be very different reasons for B to succumb to A's influence; so we arrive at a much too diffuse concept of power embracing motivation by rationally convincing someone, by appealing to his or her sense of solidarity, by presenting some incentive, or by threatening some sanction. Bacharach and Lawler do not see these deficiencies in the definition concerned, but what they do criticize is that it does not allow any distinction to be made between power mobilized in bargaining and the outcome of bargaining. It becomes identified with the outcome and cannot be used to predict that outcome. This is possible, however, if power is defined as the potential to influence the actions of another party. Accordingly, Bacharach and Lawler are in favor of this definition. Nevertheless, we have to make the criticism that this definition suffers from the same diffuseness as the first one. The third definition understands power as the ability of a party to tactically impress the other party and hence exert influence upon that party. Bacharach and Lawler accept this definition, in combination with the concept of power as potential, as being the most appropriate for their approach. However, it is as diffuse in its meaning as the other two.

In order to correct Bacharach and Lawler, we should recall the definition of power we know from Max Weber (1922/1972c: 28):

> Power is any chance one party has to enforce its will on another party, even in the face of resistance from that other party.

This type of means one party uses to motivate another can clearly be distinguished from other types of motivation, such as rationally convincing another party, appealing to solidarity, and offering incentives. Power according to this definition is produced subject to specific preconditions and gives rise to specific consequences, very different from those found with the other types of interpersonal motivation. In contrast to Bacharach and Lawler, we have to keep in mind this understanding of power when we continue with their analysis of the bargaining process.

Bacharach and Lawler (1981: 52–60) discuss three different approaches to determining the basis of power: (1) attributing power; (2) ability to apply sanctions; and (3) dependence of one actor on another. The attribution approach sees power based on the attribution of power to party A by party B based on the effect A's behavior has on B's behavior. This means that one party attributes *post hoc* power to another party when its behavior has been effectively determined by the other party's behavior. Bacharach and Lawler criticize this approach for not allowing an analysis of the bargaining process itself or of how it is steered by the mutual impression management of the parties. We can also say that it is much too diffuse for us to get any understanding of why and how the influence has occurred. Cause and effect cannot be distinguished. The second approach sees the origin of power in the ability of one party to apply sanctions against another party, thus preventing it from attaining need satisfaction. This is offensive control. On the other hand, a party's ability defensively to prevent another party's attempt to curtail its own need satisfaction also represents an enhancement of its power. Bacharach and Lawler see more usefulness in this approach than in the attribution approach, because it refers to the resources that can be imputed into the bargaining process. However, they make the criticism that this approach does not specify how the ability to apply sanctions is translated into the manipulative tactics of the bargaining process.

Dependence

This is where the authors introduce their own dependence approach, one that locates the source of one party's power over another party in the second party's dependence on the first if it wants to satisfy its needs. The second party's dependence gives the first party the ability to apply sanctions. Without such dependence there would be no effective sanctions. Moreover, it is the ability of the parties to manipulate each other's perception of their mutual dependence that transfers the ability to apply sanctions into the bargaining process and that determines the course of this process. Dependence means that one party needs the other party in order to satisfy its needs. Labor needs management in order to secure wage income; management needs labor in order to secure production and profit. Thus, we can formulate a first proposition (Bacharach and Lawler, 1981: 60):

Proposition 1: An increase in the dependence of bargainer A on bargainer B increases the opponent B's bargaining power.

According to this proposition, labor's bargaining power increases with the increasing dependence of management on labor in order to secure production and profit. Management's bargaining power increases with the increasing dependence of labor on management in order to secure wage income.

Alternatives and Commitment

Two different factors determine the dependence of the parties on each other. First, the availability of alternative sources of need satisfaction; second, the commitment to an issue at stake. When labor has no alternative source of income other than wages from a centrally managed organization and cannot break the relationship with that organization, as is the case in centralized socialist economies, it is much more dependent on that organization than labor that can shop around for different employers and move from one enterprise to another, from one branch of industry to another. When management has no alternative sources of labor other than its own workers, it is much more dependent on them than a management that has many alternative sources of labor in order to secure production and profit.

On the other hand, a party may have a greater or a lesser interest in an issue at stake, it may need a certain outcome of a bargaining process more or less urgently in order to satisfy its needs; and individual needs may themselves be more or less urgent than others. Thus, an increase in wages is more urgent for labor that has low wages and needs them to secure a living than for labor that has a high income. Keeping wages low is more urgent for management that makes low profits than for management that makes high profits.

Summing up, we can say that an increasing dependence of one party on another party increases the latter party's bargaining power. That dependence increases to the same degree to which alternative sources of need satisfaction decrease in number. And it increases to the same degree to which the needs involved are of primary importance to a party. We can formulate the following hypothesis of alternative outcome sources (Bacharach and Lawler, 1981: 63):

> Hypothesis 1: A decrease in one party's alternative outcome sources increases that party's dependence on the other party and thus increases the other party's bargaining power.

The commitment hypothesis is as follows (Bacharach and Lawler, 1981: 63):

> Hypothesis 2: An increase in one party's commitment to the outcomes increases its dependence on the other party and thus increases the other party's bargaining power.

Absolute, Relative, and Total Power

Power is involved in the bargaining process in absolute, relative, and total terms. Bacharach and Lawler speak of one party having absolute power as long as only the other party's dependence upon it is taken into account and there is no dependence at all in the other direction. One party's absolute power means the dependence of the other party upon it without any consideration of the reciprocal relationship. If we add one party's power to the other's and focus on the sum of the two, we find the total power involved in the bargaining process. The relative power of one party has to be determined by setting it against the total power in the relationship or against the other party's power. The first ratio determines the relative amount of power in the bargaining process one party has at its disposal. It may possess anything from nothing to all of that power. The second ratio determines how much more or less power one party has compared with the other party. It may have 0 to x times more or less power.

According to the outlined distinction between absolute, relative, and total power, we can formulate the corresponding dependence propositions and alternative outcome and commitment hypotheses in absolute, relative, and total terms (Bacharach and Lawler, 1981: 209–13). The dependence propositions are as follows:

2. An increase in the dependence of A on B increases B's absolute bargaining power.
3. An increase of the ratio of A's dependence on B to B's dependence on A increases B's relative bargaining power.
4. An increase in the sum of A's and B's dependence increases the total bargaining power in the relationship.

The alternative outcome and commitment hypotheses are as follows:

3. A decrease in A's alternative outcome sources or an increase in A's commitment to the outcomes at issue increases B's absolute bargaining power.
4. A decrease in the ratio of A's alternatives or an increase in the ratio of A's commitment to B's alternatives or commitment increases B's relative bargaining power.
5. An increase in the sum of both parties' dependence assessed on the basis of alternatives and commitment increases the total bargaining power in the relationship.

Zero-Sum and Variable-Sum Power Games

The distinction between relative and total power implies that the power game is not always played under zero-sum conditions. That is, an increase in one party's power does not necessarily cause a decrease in the other party's power. For example, labor's dependence on management may increase because of the diminishing availability of alternative jobs and other sources of income. This increases management's power over labor. However, it doesn't necessarily decrease labor's power over management. It may even happen that the availability of labor diminishes at the same time, so that management's dependence on labor also increases. Thus, the power of one party can increase or decrease without a reciprocal change in the other party's power, and the other party's power may even change in the same direction, leading to a change in the total sum of power involved in a relationship. Whenever this happens, we can speak of a variable-sum power game. Whenever one party's increase or decrease in power is accompanied by the reciprocal decrease or increase in power of the other party, we speak of a zero-sum power game. Both cases can occur. The actors in the bargaining process may perceive the process differently, sometimes as a zero-sum game, sometimes as a variable-sum game. Thus, we can formulate two different propositions. If bargainers conceive of the process as a zero-sum power game, the following proposition holds true (Bacharach and Lawler, 1981: 69):

> Proposition 5a: An increase in bargainer A's dependence on opponent B decreases the bargaining power attributed to A and increases the power attributed to B.

If bargainers conceive of the process as a variable-sum power game, the following proposition holds true (Bacharach and Lawler, 1981: 70):

> Proposition 5b: An increase in bargainer A's dependence on opponent B increases the perception of B's bargaining power, but does not affect the perception of A's power.

Options

We turn now to the options available to the parties in a bargaining process when we consider a labor-management dispute. Bacharach and Lawler (1981: 73–75) exemplify this with five options open to the workers, as derived from Albert O. Hirschman's (1970) analysis:

Exit: Workers can leave the organization.
Strike: Workers temporarily withdraw their services.
Explicit bargaining: Workers explicitly combine power and inducement in order to motivate management to make concessions.
Tacit bargaining: Without explicitly engaging in negotiations there may be signals on both sides indicating one's power and incentives to motivate concessions on the other side.
Submission: Workers give in and accept more or less willingly the conditions set by management.

Which action will be taken depends on the utility outcome expected by the parties to flow from that action. They will choose the form of action that is expected to provide the highest profit (rewards minus costs). According to Bacharach and Lawler, we can expect that actors will make more attempts to influence another party in the bargaining process the more the expected utility of that action increases. They also say that we can expect such an increase with an increase in perceived absolute and relative power. That is to say, the more the actors see their absolute or relative power increasing, the more likely it is that the bargaining process will have a positive outcome for them and the more likely it is that they will choose this option and put aside the other options. They may choose what is known as the voice option. With an increase in absolute or relative power the actors have greater faith in their own strength and enter into the bargaining process much more spontaneously. This is the meaning of the following two propositions, 3a and 3b (Bacharach and Lawler, 1981: 76):

Proposition 6a: Absolute power. An increase in the perceived dependence of B on A increases the perceived probability that an attempt by A to exert influence will secure a given magnitude of outcomes and thus increases the subjective expected utility of A's voice option.

Proposition 6b: Relative power. A decrease in the perceived dependence of A on B increases the perceived probability that an attempt by A to exert influence will secure a given magnitude of outcomes and thus increases the subjective expected utility associated with A's voice option.

When we examine the situation in terms of alternatives and commitment, we get the following hypotheses corresponding to these two propositions (Bacharach and Lawler, 1981: 77):

Hypothesis 6: If management has few alternatives, the union's expected probability of securing a given level of outcomes is greater than if management has many alternatives.

Hypothesis 7: If management has a high commitment to the outcomes at issue, the union's expected probability of securing a given level of outcomes is greater than if management has a low commitment to the outcomes at issue.

Hypothesis 8: If labor has many alternatives, the union's expected probability of securing a given level of outcomes is greater than if labor has few alternatives.

Hypothesis 9: If labor has a low commitment to the outcomes at issue, the union's expected probability of securing a given level of outcomes is greater than if labor has a high commitment to the outcomes at issue.

Concessions

In the chapter following the exposition of their theory of bargaining as outlined above, Bacharach and Lawler turn to determining the factors that influence the making of concessions in the bargaining process. Generally, they assume that a party's toughness, that is, its unwillingness to make concessions, increases with its perceived bargaining power. However, this occurs in different ways, depending on whether the parties understand the process as a zero-sum or a variable-sum power game. Playing a zero-sum power game makes them see power in reciprocal terms; thus, their toughness is influenced on both sides even when bargaining power changes only on one side. When they play a variable-sum power game, a change of bargaining power on one side affects only the toughness of that particular side. The following proposition is formulated in zero-sum terms (Bacharach and Lawler, 1981: 91):

Proposition 7: An increase in a party's bargaining power increases that party's toughness while decreasing the opponent's toughness.

In terms of dependence, we can formulate the following proposition (Bacharach and Lawler, 1981: 91):

Proposition 8: An increase in a party's dependence on another party increases the other party's toughness and decreases the first party's toughness.

In terms of alternatives, we can formulate the following hypothesis (Bacharach and Lawler, 1981: 94):

Hypothesis 10: An increase in a party's alternatives decreases that party's concessions and increases the other party's concessions.

In distinction to the zero-sum game, the variable-sum game only implies effects on one party's toughness coming from changes in that party's dependence on the other, that is, from changes in the other party's bargaining power. The proposition reads as follows (Bacharach and Lawler, 1981: 93):

Proposition 9: An increase in a party's bargaining power decreases the opponent's toughness but does not increase the first party's toughness.

In terms of dependence, the proposition reads as follows (Bacharach and Lawler, 1981: 93):

Proposition 10: An increase in a party's dependence on another party decreases its toughness.

We can formulate the following hypothesis in terms of alternatives (Bacharach and Lawler, 1981: 94):

Hypothesis 11: An increase in a party's alternatives decreases that party's concessions and has no effect on the other party's concessions.

Coming to an analysis of commitment, Bacharach and Lawler make a surprising discovery. A decrease in bargaining power in terms of commitment does not always lead to an increase in that party's concessions. The reason is that commitment to the outcome of an issue increases not only one's dependence on the other party but also the energy and efforts one puts into the bargaining process. Bacharach and Lawler call these tactical efforts. Strongly committed parties thus make more tactical efforts than weakly committed parties. Weakly committed parties may make concessions because they do not attach much importance to them and the concessions do not affect their utility outcomes very much. Strongly committed parties are much more concerned with the outcomes, and therefore they are less motivated to make concessions. They have to hold the line in order to get the results they want. Thus, we have two opposing effects of increasing commitment: (1) increasing dependence and thus decreasing toughness and (2) increasing tactical efforts and thus increasing toughness. The following hypotheses can be formulated (Bacharach and Lawler, 1981: 96):

Hypothesis 12: An increase in one party's commitment increases that party's dependence on the other party and thus increases its concessions.

Hypothesis 13: An increase in one party's commitment increases that party's tactical efforts and thus decreases its concessions.

Turning to a discussion of the total sum of power involved in the bargaining process, Bacharach and Lawler assume that it has effects on both parties, in the direction of decreasing their toughness. Confronted with increasing power on the opponent's part, each party will be forced to make more concessions. The following proposition can be formulated (Bacharach and Lawler, 1981: 99):

Proposition 11: An increase in the total power within the bargaining relationship decreases the mutual toughness of the bargainers.

The corresponding hypotheses of alternatives and commitment are as follows (Bacharach and Lawler, 1981: 100):

Hypothesis 14: A decrease in the total alternative outcome sources across bargainers decreases the mutual toughness of the bargainers.

Hypothesis 15: An increase in the total commitment across bargainers decreases the mutual toughness of the bargainers.

Bacharach and Lawler have conducted and cite various experiments that support the hypotheses outlined in the text to a greater or lesser degree.

Punitive Capabilities, Threat, Punishment Tactics, and Punitive Tactics

In the next two chapters, Bacharach and Lawler (1981: 104–56) introduce new concepts: punitive capabilities (the ability of a party to inflict damage on another party), threat (meaning the realization of such damage), and punishment tactics or punitive tactics (the tactical realization of damage in order to motivate the other party to make concessions). Two contradictory theories are discussed in these two chapters: deterrence theory and conflict-spiral theory. Whereas deterrence theory expects a reduction of threat and punishment tactics from an increase in punitive capabilities on both sides, conflict-spiral theory expects the contrary effect. We can summarize the various propositions (Bacharach and Lawler, 1981: 118–22):

Proposition 12: An increase in one party's punitive capability leads to an increase in the other party's punitive capability.

Proposition 13: An increase in one party's punitive capability decreases the frequency of threats and punishment tactics by the other party.

Proposition 14: An increase in the inequality of punitive capability in the relationship increases the frequency of threats and punishment tactics in the relationship.

We can also apply the deterrence proposition as a means of predicting concessions:

Proposition 15: An increase in a party's punitive capability increases the magnitude of the other party's tactical concessions.

The conflict-spiral theory assumes the contrary relationship of increasing likelihood of threats and punishment tactics with increasing punitive capabilities (Bacharach and Lawler, 1981: 127–28).

Proposition 16: An increase in a party's punitive capability increases that party's use of threat and punishment tactics.

Proposition 17: The greater the use of threat and punishment tactics by one party, the greater the use of such tactics by the other.

Both theories derive their plausibility from looking at opposing sides of the relationship. A party's increase in its punitive capability not only makes it more dangerous for the other party to apply threat and punishment tactics but also makes it more tempting for the party in question to convert its strength into action whenever there is an imbalance between the two parties and it feels superior to the other party. This is exactly what is meant by the inequality proposition of deterrence theory. Thus, to a certain degree, it points out one condition under which a conflict spiral can be set into motion. We can therefore say that deterrence works only so long as there is a stable perceived balance of punitive capabilities, whereas it doesn't work and is replaced by a conflict spiral whenever perceived imbalances of punitive capabilities occur, even imbalances that change over time. The conflict spiral means that as soon as threats and punishment tactics are applied, they give rise to retaliation, counterthreat, and counterpunishment.

Bacharach and Lawler point to two more conditions that make deterrence or a conflict spiral more likely. They distinguish between two orientations: maximizing gain and minimizing loss; and two situations: high stakes, that is, poor alternatives and high commitment to the outcome, and low stakes, that is, good alternatives and low commitment to the outcome. They assume that actors minimizing loss will avoid the application of punitive tactics more when the stakes are high than when they are low (Bacharach and Lawler, 1981: 142).

Proposition 18: The deterrence prediction holds true when stakes are high, and the conflict spiral prediction holds true when stakes are low.

Actors maximizing gain will avoid the application of punitive tactics more at low stakes than at high stakes (Bacharach and Lawler, 1981: 142):

Proposition 19: The deterrence prediction holds true when stakes are low, and the conflict spiral prediction holds true when stakes are high.

Influence in Bargaining

Bacharach and Lawler deal with the question of how bargainers come to consensual definitions of an issue and use power, bluffing or normative arguments in order to influence the bargaining process.

The definition of an issue is primarily influenced by the costs one party associates with meeting the other party's demands. If these are high, the issue will be seen as a matter of principle, and a highly competitive strategy will be pursued in order to enforce a party's position. Low costs mean the issue will be seen as one among many different issues, allowing a much more compromising strategy. We can thus formulate the following proposition (Bacharach and Lawler, 1981: 166–67):

Proposition 20: The more costs one party associates with meeting the other party's demands, the greater the likelihood that it will define bargaining in single issue, distributive terms; the fewer costs a party associates with meeting the other party's demands, the greater the likelihood that it will define bargaining in multiple issue, integrative terms.

Parties will define the bargaining issue(s) in the same way, that is, in competitive terms as a single issue or in compromising terms as multiple issues, when they associate the same costs with the matter at hand (Bacharach and Lawler, 1981: 167).

Proposition 21: The more congruent are parties' perceptions of the costs associated with meeting each others' demands, the greater is the likelihood that they will reach a consensual definition of bargaining issues.

We can assume that the definition of the party that is more powerful, or has more relative power, will prevail (Bacharach and Lawler, 1981: 167):

Proposition 22: The greater a party's power, the greater the likelihood that its definition of bargaining issues will prevail.

One party can influence the other party's action in the bargaining process by arguments that define the power of both parties. A party has to show that it has alternatives and is not so committed to the issue that it cannot leave the relationship. It can also show the value of its own contribution to the relationship so that the other party sees alternatives less attractive and becomes more committed to the relationship. In this way, the parties influence their mutual perception of their power. In doing so, the parties can exaggerate the amount of power available to them, thus making use of bluffing. How effective such bluffing is depends on how it can be backed up at least to some extent by real power and on how good the opponent's knowledge is of the party's true strength. Effective bluffing needs to be backed up by some real power and presupposes a low level of information on the part of an opponent.

Furthermore, bargainers can make use of normative arguments in order to influence the opponent's decisions. Bacharach and Lawler mention three normative arguments: (1) referring to equity, meaning that one gets results in proportion to one's investments; (2) referring to equality, meaning the equal distribution of benefits between parties; and (3) referring to responsibility, meaning that the more powerful actor has a responsibility to provide for the living of the less powerful actor. Bacharach and Lawler assume that the more powerful actors will make more use of equity arguments, whereas the less powerful will make more use of equality and responsibility arguments; the greater the difference between the two, the more the weak party will have to make use of responsibility arguments. The reason is that it is more profitable for the powerful to bargain in terms of equity and more profitable for the weak to bargain in terms of equality or responsibility (Bacharach and Lawler, 1981: 176):

> Proposition 23: The greater the difference in bargaining power, the greater the tendency of the higher power party to use equity appeals and the greater the tendency of the lower power party to use equality or responsibility appeals, with the latter moving toward responsibility appeals the greater the difference in bargaining power is.

When the lower power party commands a good deal of power and there is therefore a very large total amount of power in the relationship, it is more profitable for the more powerful actor also to bargain in terms of equality, because otherwise the bargaining process would consume much more time and other resources (Bacharach and Lawler, 1981: 176).

> Proposition 24: If the total bargaining power in the relationship is very high, both parties will use equality appeals.

Finally, Bacharach and Lawler deal with the conditions allowing for agreement and for durable agreement. In terms of power, the authors expect that equal power facilitates both initial agreement and more durable agreement. However, with regard to the likelihood of agreement, this holds more true for the dimension of available alternatives than for the dimension of commitment. Equal commitment implies not only equal power but also equal zeal in enforcing one's position, thus making agreement less likely. The following proposition, therefore, seems to be most plausible (Bacharach and Lawler, 1981: 190):

> Proposition 25: An increase in the mutual dependence on alternatives increases the likelihood of agreement, while mutual dependence on the commitment dimension has no effect on the likelihood of agreement.

The main argument for equal power on the alternatives dimension making agreement more likely is that under unequal conditions, the more powerful actor will try to draw more advantage from the bargain that gives rise to more resistance on the part of its opponent, who sees the equality principle violated. This is also the argument for claiming that agreements reached under equal conditions will be more durable. One could say that an agreement reached under conditions of unequal power would be as durable as one that has been concluded under equal power, because the agreement once concluded has the consent of both parties and therefore should reflect the equality principle. Thus, one could formulate the following proposition (Bacharach and Lawler, 1981: 198):

> Proposition 26: Whether power is convergent or nonconvergent has no effect on the nature of the agreement.

However, one can also argue that inequality of power is also reflected in the agreement, so that the weaker party is forced to consent but nevertheless feels that it has been treated unequally. Bacharach and Lawler see this argumentation better supported by empirical data. The following proposition should be more plausible (Bacharach and Lawler, 1981: 198):

> Proposition 27: Convergent power produces a smaller departure from equality than nonconvergent power.

Coming to a conclusion, Bacharach and Lawler are well aware that their theory of bargaining can be applied only if very specific conditions are fulfilled (Bacharach and Lawler, 1981: 207–8):

- First, there must be two parties with conflicting interests, either single actors or collective actors.
- Second, the issue or issues can be settled on a continuum of potential resolution points, either quantitatively or qualitatively. Any issue that allows only a pro or a contra position does not allow any scope for compromising. Yet that is the essence of bargaining and presupposes that the conflicting parties can meet at several points of convergence, where the agreement is more profitable for both parties than any alternative action.
- Third, the parties must be committed to compromising, acknowledge the conflict of interests, and recognize the legitimacy of each other's interests.
- Fourth, the parties must not have complete information on the payoffs or utilities, the power relationship, or each other's tactical plans. Therefore, the two cannot completely anticipate each other's actions, and each is open to tactical arguments made by the other party, including bluffing.
- Fifth, the two parties must engage in gathering information about each other's power and tactical plans.
- Sixth, the parties try to maximize their individual utility, playing games of maximizing gain or minimizing loss.

Critical Assessment

We can make good use of Bacharach and Lawler's theory in order to explain and predict the course of bargaining on the basis of the power involved in that process: Which are the conditions increasing or decreasing bargaining power, increasing or decreasing a party's expected utility from a bargain, increasing or decreasing concessions, threat, and punishment, consensuality on the definition of issues, and the likelihood and durability of agreement? However, the authors themselves say that the bargaining process takes place only under specific conditions. They enumerate these conditions, but they do not explain how they come into existence. This is the point where we have to consult theories outside the realm of bargaining.

For bargaining to take place at all and not be replaced by violent conflict, the actors have to be committed to the norms regulating the process of bargaining: respecting the opponent's interests and accepting compromise as a device of conflict resolution. Only a theory explaining the process of producing normative commitment can help us here. Furthermore, bargaining involves making claims and justifying those claims by arguments. Whether a claim is considered right or wrong and can be justified or not by arguments, and whether the parties can come to a consensus of claims depends on how far the conditions of a discourse have been realized and not on the distribution of power within the relationship. The latter influences the factual agreement but not the consideration of that agreement as just or unjust by the parties involved and by outsiders. Only a theory of discourse can give us the right information here. Bacharach and Lawler's treatment of the question of likelihood and durability of agreement addresses this question in an unsatisfactory way, because they do not take into account the conditions of discourse.

Finally, whether a conflict is settled by way of bargaining or by one party imposing a solution on the other party depends on whether at least one of them sees the issue as a matter of principle and has enough power to enforce its position. Whether there is a violent power struggle instead of peaceful bargaining depends on whether the two parties see the issue as a matter of principle and whether they lack commitment to norms of compromising. In a sense, only the realization of the six conditions mentioned by Bacharach and Lawler moves a conflict into the field of bargaining, where utility calculations and power together determine the outcome of conflict settlement. If we want to know more about violent conflict settlement, we have to consult radical theories of conflict that lie outside the realm of bargaining. Bacharach and Lawler's bargaining theory is not appropriate for dealing with this question. If we keep these limitations in mind, we get good information on the processes of a very dynamic, rapidly changing process of conflict resolution that mingles conflict strategy with economic calculation and power with inducements; this is the very nature of bargaining. If we want to understand how bargaining fits into the wider social field of discourse and conversation, commitment formation and ritual, power and constraint, we have to consult the corresponding theories addressing these fields of social action.

EIGHT

POWER AND THE REPRODUCTION OF SOCIAL STRUCTURE AND CULTURE: PIERRE BOURDIEU

A CONTRIBUTION to French social theory's focus on power, which has become increasingly influential in recent years, has been provided by Pierre Bourdieu. He has worked out a multidimensional view of power by differentiating economic, social, cultural, and symbolic capital as power resources (Bourdieu, 1971, 1972, 1979, 1984b, 1986, 1987; for translation, see 1977, 1984a, 1985; Bourdieu and Passeron, 1964, 1970; for translation, see 1977, 1979). Before we come to an analysis of these dimensions of power, we have to introduce Bourdieu's (1971, 1972) general view of social action, the interrelationship between society and societal development.

Class, Praxis, Habitus, and Reproduction

Bourdieu starts with the assumption that social action is "praxis." In placing "praxis" at the center of his approach he relates to the tradition of Marxist thought (Bourdieu, 1972: part 2, chapter 1; 1979: part 2, chapters 2, 3, 4)

Praxis is more than social action seen as an isolated event; it is an activity by which human individuals produce and reproduce society in its cultural, social, and economic dimensions. Praxis mediates between individual human action and societal development. As praxis, individual human action becomes part of societal development, which means producing and reproducing its culture, its social structure, and its economic wealth. A worker who does work at a workplace not only acts individually but also takes part in an overall process of producing and reproducing society's economic wealth. The worker's action is determined not only by an interest in making a living but also by the overall organization of economic production and reproduction — in Marx's terms, by the relations of production. The worker's collective action, striking for higher wages and a shorter work week, is determined

139

by his or her collective interest and also by the overall organization of worker-entrepreneur relations and the ways in which access to economic property, economic decision making, and labor-industry relations are organized.

Economic praxis mediates between individual and collective interests of workers, managers, entrepreneurs, stockholders, bankers, and governments on the one hand and the social organization of economic production and reproduction of society's wealth on the other. The outcome of this economic praxis is, for one thing, a certain level of satisfaction or dissatisfaction of individual or collective interests and, for another, the renewal of the social organization of production and reproduction of society's economic wealth and, finally, a given renewed level (higher or lower) of economic wealth and the renewed or changed distribution of such wealth between individuals, groups, strata, and classes.

This is a conceptualization of social action, praxis, and social development that draws upon Marx's concept of praxis and tries to avoid the objectivist and the subjectivist fallacy at the same time. According to the objectivist interpretation of Marx drawn primarily from his later work, particularly *Capital,* the praxis that eventually leads to the revolutionary replacement of capitalism by communism and its societal organization of economic production and reproduction is just an outcome of the quasi-natural laws of capitalist production. According to the subjectivist view, which draws primarily upon the early Marx as seen in his *Ökonomisch-philosophische Manuskripte* (Marx, 1844/1968), praxis is a spontaneous process of becoming conscious of one's interests and of enforcing these interests in political struggle, perhaps under the leadership of a vanguard political party. Contrary to these objectivist and subjectivist fallacies, Bourdieu tries to build a truly dialectical theory of social development centering on praxis as the mediating link between individual and collective action and social structure or social organization of the production and reproduction of society.

In doing so, Bourdieu (1979: part 2, chapter 3) introduces a further mediating theoretical element: the concept of habitus. He says the social structure and organization becomes incorporated, or "interiorized," by individuals, while in their action individuals "exteriorize" their individual interests, worldviews, and dispositions to act to make them part of social praxis, which again renews social structure and organization. Inasmuch as individuals share the conditions under which they incorporate social structure and organization, they develop the same habitus. People living under the same conditions in groups, strata, classes, and societies take on that same habitus.

What is a habitus? It is a certain disposition to view the world and to act when confronted with a specific situation. The worker's disposition to accept a limited standard of living as something that is natural to his or her position and a person's style of consumption, eating and living habits, TV watching, and sports watching are part of this habitus. It is an acquired, relatively coherent set of potential views of the world and activities that become actualized in situations of action. The habitus of one worker and the collectively shared habitus of workers as a whole are more enduring than their situational desires and interests; habitus is the representation of the enduring social structure and organization within their personality.

Individuals' socially determined habitus has to be distinguished from their individuality. An individual shares his or her habitus with the individuals who have been exposed to the same conditions of living: groups, strata, classes, and societies. However, every individual goes through a unique process of interiorizing the surrounding social structure and organization, which makes up his or her individual personality and version of the overall social habitus. The individual personality mediates between the individual's spontaneity and social habitus. Bourdieu assumes that the same conditions of living and the same position in society give rise to the same habitus.

The workers of a certain level in society, for example, share the same living conditions. Other classes live on different levels. The worker's class situation involves the character of work he or she has to do, for example, manual routinized factory work, and the character of living, for example, small apartment with a low level of comfort and few appliances, small used cars, superficial health care, and low quality of nutrition and clothing. What complements this class situation of the workers is their relational class position in society. This is their relation to the other classes or, in other words, the relative position of a class within the overall class system. The relative position of the workers puts them at the bottom of the class hierarchy, which always involves looking upwards when looking at people who don't belong to the working class. The worker lives with this limitation of his or her position in society. Whatever the worker wants to do is limited by the other classes above. He or she cannot reach another place in society because these places are occupied by members of higher classes. The worker has to live within his or her assigned place at work, at home, or at leisure. There are working places, homes, and vacation areas reserved for him or her, and others are not accessible.

These are the class situation and relative class position of the workers. Both give rise to the worker's typical habitus. An elective affinity exists between class situation and position on the one hand and habitus on the other hand. The limited living conditions and the limitation of the worker's scope for action by the classes above, which occupy the higher levels of societal space, make for the typical limited outlook of the worker: not aspiring beyond one's limits, setting only limited goals for oneself, making no long-range plans leading one beyond one's natural life-world, holding on to what one has, low propensity to move, deferential attitude toward people in classes above one's own, low self-confidence regarding activities one is not familiar with, limiting one's circle of living to one's immediate relatives and fellow workers, and maintaining solidarity within one's class. These are the dispositions to act that make up the worker's habitus and are attuned to the class situation and class position of the worker. It is a consistency of meaning between objective situation and position and subjective disposition to act which we can call elective affinity between class situation and position and habitus, a concept used by Max Weber to characterize the consistency between class situation and position and ethical convictions.

Above the working class is the middle class with its factions of the older petite bourgeoisie of artisans, merchants, and lower level civil servants, the new petite bourgeoisie of nurses, social workers, animators, and body builders, and the middle bourgeoisie of middle-range managers in government, administration, and private industry, secondary school teachers, and university professors. The upper class is composed of the grande bourgeoisie of established entrepreneurs and top managers in government, administration, and private industry, and the traditionally established high aristocracy. The class situation of the middle class is characterized by moderate conditions of living; its position is characterized by looking down upon the working class and busily trying to hold it down and by looking upwards to the upper class. The lower-middle class of old and new petite bourgeoisie is closest to the working class and farthest away from the upper class. Its class situation is very moderate. The natural habitus pertaining to this situation and position is formalism at work, home, and leisure, strictly maintaining a distinction from the working class in living, eating, clothing, manners, and leisure activities, social association, and cultural consumption, the lack of any flexible self-assurance, paired with a knowledge of one's limits set by the demarcation between this class and those above it. Investments for upward mobility are made in the younger generation, which is expected to move up.

The upper-middle class of middle-range managers, *lycée* teachers and university professors lives in good conditions, looks down on the lower-middle class and the working class and up only to the small upper class. The habitus of this class is characterized by a much more self-assured approach to what makes one a distinguished person: success at work, good living, clothing, and eating, and good taste in cultural consumption.

The upper class of grande bourgeoisie and established aristocracy live in affluence without any limits and look down upon the rest of society. Its natural habitus is grandeur in celebrating a distinguished style of life, no need for anxious formalistic demarcation because the other classes are far away, and no need for relentless aspiration, because everything has been achieved.

A habitus becomes established in individuals not by the conditions of living and their relative position in the structure of classes, strata, and groups alone; the natural effect of these factors is reinforced by pedagogic action that is complemented by pedagogic authority, pedagogic work, and systems of instruction (Bourdieu and Passeron, 1970). Every pedagogic action is communication, which applies power rooted in a certain authority structure and contributes to reproducing the typical habitus of a group, stratum, class, and society, thereby reproducing the culture, social structure, and distribution of economic wealth and reputation that make up the power structure of society. The young worker learns from the beginning in the family to live in limited conditions with limited aspirations; he or she also learns this at school and at work. The young petit bourgeois learns in the family to strictly organize his or her life in order to be distinct from the working class and to have limited aspirations. The member of the upper-middle class learns in the family, at school, and at university to live well, with distinguished taste and behavior, and to have strong aspirations. The member of the upper class learns in the family, at school, and at university how to behave with grandeur and how to live up to high standards of life-style. Pedagogic action is part of the overall power structure of society and works in the direction of reproducing this structure by implanting in people the habitus that corresponds to their class situation and relative position.

It is the habitus established by the differentiated conditions of living, the relative position of people in society, and pedagogic action that reproduces their linkage, which is the element that makes an analytically constructed class a real phenomenon that makes a difference in social life. This is how Bourdieu endeavors to solve the classical problem of relating analytically constructed classes to real life phenomena. Marx tried to solve this problem by distinguishing class in itself and class for itself, the latter being a number of people who conceive of themselves as being in the same situation and relative position and have a shared consciousness of this.

A class that combines an objectively stated situation and relative position in society and a common consciousness of that situation and position is a class in itself and for itself. However, how does an objectively stated class acquire a common class consciousness? For Bourdieu neither the objectivist approach, which expects the convergence of objective class and subjective class consciousness by the working of the laws of social development, nor the subjectivist approach, which expects the same from the education of the members of a class by an avant-garde, provides satisfying solutions. He sees an advantage in his approach because here the interrelationship of class situation and relative social position on the one hand and habitus on the other establish classes that are rooted in the objective structure of society and embrace people who are disposed to act in the same way because they share the same habitus, *independently of whether they are conscious of their common situation and position.* They don't need additional instruction in order to act in the same way. Their habitus leads them into a common praxis that works in the direction of reproducing the societal power structure in its cultural, social, and economic dimensions.

The habitus of individuals is the element that represents the established power structure of society in every individual situation of social action. It turns individual action into a social praxis that is rooted in an established structure of society and reproduces just that structure, including its transformation. The interaction between two or more individuals, its process, and its outcome are determined not just by factors pertaining to the situation of interaction but also by their habitus, which corresponds to a certain class, stratum, or group. What they do, how they approach one another, and their relative power to succeed are influenced by their habitus, which represents their class situation and position. Because of this representation of the societal structure in the habitus of individual actors, every single act is related to the wider structure of society and hence represents praxis working on reproducing society.

What is the relationship between habitus and praxis? In Bourdieu's view, the habitus is a generative scheme. It is a scheme that generates many different yet related actions under specific situational conditions. The relationship between habitus and action is the same as between language and an individual speech act. A language consists of a grammar and a vocabulary. Every speech act constructs individual sentences from the established vocabulary according to the rules of grammar. A habitus is a set of rules and a collection of potential acts. In a concrete situation an actor chooses a sequence of actions according to the rules prescribed by the habitus. For example, acting aggressively and acting deferentially both belong to the acting potential of a working-class male. His habitus defines the rules according to which he actualizes aggressive or deferential action in concrete situations. The rules prescribe that he should act deferentially when approaching his superiors, and they prescribe that he should react aggressively when attacked by someone in the same rank or a lower one.

The habitus, in this way, establishes schemes for actions, practices, and work that can be classified as pertaining to a specific class. In the same way, the habitus establishes schemes for perceiving and evaluating the world, society, other people, actions, practices, work done, and so on. The worker sees a command from his or her superiors as a legitimate expectation that the worker has to fulfill. He or she sees the same command coming from a worker in a level below him or her as an illegitimate expectation that needs correction. The worker regards elegant clothing among his or her superiors as normal but regards the same elegant clothing worn by fellow workers as a deviation from normal dress.

The schemes for producing practices and work and schemes for perceiving and evaluating them are applied in specific situations and give rise to specific practices and work in these situations, which are at the same time classified as practices and work pertaining to a specific class by members of that class and by those of other classes. Practices and work that are thus classified, together with further practices by which members of classes perceive and evaluate them, comprise what we can call the life-style of a certain class.

The life-style of a class is a product of its practices and work and their classification by its members and the members of other classes. What is appropriate for a male worker is defined not only by himself but also by his superiors, who belong to classes above him. The worker who reacts aggressively to the command of a superior and hears from his superior that this is not appropriate behavior is guided in his practice by the evaluation of his superiors, who participate in defining appropriate working-class behavior. On the other hand, the worker is not in a power position that allows him to apply similar criticisms to his superior. Nevertheless, a superior who loses his or her reputation with workers due to unreliability is evaluated by them and reminded of the appropriate life-style for a person in a responsible position. In this way, workers participate in defining the appropriate life-style of middle-class people. Life-style becomes the property that makes a class distinct in character.

In summary, the living conditions of a society, class, stratum, or group and its relative position in the world or society give rise to a specific habitus, which is also implanted by way of authoritatively structured pedagogic work in family and school. The habitus is structured by living conditions and relative position, yet it also — as a scheme of producing, perceiving, and evaluating practices and work — structures precisely those practices and work that comprise the life-style of a society, class, stratum, or group consisting of both classified and classifying practices. In this way, distinction between societies, classes, strata, and groups is produced and permanently reproduced. We close the circle when we say that the practices and work reproduce the living conditions and the relative position of a society, class, stratum, or group, thus creating feedback effects on just those conditions that give rise to the practices and work.

We have to make clear that it is not only isolated class practices that contribute to reproducing the structure of society. Some of Bourdieu's argumentation tends toward that view. People are also engaged in practices that bring together members of different classes, strata, and groups. A worker who does his or her work in carrying out a command is engaged not only in working-class behavior but also in the societal behavior of producing the economic wealth of society, which also involves his or her superiors who are members of other classes. Workers and superiors are engaged in a common praxis that produces and distributes the economic wealth in society. Inasmuch as they have incorporated schemes of cooperating in this praxis they act according to a habitus that reaches beyond class boundaries and represents the societal organization of economic production. Certainly, the worker and his or her superiors go about this in different ways, and their habitus as worker or upper-middle-class person is involved in their cooperation, yet this is not the whole story. In addition, they know, perceive, and evaluate how they coordinate their practices from the point of view of the societal organization of economic production. Otherwise, they would not be able to coordinate their action in a common praxis.

However, people live not only in a class, a stratum, or a group but also in a society, which has its specific situation of material conditions and a specific position in the world relative to other societies. What pertains to the situation and relative position of a class in a society pertains to the situation and relative position of a society in the world. According to Bourdieu's preoccupation with power as the major force in society, we would have to conceive of the common societal praxis, for example, of economic production, as determined by the established power structure in society. The classes, strata, and groups who have more power are capable of imposing their will on organizing common practices. However, we need such an extension of the argument beyond isolated class practices to common societal practices in order to fully understand the societal reproduction of society. This is the reason why we did not speak only of classes, strata, and groups when discussing the constitution of habitus but included society into this collection of places in which it is generated.

The Dynamics of Reproduction and the Struggle for Distinction

Bourdieu (1979: part 2, chapters 1 and 4) distinguishes three fields in the social space in which praxis takes place and in which society is produced and reproduced: the economic, the social, and the cultural fields. Labor coping with scarcity and competing for opportunities to acquire income, the production and the distribution of goods and services, and the exchange of goods, services, and money constitute the economic field. The economic production and reproduction of society means the production and renewed production of goods and services to cope with scarcity and to build up the wealth of society. Economic production and reproduction always implies a certain distribution of the products among individuals, groups, strata, classes, and societies.

The social field is made up of the groups, strata, and classes to which individuals belong according to their social origin, their relationships to other people, and their association and familiarity or dissociation and unfamiliarity with people. The social production and reproduction of society means producing and reproducing new relationships between people, associations and dissociations, groups, strata, and classes. This also involves the distribution and redistribution of social associations and solidarity among individuals, groups, strata, classes, and societies.

The cultural field embraces the acquisition of education, certificates, titles, world-views, products of the arts and mass culture, sports activities, styles of consumption, dress, living and eating, and a taste for the right things. The cultural production and reproduction of society means producing, and producing anew, these elements of culture. This also includes the distribution and redistribution of cultural products among individuals, groups, strata, classes, and societies.

Each of these fields is guided by its own laws and implies a specific game played by the actors on a certain field. Different investments are required to succeed economically, socially, or culturally. Achieving economic success involves making money either in terms of wages or capital. To do this, one has to be able to provide scarce goods or services for other people that draw the exchange activities of many people to oneself, thus achieving the opportunity to extract a good profit from the exchange. Being socially successful means being someone many other people want to associate with, being someone who draws the attention of many people, being "in demand." In order to be socially successful, one has to be able to rely on relationships to many other people, to be able to count on other people. Having relationships to many people brings one into a position of attracting even more new contacts. Being culturally successful means having distinguished taste in living, eating, and dressing and in consuming and evaluating works of art, literature, theater, music, dance, and movies. To be culturally successful one has to acquire the right education.

These three fields of the social space also have some features in common: They are all arenas for the production and reproduction of society and for the distribution of their products. They are places of societal praxis in which individuals, groups, strata, classes, and societies cooperate in producing and reproducing culture, social association, and economic wealth and compete over the distribution of these products. The struggle over the distribution of cultural, social, and economic products is what Bourdieu places at the center of his analysis. The economic, social, and cultural reproduction of society is always a reproduction of the distribution of the corresponding products among individuals, groups, strata, classes, and societies and is always a reproduction of social inequality on a new level, including transformations to new distributions of products. In Bourdieu's terms, what individuals, groups, strata, classes, and societies draw from economic, social, and cultural production and reproduction is economic, social, and cultural capital. Economic capital is built up by money income in the form of wages or profits. Social capital is the number and intensity of social relationships upon which a person can rely. Cultural capital is the degree of education one has reached, which makes one able to demonstrate good taste in one's style of life.

Economic, social, and cultural capital are drawn together to become symbolic capital when their possession is evaluated by other people. People hold those persons in high esteem who have acquired much economic, social, and cultural capital. Symbolic capital is the reputation one has because of other people's evaluation of one's acquired amount of economic, social, and cultural capital.

The distribution of economic, social, and cultural capital among individuals, groups, strata, classes, factions, and societies is the object of real struggles. The distribution of symbolic capital is the object of symbolic struggles about the evaluation of economic, social, and cultural achievements, particularly between factions of classes who rely primarily on one or two forms of capital.

Each field is a market in which individual and collective actors (groups, strata, classes, factions, societies) compete for the accumulation of capital; they want to accumulate as much capital as they can. In this process, other actors are partly cooperators and partly competitors. The worker's colleague cooperates with the worker in producing a certain product and competes with him or her for a better position that yields higher income. The worker and the company proprietor cooperate in increasing the firm's success on the market, but they compete when it comes to distributing the firm's accumulated capital between profit and wages. Students cooperate in acquiring a certain educational certificate, but they compete in turning this certificate into a job. Because an increased number of certificates devalues each one, people who want to acquire a distinguished taste necessarily compete to reach ever higher levels of education. It is the very nature of cultural distinction that makes something distinct and therefore of high cultural value only if not everybody has it. Thus, the striving for cultural distinction gives rise to a never-ending competition to reach ever higher levels of education.

People can cooperate in making friends when one person introduces another to a third person. However, they often compete for reliance on another person, because the value of that other person's support is higher the more exclusively one can rely on that person. Someone who has to support everybody cannot give much support to any one individual. Thus, there is always competition between people for the support of other people, which they need to be socially successful.

Thus, we have an economic, social, and cultural market, and in each market individuals and collective actors compete to accumulate as much capital as possible. They compete inasmuch as one actor's capital is accumulated at the cost of another actor's accumulation. The worker who obtains a promotion does so at the cost of his or her colleagues. The entrepreneur can increase his or her profit at the cost of the worker's wage. A salesperson who wants to contract with a new firm relies on the recommendation of another firm at the cost of another salesperson who will not obtain that same recommendation. A student who achieves a high level of education does so at the cost of other graduates whose educational certificate suffers a loss of exclusivity and thus of cultural distinction.

What are the means an actor can apply in order to succeed or at least to withstand the competition on the economic, social, and cultural markets as much as he or she can? The means an actor needs is the relevant capital. A person has to invest economic capital in order to accumulate economic capital, social capital in order to accumulate social capital, cultural capital in order to accumulate cultural capital. Beyond this natural relationship between capital investment and accumulation there are legitimate cross-cutting relationships. Which of them are legitimate and which are not is the outcome of symbolic struggles over the evaluation of capital forms and on their transaction from one field to the other. In traditional societies, social capital in the sense of social origin determined access to economic and cultural capital. In modern societies, social capital has lost much of its importance but still counts in secondary ways, supporting the other forms of capital. The main transaction is now one in which cultural capital acquired through education is used to gain access to social and economic capital. The latter can give access to the other forms of capital only through economic investments in educational achievement.

In each market, an individual or collective actor starts with a certain amount of capital that is invested in order to achieve in competition with other actors. The more the actor can invest, the better the actor's position in competition. With more economic capital, one can beat economic competitors who have less economic capital. The same is true of social capital in the social field. Someone who has twenty friends is likely to meet more potential friends through them than someone who has only ten friends. A person who knows important people gets access to more important people than others do. Someone who is well brought up at home finds it much easier to do well at school.

The conditions of competition on these markets are not equal. Thus, there is no ideal market in terms of economic theory. The markets historically have evolved from hierarchically structured societies stratified into lower, middle, and higher estates. Thus, the open competition for the accumulation of economic, social, and cultural capital, which became established with the evolution of modern society, started with unequal conditions that were transformed into unequal achievements. On the other hand, competitive markets always allow the rise of innovators. The rise of the bourgeoisie as the dominating class in modern society was initiated by expansion of the economic market at the cost of social origin. The success of the bourgeoisie was the success of innovators on the economic market.

However, though markets always give chances of achievement to innovators, past success on the market improves one's position on the market and creates better preconditions for further achievement. The successful begin the next round of competition on a higher level. The market then works into the hands of those who have and out of the hands of those who have not, according to the Matthew principle: "For whosoever hath, to him shall be given" (Merton, 1949/1968). Therefore, after a while, the market itself internally restricts the chances for innovators and corroborates established inequalities of success. Those who have more money can make more money on the market than others; those who have more (and more important) social relationships can make more (and more important) social relationships; those who have more cultural education can improve their education more easily than those who have less education. The competition on the three markets works in the direction of reproducing the inequalities that have resulted from traditional hierarchies and earlier phases of competition on higher levels.

Thus, economic production increases overall and improves everyone's standard of living, but it improves that standard for the middle and upper classes more than for the lower classes. Networks of social relationships expand for everybody, but those of the middle and upper classes expand more and to a more important level than those of the lower classes. Everyone's cultural education is improved considerably, but with the effect that being working class, middle class, or upper class requires more education than before. In this way, economic, social, and cultural standards of living rise considerably for the whole society, but at the same time the competition for higher status is extraordinarily intensified. In previous historical epochs, one was born on a certain level in society and was sure of keeping that level in one's future life. Today, this is no longer true. One is born on a certain level, but whether one will keep up with this level depends on one's success in a very competitive market. The expansion of enrollments in higher education increasingly provides nearly everybody with a certificate of higher education but one that becomes devalued in that very process because it brings neither cultural distinction nor a higher level job. The demands for cultural distinction and economic success become stronger at the same time. This is the fate of the many university graduates who cannot find a respected and well-paid job. They have to fight against the declassification of their achievements.

Thus, there is a paradoxical effect: Economic, social, and cultural reproduction are permanently pushed to a higher level of economic wealth, social solidarity, and cultural education, but at the same time economic, social, and cultural competition shifts to higher levels and increases the demands on achievement. Competition intensifies. What appears to increase equality of opportunity—for example, broadening access to higher education—turns out to be a raising of the requirements for economic, social, and cultural achievement. The education that previously gave access to top cultural distinction and top managerial positions is now a must for reaching middle-level distinction and appointments. We do not approach more equality in this way but only a reproduction of inequalities on higher levels of achievement (Bourdieu and Passeron, 1964, 1970).

The struggles in the economic, social, and cultural fields are always accompanied by symbolic struggles about the evaluation of economic, social, and cultural achievement (Bourdieu, 1979: part 2, chapter 4). Individuals, groups, strata, classes, and factions that rely on a certain form of accumulated capital try to raise the evaluation of that achievement in society. Workers praise the worth of manual work, administrators that of administration, business people that of economic achievement, and teachers, clergy, and professors that of cultural education. According to the logic of symbolic struggles, those with higher reputation, that is, more symbolic capital, can make use of that capital in order to increase or decrease the estimation of economic, social, and cultural achievement. The individuals, groups, strata, classes, and factions with the highest reputation have the most defining power in this process of estimating achievement. Here, again, those who have reputation from traditionally assigned higher status or from achievement in competition can make use of that reputation in order to define the value of their own and of others' achievements in public opinion formation. Nowadays, the media of communication have occupied a central position in these symbolic struggles. Groups, strata, classes, and factions have educated spokespeople who participate in the permanent struggle for reputation. Public relations work has achieved central importance in this struggle. To participate permanently in that struggle with public statements, reports, and evaluations is a must in order to maintain reputation. It is the same with economic, cultural, and social competition. No individual, group, stratum, class, or faction can rely on previously acquired reputation and be sure of maintaining it. Reputation has to be confirmed on ever higher levels of public demand. The medical profession, for example, may have lived from traditionally established esteem for a long time, but now the growing number of physicians and increasing pressures for success and the public discussion of reputation work in the direction of increasing the requirements for establishing a higher reputation. The medical profession is forced to emphasize its achievements in public discussion.

Particularly interesting in Bourdieu's approach is that he does not separate the concept of power from the concepts of economic, social, cultural, and symbolic capital. He conceives of the latter as different forms of power resources. Hence, though he does not use the concept of power frequently in the literal sense, the concept is nevertheless omnipresent, because the four types of capital represent the four types of power. Having economic capital at one's disposal gives one the power to achieve economically against economic competitors. Likewise, having social capital gives one the power to achieve socially against social competitors, and the same applies to cultural capital and symbolic capital in their respective fields.

According to Max Weber's famous definition, power is the chance to enforce one's will even against the resistance of others. Competitors are those who put up resistance to one's own achievement. To be able to achieve in the face of that resistance is to have power. Resistance in competition means that competitors who achieve more quickly than I am able to do occupy a place that I want to move to but that is no longer open to me. They have succeeded; I do not have enough power to overcome their resistance. Having more power means for me that I have more money to make the investments on a specific market earlier than my competitors. It means that I have relationships to more important people than my competitors, enabling me to conclude contracts with third parties more quickly and before the others are able to intervene. It means that I have more cultural education from home so that I can achieve culturally at school ahead of my competitors and before they have occupied the top places in class. It means that I have a greater reputation, which enables me to reach people with my message and my approach to evaluating achievements more quickly than less-reputed people. This is how economic, social, cultural, and symbolic capital is transformed into power applied to achieving against those people who compete for the same achievements.

Summary

1. Social action is not an isolated event but praxis, which mediates between individual and collective interests on the one hand and social structure, organization, and culture on the other.
2. Praxis is an organized activity that produces and reproduces the economic wealth, social structure, and culture of a society on the one hand and the individual personality on the other.
3. The interrelationship between social structure and praxis is mediated through the habitus of actors.
4. A habitus is an organized set of an individual's dispositions to act; it is a scheme for producing practices and work and for producing perceptions and evaluations of practices and work, whether one's own or others'.
5. The practices and work of individuals comprise their life-style as a system of classified and classifying practices, that is, of signs of distinction.
6. The habitus of individuals emerges from their conditions (situations) of living and their relative positions within the structure of living conditions, as well as from authoritatively structured pedagogic work that reproduces the power structure of society.
7. The habitus of individuals corresponds in its meaning to their living conditions and their relative positions within the structure of living conditions according to an elective affinity.
8. The habitus is structured by living conditions and relative position; but the habitus also structures the practices and work of individuals and their perceptions and evaluations of those practices and work.
9. People who share the same living conditions and the same relative position develop the same habitus and thus form a group, stratum, class,

faction, or society that makes a difference in determining social life and overcomes the gap between class in itself and class for itself.

10. Whenever people act socially, they represent social structure and reproduce that structure in their praxis via their habitus; thus, every situation of interaction relates to society.

11. Society is produced and reproduced in its social, economic, and cultural structure in the praxis of people based on their class habitus (and, we may add, based on their overall societal habitus).

12. The production and reproduction of society produces and reproduces its economic wealth, its social relations, and its culture; it also involves the distribution of these products among individuals, groups, strata, classes, factions, and societies.

13. Production, reproduction, and distribution occurs in three fields: the economic, the social, and the cultural.

14. Production, reproduction, and distribution involves cooperation and competition.

15. The more economic, social, or cultural capital one can invest, the more one can achieve against competitors.

16. Competition proceeds according to the Matthew principle: Unto those who have shall be given.

17. Competition in the three fields reproduces the established structure of inequality on an ever higher level of demands for achievement, thus continuously intensifying competition.

18. The evaluation of economic, social, and cultural achievement by others gives rise to symbolic capital (reputation).

19. Symbolic capital is defined and attributed in a symbolic struggle over the evaluation of economic, social, and cultural achievements.

20. The more reputation one has, the more successfully one can define and attribute symbolic capital (reputation).

21. Economic, social, cultural, and symbolic capital work as resources of power.

22. The more resources of power one has, the more one will achieve against competitors in the market.

Critical Assessment

We come to a final evaluation of Bourdieu's theory of praxis, production, and reproduction of society. His first achievement is his analysis of the mediation of social structure and individual action by praxis and of social structure and praxis by the habitus of individuals. This analysis yields deep insights into the interrelated nature of social action as praxis, relating every situation of interaction to what has gone on in society in the past and to what will go on in the future as a result of this interaction. This is an analytical instrument for analyzing the interpenetration of social structure and individual action and the ongoing reproduction of individual and society in this interpenetration. His theory can be interpreted as a theory of structuration, a theory that points out how social structure and the individual personality are produced, reproduced, and transformed in praxis, which is the mediating link between them. However, Bourdieu has a structuralist bias and therefore sees the relationship too one-sidedly, from structure to habitus to praxis to life-styles, and not in the converse direction, from life-styles to praxis to habitus and to structure. His schematic representation of that relationship in *La Distinction* (1979: part 2, chapter 3) lacks the arrow pointing back from life-styles to structures. This tells us much about his structuralist bias.

We have to note that, contrary to Bourdieu, praxis also involves much situational variation, negotiation, bargaining, interpretation, communication, discourse, and association, which introduce a lot of innovation into praxis and which depend on situational achievement and push praxis much more in a direction working toward transforming structures rather than reproducing them in their established way. Bourdieu does not leave any theoretical doors open for these innovational effects on praxis, habitus, and social structure. We can learn about these effects much more from theories of negotiation, bargaining, communication, and association.

If the causation really flows unidirectionally from structure to habitus to praxis to life-styles, how should change occur? We can make use of Bourdieu's analysis of competition on the economic, social, and cultural markets in order to correct this mistake. Here Bourdieu argues that competition pushes the requirements of achievement to ever higher levels, thus forcing individuals continually to improve their economic, social, and cultural achievement. However, this necessarily involves tremendous transformation of the habitus of individuals. Thus, a lot of workers and middle-class people are forced to achieve educationally much more than their fathers and mothers. Their educational practice transforms their habitus tremendously and changes their living conditions and relative position in the structure of society. They no longer live on a minimum level limited by the classes above them such that they accept their own position, but now live on a much more equal level with other classes and see them and are seen by them much more as competitors. The result is that we no longer have a clearly stratified society with separated classes but a mixture of classes, factions, strata, and groups that are much closer to one another and thus compete much more fiercely. Social structure is transformed by social praxis directly through the transformation of individuals' habitus.

Another example is the rise of the bourgeoisie within traditional society. This would not have happened if Bourdieu's scheme were true. The traditional hierarchical structure assigned to the bourgeoisie a definite middle position. However, achievement in economic praxis on the market as inno-vators gave rise to the bourgeoisie's rise to the top of society and to the corresponding transformation of the social structure of society. A further example of such transformation is the revolutionary overthrow of an estab-lished social structure in political struggle. We learn more about this by using theories concentrating on the action of conflict settlement.

Thus, Bourdieu's first achievement is accompanied by a deficiency that we have to correct in order to make good use of his achievement. The same applies to his second achievement; Bourdieu relates power to the economic, social, and cultural field and thus generates a complex understanding of the working of power, paying particular attention to its economic, social, and cultural resources. We can understand his theory at least partly as a theory of the economic, social, and cultural production of power. His theory informs us how the production and reproduction of power works in eco-nomic, social, and cultural terms. It is not just physical force or command over the means for satisfying the needs of other people that gives one power. One needs money to be economically powerful, social relationships to be socially powerful, education to be culturally powerful, and reputation to be symbolically powerful. There are also specific rules that guide the acqui-sition of these resources of power. Moreover, Bourdieu inserts power into a complex field of market competition. In this way power becomes speci-fied to market power, as the ability to achieve against competitors.

Bourdieu is well aware of the internal laws of the different fields that set structural limits on achievement in the power game in those fields. Nevertheless, there is a tendency in his argumentation to give the power game primary significance, which would subsume the internal logic of the differ-ent fields under the rules of that game. In this case we would lose the insights provided by an analysis of the laws uniquely applicable to those fields. To be sure, both relationships are empirically possible. There can be a structu-ration of the power game by the laws of the economic, social, and cultural fields. However, there can also be a structuration of those fields by the rules of the power game. Theory has to provide a sharp analytical differentiation of these and an insight into the working of the internal laws of the eco-nomic, social, and cultural fields and of the power game *per se*. In a second step, we can look at the effects that come about with the structuration of one such field by another. For a detailed understanding of these processes we have to go beyond Bourdieu's theory and learn from theories that con-centrate more on one or another of the different fields of social action.

A theory that sees social reality primarily in terms of a power game subordinates the economic, social, and cultural fields to power, conceiving of them as power games pure and simple. Thus it cannot explain the specific laws of the economic, social, and cultural fields that come into play inas-much as they operate independently of power. In terms of power, economic achievement is always an outcome of previous power. Such a theory of economic achievement would make no allowance for the achievement of innovators in the market. However, this does occur in markets, contrary to the power theory of economic achievement. We need an economic theory of achievement if we want to come closer to an explanation of innovation. Here we have to extend power theory using economic theory.

Similarly, a theory of social achievement in terms of power does not correctly cover the internal logic of social association. If the question is viewed in these terms, people do not associate in order to increase their social capital but only to maintain the social relationships they are familiar with, independently of whether this increases their social capital or not. Their established social relationships very often set limits on increasing social capital and on social competition. Therefore, we have little competition and little change in this field, a specific feature that is overlooked by preoccupation with competition and market power.

The same is true for the cultural field. This is the field where communication and discourse takes place, mutual understanding has to be reached, and truth has to be found out. However, the power game theory's view would make understanding and finding truth contingent on the power one can invest in communication and discussion. This occurs when power dominates. However, this is not universally so. Whenever communication and discourse proceed on their own terms, independently of power-based competition, they lead to mutual understanding on equal terms and to the construction of intersubjectively valid views of the world and not to world-views that are imposed on society by way of superior market power.

Finally, the view of symbolic power in terms of the power game suffers from the same deficiencies. Reputation can emerge from symbolic power struggles, but inasmuch as it emerges from cultural discourse it has to meet requirements of justification and legitimation, inasmuch as it emerges from social association it has to meet requirements of conformity to the norms of a community, and inasmuch as it emerges from economic competition it has to meet the requirements of economic achievement, which depends on the ability to innovate.

An approach to social reality primarily in terms of a power game does not give full attention to the internal laws of the economic, social, and cultural fields or to the effects of the uniquely characteristic laws of these fields on the acquisition, accumulation, and application of power itself. Economic competition introduces an element of change into the power structure, allowing the rise of previously unknown innovators in the power structure. Social association sets limits on power competition by keeping actors from competing with everybody and by imposing norms of competition on them. Pure power game theory doesn't explain why actors use only the peaceful and definitely prescribed means of accumulating economic, social, and cultural capital in competition. Why don't they make use of force and deceit in order to overcome competition? Power competition is a very regulated form of power struggle, which proceeds in a very peaceful way and depends in this respect on the normative control of associated people beyond the boundaries of classes, factions, strata, groups, and individuals. Communication and discourse exert pressures of legitimation and justification with regard to general ideas, values, and norms on the acquisition, accumulation, and application of power. The norms of power competition are under permanent pressure to change toward closer consistency with basic ideas of free and equally based competition, necessitating permanent corrections of the unequal outcomes of competition inasmuch as they destroy equal conditions of competition. Power competition is then measured against the norms of freedom, fairness, and equal conditions. These are the corrections that we have to apply to any power game theory from the point of view of economic, normative, and communicative theories in order to transform it from a constricted power theory to a more comprehensive theory of the production, reproduction, and transformation of the individual and society.

Ultimately, we have to correct the theory of market power from the point of view of a strictly formulated theory of power. In its terms, power is conceived of as market power in competition. The genuine source of power, however, is physical force, which can be used in order to overcome any resistance, including any kind of market power. We have to keep this in mind in order to know that Bourdieu's power games work only as long as this true source of power is kept under control and set apart from any involvement in economic, social, and cultural competition. It has to be controlled by a legal system rooted in a societal community that reaches beyond the boundaries of classes, factions, strata, groups, and individuals. Otherwise, we could not explain why these classes, factions, strata, groups, and individuals play the power game of peaceful competition at all (for a detailed assessment, see Janning, 1991).

NINE

ACTION, MOVEMENT, AND THE SELF-PRODUCTION OF SOCIETY: ALAIN TOURAINE'S THEORY OF SOCIAL MOVEMENTS

SOCIETY IS not a system based on metasocial entities like God, values, or economic contradictions but a continuous productive process located in the action of historical actors. Social movements make up the very heart of this "self-production" of society. This is the starting point of Alain Touraine's theory of social movements, which is assumed to be the core of a general theory of action and society (Touraine, 1965, 1969, 1973, 1974b, 1978, 1980; for translation, see 1974a, 1977, 1981).

Toward Postindustrial Society

Touraine is particularly concerned with searching for the new social movements that are involved in the transformation of industrial society into post-industrial, programed society, as he wishes to call the new society (Touraine, 1969). Industrial society was created by the movement of the bourgeoisie, which was counteracted by the labor movement. The new programed society that is growing out of the seedbed created by industrial society is being brought forth by the technocrats residing in the centers of management of public administration and private enterprise. It is increasingly being counteracted by the peace, ecological, antinuclear and antitechnocratic movements (Touraine, 1973, 1978, 1980). The latter form the new social movements that are increasingly replacing the labor movement as the major forces of historical change. The labor movement has lost its prominence as a force of historical change in the core capitalist societies the more trade unions have become part of the political establishment and participate in institutionalized decision making.

On the other hand, industrial culture has come under general attack, leading to radical doubts about its purported rationality that go much beyond the labor movement's claim to its share in the wealth produced by industrial society. Sharing the wealth of industrial society is no longer the aim of the new social movements, which seek instead to resist the very premises of that society: economic expansion and technological progress. Liberation from the iron cage produced by industrial society and expanded by programed society is the great theme of the new criticism. Finding one's personal identity and living in a true community become the general thrusts of the search for new forms of living.

There emerges a new populism of movements gathering the solidarity of people against technocratic powers. From the periphery the populist movements in the Third World, from Latin America to Africa, attack the domination of industrial society over the rest of the world. The antitechnocratic movements make up the new social movements that have become the most important critical force counteracting the established domination of programed society over its people. It is no longer the worker who mainly suffers from inhuman working conditions and poor living standards. In the highly developed, programed societies, people living in material wealth suffer from being dominated by an all-embracing technocratic system that controls the people instead of being controlled by the people.

This is Touraine's image of society, which explains why Touraine gives social movements such a central role in his theory of society. Society as it is has been produced by the historical struggles of social movements; it will be petrified if there are no new social movements struggling for change (Touraine, 1978).

The Self-Production of Society

Human societies do not function only according to natural laws; they do not develop only according to laws of evolution; they are not wholly governed by metasocial entities like God, by the state or the economy, or by superimposed values. Rather, they are capable of acting on their own account, of producing themselves in historical action. With this image of the self-producing society Touraine separates his approach from any type of objectivism in social science and conceives of this approach as an actionalist sociology, placing action at the center of sociological theory. Whereas the societies of the past — agrarian, mercantilist, and industrial societies — developed the capacity of self-production only to a limited degree, the postindustrial programed society makes full use of this capability.

There are three components that make up that society's capability of self-production: knowledge, accumulation, and a cultural model (Touraine, 1973: chapter 1). Society advances knowledge of nature and of itself and gains the ability to produce itself in the light of advancing knowledge. It does not blindly continue traditional practices but reviews and changes them in light of its acquired knowledge. Society is capable of saving some of its products and of investing them in further production, thus improving its capacity of production, leading to ever more accumulation of products that can be used again for improving production. This society also acts on the basis of a cultural model. This is an image of creativity, a means by which society can reflect on itself. The cultural model of the programed society is science, that is to say, science is conceived of as society's resource of creativity. Society is seen as being capable of producing itself, of transforming itself by the means of science. The cultural model is not a value system, says Touraine. In his view, science just happens to be the cultural model that is used in producing and transforming society, independently of whether it is seen as good or bad in its consequences. Science is also not simply the dominant ideology, because it is used throughout society by all classes and social groups.

Touraine calls the fact that human societies reproduce themselves in the way outlined thus far their historicity. This means that people make their own history and do not just fulfill the laws and functions of social systems. Historicity implies that the development of societies does not proceed according to laws of evolution, but involves human action, conflict, and struggle. There is not necessarily an upward evolution to higher levels of rationality in human history. Change from one societal type to another is not a necessary sequence in an evolutionary process advancing toward higher levels of human organization. Rather, it is a transformation involving struggles from which a new society emerges because it becomes successfully established by the more successful historical actors. The new society does not automatically attain higher levels of rationality; it is just a more successful alternative. The driving force of societal development is not a law of evolution but the action of historical actors, which is particularly contingent on the power available to them.

These considerations lead immediately to a qualification of the idea of the self-producing society. It is not society as a whole community that acts in this way but a group of innovators and dominators who take the lead. This is the ruling class, which acts as the main historical actor in producing society by way of advancing knowledge, of accumulation and orientation toward the cultural model. It is the ruling class that primarily exercises historicity, thus establishing its domination over society and over the popular class in particular. Inasmuch as the popular class, for its part, challenges its domination by the ruling class, it tries to win back historicity for itself. It struggles with the ruling class over the production of society.

Historicity

Two opposing processes govern the formation of society. On the one hand, historicity is converted into organization and transformed into order and power exerted on people. On the other hand, countermovements aim at cultural innovation, involving conflict and historical struggles, and thus intend to reintroduce historicity. Social movements are the major agents in any attempt at regaining historicity. Because the ruling class identifies with the established order, cultural innovation always has to pass through class conflict and involves classes as major historical actors.

The self-production of society brings actors together in social relations. An interrelated set of social relations forms a social field. The constituting feature of social relations is that they always involve power: "All social relations are relations of power" (Touraine, 1978; for translation, see 1981: 33).

Touraine also says that social relations always imply inequality. He has the relation between the ruling class and the dominated class in mind when he speaks of social relations. Wherever there is equality there is one unity, not a relation between different unities. However, action not only occurs in social relations but also takes place in a cultural field. The actors act on the basis of cultural orientations that are related to one another in cultural debates. The cultural field is defined by the cultural model of society that is used by the actors in their struggles.

Touraine opposes this actionalist sociology to objectivist sociologies, which see the motor of society and its development in an opposition between fixed rules and innovators, in the agency of the state alone, in the forces of production, or in society's normative order. In distinction to these objectivist sociologies, Touraine concentrates on the action of historical actors that takes place in social relations and in a cultural field necessarily involving conflict and class struggle. There are three levels on which this action takes place: the levels of organization, institutions, and historicity. On the organizational level, for example, action refers to the organization of work in an enterprise, perhaps addressing improvements in working conditions. On the institutional level, action refers, for example, to the relationship between entrepreneurs and trade unions in running the economy. On the level of historicity, action refers to the class relations in society and to the overall organization of society. The more the level of historicity is reached in action, the more the continuation of a societal organization or its transformation is at stake.

The major historical actors are the social classes, the ruling class, and the dominated popular class (Touraine, 1973: chapter 3; 1978: chapter 4). Inasmuch as a class acts as an historical actor it does so on the basis of a class consciousness (meaning that it knows its position in society), of a cultural orientation (meaning the maintenance or realization of cultural ideas in society), and of power applied in the struggle for historical achievement.

There is a double dialectic of the social classes. The ruling class identifies itself with historicity primarily by directing investment into production. However, it moves toward the position of domination by turning the change it has brought forth into order, thus identifying the established system with its particular interests. The popular class is dominated and reacts by adopting defensive strategies, thereby becoming antiestablishment and acting not only in its particular interest but also with a view to regaining historicity for the whole society, that is, opening up options for change.

Touraine formulates a four-dimensional model of society opposing action and crisis, order and change (Touraine, 1978: chapter 4). The action of classes as historical actors on the level of historicity leads to the establishment of class relations and is then sedimented in institutions and organizations. The order established in this way is based on repression and is progressively stabilized by rules and procedures of reproduction. The established system is developed, adapted to its environment, and modernized in continual processes of change, mostly based on the state as the agency of change. On the other hand, the established order gives rise to dysfunctions on the organizational level, rigidity on the institutional level, and domination on the level of class relations, leading in the long run to decadence. These are features of progressing crisis. Once the crisis reaches the level of class relations, historicity becomes reestablished, with class struggles leading to the transformation of society, which again moves toward organization and reproduction of order.

Social Movements and Historical Struggles

Social movements are the major actors that transform class relations into concrete social struggle (Touraine, 1973: chapter 6; 1978: chapter 5). They are conflictual in character, culturally oriented, perform class action, and do not create a more advanced society but go out in search of an alternative to the established society. They are guided by three principles: identity, opposition, and totality. They act on the basis of their own identity, which includes their class position in society, interests, and cultural orientations. They act against an adversary. And they act within certain areas that are at issue between themselves and the adversary.

Touraine distinguishes between positive and negative critical struggles, which can take place on the three levels of historicity, institutions, and organization. Positive struggles aim at improving the position of an actor in a particular field. Critical struggles react against domination that is in crisis and is seen as not being legitimized:

- Positive struggles on the level of historicity involve social movements and the clash between classes in class struggle.
- Positive struggles on the institutional level involve institutional or political pressures, for example, trade union pressure.
- Positive struggles on the organizational level involve claims and protests, for example, workers protesting against working conditions.

- Critical struggles on the organizational level involve crisis behavior, that is, attempts to reconstitute order, such as attempts to reduce unemployment.
- Critical struggles on the institutional level involve pressures against obstacles, for example, strikes in order to resist the closure of enterprises.
- Critical struggles on the level of historicity involve revolutionary action aiming at the transformation of society.

Social movements are the fabric of social life; they are agents of historical change. Two levels of sociological analysis address social struggles and the involvement of social movements in these struggles: synchronic and diachronic analysis. In synchronic analysis, we look at the ongoing struggles within one societal type. In diachronic analysis, we look at the struggles that lead to the transformation from one societal type to another.

The State in Historical Struggle

Beyond the ruling class and the popular class and the corresponding social movements, historical struggles leading to the transformation of society involve the state as the center of political power (Touraine, 1978: chapter 6). The state acts in this case as an agent of social change. It has established sovereignty over a territorial block and is governed by a ruling elite, which has to be distinguished from the ruling class in society. The political ruling elite can be part of the ruling societal class, but it need not be. In studying historical struggles we have to take into account their relationship to each other.

Development involving the passage from an old system to a new system can be broken down into the economic level and the social level, each one being composed of two elements. As long as the old system exists there must be a state of crisis (1) on the social level; on the economic level there must be an outside stimulus (2) that gives rise to investment (3) in new production in a new system on the economic level; and these are then accompanied by new forms of social participation (4) on the social level.

Touraine distinguishes three patterns of development: liberal, voluntarist, and contractual. In liberal development, the economic level occupies the central place, originating from crisis and involving stimulus, investment, and participation in that sequence. In voluntarist development, the social level is placed in the center, including the state as a central agent of change. The sequence moves from stimulus to crisis to participation to investment. In contractual development, neither level predominates, but both are involved in communication in political institutions.

In general, the state's autonomy increases in times of crisis and rigidity, when reproduction dominates over production. The state can then act as the guarantor of reproduction. It can establish an illusory order without a true correspondence in social class relations. Social movements aiming at transformation have to engage in a double fight against the state and against the ruling class. These struggles involve the following four levels:

- The establishment and maintenance of order by the state;
- Popular behavior in opposition to order;
- The role of the state in historical change, which is what I call here the mode of state intervention;
- The action of the social forces that respond to this intervention by the state. (Touraine, 1978; for translation, see 1981: 116)

Touraine emphasizes that the state in the central capitalist societies (Great Britain, the United States) has always been only an aid to the power of the ruling class as the predominating social force, performing the role of supporting modernization and of regulating conflict by way of reform. Outside the capitalist core societies, the state has played a much more active intervening role in social affairs. Touraine distinguishes four types of such state intervention, depending on whether the state acts as an agent of order or of change and whether the social forces work in historical action or in crisis. In historical action, the social forces predominate; in crisis, it is the state that predominates. In order, state intervention tries to sustain social evolution, whereas in change the state is oriented toward the solution of national problems. The four types of state intervention resulting from the combination of these factors are the following:

- The social democratic state aims at improving social order via social evolution and is based on a predominance of the social forces in historical action.
- The national popular state acts as an agent of change in order to solve national problems in historical action, together with predominating social forces.
- The communist state aims at improving social order via social evolution in crisis, with the state predominating over social forces.
- The state of communitarian socialism acts as an agent of change in order to solve national problems in crisis, with the state predominating.

The association between state and social forces is unstable in state intervention. It can break down, leading to the state working either as a pure agent of power or as an instrument for shaping a ruling class. The four types of state intervention can break down to the following extremes, power states at one extreme and instruments of the ruling class at the other:

- Social democracy can break down into fascism or social capitalism.

- The national popular state can break down into military dictatorship or peripheral state capitalism.
- Communism can break down into ideocratic dictatorship or state technocracy.
- Communitarian socialism can break down into patrimonial dictatorship or to an authoritarian neocolonized state.

According to the types of state intervention, we can distinguish types of historical struggle:

- In the central capitalist states, the labor movement joining parts of the middle class aiming at democratization is the major force of historical change. In the modern programed society, it is superseded by the antitechnocratic movements.
- In the social-democratic state, the main actors in historical struggles are the trade unions and labor parties. In cases of breakdown, either antifascism or a struggle for self-organization becomes prominent.
- In the national popular state, populist movements are the major historical actors, fighting in cases of breakdown for revolutionary nationalism or for revolutionary class action.
- In the communist state, a social and national liberation party is the major historical actor. In cases of breakdown, a movement for democratization or for popular defence becomes prominent.
- In communitarian socialism, communitarian mobilization becomes the major force in historical action. In cases of breakdown, ethnic defence against the state or establishing the class ideology of a counterelite becomes important.

Finally, Touraine (1978, chapter 6) points to two divergent effects of social movements, depending on whether they act in a liberal society, the development of which is controlled by the ruling class, or in a voluntarist society, with the state in a predominant position. In a liberal society, a social movement exerts institutional pressure that leads to organizational claims, which then lead to participation in authority. This again leads to participation in influence and to comanagement, which finally leads to the movement's incorporation in the center of domination. In the voluntarist society, the social movement is engaged in critical action that leads to the formation of a counterelite, which establishes its own elite that forms a ruling class and then becomes a privileged dominant class.

Sociological Intervention

Touraine formulates his credo in the following words:

Thus it is by studying social movements that one becomes able to construct a new image of society. The principal stakes in a sociology of action are: overthrow the old subjugation of social facts to a metasocial order, and in particular the submission to economic facts and to the supposed laws of evolution; battle against the reduction of liberated historicity to an absolute state power; prepare the popular counteroffensive which, beginning from a defensive withdrawal towards communitarian utopias, should reconquer the entire system of action in order to obtain the joint triumph of social conflict and cultural innovation. (Touraine, 1978; for translation, see 1981: 137)

Touraine (1978: part 2) argues for sociological intervention as the specific method of studying social movements in their central role as historical actors and cultural innovators. Sociological intervention proceeds according to the following four principles (Touraine, 1978: chapter 7):

1. The sociologist enters into a relationship with the social movement itself.
2. The sociologist has to apprehend the group in its militant role, to confront it with the opponent and with representatives of other levels of action, thus working as an interlocutor between the opponents.
3. The sociologist has to engage the group in discussions aiming at bringing to light the totality that is at stake, the deeper grounds underlying its action.
4. The sociologist has to sustain the group's self-analysis, so that it can reach the level of a movement acting on the level of historicity reaching beyond the organizational and institutional levels.

In doing so, the sociologist becomes involved in the social movement but also keeps a distance in his or her role of interlocutor. The sociological research team has to combine the roles of secretary or analyst, who notes down what goes on, and of agitator or interpreter, who actively takes part in debates and self-analysis. In doing this job, a group is led from analysis to interpretation. As such, sociological intervention goes through the following phases:

A national group becomes a witness of historical action; sociological intervention first turns it into an image group, a group that acts according to an image. Further conversion turns it into an analyst group. Interpretation moves it toward a mixed self-interpretation group, which contributes to permanent sociology as an interaction between social movements and sociological analysis. Finally, the group goes on as a national group on a higher level of historicity after the sociological intervention has been terminated.

In the above processes, the sociologist fulfills two tasks: First, he or she reveals social relations that lie below the surface of everyday action by initiating confrontations between opponents. This is a precondition for sociological analysis. Second, he or she contributes to society's cultural innovation. Thus, the sociologist works as an analyst and as a cultural innovator without becoming an ideologist of a social class or a social movement. Sociological intervention lies between unaffected observation and ideological commitment.

Summary

1. The more industrial society is replaced by programed society, the more the labor movement's importance and influence will be replaced by those of the antitechnocratic movement.
2. The more human society moves from the agrarian to the mercantilist to the industrial and finally to the programed type, the more it will develop the capacity of self-production in advancing and applying knowledge on nature and on itself, in investing in production allowing the accumulation of ever more wealth, and in orienting itself to a cultural model serving as an image of creativity.
3. The more a society develops the capacity of self-production, the more it will be characterized by historicity, that is, the more it will decide on its fate in historical action rather than being determined in its fate by God, laws of evolution, modes of economic production, or values.
4. Whenever social change takes place, it will proceed in social struggles between historical actors.
5. Whenever social change takes place, it will not necessarily lead to higher rationality in an evolutionary way but may lead to a new alternative of social organization established by historical actors succeeding in historical struggles.
6. The more a society develops the capacity of self-production, the more it will do so under the guidance of a ruling class that is opposed by the popular dominated class.
7. Whenever social struggles are fought out in epochs of salient historicity, they will eventually lead to the establishment of class relations, institutions, and finally organizations, thus leading to a decline of historicity.
8. Whenever historicity is suppressed by organization, countermovements aiming at regaining historicity will be provoked.
9. Whenever human action takes place, it will do so in social relations involving inequality and power, and it will be oriented to a cultural field.

10. The more action moves from the level of organization to that of institutions and eventually to that of historicity, the more far-reaching its consequences will be.

11. Whenever social struggles take place, they will involve a struggle between the ruling class and the dominated popular class.

12. Whenever a social class enters a social struggle, it will do so on the basis of class consciousness, cultural orientation, power, and a social movement.

13. Whenever a social class establishes its power in society, it will turn historicity into organization to further its own particular interests, whereas the dominated class will act against the established order, thereby aiming at regaining historicity for society (this is the double dialectic of social classes).

14. The more historical action proceeds in time, the more it will move from historicity to the establishment of class relations, institutions, and organizations, involving the establishment of order in a sequence of repression, rule, and reproduction but then giving rise to crises appearing in dysfunctions, rigidity, domination, and decadence; subsequently, this will provoke attempts (by the state) to bring about change through development, adaptation, and modernization, but it will also provoke social movements aiming at regaining historicity, beginning the process anew.

15. The more social movements enter upon the scene, the more class relations will be turned into social struggle.

16. Whenever a social movement acts, it acts on the basis of its identity against an adversary and oriented to the totality of underlying areas at stake.

17. Positive struggles aim to improve the position of an actor in a particular field; whenever they take place, they will appear as social movements on the level of historicity, as institutional pressures or organizational claims and protests.

18. Critical struggles react against the worsening of the position of an actor in a particular field; whenever they take place, they will appear as organizational crisis behavior, institutional pressures against obstacles, or revolutionary action.

19. The weaker the ruling class, the more important will be the role of the state as an agent of order and change.

20. In a liberal society with a strong ruling class, whenever there is a crisis and an outside stimulus, investment and thus social participation will bring about a transformation of society.

21. In a voluntarist society with a strong state, whenever there is an outside stimulus that brings about crisis, social participation and then investment will bring about transformation.

22. In a contractual society, where the ruling class and the state have a contractual relationship, communication between them involving stimulus, crisis, investment, and social participation will bring about transformation.

23. Whenever social struggle takes place, four levels will be involved: the establishment and maintenance of order by the state; popular behavior in opposition to order; the state as an agent of change; and action of social classes responding to the state's intervention.

24. Whenever the state acts in a central capitalist society, it will act as an aid to modernization and reform.

25. Whenever a social democratic state acts based on strong social forces in historical action, it will aim at improving social order via social evolution.

26. Whenever the national popular state acts in historical action along with strong social forces, it will act as an agent of change in order to solve national problems.

27. Whenever the communist state acts in crisis and is stronger than the social forces, it will aim at improving social order via social evolution.

28. Whenever the state of communitarian socialism acts and is stronger than the social forces, it will act as an agent of change in order to solve national problems.

29. The more the relationship between the state and social forces breaks down, the more there will be a transformation of the social democratic state toward fascism or social capitalism, of the national popular state toward military dictatorship or peripheral state capitalism, of the communist state toward ideocratic dictatorship or state technocracy, and of communitarian socialism toward patrimonial dictatorship or authoritarian neocolonized state.

30. The more there are historical struggles in central capitalist societies, the more the labor movement will act as the major force of historical change but will be increasingly replaced by the antitechnocratic movement, with the transformation from industrial to programed society.

31. The more there are historical struggles in the social democratic state, the more trade unions will act as the major force of change, with movements toward antifascism or struggles for self-organization in cases where the balance between the state and social forces breaks down.

32. The more there are historical struggles in the national popular state, the more populist movements will act as major forces of change, moving toward revolutionary nationalism or revolutionary class action in cases where the balance between the state and social forces breaks down.

33. The more there are historical struggles in the communist state, the more a social and national liberation party will act as a major force of change,

with movements aiming at democratization or popular defence in cases where the balance between the state and social forces breaks down.

34. The more there are historical struggles in communitarian socialism, the more communication mobilization will act as a major force of change, with movements aiming at ethnic defence or establishing the class ideology of a counterelite in cases where the balance between the state and social forces breaks down.

35. Whenever a social movement proceeds successfully in a liberal society, the development of which is controlled by the ruling class, the movement will exert institutional pressure leading to organizational claims, which leads in turn to participation in authority, then to participation in influence and to co-management, which finally lead to the movement's incorporation into the center of domination.

36. Whenever a social movement proceeds successfully in a voluntarist society with a strong state, the movement will engage in critical action that will lead to the formation of a counterelite, which will then establish an elite that will go on to form a ruling class and then become a privileged dominant class.

37. The more the sociologist works as an interpreter and an analyst of social movements, the more he or she will engage in permanent sociology and the more he or she will improve sociological analysis and cultural innovation at the same time.

Critical Assessment

Evaluating Touraine's actionalist theory of society, we can share his central thesis that the development of society cannot simply be explained by the working of God, laws of evolution, or superimposed values, but always involves social struggles between historical actors. We cannot explain the emergence of capitalism as necessarily evolving from the contradictions of feudalism, as a naturalistic reading of Marxist theory would have it. Without the successful struggles of the bourgeoisie against the aristocracy, the rise of capitalism would never have occurred. And without the successful struggles of the labor movement against the bourgeoisie's domination and against inhuman working conditions, the incorporation of the trade unions and of the labor parties into the center of domination in industrial societies would never have occurred. The precondition for such a transformation of society is the mobilization of as much power as necessary in order to force the dominating opponent to give in.

Power is the decisive force in maintaining order or bringing about change. Without such mobilization of sufficient power, neither the bourgeoisie nor the labor movement would have been successful in their historical struggles. It is right that these struggles involve the struggle between opponents and a reference to the totality of social organization that is at stake. It is also right that a liberal yet strong ruling class will normally give rise to the incorporation of opposing movements in the center of domination, whereas an authoritarian ruling class will react by repressing an opposing movement but is more likely to be replaced by that movement the weaker it is. These and the many more special principles of Touraine's actionalist theory of society can be fruitfully applied in explaining the course and outcome of social struggles as major factors of social transformation as long as we want to know the effects of power on the outcome of these struggles. However, power is not all that is involved in social action oriented toward maintenance and change of social order; nor, contrary to Touraine's premise, can social relations be completely reduced to power relations. We would lose a lot of information and precision in sociological analysis if we followed this line.

Take only the course of social struggles and the success of social movements. The ruling capitalist class makes concessions to the demands of workers by improving working conditions, expanding participation in decision making, and increasing wages not only in cases of superior pressure based on the power of the trade unions but also in many cases just to give incentives to work harder and more responsibly and to provide the material basis for broader consumption, which is a precondition for increasing profit. Thus it is frequently an economic incentive and not pressure, that is, money and not power, that motivates the representatives of capital to raise the living conditions of workers without being forced by a strong social movement. In present times, progressive companies negotiate with their employees successfully in this way at the cost of the trade unions, which may lose much of their influence. In this way employees are motivated to contribute to their company's wealth because they expect to make economic gains for themselves from such economic advancement. On the other hand, they explicitly motivate their company to improve working and living conditions in order to enhance their productivity.

What goes on in these interactions is not so much a fight on the basis of power, where one party's gain is the other party's loss, but an exchange based on money and other incentives where both parties expand their gains. These are interactions in which important changes take place and that have become more and more important in the central capitalist societies, very much at the cost of the decline of trade unions' influence on workers. Touraine notes the declining importance and influence of the labor movement and the trade unions, but he explains this only in terms of the trade unions' incorporation into the center of domination based on their power. What he completely misses is the change of capital-labor relations from power struggle to economic negotiation even in the relationship between companies and trade unions, but resulting also in a declining influence of the old-fashioned trade unions. Because his actionalist theory of society is exclusively based on power and power struggle, he has no theoretical instrument with which to explain this phenomenon. What we need here is a theory of economic transactions with money, not power, at its center.

However, neither power struggle nor negotiation is all that is involved in the transformation of capitalist societies from the point of view of the capital-labor relationship. Inclusion is a further relationship that is important; it cannot be reduced to terms of power, but needs to be explained in terms of commitment and influence. The building of nation-states and the participation of the whole population in the wars between these nation-states has contributed to establishing national solidarities leading beyond class solidarities. The extension of rights of citizenship, that is, economic rights to property, political rights to vote, social rights to social welfare, and cultural rights to education began with the formation of national solidarities in the building of the European nation-states. The extension of these rights does not mean incorporation into the center of domination in the first instance, but inclusion in the societal community and the establishment of national bonds of solidarity crossing over class boundaries. Only in a secondary way can participation in domination arise from this inclusion. The European nation-states have been successful in bringing about this inclusion to very different degrees. And this is important for explaining the transformation of the capital-labor relationship in these societies. Where this inclusion came about very late and to a limited degree, the labor movement has remained much more radical and violent than in societies where inclusion began earlier and reached farther. This explains why the labor movement is still more radical and violent in France and Italy than in Britain and in the Scandinavian countries, where the labor movement is strong but not radical and violent in its aims and means regarding the societal system itself. Touraine has no theoretical device for explaining such differences because he does not give inclusion, solidarity, commitment, or influence a position independent of power in his theoretical scheme. We need a theory that gives these variables an independent status in order to explain such phenomena. The extension of citizenship rights is a central feature of the transformation of the capital-labor relationship in capitalist societies, as T. H. Marshall demonstrated in his *Class, Citizenship, and Social Development* (Marshall, 1964/1976). This transformation calls for an explanation in terms of processes of inclusion that cannot be reduced to economic negotiation or to power struggles. The latter play a part in this process, but they cannot replace the inclusion process in itself.

Finally, the transformation of the capital-labor relationship involves processes of discursive justification of claims that have their own quality and effects and cannot be reduced to terms of the power struggle. Certainly, the struggle between capital and labor has been very much a debate as Touraine would see it, which means that the claims are ideological in nature, representing particular class interests, and are successfully validated by way of factual enforcement based on the mobilization of power. It is true that power often sustains the successful enforcement of arguments. However, this is not the whole story. Discussions also display a logic of their own. After the Enlightenment had enshrined the values of freedom, equality, and rationality for everybody as the cultural idea of the bourgeois movement, it set in motion a process of discourse that could not be limited to legitimating the freedom and equality of the bourgeoisie and the rationality of capitalism alone without contradicting the very nature of the ideas: their universal validity for everybody.

Thus, the farther this discourse progressed, the more it could be turned against the constraints, inequalities, and irrationalities of capitalism, setting enormous demands for legitimation. That these demands are continually broadened is a logical process because discourse in itself moves toward universalization. Every constraint, inequality, and irrationality can be attacked in the light of the universal values of freedom, equality, and rationality. This is an enormous factor of change, which directs societal development toward higher levels of freedom, equality, and rationality. However, because every change caused by such criticism brings about new constraints, inequalities, and irrationalities, this is a never-ending task for modern societies, initiated by the very idea of mastering the world by moving it toward more freedom, equality, and rationality. In this way we produce an artificial world, which sets the new problems we have to solve. In the process of emancipating ourselves from nature, we have built up an artificial world of institutions and technology from which we have to emancipate ourselves again, creating new institutions and technologies that exert their domination upon us. This is the never-ending, Sysiphian task that has been set in motion by the ideas of the Enlightenment.

These are transformations taking place in modern societies and having enormous effects on the capital-labor relationship that cannot be explained in terms of power struggle between classes. The logic of discourse and argumentation is at work here and we need a theory of discourse on its own in order to understand and explain these processes. Touraine misses this dimension of societal transformation because the power struggle unduly dominates his actionalist theory of society. This is also a decisive failure, making his method of sociological intervention an arbitrary contribution to the power struggle. Because reason has no place in Touraine's theory, there is no reason for one sociological intervention to be better than any other. Founded on rational discourse, sociological intervention would have to meet the demands of rational justification in contributing to the self-analysis of a group and to the interpretation of the underlying areas at stake. Sociological intervention would have to set in motion processes of discourse beyond the limits of a specific movement in order to give rational justification for its work. Limited to Touraine's preoccupation with power struggle, sociological intervention cannot be any more than a particularistic contribution to the battle between particularistic positions. There is no escape from power struggle as long as we subscribe to Touraine's perspective on society.

TEN

POWER AND AGENCY: ANTHONY GIDDENS'S THEORY OF STRUCTURATION

AFTER ITS classical foundation by Spencer's evolutionism and utilitarianism, British sociology developed very much in correspondence to the labor movement (see Abrams, 1968; Abrams, Deem, Finch, and Rock, 1981). The class structure of British society became the predominant research subject and has been so particularly since World War II. It is therefore no surprise that class, power, and conflict became the major categories of British sociology in approaching social reality. Conflict theory of the Marxist type, concentrating on the analysis of class conflict, flourished on this ground. Sociologists like John Rex (1961, 1981), David Lockwood (1956, 1958, 1960), John Goldthorpe (1968, 1980), and Ralph Miliband (1982) represent this British version of conflict theory.

This is the intellectual context within which Anthony Giddens has developed his own theory of society. However, Giddens has taken up ideas from other intellectual contexts that have led him well beyond the boundaries of the traditional British type of class-conflict theory.

Giddens has attracted much attention in his endeavor to build what he calls a theory of structuration in contemporary sociological discourse (Giddens, 1976, 1979, 1981, 1982, 1984, 1985, 1987, 1989). He places the human agent, his or her knowledgeability, and his or her power to get things done and to make a difference in the course of events at the center of his theory. This is the reason why we can examine Giddens's undertaking under the heading of theories of power and conflict, though he claims more comprehensiveness than the traditionally established sociological theories.

Objectivism and Subjectivism

Giddens begins his endeavor with a critique of the established schools of objectivism and subjectivism (Giddens, 1984: xiii–xxxvi, 1–5). In his view

175

the school of objectivism, comprising the approaches of Marxism, functionalism, and structuralism, explains the continuation and transformation of social structures in terms of functional needs or structural laws without reference to the activities of human individuals (Giddens, 1984: 162–226). The action of individuals is explained by the constraining forces of structures according to the view of objectivism. Human individuals cannot do anything other than to act out whatever is predetermined by structural constraints. On the other hand, the subjectivist school, which embraces approaches like symbolic interactionism and ethnomethodology, explains the establishment, continuation, and transformation of social structures as an outcome of the freely chosen activities of individuals (Giddens, 1976). The origin of individuals' actions lies in their subjectivity and free will.

The Duality of Structure and Agency

Social theory is split into these two traditions, and it is the aim of Giddens to overcome this dualism by synthesizing objectivism and subjectivism in the new approach of structuration theory. The central concept expressing this synthesis is the "duality of structure," or, as Giddens sometimes also says, "the duality of structure and agency" (Giddens, 1984: 5–28, 297–304). The core meaning of this concept is that neither structures nor actions exist *per se* but are closely intertwined. There is no structure without action, and there is no action without structure. In stating his theory, Giddens chooses the concepts of "agent" and "agency" rather than "actor" and "action." The latter have been used by subjectivist theories of action, which do not sufficiently take into account that action starts out from structures and results in structures or properly consider the central importance of power for carrying out action with these features and the knowledgeability of human individuals engaged in this process.

An agent is not just the abstract subject of an act but is an individual who is engaged in social praxis and therefore exerts his or her influence on the course of that praxis; that is, he or she makes history. An actor is the subject of an isolated action that is composed of isolated acts. An agent is the subject of social praxis that makes history. Making history means that action is embedded in social praxis that starts from given social structures and contributes to their continuation or transformation. It is in this way that social systems, for example, societies, are reproduced. Agency is more than an isolated action; it is an action that is part of social praxis engaged in reproducing society. When a worker sells his or her labor power to the capitalist entrepreneur, that worker is not just an actor who performs an isolated action in an isolated situation but is an agent of historical development whose agency is part of an overall social praxis spreading in time and space beyond the individual situation of contract concluding, related to the previously established structure of the capital-labor relationship, and contributing to the continuation of just that structure of the capitalist economy. In this sense of the worker's active involvement in making history by starting from established structures and contributing to their continuation or transformation and thereby to the reproduction of society, the worker is an agent and the selling of his or her labor power is agency.

Agency and Knowledgeability

Beyond this first differentiation of agent and agency from actor and action there are further properties that make up the distinctive character of an agent and his or her agency. The first major feature that has to be introduced here is termed the knowledgeability of agents (Giddens, 1984: 3–4, 21–22, 26–27, 90–92, 281–82, 289, 327–34, 375). According to Giddens, humans are not blind and dull objects of structural constraints who carry out whatever is predetermined by structures; they are agents who know a lot of the social circumstances, the conditions of their agency, and its outcomes and who make use of that knowledge in order to carry out their agency. Moreover, this knowledge makes a difference in the organization of agency. The knowledge of agents becomes a central place for mediating between established conditions and structures, praxis, and outcomes of agency in the continuation or transformation of structures.

Human agency does not proceed like a billiard ball that has its course immediately determined by the impact of another ball, where a cause effects a determinate movement toward a specific goal. Human agency always involves the processing of knowledge of the situation and its relation to precedents and outcomes by an agent. The worker who concludes a labor contract with an entrepreneur does so with knowledge. He or she is not driven into that contract by the structure of the labor-capital relationship as an external constraining force.

As Marx put it, the establishment of wage labor as a constitutive element of capitalist commodity production directed toward the accumulation of capital as a goal in itself was made possible by setting the worker free from the personal authority of feudal lords. The structure then is a mass of free workers who need to sell their labor power on the labor market in order to make their living and capitalists who need to buy that labor power in order to extract from it the value added derived from the production process and then sell the commodities thus produced on the market. Neither the worker nor the capitalist is blindly driven into the contract by this structure. What they do depends largely on what they expect from the contract, which alternatives they see, how they interpret their relationship, and what they know about the rights of the contracting parties. In many cases, workers will expect just a chance to make their living from the contract; they will see no alternative and will interpret the relationship simply as a submission to an established power, and the capitalist will have a complementary view of the situation. However, their knowledge is crucial to what goes on; their praxis and knowledge can change; here is a major source of change in established practices, resulting in the change of structures. The worker can look for alternative ways of acting in order to improve his or her position in the relationship to the capitalist. The worker can realize that forming coalitions with fellow workers strengthens the workers' position so that they can change the terms of contracting to their advantage, resulting in an improvement of their working and living conditions. The individual worker knows well that he or she is forced to sell his or her labor power in order to make a living. There is this constraining feature of the given structure of capital-labor relationships. It is constraining for the worker inasmuch as he or she does indeed choose to make his or her own living and not to die of starvation or to live from charitable care.

However, this constraining force of the capital-labor relationship is mediated by the worker's knowledge of that structure, the ongoing praxis and its outcomes. The worker's idea that a coalition with fellow workers may improve the worker's position vis-à-vis to the capitalist changes the influence of the established capital-labor structure on that praxis quite remarkably. Now the worker does not just comply with the capitalist's demands but actively resists the bluntly exploitative demands, also making at least minimal demands of his or her own for certain wage and working conditions, such as shorter working hours, breaks, better security, health care, recreation, or participation in decision making. The outcome of this praxis is a transformed capital-labor structure in terms of the distribution of power in the relationship. Before the change of workers' praxis based on their knowledge of structure, praxis, and outcome, the capital-labor structure was characterized by an extreme inequality of power. The capitalist was able to enforce everything; the worker was not able to enforce anything. Now the capitalist still may be able to enforce quite a lot within the factory, but the worker can enforce much more than before at the cost of the capitalist's ability to enforce everything. Whereas the praxis of the worker contributed to the continuation of the capital-labor structure for a long time, it contributes to its transformation after the worker has changed his or her knowledge of structure, praxis, and outcomes.

Praxis is not a one-sided process, and it involves more than one agent: in this case, besides the worker and his or her fellows, the capitalist and his or her own fellows and competitors. What the capitalist does also does not depend directly on the structure of the capital-labor relationship but is mediated by his or her knowledge. The capitalist may have seen prolongation of the working day and keeping the wage as low as possible as the best means for exploitation and thus as the source of profit for a long time.

But the capitalist, too, changes his or her knowledge of the structure, praxis, and outcome, expecting an expansion of consumption and thus higher profits from selling commodities as a result of raising wages and reducing the length of the working day. Thus, the capitalist changes his or her practice in concluding labor contracts. And this praxis transforms the capital-labor structure, reducing the level of suppression imposed on the worker.

The process may go on so that the worker gets to know about the capitalist's knowledge and the capitalist about the worker's knowledge. In this way, *mutual knowledge* becomes constituted and plays a central role in shaping the ongoing praxis. The worker knows that the capitalist knows about the profit-increasing results of increasing the level of consumption via higher wages and shortening the working day. The capitalist knows that the worker knows about the improvement of his or her bargaining position to be had by joining with fellow workers and the danger to capital accumulation of their collective refusal to comply in a strike. This mutual knowledge becomes a constitutive element of their agency in social praxis. And this knowledge becomes increasingly complex. The worker includes rights of freedom and equality in his or her knowledge; the capitalist includes the productive effects of institutionalizing such rights in caring for workers' self-development in work and involving workers in the decision-making process. With the involvement of such rights and means of increasing productivity in the worker's and the capitalist's knowledge, the mediation between capital-labor structure, praxis, and outcomes becomes increasingly complex. What goes on in praxis and what will result from this for the continuation or transformation of the capital-labor structure is directly determined less by the preestablished capital-labor structure and more by the agents' processing of information, by their mutual knowledge.

Today, a bargaining process by union and industry is not predetermined in its course and outcome as much by the historically established structure of the capital-labor relationship as by their knowledge of the situation, its relation to conditions and outcomes, their knowledge of one another, and their knowledge of the knowledge each has of one another. This knowledge shapes the strategies and tactics that decide their success or failure, which again decide the outcome and the resulting continuation or transformation of the capital-labor structure. A momentary disadvantage in knowledge can have lasting effects. This is why human agents' knowledgeability affects the continuation or transformation of structures and thus the reproduction of social systems immediately and is of such importance for analyzing social praxis in Giddens's eyes.

Levels of Agency

Having explained Giddens's idea of agents' knowledgeability, we can further point out its relation to action by introducing three levels involved in the process of agency: (1) the motivation of action; (2) the rationalization of action, and (3) the reflexive monitoring of action (Giddens, 1984: 5-15, 41-45). By and large, three levels in the individual's mind correspond to the three levels of agency: (1) unconscious motives and cognition; (2) practical consciousness, and (3) discursive consciousness. In this way, the concept of knowledgeability becomes differentiated. It embraces levels 2 and 3 in agency and consciousness. The motivation of action is what is closest to the immediate course of action. When working in a team of fellow workers, the individual worker may just carry out a routine that he or she has learned. Carrying out this routine does not involve much attention, calculation, and conscious processing of knowledge. It involves just his or her motivation, to earn some money, the unconscious view of the situation as a work situation, and the unconscious compliance with the routine and the authority relationship that lies behind it. Immediate motivation to work hard for money and unconscious compliance with routine and authority complement each other. This is the normal praxis that goes on in everyday life and contributes to the continuation of the routine and authority structure.

However, this very praxis can become the object of attempts at rationalizing action that involve the working of the individual's practical consciousness of how to do things best in order to attain one's goals. The worker's established routine can be conceived of as a rational way of producing something and of earning a living. And the worker's practical consciousness contains the practical knowledge for solving problems arising within his or her routinized work. The worker knows how to do his or her job and also how to repair minor breakdowns occurring in the production process. Inasmuch as the worker's task within the production process is related to a specific goal it can be measured according to the degree to which it reaches that goal, for example, maximum output at maximum quality, and it can be compared with alternative modes of organizing production. This measuring and comparison is part and parcel of the praxis itself, and the more it takes place, the more the work process will be rationalized. Correspondingly, the worker's practical consciousness becomes rationalized.

Whereas the rationalization of action and practical consciousness are an immediate part of daily action itself and are confined to the circumstances of that action, we reach a new level of knowledgeability the more there is talk about that action. The worker who is asked by an inspector from the state bureau of health about the organization of the work and the reasons why he or she does something in one way and not in another gives descriptions of and reasons for what he or she is doing. This is what Giddens calls reflexive monitoring of action involving the discursive consciousness of the individual. Compared to the immediate rationalization of action, the reflection about what is done and why it is done becomes much broader in reflexive monitoring, including many more aspects and goals for action than just production and its relation to output and quality.

Here is the level where criteria of autonomy and health can come into play. Reflexive monitoring and discursive consciousness provide the image of one's actions and reasons, justifications, and legitimations for it. The more reflexive monitoring and reflexive consciousness become separated from the immediate rationalization of action and from practical consciousness, the more it can give images, reasons, justifications, and legitimations that do not correspond to the immediate motivation and unconscious motives and to the rationalization and practical knowledge of that action. Reflexive monitoring and discursive consciousness can then produce ideologies that hide the true reasons for action. How the worker carries out his or her task may be motivated by an unconscious reliance on an established routine. When asked for reasons, the worker may answer that he or she believes it is the most productive way of doing things.

What we have explained with the example of a worker's routine we could also explain with our example of the labor contract. The motivation of action for both labor and industry is to make money and involves the unconscious leaning toward reiterating established routines of concluding contracts. The rationalization of action and practical knowledge imply know-how in concluding contracts that are most useful for both parties. Here, we enter the level of thinking about the contract explicated in the previous parts of this chapter. The more the agents give descriptions, reasons, justifications, and legitimations, the more they reach the level of reflexive monitoring and discursive consciousness. The disjunction of discursive and practical consciousness means, for example, that the capitalist refers to the rights of the worker in his or her concessions but actually makes the concessions because he or she expects higher levels of productivity and consumption. Social praxis is an interplay of the outlined levels of motivation, rationalization, and reflexive monitoring of action involving unconscious motives and cognitions, practical consciousness, and discursive consciousness.

Unacknowledged Conditions and Unintended Consequences of Action

The more agency involves levels 2 and 3, the more the course of social praxis and its relation to preceding structural conditions and resulting continuations and transformations of structures will be shaped by the agents' knowledgeability. Nevertheless, not everything is under the control of agents' knowledge; agents may not be conscious of given structural conditions and may not know every effect resulting from their actions. Therefore, we also have to pay attention to the unacknowledged conditions of an action and the unintended consequences of that action.

For example, in a tribal society the people scattered over a wide territory regularly come together to perform certain ceremonial activities. The condition they think gives rise to this gathering is their dependence on certain demons for rain and a good harvest. Their intention in performing the ceremony is to influence the demons in order to bring rain and a good harvest. However, the unacknowledged condition is the fact that they are scattered over a wide territory but nevertheless feel a mutual belongingness and common identity. Thus, they have a motivation to come together from time to time, and this gathering has the unintended effect of reinforcing their feeling of belongingness and of a common identity that contributes to continuing the structure of a feeling of belongingness and common identity in scattered living conditions. This again gives rise to the praxis of ceremonial gathering, and so on. Here the mixture of unacknowledged conditions and acknowledged conditions (depending upon rain and a good harvest) relates to a social praxis, which has the unintended consequences of continuing the unacknowledged conditions of that praxis.

In functionalist terms, providing for rain and a good harvest is the manifest function of the ceremony, whereas the production of a common identity is the latent function. However, such a functionalist explanation of the ceremony relies on the assumption that the tribal society has a need for common identity. Giddens correctly criticizes that we cannot attribute such a need to a society as a unity, because the society is not a subject that could think about a way of fulfilling such a need. Only deliberate knowledge of the tribal collective of such a need and its satisfaction by ceremonial gatherings could remedy this mistaken explanation. But this would turn the latent function into a manifest one, thus abandoning the whole concept of latent functions. Certainly collectives can get to know about this process and consciously organize ceremonial gatherings. However, Giddens points out with the above analysis how we can give an explanation of ceremonial gatherings without referring to either manifest or latent functions: They are practices organized by agents who feel a belongingness and common identity under the condition of scattered living, and these practices contribute to the very continuation of the same structural conditions (Giddens, 1984: 12–14, 293–97).

This is a feedback loop of unacknowledged conditions, social praxis, and unintended consequences continuing with the unacknowledged conditions. However, we have to recognize that the knowledge of the agents remains an important mediating link in this feedback loop. The structural conditions do not causally determine the ceremonial praxis. Occasionally, the mixing of the agents' false knowledge about demons, rain, and a good harvest with the unconscious motive of regularly meeting people one feels one belongs to brings about the praxis, and that praxis reconfirms the feeling of belongingness. The unconscious motives and the agents' knowledge play a major part in relating structure to social praxis and this to structure again. This is what distinguishes Giddens's explanation from a purely structuralist or functionalist one. However, we have to correct him in one respect. He says that the "unintended effects form the *acknowledged* conditions for further action" (Giddens, 1984: 14) in this case. These unintended effects *may* become acknowledged conditions of further action but *need not* necessarily do so in order to keep the feedback loop going.

Giddens gives two further examples of unintended effects. First, one event may eventuate in a sequence of consequences; second, a number of actions by different actors may result in one consequence. In the first example, a man who switches on the light in his house may occasionally cause a burglar to flee down the street, where he is arrested by the police and then brought to the district judge, who sentences him to three months in jail. A number of additional actions of other actors have to contribute to the initiating action in order to give rise to the eventual result of sentencing the burglar to jail. In the second example, if we start with a situation of an ethnically mixed neighborhood, the decision of actors not to live in a neighborhood where they form a minority leads to the consequence of complete ethnic segregation of neighborhoods. Here a number of independent actions have a definite structural outcome.

Agency and Power

In Giddens's perspective, power is an immediate property of agency and action in general (1984: 14–16, 281–85). Action and agency presuppose power. To carry out an action means

> to intervene in the world or to refrain from such intervention, with the effect of influencing a specific process or state of affairs. . . . [An action] make[s] a difference to a pre-existing state of affairs or course of events. (Giddens, 1984: 14)

This means that an action changes the world; it has some consequences for that world, which is then not the same as it was before. Thus, whenever an individual carries out an action, he or she deploys some causal effect on the world, which includes the actions of other individuals and their deployment of causal effects. The exertion of power is not a specific type of conduct alongside other types, like association, communication, and exchange, but the very essence of any action, whatever type it may otherwise be. Giddens makes the exertion of power the key concept of his theory of structuration; concepts like influence, inducement, value commitment, reason, and legitimation can have only secondary status compared to the concept of power. Whenever an actor acts, he or she exerts power; otherwise the actor would not be able to carry out the action.

A tennis player who plays the ball from one corner of an opponent's field to the other and makes the person run from one corner to the other exerts such power in his or her action. It is an action carried out with a definite consequence — making the other player run from one corner of the court to the other. Without the first player's action taking place, the second player would not run from one corner of the court to the other. The capitalist who concludes a labor contract with a worker exerts power because he or she makes the worker obey commands, which the worker would not do if the capitalist had not concluded the contract with the worker. The police officer who captures a burglar exerts power because he or she makes the burglar comply with certain commands, which the burglar would not do if he or she had not been captured by the officer.

A person who orders a cab exerts power when he or she tells the taxi driver to come to the hotel in order to pick him or her up and drive to the airport. Without the person's order, the taxi driver would not do so. Another person coming a moment later has to wait for another cab, which he or she would not have had to do if the first person had not taken the cab. A person who enters a restaurant and asks to be seated exerts power, because the person makes the waitress seat him or her and makes other people take other tables. Neither the waitress nor the other people would do this if the person had not occupied a table. The bus driver who warns a passenger who is getting out to "Watch your step!" exerts power because the passenger now slows down and takes care, which he or she would not have done if the bus driver had not said "Watch your step!"

A woman who invites guests for dinner exerts power because she makes her guests come to her home, which they would not otherwise do at that time. A union leader who calls on workers to join a strike exerts power because he or she makes the workers join the strike, which they would not do if not called out. A professor who teaches students sociological theory in structurationist terms exerts power because he or she makes the students see the social world in structurationist terms, which they would not do if they had not been taught that theory. A discussant who gives evidence for the falsity of a statement of another discussant exerts power because he or she makes the other discussant revise his or her statement, which the person would not have had to do if the first discussant had not given the evidence. A person who spends an evening reading one of Giddens's numerous books on structuration theory exerts power because he or she prevents the authors of other books from being read by him or her and also makes his or her friends spend the evening without his or her company. A man who moves from Europe to the United States exerts power because he makes his European friends spend all their time without him while his American friends can see more of him. A person who commits suicide exerts power because that person makes his or her friends live on without him or her.

In order to exert power, an individual needs resources. What are such resources? Giddens distinguishes two types: allocative and authoritative

(Giddens, 1984: 31, 33, 258–62). Allocative resources are (1) material features of the environment (raw materials, material power sources); (2) means of material production/reproduction (instruments of production, technology); and (3) produced goods (artifacts created by the interaction of 1 and 2). Authoritative resources are (1) organization of social time-space (temporal-spatial constitution of paths and regions); (2) production/reproduction of the body (organization and relation of human beings in mutual association); and (3) organization of life chances (constitution of chances of self-development and self-expression).

In the previous examples, the capitalist and the persons ordering a cab and occupying a table in a restaurant have money, an allocative resource, which enables them to carry out their action. The worker, the taxi driver, and the waitress need the money; therefore, the persons with money can make them conform to their commands. All the other persons in the examples possess authoritative resources of different kinds; the tennis player and the policeman possess superior physical abilities, supported by their equipment; the bus driver, the professor, and the discussant have knowledge that the other persons do not have; the woman and the union leader make use of their reputation in a certain social circle; the reader, the man who moves, and the person who commits suicide make use of their ability to make a decision that has consequences for other persons. Looking at the examples shows us how widespread Giddens's use of the concept of power is and particularly how widespread his use of the concept of authoritative resources is. The consequence is that he has to blow up the meaning of power and allocative and authoritative resources so that power does not tell us any more than action itself, making exchange, association, communication, and domination all forms of an overall understanding of the exertion of power. Alternatively, he could give exchange, association, and communication a derivative status with regard to the exertion of power. Giddens does both, but he tends mostly toward the second solution of his dilemma. In doing so he necessarily commits the mistake of subordinating truth to power, a mistake that he criticizes in the work of Foucault. The professor who teaches his or her students structuration theory and the discussant who gives evidence on the falsity of another discussant's statement do exert power, because they are in a position to make decisions that have consequences for other persons. It is the power of argument that they deploy. However, is that power all that makes an argument effective? And where does this power originate? It is precisely the difference in the origin of the power exerted that may make the biggest difference in the consequences of actions, and that is not always the same thing as power itself. What gives the teaching of structuration theory power to transform a student's view of the social world is its convincing justification by reasons generally accepted as valid in sociological discourse.

Thus, the power of the professor's teaching derives from valid reasoning on the basis of the rules of discourse. And this derivation from valid reasoning makes the professor's power very different from that of the police officer, the capitalist, or the union leader. His or her teaching exerts power only inasmuch as it is backed up by valid reasoning. The police officer's power does not immediately need such backing up by valid reasoning; this does not come into play until the suspect is interviewed at the precinct station. The professor acquires and applies his or her power according to very different rules than those of the police officer or the burglar who gets his way with a gun, the tennis player, or the union leader. The effects are also very different. The police officer's power lasts only as long as he or she can hold the burglar in hostage. The power of the professor's teaching of structuration theory lasts as long as it isn't superseded by a more convincing theory.

Another source of the professor's power is being in a position to decide on a student's exclusion from class. Some students may submit to a professor's teaching just because they fear they may otherwise be excluded. In this aspect the professor's power is closer to, but still different from, that of the policeman. Yet another source of the professor's power may be that the students like him or her. In this case, they adopt the professor's view because they do not want to lose his or her sympathy. A further source of power may be that the professor is in a position to give the students good grades for adopting his or her views. Here the students may take over the professor's views because they don't want to get bad grades. In all these aspects the professor's power derives from very different sources with very different requirements for their mobilization and application and with very different results.

Valid reasoning has to conform to the rules of discourse and changes the *mind* of a student; sympathy has to conform to the rules of association and changes the *heart* of a student; exclusion from class has to reside on physical force and changes the *physical location* of a student; and grades have to work as incentives and change a student's *interest* in a subject. Thus, the professor's action has different consequences depending on the power resources that are applied in the action. And the consequences may differ in their persistence depending on the counteraction coming about after the professor has finished his or her teaching. The student's interest in structuration theory can quickly turn toward another subject when the student tries to improve his or her grades in other classes. The threat of excluding the student from class will commit him or her to structuration theory no longer than the teaching in class goes on. The student's sympathy for structuration theory will last as long as he or she keeps in touch with the professor or at least maintains a sympathetic image of him or her and as long as it isn't displaced by growing sympathies for other professors. The student's conviction of structuration theory's validity will last as long as no criticism is voiced that succeeds in replacing the theory by an even more convincing alternative.

As with the different resources of the professor's power, so it is with the different persons in our examples. They have to be separated analytically in order to reach more precise statements about their effects. The worker, the taxi driver, and the waitress will submit to the power exerted upon them only as long as there is no better alternative to serve their interests; as soon as there is one, they will refuse to comply. The tennis player and the police officer will exert their power only as long as their opponents cannot mobilize superior power. The woman will be a successful hostess only as long as she appears sympathetic to her guests. The union leader will successfully call on the workers to join a strike only as long as the workers feel committed to their union. The discussant will successfully make another discussant revise his or her statement only as long as no contradictory evidence is presented. The persons who move or commit suicide will exert effects on their friends' behavior only as long as they feel a belongingness with those persons. And it is important that interests, physical location, sympathy, and conviction of truth are reproduced in very different ways: market competition, exertion of physical force, establishing a feeling of belongingness, and discourse. Unfortunately, these very different resources of power are leveled out in Giddens's concepts of power, allocative, and authoritative resources. Taken to its logical conclusion, a gun is the same as an argument in this perspective. I am sure Giddens does not want to have it this way, because otherwise he could not criticize Foucault for submitting truth to power. However, the very core of his structuration theory, willingly or not, has the same consequence.

It is not only insufficient internal differentiation of power resources and the resulting differentiation of the exertion of power and its effects that is deficient in Giddens's structuration theory. It is also the insufficient differentiation of the exertion (execution) of power from other dimensions or forms of social interaction: exchange and negotiation using money, association and joining in solidarity using influence, communication and discourse using value-commitments, truth, and arguments. An actor who has power is in a position to impose a certain way of acting on another actor, so that the other actor has no choice other than to comply. Thus, the second discussant has to revise his or her position because the first discussant has evidence that does not allow him or her to maintain his or her statement according to the rules of discourse. The people invited by the woman to her home have no other choice because they would risk losing the woman's sympathy. The taxi driver has no other choice because he needs the money. The burglar has no other choice because otherwise he would lose his life.

Being able to reduce the alternatives of action for other people to one single choice means having power. However, this is not the primary property of money, or of an argument, or of influence based on a sense of belongingness. It is only a secondary way of turning these sources of action into power resources. With money I have to make an offer that can compete on the market. The employer has to make his or her offer of money more attractive, the more alternatives the worker has. Money is an incentive that always has to compete in the market and thus is limited in its capacity to serve as a power resource. And it buys only specific services without further limitations on action. The worker, the taxi driver, and the waitress can do what they want with their money. For the worker, taxi driver, and waitress, the money received in the transaction is not something that narrows their alternatives to act; rather it is something that offers new alternatives. Money received in transactions is not a limitation on action but an opportunity to do more things than before!

Influence also works in a different way than power. It is exerted within a community on the basis of mutual feelings of belongingness. It enables members of a community to motivate their fellows to join them in certain actions according to the norms of the community. Here there are no alternatives that have to be reduced explicitly, and there is a limited set of actions that appear self-evident when asked for by a member of the community. When the union leader calls on the workers to join the strike, he or she does not have to reduce the workers' alternatives so that they have no other choice. The leader's call is self-evident in its own right, and the workers' joining the strike is self-evident, too. Thus, there is neither a narrowing nor a widening of the workers' scope for action. It is just left as it is. It is not the union leader who narrows the workers' range of choice but their community that does not allow any alternative to come up even in the worker's imagination.

The discussant's argument is part of an ongoing discourse in which both discussants are in search of truth. Whenever one discussant's argument leads to the revision of another discussant's statement, this does not at all narrow his or her scope for action. On the contrary, it is an opportunity to put the statement on a more generally valid footing and to cover more of the world than before. However, contrary to these examples the policeman really exerts power over the burglar in a primary sense. The burglar sees many alternatives to going to jail, but is forced by the police officer to do so.

To briefly summarize, the difference between the four types of motivating action is this: The burglar has not lived in prison but is now forced to do so. His or her scope for action is extremely constrained. The taxi driver has not lived in prison and isn't forced to do so. His or her scope for action is widened. The union member has lived in a prison (the community) and goes on doing so. His or her scope for action remains narrow. The discussant has lived in a prison to a certain extent, because his or her mind was narrowed by false statements; the discussant now becomes slightly liberated from that prison, because his or her mind has been widened. Giddens's preoccupation with the concept of power taken to its logical conclusion reduces these very different processes of interaction to one. It makes the taxi driver, union member, and discussant share the fate of the burglar. This is too much power; we have to liberate ourselves from that power exerted by structuration theory by way of more convincing reasoning.

Structure and Structuration

Giddens's false reduction of agency to the execution of power also has narrowing effects for his understanding of structures, structuration, the continuation and transformation of structures, and the reproduction of social systems (Giddens, 1984: 16–34, 162–226, 319–27). Power struggle becomes the primary force in making history.

Social systems consist of social relations patterned across time and space. The members of a football team build up a system because they are related to one another. The game between two teams is a wider system because here the interrelations within each of the teams are mixed with interrelations between the two teams. The professional organization of football teams embraces them all in one even more comprehensive system. A market is a system insofar as it draws together buyers and sellers in complex interrelationships. Sociology as a social system relates sociologists as discussants to one another. Modern societies based on the foundation of nation-states are social systems that draw their members together on the basis of common citizenship and occupation of a certain territory. By social systems, Giddens means the drawing together of members in social relations with more or less open boundaries regarding interrelationships with other systems and membership.

Social systems are integrated socially by the reciprocity in immediate interaction of co-present actors: social integration. They are integrated systemically by the reciprocity of actors or collectivities across extended time and space: systems integration.

Social structures are properties of social systems; they are a specific delineation of the social relations in the system. Structures determine which type of behavior is more likely in a system and which type is less likely. Structures are rules and resources for action. Rules of social life are

> techniques or generalizable procedures applied in the enactment/reproduction of social practices. (Giddens, 1984: 21)

Thus, it is a factory rule that the workers check in every morning at 7:00 A.M. and check out every afternoon at 4:30 P.M., whereas the white-collar employees come at 8:00 A.M. and leave at 5:30 P.M. and the management comes at 8:30 A.M. and leaves sometime in the late afternoon. It is

a rule of a family that Mom gets up at 6:00 every morning in order to prepare breakfast, then wakes up the rest of the family to have breakfast with
one another. The family uses the bathroom in a specific order from 6:30
A.M. to 7:00 A.M. and leaves home in a specific order from 7:15 A.M. to 7:45
A.M. These rules describe recurrent procedures as they occur but are also
understood as counterfactual prescriptions, because deviations provoke activities to reinstitute the rules. On the other hand, they also express a certain
order of privileges and power relations between both the members of the
factory and members of the family: the managers are above the middle-
range employees, who are above the workers. Dad and Mom rank above
the children. The rules define the actions that are likely to occur in the factory and the family, thereby making up a structure. According to this structure, not everything can happen within the systems. What can happen and
what cannot happen is defined by the rules.

Insofar as structures made up of rules preclude the occurrence of certain actions, they are constraining in character. In Durkheim's (1895/1973a)
sense they are external to the individual worker. Keeping to our example,
they range over time beyond the employment period of any single person,
are binding for every worker, and call for negative sanctions in case of deviations. Beyond the constraints of rules, the physical environment and the
physical limitations of the body also exert constraints on the individual's
actions (Bhaskar, 1979).

However, it is a major point of Giddens's theory that structures are not
only constraining rules but also enabling resources for action. The organization of workers' clocking on and clocking off times is a resource for them
to mutually predict exactly when they come and go and thus a resource for
organizing cooperation. The family rules for getting up, having breakfast,
using the bathroom, and leaving home are important resources for being
able to talk to each other in the morning, to have breakfast, to be able to
wash, and to leave home at the right time. Without the rules they would
not be able to do all these things. The offside rule is a constitutive rule of
the soccer game that constricts the actions of the players; however, an intelligent team explicitly makes use of that rule in order to improve its position
by playing with an offside trap.

Though Giddens usually speaks of rules and resources, he means that
the rules that make up structures also function as resources for action.
Beyond this immediate relationship between rules and resources we can also
say that the distribution of power resources in a social system in the sense
discussed above is part of its structure and a basis of agents' resources. The
capitalist has more power resources than the worker unless the workers form
a strong union. This distribution of power resources is part of the structure
of the economic system.

Giddens distinguishes three types of structure: structural principles,
structures, and structural properties (Giddens, 1984: 185–93). Structural prin-

ciples are principles of organization of societal totalities, like private owner-ship of the means of production in capitalist society. Structures are rule-resources sets, like the capital-labor structure of the economy. Structural properties are institutionalized features of social systems that stretch across time and space, like the degree of concentration of capital in the economy. There is a rising level of abstraction from structural properties to structures and then to structural principles.

Of central importance for Giddens's theory is the process of structura-tion. This means that structures are not predetermined once and for all but made in social praxis. All social praxis starts with a given structure that has emerged from previous praxis, provides an instantiation of that structure in social action, and results in contributing to the continuation or transfor-mation of the structure. This is how the social system that displays this struc-ture and process is reproduced. Because structure is both the medium and the outcome of social praxis, structure has the central feature of duality. It is objective and subjective, constraining and enabling at the same time.

This is the duality of structure. The worker who checks in at 7:00 A.M. at the factory and checks out at 4:30 P.M. relates to a structure that has been established by previous praxis. That is, the workers have always kept to those times. At the same time, they give an instantiation of that structure in their action. Without that instantiation the structure would not exist as part of the present situation of action. And in making this instantiation the work-ers contribute to the continuation of the structure and thereby to the social system of the factory because they continue to maintain their social rela-tions. The clock-on clock-off rule is the medium that is used by the worker in his or her action, and it is the outcome of that action.

The workers may make use of their knowledgeability and deliberate about ways of rationalizing their action with regard to making a living. They may organize a union and demand a shorter working day. They know they will reduce production too much so that there will be enormous losses. Thus, they threaten to go on strike unless the working day is shortened to 7:30 to 4:30 at the same pay as before. If the capitalists give in, social praxis will transform the working-day structure, thereby reproducing the social system because the social relations still continue to exist. What becomes the major transformative force here is the knowledgeability of the agents involved in social praxis.

According to Giddens's understanding of power as the major element of agency, the continuation or transformation of the structures is an out-come of power struggles. However, this is a much too narrow view of social praxis, as we have seen in the above discussion. It does not catch sight of the processes of exchange and negotiation, association and solidarity rela-tionships, and communication and discourse, which exert their own features on the process of structuration. In exchange and negotiation, labor unions and industry may both benefit from continuing or transforming structures and thus work more with incentives than with power in the negotiation process. In an industrial enterprise, union and management may share leadership so that they feel a mutual solidarity and therefore continue with established structures just because they are both committed to them, or they may transform them in order to reinforce this solidarity. Again, the process is different from that of a power struggle. Structures of industrial production may become the object of public discussion. In this case, whether a structure is continued with or transformed depends at least partly on valid reasoning. When public discussion, for example, concentrates on reducing the working week from 40 to 38.5 hours in order to give opportunities for creating new jobs for the unemployed, it is much less a question of power than one of insufficient legitimation that puts the employers on the losing side in trying to maintain the 40-hour week. Because Giddens builds up his theory of structuration from the concept of power as its key term, his theory does not give us adequate access to the complex nature of processes of structuration. It is a very limited theory of structuration, reducing social action to strategic power struggle and closing out any access to negotiative, associative, and communicative aspects of social action.

Institutions

This shortcoming of Giddens's theory of structuration is also apparent in his dealing with institutions and their interrelationships. He distinguishes four major institutional orders of society: (1) symbolic orders/modes of discourse; (2) political institutions; (3) economic institutions; and (4) legal institutions (Giddens, 1984: 28–34). However, he reduces these four to three structures: (1) symbolic orders/modes of discourse to signification, with interpretative schemes as the modality and communication as the type of interaction; (2) political and economic institutions to domination, with facilities as the modality and the execution of power as the form of interaction; (3) legal institutions to legitimation, with norms as the modality and the execution of sanctions as the form of interaction. He conflates the economic and the political sphere in an overall structure of domination based on the execution of power. In doing so he loses any chance of adequately spelling out the distinctive character of economic action and process, praxis and structure. And because he gives domination and power the prominent rank in his theory, he necessarily has to reduce signification and legitimation to domination, whether he wants to do so or not. The very conceptualization of agency and power leaves him no other choice.

There is no way of reaching an intrinsic understanding of the features of the economic sphere, signification, and legitimation in terms of Giddens's theory of structuration, only an understanding of the economic sphere, of signification and legitimation in terms of power. This power bias may provide adequate explanations for cases in which there is such an order of institutions in reality; however, it doesn't provide adequate explanations for cases departing from this type. Nor does the theory provide an adequate understanding of the economic sphere, signification, and legitimation in themselves. In order to gain such insights we can learn much more from theories of economic, normative, and symbolic structuration. What Giddens provides is a restricted theory of political structuration.

Applications

What we have said about Giddens's theory of structuration in general can also be demonstrated with his applications. For example, he is rightly critical of overgeneralized schemes of evolution stressing the fact that historical development depends on many instances of social praxis leading forward, sideways, and backward with no uniform direction (Giddens, 1984: 227–80). However, when he characterizes this praxis, he reduces it to the execution of power, leaving out the effects of processes of exchange and negotiation, association and formation of solidarity, communication and discourse. He also drops the acceptable elements of evolutionary theory because of his preoccupation with making history by human agency. Evolution takes place on the level of symbolic codes by way of the interaction of these codes with social structures mediated via genotypes and phenotypes in social praxis. Giddens fails to conceive of social praxis as an element of the evolution of symbolic codes (not of societies). At least in science we accept such a position as long as we believe that we can make progress in approaching truth. And we also believe so with regard to the moral world. Relating this assumed ability to progress to social praxis is what a contemporary evolutionary theory has to do. This is much less than a formulation of overgeneralized evolutionary schemes but more than reducing history to the struggle for power.

Dealing with T. H. Marshall's (1964/1976) study on the emergence of civil rights in the seventeenth and eighteenth centuries, political rights in the nineteenth and twentieth centuries, and social rights in this century in Britain, he rightly points out that this is not a necessary evolutionary process stepping from one level to the next but a historical process involving steps forward and backward. However, he does so primarily in terms of political struggle and does not address sufficiently the important role played by processes of negotiation, association as citizens, inclusion, and public discourse (Giddens, 1982: 163–80).

Giddens cites a study of Willis's (1977), pointing out how praxis at school instantiates school structure and leads to its continuation and to the continuation of an overall societal structure (Giddens, 1984: 289–309). The school works with an authoritative structure; the group of "lads" is well aware of that structure but "plays" with it, making jokes about the teachers and maintaining indifference. It is their way of instantiating that structure and also of living with that structure. And in their praxis they contribute to the continuation of that very structure as well as to that of the structure at work in which the situation at school is repeated. They learn how to cope with domination that does not provide much reward for them. They make up the mass that is resigned to carrying out dull jobs. In this way, school praxis involving the "lads'" deviant behavior contributes to the continuation of its own structure and an overall societal structure. However, Giddens interprets this praxis by referring to the "lads" only from the point of view of a power game between teachers and pupils, excluding processes of negotiation, association, and communication from explicit consideration.

The same holds true for his interpretation of a study by Ingham (1984) on the reasons why the City of London was able to maintain its outstanding position as a financial center compared to the industrial centers of the country even after the decline of British industry (Giddens, 1984: 319–24). According to Marxist theory, one would have had to predict the decline of the City because of the inevitable ascendancy of industrial capital relative to financial capital in the course of capitalist development. However, the contrary development took place. Ingham's explanation is that the City's position was backed by some fiscal reforms in the early nineteenth century, whereas in the twentieth century it was able to establish itself as a world financial center, the position of which became independent of the fate of British industry. Giddens rightly points out that this study shows that there is no unidirectional evolution as predicted by Marxist theory, and that the supremacy of the City was based on different grounds in the nineteenth and the twentieth centuries. However, his preoccupation with power closes his eyes to the contribution of processes of negotiation, the establishment of trust and reputation, and the communication of reasons to establishing its outstanding position.

Giddens refuses to formulate propositions (Giddens, 1976, 1982: 1–17, 1984: 343–48). His argument is that the knowledgeability and agency of agents based on their power to make a difference countervenes the working of laws, and that praxis is always an historically particular praxis. However, this fact of the historicity of action does not at all preclude that there are at least lawlike processes on an analytical level residing behind the knowledgeable agency of agents. Giddens confuses the concrete unpredictability of historical action with the unpredictability of analytically separated aspects of action. With regard to concrete action, he is right, but not with regard to analytically separated aspects and relationships of action. Thus, we can ask, for example, what raises the *commitment* of an actor to joining with other actors and answer that it is his or her feeling of belongingness to the other actors that raises his or her commitment to joining the other actors' action. This is a *general* statement on an analytically separated relationship between the establishment of a sense of belongingness and the growth of commitment to joining an action. The universal truth of that statement does not imply that actors are unconscious individuals who do nothing but carry out this law. As knowledgeable agents they can get to know about the phenomenon and can resist feeling a sense of belongingness by keeping away from people or can make use of it to establish just that feeling and accompanying commitment in other people. But what the actor cannot do is feel a sense of belongingness and reduce his or her commitment to joining the same people's action. This would be contrary to the theoretical proposition and a falsification of it, giving rise to attempts at formulating a better proposition. Giving up this attempt altogether means leaving the field to the historians. One then has to ask what sociologists should do other than resign from their profession and ask historians to let them enter theirs.

Summary

Giddens is not consistent in refusing to formulate propositions. At least some of his assumptions implicitly work like propositions:

1. Structure is the medium and outcome of social praxis.
2. Structure constrains and enables at the same time.
3. Social praxis involves the agency of agents.
4. Agency is carried out by the application of power.
5. Power is the ability to make a difference in a state of affairs or the course of events.
6. The outcome of social praxis resulting in the continuation or transformation of structures and the reproduction of a social system depends on the amount of power mobilizable for continuation or change: The more power that can be mobilized for a certain feature of social structure, the more it will be realized.
7. Social praxis involves knowledgeable agents.
8. The more social praxis involves the knowledgeability of agents, the higher the rate of transformation of structures.
9. The more allocative or authoritative resources an agent can mobilize, the more he or she will be able to determine the course of social praxis.
10. The more signification and legitimation are backed up by domination, the more lasting effects on the continuation or transformation of structures they will exert.

Critical Assessment

Giddens has provided a remarkable approach to analyzing the continuation and transformation of structures in social praxis involving the process of structuration and the duality of structures. However, what he claims to be revolutionarily new is not as new as he would like to have it. His notion of agency is exactly the same as that formulated by Parsons (1937/1968: 49–50) in 1937. His notion of the duality of structure is exactly the same as introduced by the major classics in sociology. Weber (1922/1972c) centered his work around the interrelationship of ideas and interests, culture, and social structure mediated in social action; this is duality of structure. Simmel (1914/1926) worked on the dialectics of subjective and objective culture; this is duality of structure. Durkheim (1914/1970, 1924/1974) made the concomitant exteriority and interiority of the moral fact a central statement of his mature position; this is duality of structure. Parsons (Parsons and Platt, 1973) made the interpenetration of the cultural system, the social system, the personality system, and the behavioral system a central statement of his mature position. This is duality of structure. Mead (1934) made the interplay of "I" and "Me" a central statement of his mature position. This is duality of structure.

What we owe to Giddens is not a revolutionary new synthesis of objectivism and subjectivism but a nice reformulation of traditional attempts at overcoming this schism. However, his reformulation is biased toward a preoccupation with power. Thus, he also has to conceive of the relationship between objective structure and subjective consciousness in strategic terms, closing out a communicative approach to this phenomenon. Established structures can only play a role as constraints or resources. They are not something on which actors can enter a discourse, thus debating the rights or wrongs of established structures according to the rules of discourse. Establishing a discourse on structures implies validating or refuting the rules lying behind them. Discourse on the working day turns an external structure into a valid or nonvalid rule. This is a liberation from structural constraint that is completely different from making the best of structural resources in a power game (see Archer, 1988).

Giddens makes much of the knowledgeability of agents, but he misses the very core of knowledgeability: discourse. What he analyzes as discursive conciousness does not reach the level of discourse in its true sense. When he speaks of discourse, it must, according to the structure of his theory, be an intellectual power game. This is also why he cannot truly formulate a critical theory, though he wants to do so. Such an attempt needs a sophisticated theory of discourse centering around discourse itself. Giddens has no such theory, and he has not learned enough from Habermas. Therefore, he is not able to take up Habermas's theory of discourse as an element of his own approach.

Related Theory and Research: Conflict Theory and Historical Sociology

The role of violence and power in historical development became a very common concern of sociologists who had turned to historical analysis well before Giddens focused the attention of theory building on that phenomenon. The reason for this affinity between conflict theory and historical sociology is the fact that major historical transformations in a relatively short time, occurring in their extreme form as revolutions, make the power struggle between groups the dominant feature of society. Because this is indeed so, it is by no means wrong to begin the analysis with studying the structure of interests, power positions, and interrelationships of the relevant political groups.

The most widely received study of this kind of structuralist conflict theory is Barrington Moore's (1966) work on the conditions under which revolutions lead to democracy, socialism, or authoritarian rule. He distinguishes five classes, determines their interests in democracy or authoritarianism as forms of government, and then looks at their constellation. The bourgeoisie's first choice is democracy; its second choice is authoritarianism if there are threats to its ruling position. The landowners' first choice is authoritarianism; their second choice is democracy in case of threats to their ruling position by the governmental bureaucracy. The government bureaucrats' first choice is authoritarianism; their second choice is socialism. The peasants are mobilized only to a small extent and may join revolutionary movements; they tend toward the weak parts of the capitalist class. The industrial workers favor either democracy or socialism.

Moore distinguishes three basic constellations leading to democracy, socialism, or authoritarian rule. The British constellation led to democracy, with the landowners driving the peasants off the land to form the working class, becoming agricultural capitalists and joining the bourgeoisie in the struggle with the Crown and governmental bureaucracy. This favored the choices for democracy, later on allowing the workers to choose the reformist path to their rights within democracy. The Chinese constellation (which was also present in France in a slightly different form) led to socialism. Here the landowners became *rentiers* and exerted pressure on the peasants, who were also under the pressure of the market. This mobilized the peasants and resulted in the revolutionary path to socialism. The Russian/Japanese constellation has the landowners producing for the market but holding the peasants on the land and exploiting them as much as possible. They join the governmental bureaucracy, which sustains the forces for authoritarian rule.

Theda Skocpol (1979) has provided an explanation of when revolutions break out, working alongside Moore's approach. She distinguishes three basic classes: the property-owning class, the producing class, and the state bureaucracy. Whereas political revolutions change only the type of government, social revolutions involve a power struggle between those three classes. They occur when the state class has been weakened by military defeat or by excessive military expenditure and then tries to extract more resources from the property-owning class. When the resulting conflict between these two classes converges with peasant revolt we have the constellation for a revolution. Skocpol's examples for proving this theory are the French, Russian, and Chinese revolutions. Because there are no longer peasants in a sufficient number to form a powerful class in advanced industrial societies, Skocpol expects that there will be no more revolutions but only parliamentary reforms.

There is no doubt that revolution primarily involves a power struggle. Thus far, Moore's and Skocpol's approaches are right. However, they turn out to be too limited in their scope when they attempt to formulate a general theory of the occurrence or outcome of revolutions by generalizing from a handful of historical cases. There are hundreds of factors that can enter the constellations of interests and power, from the number of estates, classes, strata, and other groups and factions within them, going much beyond Moore's and Skocpol's selection of classes, to factors like strength of organization, leadership, strategies in applying power, and so on. Taking into account those factors immediately connected to the power struggle renders the model so complex that it is impossible to formulate generalizations of the type put forward in Moore's and Skocpol's analyses. The picture becomes much more complex, though, when we examine other factors. For example, how was the legitimacy of the established classes undermined by cultural criticism? How much more were rising classes capable of founding their claims on legitimate grounds than the thus far established classes? Why did new coalitions between classes occur and old ones break? How did the distribution of resources between classes change according to economic transformations? These are questions that cannot be answered with the tools of conflict theory and need applications of theories of legitimation, solidarity structures, and economic transactions. There is no systematic access in Moore's and Skocpol's theories to such important questions. It is, for example, a mistake to play down the role of the bourgeoisie and its intellectual leaders in explaining the French Revolution as much as this is done in the Moore-Skocpol theory. Taking into account the factors mentioned makes the model even more complex. This demonstrates that it is impossible to find general theory on the level of historical concreteness as Moore and Skocpol seek to do. This is the level on which historical study of the concrete cases with special sensitivity to the very concrete circumstances on the levels of economics, politics, solidarity structures, and legitimation is required. We can *apply* general theory to explaining various aspects of revolutions, but we cannot *derive* theory from a handful of historical cases.

Mixing the positivistic search for empirical generalization with historical study tends to result in limitations of both theory and history at the same time. As theory, this type of analysis makes the error of generalizing from a handful of facts and never reaching the proper level of analytical abstraction that is the only one where generalization is possible. As historical study, this type of analysis constricts the view of the historical events to such a degree that it provides no sufficient explanation, because it leaves out too many of the interesting elements. Though the limitation of such sociological approaches to history are apparent, they have become a growing branch of academic study in recent years. A well-received work of this type, for example, is Perry Anderson's *Passages from Antiquity to Feudalism* (Anderson, 1974). The studies of Michael Mann (1986) have also attracted much attention. He demonstrates the role power played throughout historical development from tribal societies to the modern state. For example, he argues that the modern state developed on the basis of monopolizing military power. There is certainly no doubt that power plays a central role in historical transformations. However, to step beyond such an undebated statement to reducing the whole history of human societies to power struggles would set too narrow limits for sociological analysis. Historical sociology needs the application of better theory. Power does not explain anything more than the aspect of enforcement of action. But how about its variation because of economic change, its structuration because of solidarity relationships, and its legitimation because of cultural developments and all their various subdimensions? Historical sociology in terms of power-conflict theory cannot tell us anything about these aspects of historical development.

ELEVEN

FROM STATE MONOPOLY OF PHYSICAL FORCE TO SELF-CONSTRAINT: NORBERT ELIAS'S FIGURATION THEORY OF THE CIVILIZING PROCESS

IN 1939, the German sociologist Norbert Elias published a book entitled *Über den Prozeß der Zivilisation* (*The Civilizing Process*), which turned out to have a remarkable fate. The author had to emigrate from Nazi Germany like so many of his colleagues, and the intellectual milieu that would have supported the book broke down. Thus, it was not recognized for a long time. However, thirty years later, in the late 1960s, the book suddenly attracted the attention of intellectuals in West Germany, Great Britain, and The Netherlands (Mennell, 1989, 1990; Goudsblom, Jones, and Mennell, 1989). After this late reception, Elias's work became part of sociological discourse well beyond the boundaries of West Germany, Great Britain, and The Netherlands. This late reception of Elias' work on the civilizing process is the reason why we deal with it in the context of developments since the 1960s even though the first edition of the book appeared in 1939.

Elias's (1939/1976) study points out that the rise of modern society and its further development is characterized by a specific feature: the disappearance of physical force from everyday interaction between people and the growing affect control, self-control, and self-restraint of the individual. This is the essential feature of the civilizing process in Elias's view. He confirms his thesis by the displacement of physical force from everyday interaction, by the refinement of table manners, and by the narrowing of modesty boundaries that took place in the historical change from the life of the medieval knights to court life in the time of rising absolutism. Elias's case for demonstrating this transformation is the establishment of absolutism and refined court life by Louis XIV in seventeenth-century France, attracting the whole aristocracy to the central court in Versailles. In this process, the originally self-equipped warrior became a dependent courtier at the king's court. These are the historical facts described by Elias with a variety of examples from the lives of the earlier knights and the later courtiers. These descriptions make Elias's study particularly appealing. It is history on the level of everyday life.

However, Elias does not confine his study to the description of historical changes in everyday life. He aims to do more. He takes the described facts as instances of a more deep seated historical transformation in social life, which he calls "the civilizing process." In this process, the application of physical force in everyday interaction and the uncontrolled acting out of feelings and aggressions is increasingly replaced by self-control rooted in self-restraint. Elias takes the stronger self-discipline of the courtier in matters of physical force, affects, table manners, and modesty compared to the medieval knight as an instance of that more deep seated and broader historical transformation toward increasing self-restraint.

Furthermore, Elias not only claims a broader and more deep seated historical transformation for the change from the medieval knight to the courtier during the time of absolutism but also tries to find a theoretical explanation of this historical transformation by building a theory of the civilizing process. The theory concentrates on the figuration of powers and their effects on individual action and societal development. This is why Elias's approach is called a sociology of figuration.

The Theory of the Civilizing Process

The theory of the civilizing process can be summarized in the following statements (Elias, 1939/1976, volume 2: 312–454; for translation, see 1978a):

1. The more the competition for power between rivaling groups in society sharpens, the more a selection will take place, leading to the survival of winners and to the extinction of losers.
2. The more competitors in societal struggles for power can rely on earlier success, the more chances they will have to emerge as winners from further struggles, thus eliminating from the scene a growing number of rivals and finally leading to the establishment of a monopoly on power by one superior authority.
3. The more a monopoly of power has been established by one superior authority, the more a territory originally divided into different principalities becomes united into one kingdom.
4. The larger a kingdom with a unitary rule grows, the more the coexistence of multifunctional small power systems will be replaced by one centralized power system with a functional differentiation of subsystems specialized in the fulfillment of specific functions and the more social interaction will expand in territorial scope.

5. The more power is monopolized by one superior authority that controls a larger territory, the more physical force will retreat from the everyday interaction between people and the more interaction will be controlled by the statute laws passed by the central authority.

6. The more systems are functionally differentiated within a larger system and the more actions expand within this system, the more the interdependence between subsystems and actions will grow, and the longer chains of actions will become.

7. The longer chains of actions grow, the larger will be the scope of effects in space and time resulting from one single action and the greater will be the number of reactions provoked by that action.

8. The larger the scope of effects resulting from one single action and the greater the number of reactions by other actors, the more success in attaining goals will be achieved by the actors who calculate the effects and reactions resulting from their actions more precisely, who exert a stronger self-restraint than others, and who give less room to acting out affects spontaneously.

9. The more actors direct their actions not only after being confronted with the reactions of others but also according to their calculation of others' reactions in advance, the more external constraint will be transformed into self-restraint.

10. The greater the number of actors and strata included in the system of interdependent actions, the greater will be the number of actors and strata that will learn to control their affects by self-restraint.

11. The more prestigious are the actors who represent the avant-garde when it comes to controlling their affects by self-restraint, the more easily the model of the affect-controlled self-restraining human individual will be diffused throughout every stratum of society by imitation.

Application of the Theory

In applying his theory to the historical facts, Elias points out that the monopolization of physical force by establishing the rule of absolutism in seventeenth-century France set in motion the processes predicted by his interrelated set of theoretical assumptions leading to an ever finer control of affects by the individual's self-restraint. His paramount type of the self-disciplined individual who controls his or her affects is the courtier living at the central court in Versailles. The further diffusion of this affect control by self-restraint is carried on by the inclusion of ever broader strata in the system of interdependent actions and by the leading role of the aristocracy in matters of life-style. The aristocratic affect control becomes the role model for the rising bourgeoisie, which tries to imitate the distinction of aristocratic life.

Critical Assessment

Elias's theory of the civilizing process can easily be recognized as basically a conflict theory of social development. The struggle for power is the major force that eventually leads to the establishment of the power monopoly of a central authority, which then establishes its rule over a larger territory and replaces the coexistence of a plurality of autonomous multifunctional systems by one functionally differentiated system. The growing interdependence of actions within this system confronts each individual with a greater number of reactions. Because the individual actor no longer has as much power at his or her disposal as would be necessary to control all possible reactions from others, he or she has no other option than to calculate the possible reactions of others in advance in order to reach his or her goals. Successful performance needs affect control by self-restraint under these conditions. The power to react to his or her actions on the part of a multitude of other actors forces the individual to control his or her affects by self-restraint. External constraint based on multiple sources of power becomes transformed into the internal constraint of the rational actor.

This is a positivistic conflict theory of establishing self-restraint, because the source of this self-restraint is power located in external conditions. The social order that comes about in the interaction of self-controlled actors is caused by external conditions. Actors who are adapted to these conditions may emerge in two ways. Either they are selected unintentionally by those conditions via the survival of the self-controlled and extinction of the uncontrolled, or they learn to adapt rationally to those conditions. Both explanations of self-restraint and the corresponding social order are positivistic in character, because they do not address the problem of internalization of social control in terms of identification and/or communication. Only Elias's final and supplementary hypothesis on the diffusion of the aristocratic role model introduces an element of identification. However, his explanation of the establishment of affect control, long-term rational calculation of interdependencies, and self-restraint from proposition 1 to 10 is strictly couched in terms of a positivistic conflict theory.

Elias's theory adequately points out the results of competition in the establishment of power monopolies, which subject ever larger territories to one rule, replace the coexistence of a plurality of small autonomous multifunctional systems by one larger functionally differentiated system, and enormously increase the interdependence of actions, making affect control, rational calculation, and self-restraint the only adequate means of successful action. The theory adequately demonstrates a sequence of processes resulting from power competition in society inasmuch as actions are guided by nothing but the attainment of goals by the application of power or by the submission to superior external power. It does indeed explain the part that is played by external constraint in establishing affect control and internal constraint.

However, the theory does not give a sufficiently complete explanation of what we call self-control. It has nothing to say about the associational and communicative foundations of self-control, nothing about the establishment of moral responsibility and autonomy as fundamental aspects of self-control. The moral part of self-control is completely out of range for Elias's theory of transforming societal constraint into self-restraint. In Elias's view, self-control becomes restricted to the elements of intelligent adaptation to varying situations based on trial-and-error learning and affect-control based on self-restraint. There are, however, other elements of moral obligation based on the attachment to groups and commitment to their norms and of autonomy based on discourse and reflection. Elias's theory of the evolution of self-control is much too mechanistic in character to provide a sufficient explanation. For a full understanding of the evolution of self-control we would have to turn to the theories provided by authors like Durkheim, Simmel, Mead, Piaget, Kohlberg, and Parsons. The questions of moral learning, moral constraint, moral universalization, and moral autonomy are left unanswered by Elias's positivistic conflict theory on the evolution of affect control and self-restraint in the civilizing process.

With the deficiencies of Elias's theory come major faults in his historical account of the civilizing process. First, it is rather an arbitrary decision to view the change from the relatively rough life of the European medieval knight to the refined manners of the courtier as the major transformation from premodern and less civilized societies to modern civilized societies. The European medieval knight's manners and weak control of affects are manners warriors of all historical times have had, just as the manners of the courtier are also manners of all historical times reaching much farther back in history than the time of European absolutism.

Second, Elias's theory does not completely apply to the situation of the courtier, because the latter lives in a small circle and is not confronted with long chains of interdependent actions. His or her modesty and table manners are controlled by the permanent presence of others within a closed circle.

Third, in order to demonstrate the effects of long chains of interdependent actions on self-control, Elias would have had to study the transformations that occurred with the monopolization of power in the establishment of contract relationships and associated legal institutions for controlling economic life, and the corresponding fidelity in contract relationships. In doing so, he would have had to join Durkheim's program of studying the transformation from mechanical to organic solidarity with the growing division of labor. He would also have had to recognize Durkheim's insight that the moral aspect of self-control in organic society does not simply spring from growing factual interdependence but only from growing associational commitment.

Fourth, Elias wrongly takes the modesty and table manners of the aristocratic courtier to be the prototype of the self-controlled individual in modern times. However, there is no pathway from modesty and table manners to the self-control of the modern human individual in terms of moral self-responsibility, moral autonomy, moral universalism, and moral learning. The historical roots of this type of moral consciousness have to be sought in the idea of morality as it emerged in Judeo-Christian religion from ancient Judaism to Calvinism and to the modern secular morality formulated by the Enlightenment philosophers. In terms of social strata its roots have to be revealed in the Puritan saints and in the self-employed and self-responsible strata of the rising bourgeoisie in seventeenth-century England and America.

The self-control of the modern individual does not show up in table manners and modesty but in self-responsibility along with moral autonomy, moral universalism, and moral learning. Table manners and modesty are superficial elements of behavior compared to those elements of moral consciousness, which do not change with the superficial change of manners. They place high moral standards on the individual and open chances for extraordinary moral conduct and also for moral failure. The highest forms of devotion to justice all over the world stand next to fearless egotism, narcissistic self-love, self-realization for its own sake, and moral absolutism, which may even justify terrorism. There is often only a very small distance between morally grounded self-responsibility and its perversions; sometimes they are interconnected. This is a fundamental and unresolvable dilemma of modern moral self-responsibility of which nothing is revealed, let alone explained, in the perspective of Elias's much too positivistic theory of evolving self-control. To do this, Elias would have had to join Max Weber's historical comparative studies on the evolution of moral consciousness from ancient Judaism to ascetic Protestantism.

Further and Related Work

Elias has extended his work beyond his study of the civilizing process, keeping in line with his general approach and applying it to a variety of subjects (Elias, 1969, 1970, 1986, 1987, 1990; for translation, see 1978b). A number of scholars have begun to study his work and to carry it on to further projects (Gleichmann, Goudsblom and Korte, 1979; Mennell, 1989, 1990; Goudsblom, Jones and Mennell, 1989).

PART FOUR

The Symbolics of Social Action

>

THEORIES OF DEVIANCE LABELING: HOWARD S. BECKER, EDWIN M. LEMERT, RICHARD QUINNEY, AND EDWIN M. SCHUR

ONE OF the most successful applications of symbolic interactionism was developed in studies of deviant behavior. In the perspective of symbolic interactionism, such behavior is not taken as an objective fact but as being socially defined in processes where it is labeled as deviant. This is often said to work as a self-fulfilling prophecy in that it places a person who is labeled as deviant on the path to a "deviant career." In order to get an idea of the merits of symbolic interactionism in explaining deviant careers we will look at the contributions of Howard S. Becker, Edwin M. Lemert, Richard Quinney, and Edwin M. Schur.

The Career of the Deviant: Howard S. Becker

In his study on outsiders, Howard S. Becker (1963) paved the way for conceiving deviant behavior in terms of a career that has a sequence and in which being labeled as deviant contributes a vital part. Becker first emphasizes the socially defined character of being deviant or of being an outsider. Different people can label behavior as deviant and people as outsiders differently. What is deviant from the standpoint of one group can be conforming from the standpoint of another group. A deviant act or being an outsider is seen as breaking a rule of a group that is in the position of defining rules of proper behavior. It is breaking such rules that makes a person an outsider. But from another point of view, one could also define one's judges as outsiders if one only had the power to define the rules. It is not the single person who makes the rules but the group unisonous, by majority or by a ruling minority. Rules may have the character of formally enacted law that is enforced by the sanctioning power of the state. Or they may represent informal agreements that are enforced by informal sanctions.

With this conception of deviance in mind, Becker rejects various other definitions as inadequate:

- anything that varies too widely from the average behavior of people;
- a pathological state, a disease; or
- behavior that has dysfunctional effects on society.

Rather than using one of these definitions, Becker proposes to define as deviant such behavior that fails to obey group rules and is therefore labeled as deviant by the group. This definition of deviance allows us to see that deviance is doubly constituted: by a group's rules being broken and by the group's actions of labeling an action as deviant.

The process of labeling is by no means infallible. How other people respond to a given act and the degree to which they label it as deviant vary greatly. There are occasional drives against specific kinds of deviance; people are treated differently according to class, race, ethnicity, gender, and other criteria; some rules are enforced only when breaking these rules has consequences; these, however, are not properly observed.

Modern society is not uniform in character but composed of different groups that prefer different rules and define deviant behavior differently. Those groups whose social position gives them weapons and power are best able to enforce their values.

The double constitution of deviant behavior by the person who commits an act and the persons who label it as deviant allows us to differentiate between four types of behavior:

1. Behavior that is rule obedient but perceived as deviant. This is falsely accused behavior.
2. Behavior that is rule obedient and not perceived as deviant. This is conforming behavior.
3. Behavior that is rule breaking and perceived as deviant. This is pure deviant behavior.
4. Behavior that is rule breaking but not perceived as deviant. This is secret deviant behavior.

Deviance is not simply a consequence of simultaneously working causes. Rather, it is produced by causes that operate at different stages in a sequence of deviant behavior. For example, the drug addict must first have drugs available, then has to experiment with them, and then has to continue using them. With this sequential understanding of deviant behavior in mind, Becker introduces the model of a deviant career. This means that a person does not become an outsider instantly but becomes involved in a deviant career step-by-step. The earlier the stage one has reached in such a career, the more opportunities there will be for continuing to deviate *and* for returning to conforming behavior. The later the stage, the fewer opportunities for conforming behavior remain and the more opportunities for deviance open up. There is a growing commitment to deviance as the deviant career progresses.

The beginning of a deviant career is marked by the individual's committal of a nonconforming act, which can result from different causes: innocence, experimentation, participation in gang behavior, or opposition to authority. If the person is highly involved in a conventional career and has established a reputation in such a career, he or she is drawn back to norm conformity by his or her own intention of maintaining such an identity and by the reactions of others who count the nonconforming act as occasioned by specific circumstances. These are forces that hold the person on the path of a conventional career. However, the more a person lacks such an involvement in a conventional career, the less he or she has to lose and the more his or her behavior will be treated as durably deviant.

Furthermore, as the individual moves progressively farther into deviance, this behavior needs to be justified in order to settle the conflict between the commitment to conventional norms and the violation of these norms in his or her behavior. Such justifications enhance the person's ability to live with deviation from conventional norms. Becker refers here to the techniques of neutralization introduced by Sykes and Matza (1957): denying one's responsibility for an action, downgrading the harm produced by the deviant act, conceiving an act as not wrong in the light of the circumstances in which it is committed, condemning one's condemnors, loyalty to the smaller group, definition of an act as legitimate.

The next step in a deviant career is learning deviant motives, interests, pleasures, and vocabularies, which occurs in social relationships.

Being caught and publicly labeled as deviant is a most crucial step in a deviant career. Now the individual moves from being a person who has committed some nonconforming act to a person who *is* deviant. He or she acquires a deviant identity. The more other people see a person as a deviant, the more being a deviant will become a so-called master status trait that is perceived as connected with secondary auxiliary traits. Whatever one does and whatever one is, it is treated as dependent on one's master status as a deviant.

A further decisive step is being cut off from conventional life. There are then no social forces that draw the person back to conforming life. He or she is then drawn more and more to organized deviant groups. The person who becomes a regular member of such a group gets support from that group and learns still more deviant motives, techniques, and rationalizations of deviant behavior.

Summary

When a person commits a nonconforming act, he or she will step into a deviant career sequentially the less the person is involved in a conventional career, the more he or she can make use of techniques of neutralization, the more he or she learns deviant motives, interests, pleasures, and vocabularies, the more he or she experiences being caught and publicly labeled as deviant and having a deviant identity, the more being deviant becomes a master trait and everything else an auxiliary trait to that, the more he or she is cut off from conventional groups and life, and the more he or she becomes a regular member of an organized deviant group.

Secondary Deviation: Edwin M. Lemert

Edwin M. Lemert (1972) introduced the notion of secondary deviation in dealing with the process of labeling behavior as deviant. He takes primary deviation to be an initial act that violates the rules of a group or wider society. This act may provoke two different types of response. There may be responses that contribute to normalization, that is, to bringing the deviant back to the conventional ways of life. There may, however, be responses that contribute to stigmatization, that is, to attributing traits to the deviant that make him or her an outsider, someone who has a special stigma that makes him or her different compared to conventional people.

When such stigmatization has set in, the deviant has to cope with this situation; he or she has to respond to the other people's response to his or her primary deviation. This response of the deviant is what Lemert calls secondary deviation. The responses of other people to primary deviation apart from stigmatization may include punishment, segregation, and social control, such as imprisonment. These reactions by other people create problems for the primary deviant person that call forth attempts to solve them. The life and identity of the deviant become organized around the facts of his or her deviance. The less the deviant is capable of dealing with his or her deviance in ways that bring him or her back into normal life, the more likely the person's activities of coping with the new situation will lead him or her even farther away from conventional life and identity. The stigma of the deviant will be created, maintained, or intensified. The result is a loss of control leading to hopelessness. Whatever the deviant person does, his or her stigma as a deviant will be confirmed. There is finally no way out.

Several factors lead a person along the path to secondary deviation. The person may first drift into primary deviance. Then the societal reaction sets in. The less it leaves open any way of returning to a conventional identity and the more it establishes a stigma, the more the person will drift into secondary deviation. This is particularly true when the societal reaction to primary deviance generates a sense of injustice, of not having been fairly treated.

The process of social control that sets in after primary deviance contributes to leading a person into secondary deviance. The person is treated in a way that gives him or her a morally inferior status; he or she acquires special knowledge and skills in order to cope with control, which again involve deviant behavior; he or she establishes an integral attitude and world-view of the deviant, perceiving the world in terms of an outsider; he or she learns to live with a distinctive self-image of a deviant person; finally, the person reaches a stage in his or her career as a deviant that establishes him or her as a deviant person once and for all. The person has then reached the point of no return in his or her deviant career.

After first merely drifting into secondary deviance, a person then learns to play the role of the secondary deviant. Various factors contribute to playing that role with more or less success: (a) the clarity of definitions of deviant roles, (b) attributes, knowledge, and skills to enact, improvise, and invent deviant roles, and (c) being motivated to play the role of the deviant, which very often comes with success in playing that role.

The more a person has drifted into secondary deviance and the more successfully he or she plays the role of the deviant, the more deviance will become the most effective behavior in satisfying the person's needs: (1) defining oneself as deviant then becomes instrumental in seeking out means of satisfying needs and of mitigating stigmatization; (2) the value hierarchy of the deviant who then is a degraded person changes; he or she turns down conventional approval and overstates disapproval by his or her hated enemies; (3) what is immediately attainable receives primacy over any long-term career plans; changing one's deviant status would involve too much effort and too many costs, and would be almost impossible to achieve. Thus, it is more beneficial to stick with one's deviant identity.

In very extreme cases, secondary deviation involves a disposition to engage in self-defeating behavior. The person has acquired a totally negative self-image and engages in deviant behavior that contributes to maintaining this negative self-image.

Summary

The more the societal response to primary deviance involves stigmatization, punishment, segregation, and social control that shut off paths back to normalization, arouse a sense of injustice in the deviant, give him or her a morally inferior status, provoke the learning of special knowledge and skills of deviance, establish an integral deviant attitude and world-view and a distinctive self-image as a deviant, lead to a point of no return, contribute to playing the role of the deviant by way of clarity of role definitions, attributes, skills, and knowledge to enact, improvise, and invent roles, and motivate him or her to play the role, then the more deviation will become the most effective behavior; the person defining him- or herself as deviant is instrumental in seeking out means of satisfying needs and mitigating stigmatization, changing his or her value hierarchy, orienting the person to what is immediately attainable, making any change of the deviant status too costly, and leading to self-defeating behavior.

Labeling Deviance and Class Conflict: Richard Quinney

In the 1970s, labeling theory made a turn toward interpreting the labeling process in terms of conflicts between groups. In this way labeling theory became a conflict theory of symbolic processes of labeling. For an example of this turn we can take Richard Quinney's (1970: 15–25) approach to labeling as conflict between groups. Quinney presents his theory in six basic propositions:

1. Crime is a definition of human conduct that is created by authorized agents in a politically organized society. (P. 15)
2.1. Criminal definitions describe behaviors that conflict with the interests of the segments of society that have the power to shape public policy. (P. 16)
2.2. The greater the conflict in interests between the segments of a society, the greater the probability that the power segments will formulate criminal definitions. (P. 17)
3.1. Criminal definitions are applied by the segments of society that have the power to shape the enforcement and administration of criminal law. (P. 18)
3.2. The probability that criminal definitions will be applied varies according to the extent to which the behaviors of the powerless conflict with the interests of the power segments. (P. 18)
3.3. The probability that criminal definitions will be applied is influenced by such community and organizational factors as (1) community expectations of law-enforcement and administration, (2) the visibility and public reporting of offenses, (3) the occupational organization, ideology, and actions of the legal agents to whom the authority to enforce and administer criminal law is delegated. (P. 19–20)
4.1. Behavior patterns are structured in segmentally organized society in relation to criminal definitions, and within this context persons engage in actions that have different relative probabilities of being defined as criminal. (P. 20)
4.2. The probability that a person will develop action patterns that have a high potential of being defined as criminal depends on the relative substance of (1) structured opportunities, (2) learning experiences, (3) interpersonal associations and identifications, (4) self-conceptions. (P. 21)

5. Conceptions of crime are constructed and diffused in the segments of society by various means of communication. (P. 22)
6. The social reality of crime is constructed by the formulation and application of criminal definitions, the development of behavior patterns related to criminal definitions, and the construction of criminal conceptions. (P. 23)

This final proposition is a summary of Quinney's model of the social reality of crime.

Quinney (1973) uses this conflict-theoretical turn in symbolic interactionist labeling theory to present a Marxist approach to explaining crime control in capitalist society. He starts by distinguishing four approaches to studying legal order and deviant behavior:

1. Positivism looks at facts as they appear to be.
2. Social constructionism sees facts as a result of social construction.
3. Phenomenology looks for the essence of things underlying their appearance.
4. Critical philosophy criticizes the real from the point of view of the valued possible.

The latter expands on the insights of the first three approaches and can be seen as their completion. Quinney's analysis of crime control in capitalist society can be broken down into six statements:

1. Capitalism divides society into a ruling class and a ruled class.
2. The ruling class uses the state to serve its interests: maintaining capitalism.
3. Criminal law is the state's and ruling class's means of maintaining the existing economic and social order.
4. The institutions of crime control serve the enforcement of criminal law and thereby the maintenance of capitalist society.
5. The contradictions of advanced capitalism require the oppression of the subordinate classes through the coercion and violence of the legal system.
6. Only the collapse of capitalist society and the establishment of a socialist society will solve the crime problem.

Labeling as Political Struggle: Edwin M. Schur

Quinney's Marxist approach represents a rather simplifying turn of labeling theory from symbolic interactionism to a Marxist conflict theory that was very *en vogue* in the 1970s. In the 1980s, however, more variation and sophistication was again introduced in labeling theory, while the basic approach of what we can call conflict symbolic interactionism was maintained. The work of Edwin M. Schur (1980) represents this kind of labeling theory. He sees processes in which behavior is defined as deviant as a political struggle between a variety of groups, not simply between a ruling and a ruled class. We can summarize his approach in the following statements:

General Assumptions

1. What is defined as deviant is the outcome of political struggle and gives rise to further political struggles.
2. The political struggle cannot be simplified to a conflict between a ruling class and a ruled class. It involves many groups, factions, coalitions, and movements with different interests, views, and values, and also ambiguous and multiple interests.
3. Definitions of deviance reflect and determine configurations of power.
4. Defining deviance is a stigma contest.
5. The deviantizing process is self-fulfilling in character: self-fulfilling stigmatization and self-fulfilling fear of crime in the community.
6. Deviantizing is a collective definition of what is deviant and involves (a) moral crusades by moral entrepreneurs, (b) a perceived threat, and (c) politicization.
7. Deviantizing takes place on the following levels: (1) the micropolitics of deviance: (a) intrinsic and (b) situated; (2) the institutional politics of deviance; (a) general, (b) organizational, and (c) professional; and (3) the collective politics of deviance: (a) conceptual and (b) official. (Schur, 1980: 27)
8. The politics of deviance involves social change.

Case Studies

Psychiatry and Mental Illness

1. Mental illness had been taken as a matter of fact for a long time: a deviation from normality.
2. Psychiatric definitions of mental illness are not intrinsically psychiatric but very much the outcome of social norms.
3. Psychiatric treatment has established close social control of mental patients.
4. Psychiatric treatment has been less a help for the individual but much more an agent of society's social control.
5. In the 1960s and 1970s, psychiatry came under attack.
6. A social movement aiming at liberating mental patients became established.

7. This social movement met with the interests of the tax-cutting movement to reduce the costs of maintaining social welfare institutions.
8. Mental illness was redefined. Many people who had been in mental hospitals were sent home or to the streets to join the homeless people.

The Abortion Conflict

1. Abortion had been defined as a violation of criminal law for a long time, except in cases of danger to the mother's life.
2. This led on the one hand to a practice of close control in hospitals, the board system, but on the other hand to a widespread black market.
3. On the black market, poor women were disadvantaged.
4. Beginning with criticism in the 1950s, a movement for changing abortion law became established in the 1960s.
5. The issues became politicized and involved a stigma contest between pro-abortionists ("pro-choicers") and anti-abortionists ("pro-lifers").
6. A Supreme Court decision in 1973 changed the situation in favor of liberating abortion.
7. However, the battle between pro-choicers and pro-lifers is still not settled. The former fight for the basic rights of women, the latter for the rights of the unborn child.
8. Each party makes use of techniques of stigmatization, saying that the other party has no respect for the rights of women (the "fetal container" accusation) or no respect for the rights of the unborn (the "infanticide" accusation).

Critical Assessment

Studies in labeling deviance are some of the most convincing applications of symbolic interactionism. They point out clearly and dramatically how social definitions of the situation play a part in making reality. Howard Becker's study on outsiders has become a classical sociological study that paved the way for a whole series of further investigations into the processes of labeling behavior as deviant. We clearly learn to understand the power of defining situations and behavior and its self-fulfilling effects on further behavior. However, we would like to know more precisely how different social conditions result in different forms of labeling. We would like to know how closed communities exert constraint on defining behavior in a uniform way, how the power to define allows certain agents of society to enforce certain very selective definitions, how struggles over defining situations and behavior bring about a rapid change of definitions, and how discourse allows only legitimate definitions of situations and behaviors to be accepted generally. The development of labeling theory first moved toward a simplistic conflict interpretation of the labeling process in the 1970s and then to a more sophisticated conflict interpretation in the 1980s. However, conflict is not the only element that is involved in processes of symbolic definitions of situations. First there is the communicative process itself with its roots in discourse, then the association of people, then their mutual adaptation, and finally their conflict and competition. Also present is the institutional framework within which these processes take place. We need more elaboration of these features in a systematic approach in order to attain a more complete understanding of the labeling process.

THIRTEEN

NEGOTIATED ORDER: ANSELM STRAUSS

WE HAVE seen that Herbert Blumer's paradigm of symbolic interactionism tends toward conceiving of social interaction in general and of communication in particular as a process of negotiation. Anselm Strauss (1978) has put negotiation at the center of his symbolic interactionist approach to studying social action and order. What he propagates is a negotiated order approach to studying social organization. This negotiated order approach has been formulated by Strauss and his colleagues who share his perspective as an opposing approach to the deterministic view of social order and structure (see also Strauss, 1959; Strauss et al., 1963, 1964; Glaser and Strauss, 1965, 1967). According to the deterministic view, social order and social structure, like the organizational structure of an industrial firm, is a social fact that exists independently of the individual members and exerts its constraint on individuals' actions. The individual members must comply with the rules imposed on them by the existing order or find a way to cope with them in secondary adjustments, or else deviate from them at the cost of being punished, unless they can conceal the deviation. Seen in this way, even a deterministic approach to the relationship between social order and individual action not only allows for strict compliance with the existing order in individual action but also allows for ways of coping with the order and of deviating from its rules. However, what is not covered by the deterministic view — according to Strauss's assessment — is the change of that order by individual action, particularly by processes of social interaction and negotiation.

According to Strauss's criticism, even Goffman's view of social order does not provide sufficient insight into the processes of change, though Goffman's view gives room to the individual's strategies and tactics in order to make the best of an existing order for the individual's interests. In his analysis of total institutions, Goffman demonstrates how inmates apply specific strategies and tactics in order to adjust to the institution in a way that allows them to maintain a minimal degree of freedom. However, as Strauss (1978: 31–38) criticizes, neither the personnel nor the patients can change the order itself. Goffman describes comprehensively the various primary and secondary strategies and tactics used by personnel and inmates to adjust to the established order of the total institution of a mental hospital. He reveals the "underlife" of the total institution, but (as Strauss criticizes) he does not reveal the processes that lead to change in the institution's social order. There may be a great deal of deviance from the official order, but Goffman does not show when and how this official order changes. Personnel and inmates are engaged in individual strategies and tactics of enforcing the established order and of adjusting their own needs and wishes to that order, but they are not engaged in changing that order. If they were engaged in such activity, negotiating its meaning would have been a major part of what they were doing. This is the central thesis of Strauss's approach to the study of social order and action.

The Negotiation of Order

According to Strauss's approach and contrary to the deterministic view, social order always undergoes social change at least in parts of the overall order. Social order is always the object of the activity of human actors, who aim at interpreting, applying, adjusting, and changing the order according to their ideologies and interests. Because they are mostly confronted with other actors who want to do the same and do not have superior power on a once-and-for-all basis, they have to engage in negotiations with others concerning the meaning, interpretation, application, adjustment, and change of the rules of social order. Strauss, in the introduction to his book *Negotiations* (1978: 5–6), summarizes his view of social order representing negotiated order as it was stated a decade previously and then adds what has become important for his perspective in the meantime:

1. Social order is negotiated order. The organizations studied all displayed negotiation as an important feature in the making of their social order.
2. Negotiations depend on specific structural conditions: who negotiates with whom, when, and about what. The negotiations are patterned, not accidental in character. They depend on specific conditions that form their character, and this in turn leads to specific consequences for persons and organizations.
3. The products of negotiation, namely, contracts, understandings, agreements, or rules, are temporarily limited in their existence. They are always being reviewed, reevaluated, revised, reevolved, or renewed.

4. Negotiated order is continually worked out and reconstituted.
5. The negotiated order existing on any given day consists of the organization's rules and policies and all the overt or covert agreements, understandings, pacts, and contracts currently in force on each level of the organization.
6. Every change that affects the negotiated order—such as a new member of an organization, a disrupting event, a betrayed contract, the introduction of a new technology or ideology—results in negotiation, reappraisal of order, and change.
7. The reconstitution of social order proceeds in a complex interrelationship between daily negotiations of specific agreements and periodic appraisal of the more formal and permanent organizational rules. The negotiation process exerts a pressure for change on the organizational rules, whereas the latter set limits for negotiators.
8. When we look at the daily negotiation process, the more permanent organizational rules make up the background for the current working agreements in the foreground. Looking at the periodic appraisal of the more permanent rules, we see the daily working agreements as background for the periodic appraisal of the more permanent rules in the foreground. Both processes play into each other in the evolution of social order.

These are the features of negotiated order as stated in Strauss's earlier work. He now adds the following characteristics (Strauss, 1978: 6–7):

9. Negotiation is one of a set of alternative ways to get things done and goals to attain that are more or less readily available to actors. Different modes of action are negotiation, persuasion, education, appeal to authority, or the use of coercion or coercive threat.
10. The actors' theories of negotiation shape the process and determine the course of negotiation considerably.
11. Negotiation itself differentiates into subprocesses like making trade-offs, obtaining kickbacks, paying off debts, and negotiating agreements.
12. Negotiation takes place within a specific structural context that is composed of the basic institutional patterns underlying the process of negotiation within a specific institutional sphere in society. Negotiations in American courts are shaped by basic features of the American judicial system; negotiations in an American mental hospital are shaped by properties of American medical care, psychiatry, caring professions, and the division of labor in mental hospitals.
13. A final aspect is the negotiation context that is directly related to the wider structural context and to the process of negotiation itself. It mediates between structural context and negotiation. The negotiation context surrounds and affects the process of negotiation directly. The

following properties have to be taken into account in order to specify the negotiation context:

- The number of negotiators, their relative *experience* in negotiation, and whom they *represent.*
- Whether the negotiations are *one-shot, repeated, sequential, serial, multiple,* or *linked.*
- The relative *balance of power* exhibited by the respective parties *in* the negotiation itself.
- The nature of their respective *stakes* in the negotiation.
- The *visibility* of the transactions to others; that is, their overt or covert characters.
- The *number* and *complexity* of the *issues* negotiated.
- The *clarity of legitimacy* boundaries of the *issues* negotiated.
- The *options* to avoiding or discontinuing negotiation; that is, the alternative modes of action perceived as available. (Strauss, 1978: 99–100)

These properties of the negotiation context shape the course of negotiation and its outcome. However, Strauss does not tell us anything about the direction in which these properties lead the course of negotiation. We only know that they have an influence on the course of negotiation, but we do not know their specific effects upon it.

Case: Experimental Psychiatric Wards

Strauss presents a number of case studies that he interprets in the light of the outlined view of making and remaking social order in processes of negotiation. The first case presented is a study of experimental psychiatric wards carried out by Rue Bucher and Leonard Schatzman (1964) in the context of a broader research project undertaken by Strauss and several colleagues in the late 1950s. We can take Strauss's (1978: 107–22) interpretation of this case study as an example of the application of his negotiation perspective to the analysis of the evolution of social order within an organization in processes of negotiation.

Strauss begins by describing the structural context of psychiatry in the United States at that time. For about one hundred years, persons defined as severely or dangerously mentally ill were held in custody in special hospitals, often run by the state. The attitude toward patients was custodial; therapy aiming at curing their illness did not exist to an effective degree. The hospitals were managed by physicians or psychiatrists assisted by lay personnel and a few physicians and nurses trained only in medical care. During the 1950s, a movement aiming at abandoning the purely custodial system and at turning toward effective therapy in order to cure patients as far as possible became established. The traditional ideology favored the custodial system and drug treatment; the modern ideology argued for psychotherapy. A third ideology that entered the discussion proposed milieu therapy. Psychiatry endeavored to establish for itself a more respected place within the medical system. Psychologists and social workers found more and more access to mental hospitals.

The hospital studied by Bucher and Schatzman was headed by a director who wanted to introduce modern psychiatric therapy. He attacked the traditionalists by reorganizing the experimental wards completely. He hired young psychiatrists and gave each a ward and a professional team composed in a multidisciplinary way. The team consisted of the psychiatrist, a social worker, and a recreational or occupational therapist.

Five wards were built up in this way. They shared the following conditions: inadequate physical facilities; sixty-five to eighty-five patients; random admission of patients except by gender; a wide range of diseases, however, primarily schizophrenia; and a mandate to organize the treatment of patients in order to have them discharged on improvement.

Each of the five wards had a different structure: First was the radical patient government system that tried to include the patients in running the ward as a therapeutic community as much as possible. Second was the representative system in which arbitrarily divided groups of patients were represented by one professional in the team. Third was the psychotherapeutic authority system that was led by the psychiatrist according to the psychotherapeutic model but in the traditional authoritative way. Fourth, the somatic system was administered by a physician not committed to psychiatry in an eclectic way. The fifth system was unresolved, because the new chief was not yet able to introduce an overall binding system; it was characterized by the conflicting ideas of the different team members.

The negotiation context displayed the following features: In each of the wards a division of labor had to be worked out. This was not completely predetermined by the hospital's organizational structure but had to be established in processes of negotiation. The organization of treatment not only reflected the viewpoint of the director but also was influenced by the different viewpoints of the different team members. The social structure, particularly the authority structure, was neither firmly preestablished nor completely disorganized. Thus, there was a lot of scope for negotiating the organization of treatment, responsibilities, authority, and the division of labor.

The negotiation context was further characterized by the novelty of many negotiations for the team members, who were inexperienced; they were young and recently recruited. Therefore, negotiations took up a lot of time with many unexpected results for the team members and many renegotiations of earlier agreements. The stakes were both common and very different; team members had in common the interest in getting the work done but were different in their ideological outlooks and in their interest in doing the work that was most satisfying for each one of them. This also contributed to making negotiations difficult and time consuming and required many renegotiations. Moreover, there was no clear understanding of what was legitimate and what was not legitimate in treating patients. This meant that the team members had no firmly established guideline in legitimating their claims, so that negotiation also reached the level of discussing what is legitimate and what is not legitimate. Not only was coming to mutually accepted agreements difficult and time consuming, but every agreement was fragile and in danger of being questioned and renegotiated.

Sometimes team members negotiated for themselves, sometimes for the team, sometimes for their profession, and sometimes for an ideological position. The negotiations involved individuals, alliances, or the whole collective who wanted to handle matters in certain ways. This feature of the negotiation context made it very difficult for the team members to get to know the true purposes of their partners in negotiations and made negotiations difficult to assess and their outcomes difficult to predict.

Many negotiations were linked with other negotiations. Inasmuch as this was overlooked, conflict arose because of a lack of coordination. This contributed again to making negotiation time consuming and fragile, leading to many renegotiations. There was mostly no clear-cut power structure, with the chief psychiatrist giving authoritative commands. Rather, the different team members based their stakes on different power resources. These could be the right of a formal position to give commands, the traditional status of a profession, the amount of specific experience on a specific ward, support of one's position through alliances, or ability to further the interests of other team members. This complexity of the power structure was mostly responsible for the fights in the processes of negotiation and contributed to making negotiations time consuming, fragile, and apt to be renegotiated.

One ward displayed the described features to the most extreme degree: the so-called unresolved system. It was characterized by a battle between the psychiatrist and the physician regarding their authority and the psychotherapeutic or somatic treatment of patients. Because of the long period of unresolved conflict, many relationships and task assignments concerning the other team members were left undecided for a long time. Private agreements between individual members were concluded in the meantime, but often only for a short time, so that renegotiation occurred continually. Some negotiations were overt, while some were covert, as was also the case in the other wards. Here, as in all the wards, negotiation subprocesses included trading off, mediating, exploring legitimate boundaries by proffering advantages and territorial claiming, bypassing of negotiation, and the renegotiation of previous agreements. The members of this ward, as those of all wards, also made use of alternative modes of action: refusal to negotiate or breaking off of negotiation, appeals to rules or authority, attempts at education and persuasion, the manipulation of events, and even some forms of coercion. Above all, though, the social order evolving under these structural and negotiation context conditions was a negotiated order.

The structural and negotiation context conditions in this case were all of one kind: they made the situation of action for the actors very complex, insecure, and unpredictable. On the structural level, there was the clash between the traditional somatic and the modern psychotherapeutic ideologies, between the authority claim of the traditional medical profession and that of the young psychiatrists, compounded by the rise of new professions: psychologists and social workers. On the level of the negotiation context, the number of negotiators was greater than in traditional wards because of the less authoritative structure of the wards and because of the individual self-consciousness of the team members. They were rather inexperienced, and it was not always clear what they represented: themselves, their profession, the team, or the ward as a collective. The negotiations were multiple and linked, less one shot, repeated, and serial, so that they lacked order and predictability. The balance of power was fragile, because the different team members had access to different and changing power resources and because frequent replacements shifted the power balance. The stakes were at the same time common and different, making agreements difficult to achieve. The transactions were partly visible but partly invisible, making it very difficult to master the whole situation. The issues negotiated were numerous and complex. The legitimacy boundaries of the issues negotiated were unclear. There were fairly open options of alternative modes of action, so that negotiations were always in danger of breaking down. Negotiations involved many different subprocesses like trading off, mediating, exploring legitimate boundaries via proffering advantages and territorial claiming, bypassing of negotiation, and renegotiation. This differentiation of subprocesses contributed to the complexity of the situation and to the low mutual predictability of actions.

All these properties of the structural and the negotiation context lead in one direction: social order was not well established and left much room for negotiation and alternative modes of action. Negotiation itself even reached the level of the legitimacy of treatment practices and thus was not limited to narrow issues. Since it penetrated nearly every action, its outcome was unpredictable. Agreements were difficult to achieve, because of the complexity of stakes and because of the lack of consensus on legitimacy. And agreements achieved in negotiations were fragile and usually had to be questioned, reviewed, and renegotiated. Therefore, social order was permanently in the process of change by way of negotiation and renegotiation. Because negotiation and renegotiation were common, change tended to occur continually in small steps rather than abruptly in big steps. The division of labor arising from the negotiation process was very different in the different wards because the course of negotiation went in different directions. Tasks were sometimes gained by making claims based on legitimation, or they were proffered by some professionals according to a specific interpretation of the ideology, or sometimes team members were stripped of some tasks because, it was argued, they were no longer able appropriately to carry out the tasks according to their qualifications in the light of the preferred treatment ideology. Legitimation was often put differently according to the different ideological positions of different team members.

Strauss summarizes the consequences of the structural and negotiation context as follows:

> Given those salient structural and contextual properties, here is what typically happened on these wards. Almost any task undertaken or sought by a professional was subject to review and denial. Even tasks backed by law and constitutional authority were called into question. Also, claims that had been won earlier were not insured against loss, and new ones could emerge with changes of personnel or the appearance of new ward contingencies. The claim might be to an area of competence and to particular associated tasks that might long have been successfully claimed by the team member's profession — then he was reiterating traditional rights — but the area and tasks might be quite new.
>
> In either case, justifying rationales had to be given in negotiating for those areas of work, unless there was no contest over the traditional areas, and that was not necessarily always so. The legitimating rationales were grounded on such bases as legality (certification), appointed authority (institutional authorization), tradition, formal education (including degrees), prior experience with the task in question, current need or expediency, and a desire or wish to perform a task ("try it"). Understandably, personnel used those particular rationales that fit their respective situations.
>
> What they judged as their situations were linked with their perceptions of the audience with whom they were negotiating. (Strauss, 1978: 112)

Summary

So far, reviewing Strauss's interpretation of the psychiatric wards study has brought us closer to some assumptions about the structural and contextual conditions that enlarge the part of negotiation in making and remaking social order and about the properties of negotiations arising from specific structural and contextual conditions and about the processes of negotiation and renegotiation. We can go farther in explicitly formulating these assumptions than Strauss himself. He does no more than provide us with a vocabulary and describe cases with this vocabulary, sometimes giving implicit hints for propositional assumptions about what follows from what. However, we have to do that more explicitly than he does. We can formulate the following propositions:

1. The more ideologies compete on the level of societal social structure, the more the legitimation of social order involves processes of negotiation, provided there is a relative balance of power, mutual toleration of stakes, willingness to come together, and willingness to compromise.

2. The more professional groups compete for authority in the social structure of society, the more the establishment of authority in social order involves processes of negotiation, provided there is a relative balance of power, mutual toleration of stakes, willingness to come together, and willingness to compromise.

3. The greater the number of negotiators, the less experienced the negotiators are, and the more different people they represent, the less predictable and the more time consuming the negotiations will be and the more fragile the agreements will turn out to be, which implies the need for renegotiations.

4. The more negotiations are multiple and linked and the less they are one shot, repeated, sequential, or serial, the less predictable and the more time consuming they will be and the more fragile the agreements will turn out to be, implying renegotiations.

5. The more different power resources different negotiators can mobilize and the more frequently changes of membership occur, the less predictable and the more time consuming the negotiations will be and the more fragile the agreements will turn out to be, implying renegotiations.

6. The more different common and individual stakes negotiators introduce into the process, the less predictable and the more time consuming the negotiations will be and the more fragile the agreements will turn out to be, implying renegotiations.

7. The less visible transactions are to actors, the less predictable and the more time consuming the negotiations will be and the more fragile the agreements will turn out to be, implying renegotiations.

8. The greater the number and complexity of issues negotiated, the less predictable and the more time consuming the negotiations will be and the more fragile the agreements will turn out to be, implying renegotiations.

9. The less clearly legitimacy boundaries of negotiated issues are defined, the less predictable and the more time consuming the negotiations will be, reaching deeper levels of legitimation, and the more fragile the agreements will turn out to be, implying renegotiations.

10. The more alternative options to act negotiators have, the less predictable and the more time consuming the negotiations will be and the more fragile the agreements will turn out to be, implying renegotiations.

11. The more the evolution of social order arises from processes of negotiation, the less stable it will be and the more renegotiation of social order will occur.

12. The more the evolution of social order arises from processes of negotiation, the more social order will change step-by-step and the less it will change abruptly in one big surge.
13. The more negotiation involves matters of legitimacy of social order, the more rapidly the legitimacy grounds of social order will change, the more unpredictable social change will be, and the less social change will move in the direction of approaching more consistency with the dominating ideas underlying the culture of a society.

Critical Assessment

Going beyond Strauss's negotiation paradigm by explicitly formulating some basic propositions out of his vocabulary and his interpretation of some case studies shows us, much more than Strauss himself does, what specific contribution has been made by this symbolic interactionist approach to the study of social order from the negotiation point of view. Whereas according to the deterministic view social order is the outcome of preestablished material, social, or cultural structures imposing their order on the individual's actions, according to the negotiation view social order is the outcome of processes of negotiation. It is a negotiated order. However, this is a way of conducting science that has hardly progressed from crawling to walking. It is not science, because science doesn't answer questions of what *is* the case but rather seeks to answer questions of *when* and *why* something is the case and *how* this occurs. It is beside the point to hear that social order is deterministic or is negotiated. What we want to know is when and under what conditions social order is deterministic and when and under what conditions it is negotiated. We want to know what are the properties of social order when it is deterministically established and when it is established in negotiation processes. Strauss and his symbolic interactionist colleagues are so interested in social order as negotiated order that they forget to explain when and under what conditions and with what resulting properties social order is negotiated. However, Strauss at least provides the vocabulary and some case interpretations that we can use as stepping stones for formulating propositions on the conditions that make negotiation the likely origin of social order and on the properties of social order resulting from processes of negotiation.

In the light of these considerations, the negotiation approach to social order of symbolic interactionism with the addition of our explicit formulation of propositions can show us, to begin with, what the structural conditions are that enlarge the place of negotiation in making and remaking social order, for example, competing ideologies and social (professional) groups. We would have to add a relative balance of power, a relative toleration of the stakes of the competing parties, a willingness to come together with competing parties, and a willingness to compromise. Without adding these conditions there would be conflict but not negotiation. Thus we must go beyond Strauss in order to formulate the qualifications that have to be fulfilled before his negotiation approach would yield propositions that could be confirmed by reality. We must qualify his far-reaching claim to very specific conditions. Though in general Strauss is cautious, he does not formulate explicitly the sole conditions under which his paradigm holds true. Thus, he universalizes a rather specific approach too much.

Strauss's symbolic interactionist paradigm explains a specific feature of making and remaking social order: negotiation. It also provides us with information about the contextual conditions that shape negotiations in a specific way, conditions that make them more or less predictable or time consuming for negotiators, and conditions that make agreements more or less fragile, implying more or less renegotiation. Finally, the paradigm explains specific features of social order as an outcome of its making and remaking in processes of negotiation: permanent change step-by-step but with no direction, rendering change unpredictable. These are the features of social order we can explain when we make use of the negotiation paradigm of symbolic interactionism by explicitly and more precisely formulating propositions.

However, social order has other features as well, in addition to permanent undirected change based on negotiation that is more or less predictable, time consuming, and fragile in its outcomes. Social order sometimes is characterized by a rigidity that implies actors doing nothing but carrying out a traditionally established program in their everyday actions. Traditional consensus is the structural condition in this case, and communal association is the vehicle that makes and remakes social order. Symbolic interactionism with its preoccupation with competition, negotiation, and situational change does not tell us anything about this feature of social order and its conditions. The same holds true for the feature of revolutionary change of social order that comes from conflict of ideologies and groups and power struggle. Conflict theory is much more helpful in this context to the sociologist looking for explanations.

Finally, the legitimacy of social order is a feature that cannot arise from negotiations, because it expresses not a compromise between competing stakes but the correctness of the legitimation of claims by deriving these claims from certain universally valid ideas under specific conditions in processes of discursive argumentation. Here we have to ask a theory of communicative action and discourse for more information. Inasmuch as symbolic interactionism shows us how negotiation is involved in processes of legitimation of claims, this paradigm gives us the right explanations for this aspect of legitimation processes, particularly concentrating on the condition of competing ideologies, negotiation, and rapid, undirected change of legitimacy. However, this again is only one aspect of the legitimacy of social order. Validity, bindingness, and enforcement are further important aspects of legitimacy, and these are not covered by the symbolic interactionist paradigm of negotiation. Validity of legitimacy claims can be explained only by a theory of communicative action and discourse, bindingness only by a theory of solidarity and consensus, and enforcement only by a theory of authority, domination, and power.

It is perplexing that the paradigm of symbolic interactionism in general and its specification to processes of negotiation only tell us about a specific secondary aspect of communication: its negotiation aspect. The primary aspect of communication, namely arriving at mutual understanding, and the primary aspect of discourse, namely arriving at valid knowledge, are out of the range of symbolic interactionism and of the negotiation paradigm. In order to understand the primary aspects of communication and discourse, we have to turn to a theory that concentrates on these features of communication and discourse: Jürgen Habermas's theory of communicative action.

FOURTEEN

THE LOGIC OF MORAL DEVELOPMENT: LAWRENCE KOHLBERG

THE GROWING influence of symbolic interactionism in the 1960s and 1970s made the symbolic part of human action a matter of dynamic negotiation between actors trying to define their common situation of action. Inasmuch as actors work out a common order and personal views of that order, of right and wrong, this is something that is constantly in a state of change dependent on the contingencies of situations and interaction. In the interactionist perspective, there is no stable reference point common to the actors and no underlying logic in the development of moral order and moral judgments. Anselm Strauss related Mead's symbolic interactionism to structuralist thought as represented by the cognitive-developmental approach of Jean Piaget. He thus opened up new perspectives for a more comprehensive treatment of the symbolic aspect in social interaction and social organization. It is to the credit of Lawrence Kohlberg, who had Strauss as one of his mentors while he was a graduate student at the University of Chicago, that Piaget's thought underwent a vital renewal in the seventies. Though Kohlberg thought of himself as a psychologist, his work is of great importance to the sociological theory of the individual's moral development. With its concentration on the structural logic of moral development, Kohlberg's theory is a logical counterpart to the interactionist preoccupation with dynamics in the development of self and social order (Kohlberg, 1969, 1975, 1981, 1984, 1987).

Kohlberg extended Piaget's studies in the development of moral judgment into adolescence and adulthood. He conducted longitudinal studies from childhood to adolescence to adult age, asking the same persons at different times in their lives for solutions of the same moral dilemmas and to give reasons for their positions. Going beyond Piaget's distinction of two

231

levels of moral development — heteronomy and autonomy — he distinguishes three such levels, with each level comprising two stages, so that there are six stages of moral development. The levels and stages make up interrelated sets of logical thinking, role taking and social perspective, and moral reasoning (1984: 173–85). These three dimensions are interrelated, so that reaching a certain level of logical thinking is a necessary precondition for reaching a certain level of social perspective, and both are necessary preconditions for reaching a certain level of moral judgment. The three levels of logical thinking, social perspective, and moral judgment are:

I. Intuitive reasoning, concrete individual perspective and preconventional morality.
II. Concrete operational reasoning, member-of-society perspective and conventional morality.
III. Formal operational reasoning, prior-to-society perspective, and postconventional morality.

Kohlberg claims that human individuals move up these three levels in a necessary sequence from level I to level III throughout all cultures; however, not every individual and not every culture moves through all levels and stages. In terms of moral levels, he says, most children under nine, some adolescents, and adult criminal offenders do not move beyond the preconventional level; most adolescents and adults remain on the conventional level; and only a minority of adults reaches the postconventional level and then only after the age of twenty. Let us now look at the individual levels and stages.

Level I: Preconventional Morality

Logical Reasoning

On Level I, the human being's capacity for logical reasoning remains restricted to concrete intuition and learning from concrete experience and observation.

Stage 1: Heteronomous Morality

Social Perspective

At the first stage, the individual has an egocentric view of the world. He or she cannot take into account the difference of interests and perspectives of different actors and confuses his or her own perspective with that of (adult) authority. Action is seen only in its physical aspects, not in its meaning and intention.

Moral Judgment

The individual sees as right what avoids punishment and wrong what is sanctioned with punishment. The reason for doing right is to avoid punishment by the superior power of authorities.

Stealing from a Store

A person is asked: Why shouldn't you steal from a store? The answer is: Someone could see you and call the police.

Heinz's Dilemma

Heinz's wife suffers from a rare kind of cancer and is near death. A druggist in town has discovered a new medicine, a form of radium, which may heal the illness. He charges $2,000 for the medicine, ten times the level of his costs. Heinz does not have the money and borrows from everybody he knows, but he gets only half the money he needs. The druggist, though, does not sell the medicine at a lower price. So Heinz decides to break into the druggist's store to steal the drug for his wife. The question then is: Is he right to do so, and if so, why?

The answer at moral stage 1 would be that Heinz is right as long as he isn't caught by the police, because he can then help his wife. But he is wrong if he gets caught by the police. Then he cannot help his wife.

Stage 2: Individualism, Instrumental Purpose, and Exchange

Social Perspective

At Stage 2 the individual learns that different people have different interests and views of the world, so that they are in conflict, which necessitates adjustment of interests.

Moral Judgment

For the individual it is right to follow rules when to do so is in his or her immediate interest. But one also has to let other people do the same. Therefore, it is also right that exchanges, deals, and agreements should serve the interests of all the parties involved on fair terms. The reason for doing right and, in doing so, for recognizing the interests of others is that one gets repaid for everything one does.

Stealing from a Store

The storekeeper will not like it and will keep you out of the store whenever you want something else.

Heinz's Dilemma

The life of Heinz's wife is more important to Heinz than the medicine is to the druggist.

Level II: Conventional Morality

Logical Reasoning

On this level, the individual has managed to carry out partial logical operations with regard to concrete phenomena.

Stage 3: Mutual Interpersonal Expectations, Relationships, and Interpersonal Conformity

Social Perspective

The individual is now aware of the group to which he or she belongs and of the feelings, expectations, and agreements he or she shares with the others. The person is capable of subordinating individual interests to those that he or she shares with others and of putting him- or herself in the shoes of others.

Moral Judgment

To do right means to live up to what is expected of one by one's immediate fellows: family and friends. One has to be loyal to one's fellows. The reason for doing right is to be seen as good by one's fellows. One wants to be a good person in their eyes.

Stealing from the Store

Your family and your friends would think badly of you.

Heinz's Dilemma

Heinz has to steal for his wife because otherwise he would not be good to her.

Stage 4: Social System and Conscience

Social Perspective

The individual is capable of taking the point of view of the whole societal system, which reaches beyond interpersonal relationships between friends and fellows. Individual relations are placed within the total social system of society.

Moral Judgment

Doing right means doing what is prescribed by society's laws. The reason for doing so is that society's order would break down if everyone did what he or she wanted without any regard for the system as a whole.

Stealing from the Store

It is against the law. Society would break down if everybody could take what he or she wanted from anybody else.

Heinz's Dilemma

It is against the law to steal. But it is also against the law not to help someone who is in danger of dying. Because the life of its members is more important to society than any material property, Heinz does the right thing.

Level III: Postconventional Morality

Logical Reasoning

The individual is capable of carrying out abstract logical operations.

Stage 5: Social Contract or Utility and Individual Rights

Social Perspective

The individual sees social relations as being regulated by voluntary contractual agreements on the basis of equal rights and social opportunities.

Moral Judgment

Doing right demands taking into account the rights of other individuals. One has to establish agreements with others that guarantee the rights of everybody. The reason for doing so is that all human beings are born equal and have the same rights and live together under a contract that guarantees their rights. Thus, one has to carry out this contractual agreement in concrete action. When the law violates rights, one has to oppose the law and to realize the rights.

Stealing from the Store

Stealing is a violation of other people's rights of property ownership.

Heinz's Dilemma

Everybody has a right to life and to property. Here the wife's right to life is in conflict with the druggist's right to property. However, life is a higher right when in conflict with property; therefore, Heinz is right.

Stage 6: Universal Ethical Principles

Social Perspective

The individual has managed to see social relationships from the perspective of universal standpoints of humanity and reason.

Moral Judgment

Doing right is doing what can be justified by universally valid principles. When the law cannot be justified by such principles, one has to deviate from the law and to oppose it. The reason for doing so is that only what holds true on universal grounds of justification, what withstands any critical examination, and what would receive the consent of everybody subjecting it to close examination may be assumed to be right.

Stealing from the Store

It is not right to steal from a store, because it is an action that is based on the arbitrary exercise of power, not lawful behavior that could be justified on universal grounds. If there are any doubts about the rightful possession of the things by the storekeeper, one has to confirm them in due process of law. Should there be any doubts about the rightfulness of property law, one is not allowed simply to steal on the basis of an arbitrary decision but must prove the illegitimacy of property law on universally valid grounds. Then one must argue for a change in property law instead of simply stealing property according to one's own arbitrary decision.

Heinz's Dilemma

Any law that does not oblige the druggist to subordinate his property right to the duty to save a human life that he sees in danger is not legitimate. The druggist who does not act to save a life violates moral law. Heinz would have to point out that the druggist is morally wrong. If he did not succeed in convincing the druggist and did not get support from courts that would enforce his wife's moral right quickly enough, he would have no other way of solving the dilemma than to do what he does. But he has to try to keep the druggist's damage as small as possible.

The Social Preconditions of Moral Development

These are the stages that Kohlberg claims make up a unidirectional logical sequence. That is, because the sequence is a logical one, there is no room for cultural variation with regard to any deviation from the sequence. This does not mean that there is no cultural variation at all. However, it is variation only with regard to the levels reached in a culture overall and with regard to the number of people who reach each level.

Thus, Kohlberg is preoccupied with working out the logic of moral development and neglects the social basis of this development much more than Piaget did. For Piaget, a change in social structure—from constraint to cooperation—is the social basis for the transformation from moral heteronomy to moral autonomy. Kohlberg does not systematically incorporate this social basis into his theory of cognitive moral development. However, he also does not deny that there is an interrelationship between social structure and moral development. He refers to the fact that a comparison between different social settings for moral development reveals the following (Kohlberg, 1984: 198–203):

An American orphanage had most children on the lowest stages, whereas an Israeli kibbutz had most children on the highest stages. The orphanage is a setting that provides little opportunity for role taking, voluntary participation, communication, and decision making, whereas the Kibbutz provides plenty of opportunities for these. Thus, we have to state that moral development is sustained by opportunities for role taking, voluntary participation, communication, and decision making. A similar effect comes from the moral atmosphere of organizations. If they are organized on moral levels above the personal levels of some of its members, for example, schools with teachers on high levels and pupils on lower levels, but do not put too much demand on the lower ranking members, the latter will tend to be raised to higher levels more than members in organizations with lower levels of moral order, for example, prisons.

Summary

1. The more cognitive training leads an individual from reasoning by intuition to reasoning by concrete operations to reasoning by abstract formal operations, the more the social perspective of the individual will proceed from the egocentric to the concrete individualistic to the interpersonal to the social system, to the contract and to the universalistic view; the more both developments proceed, the more the individual will proceed from preconventional (heteronomous, individualistic) to conventional (interpersonal, societal) and to postconventional (contractual, universalistic) morality.
2. The more social settings encourage role taking, voluntary participation, communication, and decision making, the more individuals confronted with these settings will advance to higher stages of moral consciousness.
3. The higher the level of an organization's moral atmosphere and the less it overdoes its moral demands on its members, the more the members will advance to higher levels of moral consciousness.

Critical Assessment

Kohlberg's contribution to our understanding of moral consciousness clearly and consciously concentrates on the structural logic of moral development. Where he opens the door for the social basis of this development, it is clearly the chance for training in discursive argumentation that attracts his interest. Thus, the logical steps of *growing abstraction* in moral reasoning sustained by training in discursive argumentation is the aspect of moral consciousness that he explains. There are, however, other aspects that he does not cover with this theory of logical development of moral consciousness: the binding character of moral conscience, the critical spirit of moral consciousness and its dynamic change.

In order to explain why moral principles become internally binding for the individual we have to address his or her inclusion in the solidarity of groups. In order to explain the individual's capacity for moral criticism we have to look at the conflict with the social environment in an individual's biography. The individual will build up such a critical spirit only if he or she has enough opportunities to express moral anger. When explaining the dynamic change in moral reasoning, we have to study the individual's opportunities for voluntary participation in a great variety of social activities. These are aspects of moral consciousness that call for explanations that lie outside the scope of a cognitive-developmental theory of moral consciousness.

FIFTEEN

THE LEGACY OF CRITICAL THEORY: JÜRGEN HABERMAS'S THEORY OF COMMUNICATIVE ACTION

THE THEORIES of symbolic interactionism that we have discussed in earlier chapters of this book have particularly drawn our attention to the place of meaning and communication in social interaction. None of the other paradigms that we have reviewed up to now gives communication and the production of meaning in processes of interaction such a prominent position. However, symbolic interactionism does not lead us to the core of meaning and communication. It does not distinguish sufficiently between the situation in which two or more actors try to understand each other by seeking out a commonly shared meaning of the symbolic expressions they use and the situation in which two or more actors start with a specific view of the meaning of symbolic expressions and encounter each other so that they are forced to mutually fit their interpretations in order to coordinate their actions, to be able mutually to predict their actions in order to achieve their particular goals. Negotiation is the predominant way of achieving this fitting of interpretations of meaning in the view of symbolic interactionism. Hence, symbolic interactionism primarily imposes the properties of negotiation on the process of communication.

In negotiation, actors try strategically to attain goals and have to compromise with opponents who are seeking to reach their goals. In communication, one actor wants to understand what the other means by a symbolic expression and vice versa. In order to do so, they communicate, that is, they transmit meanings until they feel they understand each other. Thus, communication is something different from negotiation. And it is this different quality of communication that we would miss if we accepted the symbolic interactionist reduction of communication to negotiation. While there are aspects of negotiation in many processes of communication, this does not imply that communication is nothing but symbolic negotiation. In fact, the character of communication makes it a form of social interaction that is essentially different from negotiation and makes symbolic negotiation a secondary form in which communication and negotiation are mixed. However, negotiation is a form of strategic action from which communicative action has to be analytically distinguished. It is this distinction that lies at the heart of Jürgen Habermas's theory of communicative action (Habermas, 1968a, 1968b, 1969, 1971a, 1971b, 1973b, 1973c, 1976b, 1981, 1983, 1985; for translation, see 1970a, 1970b, 1970c, 1973a, 1976a, 1979, 1984, 1987a, 1987b). We have to consult his theory in order to come to a better understanding of the place of meaning and communication in social interaction.

Strategic Action and Communicative Action

For Habermas (1968a, 1981: 25–203, 369–452), the distinction between strategic action and communicative action is crucial. Strategic action is a special form of teleological or instrumental action. The latter is oriented toward attaining a specific goal under given conditions with available means. Instrumental action is successful inasmuch as it attains the goal set in advance. We call it instrumental because the actor sees his or her action and also available means as an instrument for reaching a specific goal; it is instrumental for that purpose. In planful instrumental action, the actor proceeds in his or her action according to a plan that tells the actor the ways of attaining his or her goal. For example, a man wants to travel from one town to another. To arrive at the other town is his goal. After some time he arrives at a river. The river is an external condition that he has to take into account. The town remains the goal, but there is the added factor of the river between the man and the town that is an external condition. The man has to apply the right means in order to reach his goal under this given condition. He cannot just walk; he has to swim or to find or build a bridge to get across the river in order to continue toward the town. He will be successful once he has arrived at the town. This is instrumentally successful action.

We can also look at an example that involves social interaction. Here strategic action comes into play as a special form of teleological or instrumental action that relates to other actors in the same way as to nonhuman external objects: A student wants to complete a specific course in sociological theory with an "A." This is his or her goal. There are requirements, set by the professor: the student must turn in four papers during the quarter and take one final exam. In the papers and final exam, he or she has to explain at least five different sociological theories, to apply them to an example from everyday life, and to evaluate their explanatory power. This is the external condition that the student must take into account in order to get an "A." There are, then, more or less promising means of meeting these conditions on the way to an "A." Reading only an introductory book would be an insufficient means; reading the assigned original texts would be better, but still not enough without attending the professor's lectures and the discussion group. Doing all these things would be the right means to attain the goal under the conditions set by the professor. The corresponding strategic action will have been successful if the student gets an "A."

In communicative action, an actor conveys a message to a second actor, who interprets the message and talks back to the first actor. This type of action is successfully completed when the actors mutually understand each other, concur on how to interpret the meaning of symbolic expressions, and concur on how to act. In order to explain the character of communicative action, we can look at the student who takes an exam from the point of view of communicative action. The student asks the professor, "What are your requirements for getting a grade in this class?" The professor answers, "Four papers during the quarter and a final exam." The student then asks, "What type of paper and final exam do you want us to write?" The professor answers, "An explanation, application, and evaluation of a specific sociological theory in each paper and in the final exam." Then the student asks, "What are your criteria for evaluating the papers?" The professor says, "Completeness and precision of your presentation and explanation of a sociological theory. Completeness and precision of the application to an example, and completeness and precision of your evaluation." The conversation may go on with the student asking for examples of the professor's criteria, but let us assume the student now says, "Okay, I understand." This last statement by the student signals the completion of the communication between the two, and it also signals the success of the communication. The two understand each other and concur on how to interpret the meaning of terms like "paper" and "final exam" and on what to do in the paper and in the final exam. This is successful communicative action. Whether the student eventually passes the exam is not important for the evaluation of the success of his or her communication with the professor.

Habermas's differentiation of strategic and communicative action is analytical in character. We have to emphasize this much more than he does. Normally, both types of action are intermingled as aspects of concrete action, with one or the other taking the lead. Asking the professor for information is a means the student applies in order to pass the exam; thus, the student communicates with a strategic purpose. However, the criteria of communicative action determine the success of this action: Will they understand each other and come to a consensus on what to do? On the other hand, instrumental action can be part of communication aiming at mutual understanding. Student and professor may realize that they misunderstand each other regarding the meaning of the term "paper." Each question and explanation is then a means toward the end of understanding each other. This intermingling of strategic and communicative aspects in concrete action, however, does not imply that we should avoid distinguishing them analytically. We have to do that in order to understand precisely the conditions and the impact of these aspects on action.

Our next example, which will lead us further, also starts by looking at strategic action and then turning our attention to communicative action as part of that overall strategic action. Let us take an example that involves immediate interaction: A football fan wants to reenter a football stadium through the main gate after being outside for a while without his ticket. The gate official tries to stop him. Here the fan has the goal of entering the stadium. The official at the main gate trying to stop him is the external condition that he has to take into account. The fan may apply one of the following means: He may try to pass unnoticed by walking in the middle of a crowd. He can threaten to hit or can really hit the official. He may try to negotiate with the official that he will leave his watch with the official until he comes back with the ticket, which he left in his coat on the seat. He may try to convince the official that he has left his ticket in his coat which is on the seat, without offering his watch. Or he may be able to rely on the fact that the official knows him very well as a fan who regularly attends the matches and has a ticket for the whole season. His strategic action will have been successful if the means he applies gets him through the gate check.

The different means imply different types of action subordinated to the overall strategic goal of reentering the football stadium. Hiding oneself within a crowd is itself strategic in character. The fan moves in a specific way in order to reach the goal of hiding from the official. Negotiating to leave his watch with the official is strategic, because the fan offers something to the official that motivates the man to let him pass. His goal here is to offer the official a deal that leads him to change his action in favor of the fan. Both compromise. The fan reaches his goal but with some additional costs: leaving his watch with the official and being forced to return to present his ticket. The official reaches his goal of having a ticket presented by everybody who passes, but not immediately in this case. He has to wait until the fan returns with his ticket. Threatening or hitting the official is strategic in character, because the fan here again figures out how much power the official has and thus threatens with power or applies physical force in order to reach the goal of overcoming the official's resistance to his attempt at reentering the stadium.

However, passing through the gate on the basis of being known to the official is something different. Here the subordinated action that is a means toward the goal of reentering the stadium is not structured like strategic action and does not imply a means-end calculation. It is here that we enter the domain of communicative action. This does not mean that the overall action under consideration turns toward communication; it means only that the overall strategic action entails a subordinated step that is not strategic but communicative in character. We can enter a closer analysis of this inter-action taking place between the football fan and the official in order to get an idea of what makes the difference between the communicative and stra-tegic action. When the fan passes on the basis of being well-known to the official, both communicate silently on the basis of a mutual association, confidence, and silent understanding. Both the official and the fan under-stand that one must have a ticket to be entitled to attend a match. They both understand that the fan has a ticket, and they both understand that the fan has not lent his ticket to a friend because both understand this would not be right. And they both understand that the official has to check all the people who enter. It is this mutual silent understanding of sharing com-mon rules that gives the official the confidence to let the fan pass, because he knows he is acting according to the rules. And it is the same confidence that enables the fan to pass without recourse to any specific means of hid-ing, negotiating, applying power, or persuasion. Here, the successful criterion is not a particular actor's attainment of a specific goal but two or more actors' consensus on what to do and how to act in a certain situation.

This is the success criterion of associative or cooperative and silent com-municative action. Its success depends on whether a silent mutual under-standing in associative action enables two or more actors to come to a consensus on how to act in a certain situation. Whether the action is suc-cessful with regard to the goals of the actors does not matter. All that counts is the consensus on how to act, not the success of that action with regard to actors' goals. The consensus may even be of such a character that it pre-vents one actor from attaining his or her goal. The official and the fan may both understand that anyone entering and reentering has to present a ticket. The fan will not look for any other means than returning to the gate after picking up his ticket from his seat in order to present it to the official. Their consensus sets definite limits on the means that can be chosen. Communica-tive action takes the lead and goal attainment by way of strategic action becomes secondary in character. However, it can also be the other way around: the fan may calculate strategically whether consensus with the offi-cial will get him to his seat or whether he should apply another, more suc-cessful means.

In summary, silent mutual understanding is the basis for a form of com-municative action that we can call simple communicative action, because it does not involve any problems of understanding each other. The criterion of success is consensus on how to act in a certain situation. In communica-tive action, an actor conveys a message to a second actor who interprets the message and talks back to the first actor. The success criterion for this type of social interaction is mutual understanding and consensus. In our example, the communication may proceed as follows: The fan approaches the official and says, "Hi, it's me again." The official says, "Nice to see you again, go on, have a nice day." Both consent immediately to the fan's going on without having to present his ticket. This consensus rests on a lot of silent mutual understanding and confidence. There is no misunderstanding and no problem in their communication. Both understand very well what is the right way to act in a football stadium. They share a common life-world, which enables them to communicate smoothly and to come easily to a consensual definition of the situation and to a consensus on how to act appropriately in a certain situation.

Things become different the more our football fan has to enter a lengthier conversation with the official before the two come to mutual understanding and to a consensus on how to act. The fan has to persuade the official that he can let him pass. His attempt to persuade the official to allow him to re-enter the stadium is a means toward his goal; it is a form of communication that may proceed as follows: The fan approaches the official and says, "Hi, it's me again." The official asks, "Your ticket?" The fan answers, "It's in my coat on the seat." The official says, "Okay, go on." Though this is not a lengthy conversation and both still quickly come to a consensus, it takes the fan one sentence more to convince the official that he is entitled to reenter the stadium. Their conversation entails first a misunderstanding. The fan's, "Hi, it's me again," is intended to indicate: "I was out for a few minutes, as you will remember, and I just came back, so please let me pass." The official did not notice the fan going out, so he thinks he is just arriving for the first time and wants to see his ticket. However, the fan's answer satisfies him. The fan succeeds in reestablishing mutual familiarity and trust, so the official lets him pass. Nevertheless, the conversation entails a little problem: The official wants to see a ticket, and the fan has no ticket with him. This problem endangers their consensus. It is only by specifically mentioning his ticket in his coat on the seat that the fan can remedy the situation and reestablish consensus on what to do. The problem has to be resolved by way of proceeding in communication. The fan cannot just pass; he has to communicate further in order to reestablish consensus. What he has to do is to provide reasonable grounds for not being able to present his ticket and nevertheless being entitled to enter the stadium. The reasonable ground he provides is that he has a ticket that entitles him to enter but is unable to present it at the moment, because he has left it in his coat on his seat. He refers to a universal right: Everybody who has a valid ticket is entitled to enter the stadium, regardless of race, color, class, ethnicity, religion, and so on. Both the fan and the official understand that this is the sole general criterion for entering the stadium. The official cannot reject people who have a ticket because he doesn't like the way they look. The fan doesn't believe that he is entitled to enter the stadium without a ticket, just because he is a member of the fan club. Both official and fan concur on the one general ground for entering the stadium: possessing a ticket.

Therefore, what the fan must do is to convince the official that he fulfills the general requirement of having a ticket. He has to refer to the right to enter the stadium with a ticket and provide reasonable grounds for his statement that he has a ticket though he cannot present it to the official at the moment. This is why he says, "It's in my coat on the seat," meaning, "I have left my coat on my seat, and my ticket is in my coat pocket." The official's "Okay, go on" means that he accepts the fan's grounds for not being able to present his ticket as reasonable and approved. The reason he believes the fan's answer may be that he remembers seeing the fan passing with a coat and a ticket right before the beginning of the match, or that he knows him as a regular fan who always presents his season ticket, or that he thinks this man without a coat looks trustworthy so that he can be sure he has a ticket and really has left it in his coat on his seat. The official takes these observations as indicators of the fan's trustworthiness and the truth of what he says. If he has doubts, he can ask the fan for more evidence for his claim that he has a ticket. Then the fan must prove his statement with more universally evident grounds. Up to the point where the official lets the fan pass, he bases his acceptance of the fan's evidence on his very particular knowledge of the trustworthiness of the fan's words. The less he knows the fan, the less he will be able to base his consensus just on trust and the more he has to ask for evidence that is accessible to everybody. In this case, the conversation may go on as follows:

Instead of saying, "Okay, go on," the official says, "Anybody could tell me that. How do I know whether it's true?" The fan then may answer, "Well, I have a season ticket and come to every match. Don't you know me?" With this statement, he wants to establish his trustworthiness. Nevertheless, the official may not be satisfied, saying, "There are so many people who have season tickets, why should I know that you are one of them?" The fan may then point to another man and say, "Ask him. He knows that I have a season ticket." However, the official may say, "I'm sorry, but I don't know him either." In the course of this conversation, the fan cannot find any relationship that enables him to prove his trustworthiness. This forces him to send a friend to his seat and bring back his coat with the ticket so that he can present it to the official, "Here is my season ticket." The official is satisfied and says: "All right, go on." What is different from all the evidence the fan has presented before is that this evidence is trusted independently of any prior knowledge of the fan's trustworthiness on the part of the official. Everybody can check the ticket independently of knowing the owner of the ticket. It is a universally accessible piece of evidence, which finally opens the gate for the fan.

Certainly, the discussion could continue. The official could question the fan's ownership of the season ticket. In this case, the fan would have to prove his ownership of the ticket, for example, by having the number and name on the ticket checked against the files of the company that runs the sports games and the name in his passport. The debate could go on to a judicial court where the validity of the fan's claims have to be proved.

What we can learn from this analysis of the conversation between official and fan is that the more the conversation proceeds, the more the participants are forced to back up their claims by grounds and evidence that anybody would accept. The conversing parties move from an area of mutual acquaintance, particularistic trust, and silent understanding to an area where everything has to be grounded by evidence that anybody would accept without prior knowledge of the speaker. The conversation moves from simple communication to what Habermas (1981: 25–71) calls rational discourse.

Rationality, Communication, and Discourse

At this point, we can specify the different criteria of rationality of strategic and communicative action. Strategic action is rational if it applies appropriate means under given conditions and therefore successfully attains the goal set by the actor. We can distinguish two fundamental types of strategic or instrumental action: The first type is goal-oriented action. This implies the orientation of action toward attaining a single goal, where the more rational the action is, the more completely the applied means lead to the attainment of the goal. Here the actor acts according to the principle of maximizing the attainment of a specific goal. The second type is economically calculated action. This implies the orientation of action toward an optimum of goal attainment out of a set of multiple goals, where the more rational the action is, the more the applied means allow for attaining an optimum of all goals. The optimum is higher, for example, when an actor with ten equal ranking goals attains all ten halfway instead of realizing one goal completely and the other nine only at the 10 percent level. Here the actor acts according to the economic principle of optimizing the attainment of a set of multiple goals.

Communicative action is rational inasmuch as the actors can justify their statements with reasons (reasonable grounds) on which the actors agree. We can distinguish two types of communicative action: The first type is simple communication. Actors are led by mutual trust and silent understanding and try to come to a consensus on how to interpret symbolic expressions and on how to act. They act according to a principle of conformity to commonly shared norms. Rationality of this action merges with conformity to a commonly established life-world of ideas and norms. Here, justification of a statement with reasonable grounds means demonstrating its conformity to the established knowledge of a commonly shared life-world. The second type of communicative action is rational discourse. The actors have to justify their statements to a much wider public than the narrow confines of a community sharing norms and ideas of a life-world. Everybody, not only the members of a particular community, should be able to consent to a statement. This requirement of rationality implies that a statement has to survive any imaginable criticism from whoever it might come in order to be maintained as justified by reasonable grounds. Thus a statement has to be supported by universal ideas, norms, or laws to which everybody would consent after strict examination in order to be taken as valid. And it is only valid as long as no attempt at criticizing the statement succeeds. Whereas the rationality of simple communication is limited to the boundaries of the dominating knowledge of a community, the rationality of discourse reaches beyond the boundary of any single community.

A rational discourse takes place inasmuch as the following requirements are fulfilled by an ongoing communication (Habermas, 1968a, 1981: 48–49):

1. Everybody can make statements with equal right and no temporal, factual, and social limitation.
2. Everybody can question and criticize statements with equal right and no temporal, factual, and social limitation.
3. Only the justification of statements by reasons in argumentation determines the acceptance of a statement.
4. Of two competing statements, the one that can be justified by better arguments will be accepted. An argument is the better one if it can justify a statement by reasons that everybody holds true. An argument means the logical derivation of a particular statement from a more generally accepted idea, norm, or law under specific conditions.
5. As long as everybody agrees with a statement under conditions 1, 2, 3, and 4, a statement is taken as valid.

These criteria make up what Habermas calls an ideal speech situation. Only statements that get agreement from everybody imaginable as participants of discussion and criticism in an ideal speech situation can be held as valid. And this holds true only as long as no criticism can be imagined that can be backed by better arguments than the statement itself. This is the criterion of validity of statements. We have to distinguish this validity of statements based on rational discourse from the social bindingness of statements in a community based on simple communication. In simple communication, statements are supported by arguments that derive them from the dominating knowledge within a community. In rational discourse, statements are supported by arguments that derive them from ideas, norms, or laws that would receive the agreement of anybody who would be asked for criticism.

Habermas (1981: 33–44) distinguishes three kinds of statements: cognitive, normative, and value expressive. Cognitive statements are statements of fact or of relationships between facts, with singular or general variants. A singular cognitive statement is, for example: "250,000 cars crossed Wilshire Boulevard on San Diego Freeway in Los Angeles on February 26, 1985." These statements say that something is the case at a certain place on a certain time. A general cognitive statement is, for example: "Cars pollute the air wherever and whenever they are driven on roads." A general cognitive statement on a factual relationship is, for example: "The greater the rise or the decline in prosperity in a society, the higher will be the rate of suicides" (Durkheim's law of anomic suicide).

A singular normative statement is, for example: "The students of my class, Sociology 113 at UCLA in the winter quarter 1990, are required to turn in four papers and to take one final exam." We have to notice that this statement addressed to the students themselves is to be read as a normative statement; addressed to an outside observer it is to be read as a cognitive statement on the norms guiding students in a sociology class. A general normative statement is: "Everybody has to respect a person's property." A general relational normative statement is: "Wherever a first person has violated the property rights of a second person, the first person has to pay for the second person's damage."

A singular value expressive statement is: "UCLA's campus is beautiful." A general value expressive statement is: "Sunny skies are always beautiful." A relational and general value expressive statement is: "Whenever the sun rises, skies appear in a beautiful light."

We can add a fourth category of statements that Habermas does not take into account: statements on meaning or meaning constructions. A singular statement of meaning is: "Pastor Dole's sermon in today's service has given me back the meaning of my life." A general statement of meaning is: "Participating regularly in worship gives a meaning to life." A general relational statement of meaning is: When you believe in God, you will see light in the darkness of life (you will see meaning in a seemingly senseless world)."

The validity of statements of this kind has to be demonstrated in discourse. It is this question of validity that introduces a completely new quality into social interaction, which distinguishes communication from strategic action. What is right and what is wrong becomes an important determinant of action. Let us point out this difference with the example of the student-professor conversation. As long as student and professor both act strategically, it makes no difference for their action whether the form of exam the professor chooses is right or wrong, or whether what the student writes and what the professor expects is right or wrong. In this case, the professor's exam and his or her view of sociological theories is an external condition to which the student has to adjust his or her action in applying the right means in order to pass the exam, for example, learning exactly what the professor said in lectures and repeating this in answering the questions without asking whether this is right or wrong. The result of successful strategic action is the student's passing the exam by telling the professor what he or she wants to hear.

The course of the same interaction proceeding according to the criteria of communication and even discourse can be very different. Now the professor's requirements for the exam and view of sociological theories is no longer just an external condition to which the student has to adjust his or her action. They are statements that can be submitted to processes of justification. This is a fundamental difference. Student and professor can engage in a discourse on the validity of respective statements. Let us assume the student asks, "What type of exam will we have?" Let us also assume in this case that the professor answers, "We will have a multiple choice battery." The student may leave it at that, saying: "Okay, I understand." Here we have a simple communication that takes place on the basis of mutual trust and silent understanding. The student will try to conform to the professor's requirements as in the case of strategic action. However, the student does so not because he or she strategically adapts to an external condition but because he or she shares common norms with the professor. This difference has further consequences. In the strategic view, the student cannot raise questions regarding the requirements of the professor, because these are external factual conditions. One cannot question the rightness of factual conditions. They are just there and have to be taken into account.

However, as soon as the two communicate, the student can raise questions. He or she can ask for justification, "Why will we have a multiple choice battery and not an essay?" The professor may answer, "A multiple choice exam is a standardized means of checking over a wide range of knowledge, whereas papers select only certain aspects out of the whole range of knowledge." The student is not convinced and asks, "Why do you want to check the whole range of knowledge? This is only a very superficial test, whereas an essay would allow you to check the depth of our knowledge." The professor may answer, "It is a fundamental value of our college education to implant a broad range of knowledge in our students, and a multiple choice exam is the best way to test the range of your knowledge." The student may reply, "You're right. However, you don't cover the whole truth. It is also a fundamental value of our college education to allow students to concentrate on specific subjects in order to learn how to penetrate and analyze things in depth, and an essay is the best test of this ability." The professor may concede, "You're right, learning how to penetrate and analyze something in depth is also a fundamental value of college education, but not as important as in graduate academic training, where much more specialization is required. In college education, we consciously work against too much specialization too early. Therefore, the value of acquiring a broad range of knowledge ranks higher than the value of training the ability to penetrate and analyze something in depth. The complete education of a person, to someone who possesses the broad knowledge of our culture and who is able to penetrate and analyze the world in depth with this knowledge, requires both: learning a broad range of knowledge and learning how to penetrate and analyze something in depth. The best way to accomplish this task is to give learning of the elementary abilities the greatest part in the earlier phases of education, the broadening of the range of knowledge the greatest part in the middle phases and learning to analyze something in depth beginning to play a part, and then attaching the greatest importance to that in the later phases of education. In college, we have an overlap phase between the final steps of the middle phases and of the first steps of the later phases. Because this is a junior class, broadening the range of your knowledge is at least as important as learning in-depth analysis." The student takes up the professor's argument, "See, you're not saying that broadening the range of our knowledge is more important than learning in-depth analysis. We could say they are equal in our phase of education. Why don't we split our exam to have one-half a multiple choice battery and one-half an essay on a specific question?" The professor admits, "Your argument is convincing; because both educational values are about equal in importance in your junior class, we should split the exam into a multiple choice battery and an essay." The student replies, "Well, let's do that. Thank you for your willingness to consider our arguments." The professor replies, "No problem. You are right."

This is a rational discourse that starts with a singular normative statement: "Students of this junior class have to take a multiple choice final exam." This normative statement is examined in discourse regarding its justification by reasonable grounds that are more general in character. The professor first makes the following derivation: "It is a generally accepted value of education to broaden the range of knowledge. Multiple choice batteries are the best test of the range of knowledge. Therefore, an exam that is a test of knowledge should entail a multiple choice battery." The student makes the same derivation for his or her preference for an essay from the educational value of training in-depth analysis. The professor then goes on and gives an explanation of the relative rank of both values in different phases of education and has to admit that at the junior level in college both are equally important. Thus the student can derive the splitting of the exam into a multiple choice battery and an essay from the equal rank of the two fundamental values of education. His/her proposal is the one which is best grounded upon derivation from generally valid values of education.

In this discourse, the two mentioned values of education are taken for granted. Student and professor assume that everybody would agree with these values. However, the debate could also reach this level, so that the validity of these normative statements on what education has to do is examined. In this case they have to be derived from even more general normative statements on how a person should be. Such a normative statement would look like this: "Every person should have a broad knowledge of the culture in which he or she lives and should be able to penetrate and analyze the world in depth." The discourse could still go on until it reaches the level of discussing the meaning of life and the place of the human being in the world. The discourse can touch many related things such as other values that are touched by education, for example, equal assessment of exams and freedom of choice of educational subjects; the discourse can also involve questioning statements of fact related to the normative issue, for example, the statements that multiple choice batteries are the best test of the range of knowledge and that essays are the best test of in-depth knowledge. The questions that could be raised are endless. Therefore, a rational discourse can be suspended provisionally with a preliminary and temporary consensus. Nevertheless, it can be taken up whenever someone raises a new or an old question.

This endless questioning and criticism is the driving force of rational discourse that allows us to assume that statements that survive this severe criticism and examination will approach validity in the long run. This does not imply that we can be sure about any specific statement that has survived criticism, because tomorrow new criticism may be raised. However, we can be sure that criticism in rational discourse will bring us closer to validity of our knowledge in the long run, and that there is no other way to validity than the endless questioning of validity claims. Permanently generating dissent is the way to valid knowledge. Consensus is only a very fragile phase of rational discourse and not the proof of validity. We have to correct Habermas at this point of our discussion. According to his consensus theory of validity, consensus under the condition of an ideal speech situation provides the validity of knowledge. This criterion of validity still entails an element of social bindingness: Consensus occurs only for a while, because the participants take for granted some parts of their commonly shared knowledge that prevails in their community. Thus, consensus is not a true criterion for validity. There is no criterion for proving the validity forever of a statement made here and now. All that we can assume is that the endless criticism of rational discourse in the long run will lead to the survival of those statements that are closer to validity than those that did not survive. We can be sure about the never-ending process but not about any single statement that has consensus at a certain time (see Münch, 1984: 77–126).

The Nondiscursive Elements in Real Life Discourse

Habermas has been extensively criticized in the literature for having constructed a theory of rationality that rests on unreal conditions: the conditions of the ideal speech situation. They can never be completely realized, the critics say. However, this critique is completely mistaken. These critics fall into the trap of a fallacy of misplaced concreteness. Habermas's theory of rationality is an analytical statement. It singles out the structural conditions under which progress in the validity of our knowledge and progress in the corresponding rationality of action would take place if action were to be determined by nothing but the structural features of rational discourse: actors communicate, everybody has an equal right to make statements and to criticize statements, nothing but the better argument counts, and a statement is accepted only as long as it withstands severe criticism. The more the examination of knowledge proceeds in this manner, the more the resulting knowledge will be universally grounded. This statement on the progress of our knowledge and of rationality is conditional in character. Only inasmuch as the conditions of the ideal speech situation are realized will our knowledge proceed toward more universal rationality. The truth of the theory does not depend on whether or not the conditions of the ideal speech situation really exist, with nothing but rational discourse influencing the development of knowledge.

To prove Habermas's theory of discursive rationality we have only to isolate the structural conditions of discourse from other factors so that we can examine their specific influence on the progress of knowledge. This is no different than any other procedure of scientific investigation. Concrete reality is always a mixture of different factors having influence on events, behaviors, and developments. This is true with physical reality and with social reality. The laws of physical science, too, analytically isolate the relationships between specific causes and their specific effects on specific behaviors of objects. Social science always proceeds in this way. Social life seen in its full concreteness is almost never determined only, for example, by market structures or power structures or community relationships. They are mostly intermingled. However, in order to specify the specific effects of markets, power structures, and community relationships on social action and social order, we have to single them out and to state their effects analytically. Similarly, in concrete social life, the structure of rational discourse is mostly intermingled with other structures leading to mixed effects on social action and order. Nevertheless, it is the task of social science to ascertain which are the specific effects of rational discourse on social action and order. In order to do that, we have to single out the structure of rational discourse and to specify what would happen with social action and social order if they were determined by nothing but rational discourse. Stating that everything is mixed does not help us here. Those who look for such "concrete theories" do not understand what the task of science is.

Our example of the student-professor conversation, should it take place in concrete life, would very often involve nondiscursive factors that would influence the course of the discussion. Strategic elements would exert their influence. The professor would make use of his or her power position and reject the student's questions. The student could strategically refer to values that he or she knows are acknowledged by the professor and could strategically lead the discussion in the direction of writing an essay instead of a multiple choice exam, because the student knows he or she is better at writing essays. And the professor may be influenced by the student particularly because he or she feels committed to this class, which has done very well during the term. Thus, the conversation as it occurred in real life would be influenced not only by elements of rational discourse but also by elements of domination, negotiation, and communal association.

Every concrete conversation, even if the primary emphasis is on rational discourse, would imply elements of domination, negotiation, and communal association. A concrete discourse itself would need inputs of this kind in order to really take place. Participants first have to accept each other, to listen to each other, and to be trustworthy and trusting. This would not occur if there were no communal association between the participants in a discussion. However, on the other hand, this communal association sets limits on criticism and innovation. Criticism is often harmful, and it is easier to criticize an enemy than to criticize a friend. Discourse primarily needs criticism, but it also needs the acceptance of others as fellow members of a community. Building such a community, though, sets limits on innovation, because the more the community becomes established, the more the horizon of thought is narrowed to its boundaries. Furthermore, effective discourse needs leadership by a mediating chairman. This element of domination in discourse is necessary in order to concentrate discussion on specific points so that progress can be made with regard to these points. However, this leadership in discussion at the same time suppresses contributions that are necessary to broaden criticism. In order to keep conversation flexible, negotiations are necessary, so that participants can proceed with a discussion by way of accepting a compromise on preliminaries. Without such negotiation, the discussion would not go beyond the preliminaries. However, this renders these very preliminaries immune to criticism, which is against the rules of discourse.

The Effects of Discourse on Social Action and Social Order

This intermingling of rational discourse with elements of communal association, domination, and negotiation does not mean that rational discourse has no effect on the development of knowledge about social action and social order. Its effect can be as great or as small as those of communal association, domination, and negotiation, which are equally not the only effective factors influencing the course of knowledge production, social action, and social order. There is no social order that is based only on domination, negotiation, or solidarity, just as there is no social order that is based only on rational discourse.

However, every social order is established by varying contributions made by these different structural conditions, and every social order evolves in the direction of those structural conditions that prevail in a specific historical situation in a society. And it is the specific effects of those structural conditions of the development of knowledge, action, and order that we want to know. In order to meet this requirement, we have to build theories on processes, which we analytically single out and separate from other processes in order to study their specific effects on knowledge, action, and order. It is just this analytical knowledge that is provided by Habermas's theory of communication and discourse.

According to this theory we can assume that inasmuch as the development of knowledge, action, and order is influenced by the procedural rules of rational discourse, they will progress toward higher levels of rationality in the sense of developing and applying knowledge (cognitions, norms, value expressions, and meaning constructions) that has thus far survived under criticism and approaches higher levels of general validity, and with which everybody participating in a discourse would agree. Knowledge, action, and order approach higher levels of universality. Rational discourse as an element that influences the development of social order has been of prominent importance in modern Western societies since the Enlightenment broke down the previously existing boundaries for rational discourse and claimed its penetration into every sphere of societal life. In every historical epoch before the Enlightenment, rational discourse was limited to small circles of scholars. The Enlightenment philosophers were the first in history who proclaimed the building of a whole new society on the principles of rationality. The French Enlightenment philosophers of the eighteenth century were the most radical protagonists of this idea. Their alliance with the bourgeois middle class during the French Revolution was the great political breakthrough of their desire to build a new society on the principles of rationality. Though their political success was limited in French history because of the course of the Revolution and its final replacement by Napoleon's regime and the further restoration of the old powers, the Enlightenment has had lasting cultural effects throughout the world. The place of rational discourse in guiding the development of social order has become successively more and more important. This holds true for the overall development despite regressions as experienced in the fascist epoch, 1920–1945.

Let us take one example: In the United States, the Supreme Court is a central social institution that has an important influence on the evolution of social order. This institution is discursively structured to a higher degree than any other political institution with a similar influence on society anywhere else in the world. The Court has made many important decisions on what is right or wrong in American life from a normative point of view. It has made important judgments, for example, on the freedom rights of the media and of suspects and on the equality rights of minorities and women. The changes that have taken place in working against inequality of opportunity in admission to schools, colleges, universities, administrations, and companies cannot be explained without recourse to the evolution of decision making in the Supreme Court (see Münch, 1986: 439–51). And we can observe a clear development toward higher levels of universal validity of the Court's ruling.

One example is the history of Court decisions on discrimination in school admission. The cases on which the Court had to decide were Black school children seeking admission to all-white schools. There was a steady refinement of the Court's ruling from decision to decision, a steady broadening of the understanding of equality of opportunity, putting the decision on increasingly more universal grounds. In the first decision in favor of dismantling discrimination of Blacks, the Court did not vote for admission of Blacks to all-white schools, but voted for offering Blacks the opportunity to go to a similar all-Black school without consideration of its quality (1899, *Cumming v. Richmond County Board of Education*). In a much later decision, the Court voted for separate schools, but they had to have equal material equipment (1950, *Sweatt v. Painter, McLaurin v. Oklahoma State Regents for Higher Education*). The great breakthrough came in 1954 when the Court ruled against separate schools saying that this would implant forever a feeling of inferiority in the Black child (1954, *Brown v. Board of Education of Topeka*).

In these decisions, the Court examined the compatibility of admission policies of schools with the general normative statement of the Fourteenth Amendment to the U.S. Constitution. This amendment of 1868 made the Black ex-slaves citizens of the United States and prohibited all states from robbing citizens of their privileges and immunities, of legal equality, and the rights to life, freedom, and property without due process of law. The Court ruled in its decisions that certain admission policies contradict this amendment. The historical development thus led to an increasingly strict interpretation of the Fourteenth Amendment with increasingly strict requirements regarding equality of opportunity in school admission. The meaning of equality of opportunity as formulated in the Fourteenth Amendment becomes universalized to take in an increasing number of people and cases. Because of this extension of its scope of application, a greater number of cases becomes illegitimate in the light of the Fourteenth Amendment. Social facts that were long taken for granted now become visible as inequalities and are seen as illegitimate. This calls for the abolition of these illegitimate inequalities and for social order in every sphere of society to be placed on

more universal grounds, that is, for institutions with their particular norms
and practices to be changed in the direction of a closer correspondence with
the universal normative idea of equality of opportunity as stated in the Fourteenth Amendment. Inasmuch as rational discourse influences the course
of social development — as is the case when there is a powerful institution
based on discourse like the U.S. Supreme Court — social order evolves so
as to approach a closer correspondence of its institutional norms and practices with universal norms.

What we stated about the effects of institutionalized rational discourse
should not be misunderstood as a confirmation that everything in society
is determined by rational discourse and that society moves unidirectionally
toward higher levels of rationality. Whether this is so or not depends solely
on the degree to which rational discourse is firmly institutionalized in society and overrules factors leading societal development in other directions.
Also, in order to penetrate society truly, the Court's rational discourse needs
the assistance of nondiscursive factors: only a highly esteemed Court has
the *influence* to have its decisions accepted as *binding*, only *negotiations*
in Court keep the process of decision making *flexible* and *effective* in much
debated cases, only the Court's *authority* allows the strict *enforcement* of
its decisions against resistance. However, it is just this dependence of the
Court's ruling on nondiscursive elements that opens the door for distortions in its decision making as rational discourse is overruled by communal
association, negotiation, and domination. For a long time, the Court
represented only the morality of the white population, being just a part of
this community; its decision making sometimes depends on the ability to
achieve in negotiation, and its decision making is influenced by the political views of its majority. However, this intermingling of discourse, association, negotiation, and domination does not imply that discourse has no effect
at all. It is only that the effects of discourse on social order are limited by
those nondiscursive elements the more they work against the results of discourse and do not support the penetration of these results into society.
Habermas's theory of discursive rationality tells us about something that
has an effect on societal development; how much effect this is depends on
the scope of rational discourse in society.

Critical Theory

At this point we come to a fundamental property of the theory of discursive rationality that enables Habermas to continue with the tradition of critical theory of the Frankfurt school on a new level of theoretical progress,
escaping some of the dilemmas of older critical theory (Habermas, 1981:
455-534; see Adorno et al., 1969; Jay, 1973, 1984, 1986; Tar, 1977; Held,
1980; McCarthy, 1982; Bottomore, 1984). With the theory of discursive

rationality we can, on the one hand, describe and explain societal processes from the perspective of an observer who looks at the effects of discourse on the evolution of knowledge and social order in society. We can also describe and explain, from the perspective of an observer, limitations and breakdowns of rationality such as distortions of communication and rational discourse due to the invasion of strategic action like domination and negotiation into discursive procedures. We can show, for example, how the domination of the Supreme Court by conservative judges committed to the ruling white Anglo-Saxon and Protestant population distorted discourse in the Court for a long time, so that it took more than fifty years to come from the separate schools ruling in 1899 to the free admission of Blacks at any school and the integrated schools ruling in 1954. We can show how the prevailing white opinion and the conservative domination in the Court violated the rules of free access and equality in discourse, therefore, distorted communication, and resulted in the rulings that were imposed on society but have to be regarded as decisions with distorted rationality. They could not be universally valid because they would not withstand criticism as soon as free access and equality in discourse opened the door for such criticism. The opening of discussion in the 1950s and 1960s introduced this criticism and consequently led to a change of the Court's decisions in the direction of universalizing the idea of equality of opportunity.

An analysis of this kind is a contribution to rational discourse in society itself. That is, the sociologist who does such an analysis not only observes societal processes but also contributes with the same analysis to rational discourse itself. He or she switches from the perspective of an observer of societal processes to the perspective of a participant in the same processes of rational discourse. A sociologist's review of Supreme Court decisions on civil rights over the last one hundred years that is read by people who take part in public debates on Supreme Court decisions or enters into the actual deliberations made by the Court is itself a contribution to rational discourse in Court and exerts an influence on that discourse whatever the amount and result of this influence may be.

A sociologist who investigates the course of decision making in a specific case may interview the decision makers. He or she can do this from the perspective of an observer who describes and explains but can also go on talking to his or her interview partners about distortions of the decision-making process and question the validity of the resulting decision. This may cause further deliberations by some of the judges and lead to a reconsideration of the case. However, we have to notice here that the sociologist who switches from the perspective of the observer to the perspective of a participant in rational discourse has to do so on equal terms, not as an authoritative expert who advises his or her audience. He or she has to compete with alternative analyses and interpretations and with the analysis and interpretation of the interviewed judges on equal terms, otherwise the sociologist him- or herself would distort communication. The sociologist is never in the position of someone who tells his or her audience the "truth," but is one of many participants in the endless societal enterprise of rationally discussing the validity of the cognitions, norms, value expressions, and meaning constructions that make up its culture and become institutionalized in its social order. This is the point at which Habermas goes beyond the restrictions of purely hermeneutic approaches to studying society as a text, relying, for example, on Gadamer's (1960; for translation, see 1975) hermeneutics. The latter remains limited to pointing out how an interpreter can come to a valid understanding of the meaning of a text by entering into a virtual conversation with its author and reaching a mutual understanding. The question of whether the claims of the text are valid or not, however, can also be raised and has to be answered in a different discourse on the validity claims of the text.

The achievement of Habermas's procedural theory of rationality frees critical theory from the dilemma of criticizing distortions of communication and rationality in societal development and contributing to that distortion of communication and rationality by taking a stance above the accumulated knowledge of society and claiming a truth that cannot be proved once and for all. The political transformation of this claiming of higher truth unavoidably leads on to the political domination of society by an intellectual elite and turns the claimed truth into a ruling ideology. This was the fate of Marxism in the socialist countries of the Soviet and Chinese type. Habermas manages to solve this dilemma by locating rationality in the procedure of rational discourse. It is not an absolute knowledge as in Hegel's philosophy, not a scientific theory like Marx's historical materialism, not an historical subject like Lukács's class consciousness of the enlightened working class that is the carrier of rationality, but a never ending procedure: the procedure of rational discourse.

Habermas succeeds in giving critical theory a new basis for the integration of a theory of society with rational criticism of societal development. However, it is an integration that does not claim priority for any one theory of society or any one form of societal criticism over competing theories and criticisms, as was claimed by Marxism and earlier critical theory before their recourse to aesthetic criticism as the final point of escape for a nondistorted critical stance. Habermas shows how critical social science is possible, but it is a procedure that represents critical social science, not a substantial theory of society. Habermas's success has stripped Marxism and critical theory of their claims to higher truth.

However, in substantive terms Habermas continues with the tradition of critical theory. The topic of critical theory is the fate of reason, meaning, and freedom in modern society. To get an idea of this topic we have to start with the separation of cognitive "theoretical" reason and normative "practical" reason in the philosophy of Immanuel Kant (1781/1964a, 1788/1964b, 1790/1964c, 1793/1964d). According to Kant, practical questions of the validity of normative statements and theoretical questions of the truth of cognitive statements have to be answered in different ways. Theoretical questions are the domain of the (natural) sciences; practical questions are the domain of moral reasoning. The sciences answer questions on "what is"; moral reasoning answers questions on "what should be." In Kant's view, the actual course of history is one thing, while the moral evaluation of it is quite another. Moral reasoning that is oriented toward finding out what is universally valid in moral terms is a critical measure for the actual course of history and therefore an indispensable corrective of history. History has meaning only inasmuch as we never cease correcting its development according to moral measures; however, there is no intrinsic meaning in actual historical development itself. There is no chance of completely bridging the gap between moral reasoning and actual historical development. In this sense, Kant argues for a very limited philosophy of history. It cannot discover historical laws that lead to the convergence of the actual course of history and the accomplishment of meaning in history, leading to the rise of a world that reaches higher levels of reason in social order.

The philosophers of German Idealism following Kant's epoch were not satisfied with Kant's limitation of the philosophy of history to a critical measure of the actual course of history. What they were seeking was a new convergence of reason and history, and the philosophy of history had to point the way toward this reunion. It was Hegel (1807/1964–1971, 1821/1964–1971) whose philosophy of history became most influential. According to Hegel, the development of history proceeds in dialectical terms. Its origin is a primitive unity of reason and world in the primitive consciousness of man in primitive society. The rise of modern bourgeois society and modern science has broken up this original unity and divided reason and world. This is a situation of alienation of consciousness from the world that appears as something alien guided by its own laws. It is the rise of absolute knowledge superseding the epoch of modern science and bourgeois society that dialectically replaces the split knowledge of that epoch and leads to a new unity and synthesis of reason and world on a higher level of historical development. In society it is the state oriented toward realizing the universal that unites the divided classes on a higher level.

Karl Marx did not believe in Hegel's optimism regarding the reunion of reason and history in the rise of absolute knowledge and the state, but pointed out instead that the state represented nothing but the particular interest of a ruling class and that "absolute knowledge" was really nothing but the dominating ideology of that class (Marx, 1844/1968, 1845/1969, 1867/1962, 1885/1963, 1894/1964; Marx and Engels, 1846/1969, 1848/1959a).

However, he himself pursued German idealism's line of thought. He just replaced the idealist philosophy of history with a materialist one. Whereas in Hegel's view the driving force of history is the evolution of the spirit, in Marx's view it is humankind's mastering of nature in its labor. Marx claimed to have discovered the laws that direct historical development: the relationship between productive forces and relations of production. In primitive society people live in an original unity with nature and with each other in labor. It is the rise of capitalism that breaks up humankind's ties with nature and with its fellows. Commodity production becomes a system guided by its own laws, and its extension to profit seeking in itself leads to the alienation of people from the world that surrounds them and of man from man in capitalist production: the antagonism of capital and labor.

The world of commodity production appears as a world in itself, the relations between men as relations between things determined by natural laws, even though this world was created by man himself. This is what Marx calls alienation in commodity production, or commodity fetishism. The exploitation of the worker in capitalist production he calls the alienation of wage-labor and capital. However, the development of history is determined by laws that lead to the breakdown of this antagonistic system of capitalism. The contradictions of this system between developing productive forces and restricting relations of production, between labor and capital, the crises of this system coming from periodic overproduction, a falling rate of profit, the increasing destitution of the working class, the development of large organized industries, and the growing political consciousness and organization of the working class give rise to a period of revolution in which the capitalist system will be overthrown and replaced by socialism and later on communism. At that phase of historical development, reason and world unite on a new level.

Everybody knows that the replacement of capitalism by socialism after the Russian Revolution of October 1917 has resulted in a disaster from which no socialist society has recovered. It was Marx's claim that his substantive theory is the key to a new reunion of reason and world, meaning and history, that was the root of the Communist party's totalitarian rule. In the hands of this party Marx's claim to the truth was turned into the domination of people by an ideology.

Max Weber (1920–1921a/1972a, 1920–1921b/1972b, 1920–1921c/1971a, 1921/1971b, 1922/1972c) broke with this tradition of the philosophy of history in German thought. In common with the neo-Kantianism of his time at the beginning of this century, he did not believe in the convergence of meaning and history and made the separation of statements of fact and statements of norms a major point of his methodology. Only statements of fact can be objects of scientific proof, whereas norms are left to the personal decisions of individuals. We can find out the truth of factual statements by scientific methods but not the validity of norms. There is no binding method for proving the validity of norms. On norms we can decide only on the basis of personal preferences. One person's god is another person's devil. Thus, in our society there is no way to a universally binding morality. Weber starts with Kant's separation of statements of fact and statements of norms; however, he does not share Kant's belief in the feasibility of universally binding moral reasoning. This is what we can call the loss of meaning in modern society, which is accompanied by a loss of freedom. The origin of these losses is the all-embracing process of rationalization. The roots of this process of rationalization are located in Judeo-Christian religion, particularly in the highest form of its evolution in ascetic Protestantism. This religion has transmitted the rational-methodical conduct of life beyond the monastery walls into the real world, particularly into the sphere of economic production and professional work and into the administration of the world in bureaucracies. And it has transmitted the quest for truth from theology into science. But these transmissions have established forces that have become increasingly separated from their ethical origin and control in ascetic Protestantism. The capitalist economy is now a self-reproductive system with profit maximization in its own right, educating the people it needs for itself. Bureaucracy constitutes an iron cage for humankind. Science proceeds by completely eliminating magic and religion as binding foundations of life. The result is a great loss of meaning, because religion is no longer binding in an age in which everything can be questioned by scientific investigation. But science does not answer questions of ethical life, leaving this to the personal decision of the individual human being. And there is a great loss of freedom, because people live under the domination of the laws of capitalism and bureaucratic administration of life.

Thus Weber has discovered a paradox of rationalization. The process of rationalization has emancipated the human being from the authority of tradition and has established his or her mastery of the world. It has led to the triumph of rationality over tradition. However, this very process has left the individual a completely disenchanted (demagicalized) world in which he or she does not find a preestablished meaning, but has to find this individually and in conflict with his or her fellows. And humankind's emancipation from traditional powers has established the power of capitalism and bureaucracy in the modern world.

Is there any chance of escaping from this paradox of rationalism? Weber does not give us a very promising answer. Questions of morality, of the values and norms that should guide human conduct and societal development cannot be answered in a universally valid way. What should be done has to be decided by the individual on his or her own. What should be done with society and its development can also not be answered in a universally valid way. Therefore, there is no other way than to fight this out in political struggle. This is why democracy with strong leadership and parliamentary control has to play a central role in guiding societal development. Modern society needs leadership, but its leaders must be controlled by competing leaders striving for political support from the people and by a parliament that has the right to investigate every important political and administrative decision, and acts as the institution through which political leaders have to be socialized to become leaders acting according to an ethics of responsibility rather than an ethics of conviction. The ethics of responsibility demands, on the one hand, a personal commitment to values but nevertheless an acknowledgement of the ever possible contradictions between values and goals and a readiness to revise values, goals, and means in the light of new evidence showing harmful and contradictory consequences of their realization. The ethics of conviction of the fanatic true believer does not acknowledge contradictions of equally ranking values and does not have regard for the consequences of his or her action beyond the realization of the values to which he or she is extremely committed. As Weber shows, an ethics of conviction has immoral consequences in modern times; only an ethics of responsibility can be accepted under these conditions. However, this is a personal decision and not an outcome of a rational discourse according to Weber's assumption that there is no binding procedure for answering moral questions in modern societies.

Scholars trained in the tradition of German idealism and its materialist follower, Marxism, have never been satisfied with Weber's answer regarding the chances of escaping the paradox of rationalization. What they have gone on seeking even up to the present is the reunion of reason, meaning, and historical development in modern society. Georg Lukács (1923/1968), the Hungarian Marxist, was one of the most important scholars who tried to find a solution to this problem in the 1920s. He reformulated Marx's theory of alienation and fetishism in capitalist commodity production. And he located the key to escaping the contradiction between evolving reason and the irrational domination of man by the rational laws of commodity production in the development of the consciousness of the class that suffered from alienation in capitalist commodity production: in the consciousness of the working class. The class consciousness of the working class becomes the carrier of reason in this epoch of history, because it is the class whose class interest coincides with the movement of history toward reunifying reason and world, man and nature, man and man in a future communist society. However, Lukács's optimistic view of historical development was soon refuted by the establishment of Stalinist totalitarian rule in the Soviet Union and by the reconciliation of the working class with capitalism in the developing Western capitalist societies. The attempt to save his theory by differentiating a true and a false consciousness of the working class made the contradictions even more apparent, because this demonstrated that the transformation of Marxist theory into totalitarian rule has its roots in theory itself and is not occasioned only by historical circumstances. The theorist has to decide what is true and what is false class consciousness. The theory has to claim a higher truth than any competing theory, which is nothing but the establishment of its domination.

Max Horkheimer (1967, 1968), Theodor W. Adorno (1966/1973a; Horkheimer and Adorno, 1947), and their companions, including Walter Benjamin (1973, 1974), Leo Löwenthal (1980, 1981), and Herbert Marcuse (1960, 1964), created the school of critical theory at the Institute of Social Research at Frankfurt University in the late 1920s and early 1930s, which they transferred to New York during Hitler's rule in Germany and reestablished after World War II in Frankfurt. This school became the most important source of Western Marxist thought. However, when Horkheimer and Adorno formulated critical theory in the 1930s and 1940s they no longer shared Lukács's optimistic view of the convergence of historical reason and historical development in the class consciousness of the working class, nor did they share Lukács's restricted view of the origins of modern domination over man in capitalist commodity production. Adorno and Horkheimer, and in a similar way Marcuse, developed a much more general view of the process of rationalization. However, they did not share Weber's answer to the paradox of rationalization. For Adorno and Horkheimer, as formulated in their works on *Critical Theory* (Horkheimer, 1968, for translation, see 1972), on the *Dialectic of Enlightenment* (Horkheimer and Adorno, 1947; for translation, see 1972), the *Critique of Instrumental Reason* (*Eclipse of Reason*, 1947/1974a) (Horkheimer, 1967), and *Negative Dialectics* (Adorno, 1966/1973a, for translation, see 1973b), partly written jointly, partly single authored, the origin of modern domination is a very abstract development of human thought: the rise of instrumental reason, which has its roots in "identifying thought." That is, questions of truth and questions of good life and morality were originally answered by the same processes of reasoning, as, for example, in Greek classical philosophy. This unity was broken up by the rise of the modern sciences and their "identifying" and instrumental approach to the world. Now the human being no longer is a companion of what he or she investigates but an observer and a master who subordinates nature and the whole world to his or her domination based on objective knowledge.

This leads to the central process of objectification (*Verdinglichung*) of the world, which is now something external to the human being, alienated from him or her and determined by apparently unchangeable objective laws. The more people approach the world with the instrument of modern science, the more they produce the objectification of a world that for its part begins to dominate humans, because they are now subordinated to the laws of that objectified world. This process of objectification of the world increases even more the more social theory proceeds according to the rules of identifying thought and instrumental reason. A social science that tries to establish objective laws of the social process does nothing but increase the objectification of the world and establish the domination of an objectified world over humankind. Therefore, Adorno and Horkheimer have to reject the Marxist claim to have discovered the laws governing historical development toward the reunification of reason and reality. This claim is nothing but a further objectification that establishes the domination of Marxist ideology over man.

There is no way out of this dilemma for Adorno and Horkheimer. Any attempt at demonstrating a way out of the paradox of rationalization with the methods of science would just continue to produce this paradox. Therefore, they had to be true to their own logic and give up this enterprise. What remained was Horkheimer's escape to theology in his later days, Marcuse's political activism, and Adorno's retreat to aesthetic criticism. For Adorno, a work of art is the only way in which the particular is not dominated by the general, in which there remains an original companionship of the artist with the object of his work, in which artist and object remain on their own and are not suppressed by a scientific process of objectification. Both the artist and his or her object remain free. Aesthetic criticism is the only way of criticizing without establishing domination via objectification.

This is how Adorno and Horkheimer left critical theory with a failed project: There is no chance for critical social theory to demonstrate the reunification of reason and reality in a universally valid way. Any attempt to do so would fall into the failure of objectification.

Jürgen Habermas, the currently reigning descendant of critical theory, has pointed out this failing to the disappointment of many adherents of older critical theory. But he has also shown a way out of the dilemma. According to Habermas's view, older critical theory failed because it has never been able to emancipate itself from the traditional philosophy of consciousness as it was established by German idealism. In terms of this philosophy of consciousness, the domain of evolving reason had to be consciousness seen as the objective spirit in evolving history. In these terms there always has to be a higher consciousness that claims higher truth and validity compared to the consciousness of earlier epochs. Therefore, any claim to truth coincides with establishing its domination over man. As Habermas shows, the theory of discursive rationality is a way out of this dilemma, because it locates the progress of rationality not in a consciousness or a substantial theory but in a formal procedure: the procedure of rational discourse. In a certain sense Habermas returns to Kant's limited type of a philosophy of history. Inasmuch as we engage in rational discourse on historical development, that development is corrected according to the preliminarily valid values and norms evolving from this discourse.

Theory of Modernity: The Colonization of the Life-World

Habermas does not give up the task of social theory in favor of practical philosophy. He is still interested in answering questions on historical development in terms of convergence or divergence between reason and reality. As such, he reinterprets Weber's theory of rationalization. In Habermas's (1981: 445–593) view, the very process of communicative rationalization is the origin of cultural and societal rationalization. Originally, people live in a life-world in which they communicate on the basis of silent understandings that are taken for granted. This silent understanding breaks up with any question raised that is unavoidably connected with the nature of conversation. The more questions are raised, the more justifications of statements by increasingly universal grounds are demanded. This leads to the differentiation of discourse from simple communication in a taken-for-granted life-world. Questions of factual truth are discussed in science, questions of moral validity in moral reasoning and questions of value expressions in aesthetic critique. This rationalization and differentiation of spheres of specialized cultural discourse is continued by the differentiation and rationalization of the societal spheres of the capitalist economy, the bureaucratic administration, and the legal system. This process gives rise to the establishment of new media for coordinating social interaction: money, power, and law. In the life-world, communication by language is the medium of integration and coordination of action. This is what we can call social integration. Money, power, and law evolved as such media from language but are now separate media of interaction that allow for integration and coordination without language. What they produce is systems integration. The capitalist economy, the bureaucratic administration, and the legal system are now systems separated from the life-world of human communication, solely functioning on the basis of being integrated by money, power, and law as media of interaction.

In Habermas's view, it is the accomplishment of modern systems theory as worked out by Talcott Parsons (1951, 1967, 1977, 1978) and Niklas Luhmann (1969/1983, 1970; for translation, see 1982a) to have pointed out this differentiation and independent functioning of systems in modern society. However, it is their failure, as Habermas criticizes them, that they have lost sight of the origin of any societal system and any medium of interchange in the communicative processes of the life-world. Therefore, they lose any means of critically discussing the separation of systems and their functioning from processes of legitimation in moral terms. They can do no more than to state their factual development and to objectify this development as an unavoidable natural process. They either do this in an optimistic way, as Parsons did, seeing a convergence of this process with the establishment of what he called institutionalized individualism particularly in the United

States, or factually state this process as unavoidable in a neutral way, as Niklas Luhmann does in order to look down upon any attempts at evaluating this process as a return to old European thought, which is out of step with historical development.

Habermas wants to do more: he wants to reestablish critical theory by thematizing the interrelationship between life-world communication and systematic processes of the economy, bureaucratic administration, and the legal system. Taking up Weber's (1922/1972c: 387–513) view of rational law, he shows that this could be a link between life-world communication and systemic processes providing the moral guidance for economic and bureaucratic processes. However, the rationalization of the legal system has itself separated its legality from the morality established in moral discourse. Taking recourse to Weber does not open a way to reestablishing a link between life-world communication and systemic processes. In Weber's view, the communicative rationalization of the life-world has resulted in the loss of meaning; the rationalization of the societal subsystems of the economy, bureaucracy, and legal system has resulted in the loss of freedom. According to Weber, this has been an unavoidable paradox of rationalization.

Habermas accepts Weber's position in empirical terms as a description of what has happened. He even goes on to state what he calls the colonization of the life-world by the systems of economy, bureaucracy, and positive law. This means that processes of mediating social action by money, power, and law have penetrated the very home of communication in the life-world by subjugating the areas of family, school, education, and public discussion to the imperatives of economic, administrative, and judicial decision making. What he calls juridification of the life-world is such an example. It means that the areas of family life and school life become increasingly dominated by legalistic law, bureaucratic control, and economic calculation, thus destroying the roots of communication.

However, Habermas does not accept Weber's diagnosis in theoretical terms; he does not believe in the unavoidability of the paradox of rationalization. The reason is his reestablishment of moral reasoning in rational discourse. In his view the differentiation of the life-world in communicative rationalization destroys religion as a source of morality, but it does not destroy morality itself, because the very procedure of rational discourse allows us to continue discussing factual, value expressive, and normative questions with the purpose of progressing toward higher levels and toward increasingly more universal validity. This is the reason why we do not have to solely state the rise of differentiated and independently functioning systems but can also raise the question of their legitimacy in terms of relating their development back to moral reasoning in rational discourse.

This is the point where Habermas switches from the sociological analysis of a factual historical development to the task of the critical theorist who raises questions about the gap between that development and ideas of morality resulting from rational discourse. Questions of legitimacy and rational criticism then replace questions of sociological analysis. However, it is here that Habermas must enter rational discourse about these questions on equal terms with competing positions. His theory of society and societal development, which he constructed using elements from Max Weber and Parsons, cannot claim a higher truth and does not answer any question about the direction in which society should go. He has to leave the answers to this question to the procedure of moral discourse itself. However, it is exactly this point where Habermas sometimes falls back into the failures of the Marxist tradition. He sometimes overestimates the place of rational discourse in modern society with a tendency toward abolishing everything that does not proceed according to its rules. This tendency was particularly apparent in his earlier writing; however, in his recent writings, he acknowledges more the independent and necessary contributions of institutions to modern societal life that are different to rational discourse: economic markets, political markets, administrative processes, negotiations, expertise, communal association, legal decision making in competition, and so on. His position now is that we have to re-link these differentiated systems to procedures of discourse.

Summary

1. The more cultural rationalization proceeds, the more it sets in motion societal rationalization that differentiates morality, the arts, and science from religion, and the legal, political, and economic systems from the life-world.
2. The more the legal, political, and economic systems become rationalized and are internally integrated by their own technical media (law, power, and money), the less they can be controlled on the basis of moral consensus.
3. The more the rationalization of society proceeds, the more the legal, political, and economic systems expand and penetrate the life-world, thus reducing areas of communicative consensus formation to a minimum and "colonizing" the life-world.
4. The more social interaction proceeds as communication, the more it gives rise to questions of justification of statements.
5. The more questions of justification arise in communication, the more silent understandings are broken up and the more understanding and consensus becomes based on universal foundations.
6. The more rational discourse proceeds, the more it results in the universalization of knowledge (cognitions, norms, value expressions).

7. The more societal development is influenced by questions of justification in rational discourse, the more it is corrected in the direction of a closer consistency with universally valid norms.

Critical Assessment

It cannot be the task of the future to replace all differentiated societal institutions by the institution of rational discourse. To do this is to emulate the failure of Marxist theory when it promised the replacement of all economic and political institutions by communism. Many of his adherents have read Habermas in this perspective, meaning that only a society in which nothing reigns but rational discourse is worth living in. Indeed it is true that Habermas has not been very clear about that. However, close reading of his theory of communicative action reveals that he does not argue for more than giving rational discourse a place in society so that it can serve as a continuously working *corrective* of societal development. Hence, he cannot argue for the replacement of the capitalist economy, bureaucratic administration, legal system, or liberal democracy by procedures of rational discourse; but what he can do is to argue for establishing a firm link between them so that those systems are related to the moral measures arising from rational discourse. However, because rational discourse also has to take into account the imperatives of economic production, bureaucratic administration, and judicial and political decision making, the linkage has to be two sided, so that these imperatives can also set limits on moral reasoning inasmuch as the processes of that reasoning would destroy the functioning of economic, administrative, legal, and political systems. Processes of legitimation would have to link moral discourse and economic, administrative, legal, and political decision making.

These processes of decision making can be criticized from the moral point of view; however, they also have repercussions on moral discussions. For example, moral discussions have to be limited in time and come to a conclusion in order to be transmitted to political decision making. If the Supreme Court did not come to a decision, it would have no effect on political decision making. This, however, sets limits on discourse, because discourse has no end. Economic restrictions of scarcity also set limits, for example, on the distribution of products on completely equal terms. These repercussions of systemic imperatives do not change morality but force the application of moral principles to take into account specific circumstances. On the other hand, moral discourse does not change the economic, administrative, legal, and political imperatives, but it does set limits for them and guides political decision making as a frame of reference for its legitimation. In this way subsystems between moral discourse and economic, administrative, legal, and political decision making and communal association provide for their *interpenetration*: economic, administrative, political, legal, and public discourse.

Moral discourse, economic transactions, political decision making, and communal association, furthermore, not only set limits to each other when they interpenetrate but also provide necessary resources for each other for accomplishing their purpose. The first internal requirement for moral discourse is the association of discussants, negotiation of proceedings, and leadership of discussion; it also needs influence transmitted from communal association in order to be accepted, money in order to organize, and power in order to transform its results into binding decisions. Thus, there is a communal, economic, and political production of morality that complements its production in rational discourse. Each system in turn has the same need for the resources provided by the other systems. In this way societal development does not proceed in a one-way process of transmitting moral discourse into economic, political, administrative, and associational systems but in a complex process of interpenetration.

Summarizing and evaluating Habermas's theory of communicative action, we can state that it provides us with important insights into the structure and processes of communication and their effects on societal development and goes much beyond symbolic interactionism in its analysis of communication.

However, Habermas's theory of communicative action is not a complete sociological theory; in order to yield complete explanations it has to be complemented by theories on economic, political, and associational processes. As we have seen, even discourse itself needs nondiscursive elements in order to take place in real life. And the penetration of its results into society needs the contribution of nondiscursive media: money, power, influence in processes of negotiation, domination, and association.

Finally, we can state that Habermas has demonstrated how a critical theory of society is still possible in our times.

Related Theory and Research

Habermas's revision of critical theory by building a theory of communicative action has stimulated further developments in recent years (Honneth, McCarthy, Offe, and Wellmer, 1989). Klaus Eder (1985) has expanded Habermas's theory in his work explaining the development of political and legal culture in Germany from 1770 to 1870 and in his work on the new social movements. Max Miller (1986) has done the same in his work on collective processes of learning. Axel Honneth (1985) has contributed a critical theory of power. Albrecht Wellmer (1971) has tried to revitalize philosophical elements of earlier critical theory. In recent times, Ulrich Beck (1986) stimulated a broadening discussion of the so-called risk society. Though not a statement of the Frankfurt School, his approach can be interpreted as a renewal of critical theory. His main argument states that contemporary modern society has reached a level of technological development at which it produces risks of a global nature that affect everyone. Traditional class conflict is replaced by the conflict surrounding control of the risks of modernization.

SIXTEEN

COMMUNICATION AS SYSTEMIC INFORMATION PROCESSING: NIKLAS LUHMANN'S SYSTEMS THEORY

A RADICALLY different view of meaning, communication, rationality, and modernity compared to Habermas's theory of communicative action has been developed by another contemporary German sociologist: Niklas Luhmann. In line with the German tradition, his work centers around meaning and communication. This is why we have placed him in the field of the symbolics of social action. However, he proceeds by taking up systems theory and evolutionary theory from the biological sciences. In this way he turns communication into systemic information processing.

The social world is not just a sequence of events occurring occasionally, and what goes on in social interaction between actors is determined not only by the properties, possessions, and abilities of the actors. Something more determines the sequence of events, the occurrence of social acts, and the course of social interaction. According to Niklas Luhmann's theory of social systems, the fact that social reality is organized in social systems just as the world in general is organized in systems constitutes that additional factor that makes a difference in the occurrence, sequence, and course of social interaction (Luhmann, 1969/1983, 1970, 1972, 1973, 1975, 1980, 1982b, 1982d, 1984, 1986, 1988; for translation, see 1979, 1982a, 1982c, 1985, 1989).

Systems

Let us take an example from our earlier discussions: the football fan's approach to the gate official, the reaction of the official, and the course of their interaction and its outcome are determined not just by their individual abilities to associate, communicate, negotiate, or apply power;

they are also determined by the fact that the fan and the official interact and communicate within a social system that adds its own properties to the course of their interaction. The social system here is the system of official-fan relationships, which is a subsystem of the football system. For the moment we can say that this system works according to its own laws; the official and the fan are not completely free in choosing their actions. Thus, it may be a general feature of this system that officials and fans regard each other with suspicion, maybe because of earlier experiences. In seeing each other in this way the fan and the official can act in many different ways and with the best intentions, yet each will nevertheless interpret the actions of the other as threatening and will react with corresponding suspicion. This gives rise to yet more suspicion on each side of the relationship. The outcome will be that there is no other possibility than the fan's attempt to illegally enter using fraud or force and the official's attempt to capture the suspect fan by alerting the police and applying force. The system's code, which is based on mutual suspicion, directs the actions and their outcome onto this path independently of how the actors act individually.

This is how the organization of their interaction by a system makes a difference in determining the occurrence, sequence, course, and outcome of social acts. This is why systems theory can tell us something that goes beyond individualistic theories of action. Other examples may illustrate this phenomenon further: The interaction between the student and the professor regarding the form of an exam is determined in its occurrence, sequence, course, and outcome not only by the individual qualities, possessions, and abilities of the two and of their actions but also by the character, particularly the code of the social system of higher education within which both act, and the particular code of their system. Thus, if they acted in a system within which it is a common understanding that professors rigidly exert pressure on students while students try to escape this pressure, any act of the student would be taken as a self-interested escape from requirements by the professor, and any act of the professor would be taken as an exertion of pressure on students, leaving both parties with no opportunity but to apply force and/or fraud. If they acted in a system in which it is understood that students participate in decisions in order to organize their education in the most successful way, the course of the interaction would lead to cooperatively finding out the best way of testing the students' progress in learning, whatever action were taken by either side. The course and outcome of the interaction occurs independently of the individual actions.

In another example, a woman asks her husband whether he wants to go with her to the cinema to see a new movie that night. What happens next depends on the system of their intimate relationship that has evolved during the history of their interactions. If the code of their system means that the man sees his wife's wishes as pressure on him and the woman sees his reactions as an escape from sharing their lives, their interaction will move in a specific direction independently of their intentions. The man may feel the pressure and, though he doesn't want to go to the cinema, may fear the reaction of his wife. Thus he doesn't answer with a concrete yes or no, but with a "maybe" and a reference to what is on TV that night. The woman takes this once more as a refusal by her husband to share her interests and asks for a concrete answer. If the man refuses to come with her, she will be confirmed in her view and react by angrily retreating from the situation. If the man agrees to come with her, she will still be suspicious and take his action as not really motivated by his wish to share her interests, and still react angrily, which may lead to neither of them going to the cinema. Her husband's action does not change the system and thus does not lead to a mutually shared experience of going to the cinema. What happens is independent of the wife's and the husband's actions taken individually but dependent on the code of the system within which they interact.

This determination of actions by systems does not imply that no change of action is possible. There is also the other side. Systems evolve, systems break down and are replaced by new ones, and systems change. The husband can spontaneously reply to his wife that going to the cinema is a wonderful idea on that night. The woman may be surprised and still may have some suspicion that there must be something in the background that has changed her husband's mind, and the outcome may not be different. However, this reaction of the husband can also be the beginning of a change in their system and even of building up a completely new system. Change may involve a new situation such that, in general, the man still experiences his wife's wishes as pressure, and the woman views her husband as escaping from sharing her life, but in particular both come to an agreement that in order to maintain their relationship they should go once a month to the cinema. They would build up a new system if the husband's spontaneous decision to go to the cinema set a complete change of their mutual perception in motion. Their system could also break down completely, leading to divorce and to the building of new systems with new partners.

These introductory examples point out that the existence of social systems makes a difference in determining the occurrence, sequence, course, and outcome of social action and that it is worth studying their mechanisms in order to improve our knowledge of social reality. We will do this in the following sections.

Complexity

Luhmann's introduction of his functional systems theory started by going beyond structural-functional theory to raise a more fundamental question. According to Luhmann's view, structural-functional theory's primary concern was answering the question of which structural arrangements would contribute to the maintenance of a system in a specific environment. Luhmann himself raises the more fundamental question: "Why are there systems at all, and what function do systems fulfill?" Because of this turn from the function of structures for the maintenance of a system to the function of systems in themselves, Luhmann (1970: 113–14) called his theory functional-structural theory. This basic question regarding the why and wherefore of systems is still in the background of his latest version of systems theory. His answer to this question begins with a statement on a certain feature of the world: its complexity (Luhmann, 1970: 114–17; 1984: 45–51). He means that the human being experiences the world as complex in character. This complexity of the world increases with the number of events and the number of relations between events that can possibly occur. They do not have to occur in actual fact; it is enough that they might possibly occur for this to add to the complexity of the world as it appears to the human being.

In such a complex world, the human being easily becomes disoriented, cannot predict the course of events, does not know how to act, and has the burden of investigating and proving everything, yet without any result that would give the person an orientation and tell him or her how to act. The sociological anthropology of Arnold Gehlen (1950) gives the following answer to this problem for humankind: Social institutions, that is, the patterning of human conduct by sets of norms and social roles, release the human being from having to find an orientation in such a complex world just by prescribing ways to view the world and to act in the world. Because the human being is much more open to the world than the other animals and much less determined by instinctive adaptation to the world, there is an enormous lack of orientation within the individual. This gives rise to an enormous need for orientation. And this orientation is provided by social institutions. They fulfill a releasing function for the human being; they release him or her from the pressure of coping with a supercomplex world.

This is the background of sociological anthropology from which Luhmann started his undertaking of introducing systems theory. He places systems where Gehlen placed social institutions. Luhmann provides a more abstract solution to the problem of world complexity for the human being compared to sociological anthropology. Systems are more than social institutions; they can be of different kinds, including nonsocial systems, like human consciousness as psychic system, the human organism, machines, or symbolic systems. Social institutions can also be parts of social systems, though social systems cover more than social institutions alone. Even a non-institutionalized encounter between two actors can be a social system.

We can formulate in general: Systems record, process, and reduce complexity, and in doing so, they make the world adaptable to the needs of the human being for minimal order, so that the human can orient him- or herself and act in the world in a planned way. Taking our examples, it may not be very satisfactory for the fan and the official, the student and professor, and the husband and wife to be determined in the course of their interaction by the outlined social systems with regard to specific needs, yet the systems do give them orientation and thus fulfill this abstract function. The man's reaction may be harmful for his wife, but it is a predictable reaction for her so that she can orient herself and make plans to convince him. If any reaction on his part were possible, it would be much more difficult for her to live with him. For her, any order is better than no order.

This is the anthropological background of Luhmann's systems theory, which he stated in his formulation of systems theory in the 1960s. Though he has partly changed his vocabulary in the course of developing systems theory, this background remains important for understanding the core of his theory.

Double Contingency

A similar direction is taken in Luhmann's (1984: 148–90) treatment of the question of the emergence of social systems, and hence of social order in a minimal sense, in his recently formulated version of systems theory. Here he starts again with the complexity of the world as it appears to the human being, now in the specified version of two actors encountering each other in the world. For the actors, the world appears complex and contingent. It is complex because of the endless number of events and relations between them that could possibly happen, and contingent because every event that does happen could have not happened, and endless other events could have happened instead. High contingency of events means everything that is could be different. In such a world, the success of an individual's action depends on, is contingent on, the occurrence of specific events that may happen but also may not happen.

The boy's success in getting the apples from the neighbor's garden depends on external conditions, such as the fence surrounding the garden, the height of the tree, and his ability to apply the right means to climb up the fence and the tree. His success is contingent on these conditions and means. This is simple contingency. However, he also has to take into account the behavior and the expectations of his neighbor. Will he be expecting the boy and watching him, will he rush into the garden after discovering the boy's action, will he capture the boy, and will he demand compensation from the boy's father? What the boy finally does and how successful he will be depends on the expectations and the behavior of his neighbor. And his neighbor's behavior depends on what he expects from the boy. This is double contingency. The success of my behavior depends not only on what I do with regard to some external conditions but also on what another person does, which is influenced by that person's expectations regarding my behavior. A mutual intermingling of expectations and behavior characterizes social interaction and produces a double contingency, and makes coordination and mutual predictability of action very difficult and unlikely.

Nevertheless, such coordination and mutual predictability exists in social interaction. The question then is: Where does it come from? The classical answer was formulated by Durkheim (1895/1973a): Social interaction takes place not in a vacuum but in a society that gives interaction guidance via its norms and institutions. Parsons (1937/1968) generalized Durkheim's position, saying that inasmuch as social interaction takes place in a society with a basic consensus on values and norms, it is ordered, controlled, coordinated, and predictable for actors. Luhmann shares Parsons's view on an empirical basis. He says that, in many concrete instances, social interaction is coordinated and controlled by a consensus on values and norms. However, this empirical observation does not answer the question of why and how such an order emerges when one starts with the assumption of double contingency.

In Luhmann's view, Durkheim and Parsons give only a limited answer to the question of order; it is limited to the case where consensus exists whatever the reasons for this consensus. How order arises from the situation of double contingency cannot be explained in this way according to Luhmann. This more abstract question needs a more abstract answer. The classics of the seventeenth and eighteenth centuries tried to answer this question when they asked how people move from the state of nature to the state of civil society. Their answer was the social contract, emerging either from an interest in escaping the war of all against all as Hobbes (1651/1966) put it, or from the coincidence of people's interest in freedom, life, and private property as Locke (1698/1967) postulated, or from the solidarity of people living together in society as Rousseau (1762/1964) imagined, or from the insight that a civil society based on universally valid laws corresponds to reason as Kant (1793/1964d; for translation, see 1974) argued.

Luhmann does not believe in the validity of any one of these classical solutions to the problem of order. Instead of reinstituting one of them, he introduces his own solution in terms of modern systems theory, postulating the principle of order from noise. The order from noise principle says that order emerges by chance from the many possible actions and relationships between actions in a highly complex and contingent world. Because there is always the danger of disruption and breakdown, anything that allows connection and continuation in action is likely to be selected by actors. As Luhmann puts it, the very problem of contingency initiates efforts at solving this problem. In his words, an autocatalytic process gives rise to the solution of the problem and to the emergence of order from noise. How does this happen? Noise is a state of the world in which no order, for example, no specific sequence of sounds, can be discovered. Order is a state in which such a specific sequence of sounds in a melody can be experienced. However, why should the world change from noise to order if there is seemingly nothing that builds a bridge? Luhmann's answer is that just such a bridge does exist: double contingency, which is part of noise and part of order.

The experience of double contingency is something that is a first structure in noise, and that is a minimal kind of order. Double contingency is something that is always there. Thus, it is something that actors can always expect; it is something that regularly exists and is therefore an *ordered* aspect of reality. And two actors who encounter each other *converge* in this experience of double contingency. This convergence of their perspectives is a further predictable, and therefore *ordered,* aspect of reality. This is the original contribution of double contingency to the production of order. It is a production of order by way of building a system of mutually related expectations of double contingency. In this way, a *social* system emerges from the encounter of two actors with the psychic experience of double contingency. And there is a further step that leads to the establishment of order in such a system: every action that allows a connection with another action is likely to be selected and continued. However, why is this so? And where does the likelihood of continuing actions that can be connected to other actions come from? Luhmann has a whole chapter on this problem in his book on social systems; however, he does not bring the question down to this point. He stops short with the answer that everything that allows connection with something else, that is, provides order, is likely to be selected. Nevertheless, he reveals his position. He assumes the convergence of interests in negating the state of disorder and creating order by way of solving the problem of contingency on the part of the actors who experience double contingency. He writes in *Soziale Systeme* (Luhmann, 1984: 172):

> Ego experiences Alter in the same way as Alter experiences Ego. He experiences with the nonidentity of the perspectives the identity of this experience on both parts at the same time. Because of this, the situation is undeterminable, unstable, and intolerable. In this experience the perspectives converge, and this allows us to suppose an interest in negating this negativity, an interest in determination. Phrased in terms of general systems theory, this represents a "state of conditional readiness," a chance to build a system in the state of waiting which can make use of almost any causal event in order to generate structures. (My translation)

Here we encounter the anthropological background of Luhmann's early writings. It is still present in his most recent work on systems theory. It is the anthropological need for order that motivates actors who converge in the experience of disorder to accept anything that makes the world ordered and predictable, thus releasing them from the pressure of having to produce that order themselves.

Interpenetration

From this mutual awareness of double contingency in the psychic consciousness of human beings arises a social system, a system of mutually oriented expectations and actions that acquires a quality of its own. It originates from, yet is different from, the two individual consciousnesses. In this sense the social system of these two actors' mutually oriented expectations and actions is constituted by two independent sources (which are systems themselves, but psychic systems). This is why Luhmann postulates that a social system, like all systems, is multiply constituted; it emerges not from one source but from at least two sources. And a specific relationship between the two sources produces the new system: it is their interpenetration. The two psychic systems interpenetrate — both with each other and with the newly created social system.

What does interpenetration mean in this context? According to Luhmann (1984: 150, 286–345), one psychic system penetrates the other when its complexity and contingency invades the other psychic system and creates the problem of reducing that complexity in the other system. One psychic system always represents disorder for the other system and vice versa. Inasmuch as the second system, which is penetrated by the first, is capable of recording and processing that complexity in its own terms, it maintains its independence from the first system and vice versa. Thus we have two systems that penetrate each other, yet maintain their boundaries and autonomy. They do not merge into one system. Ego's expectations and actions can penetrate Alter's consciousness, but they do so only in Alter's perspective. No matter what Ego expects and/or does, Alter's consciousness can contain nothing but Alter's own perception and interpretation of Ego's expectations and actions.

This is what Luhmann means by mutually penetrating psychic systems that nevertheless maintain their autonomy. They even need the penetration in order to produce their own autonomy. Alter needs Ego's expectations and actions as raw material in order to make up his or her mind according to his or her own perspective. What emerges from their interpenetration is the social system that is made up of their communication of mutual expectations and actions. The actors communicate their expectations and actions to each other. This process is something that is different from individual consciousness and proceeds according to its own laws. If the two actors were not able to create something outside their individual consciousness, mutual understanding and coordination of action would occur only by chance and could not be produced in a regular way. In social interaction, the actors step out of their individual consciousness and communicate as social actors who converge in something: in the identical experience of double contingency and in the identical interest of solving this problem and reducing the insecurity produced by that problem.

A second interpenetration emerges in this way: the interpenetration of the psychic systems of the individual actors with the social system in which they participate. The psychic systems penetrate the social system with the complexity and contingency of their states and processes. Whatever happens in the consciousness of the actors pervades the interaction within their social system and endangers its order. Their individual spontaneity threatens to disturb the regularity of their interaction. On the other hand, their interaction needs the contribution of their individual consciousnesses; otherwise, it would proceed in an empty state: just convention, with no new ideas. However, inasmuch as the social system of their interaction has become differentiated from their individual consciousnesses, the productions of those consciousnesses are recorded and processed within the social system of their interaction according to its own terms. On the most abstract level, every spontaneous idea of the consciousness that cannot be connected to the ideas as yet communicated in the system will be suppressed, accommodated, or just bypassed, whereas every idea that can be connected to the ongoing communication will be taken up. In this way the social system is penetrated by the psychic systems but nevertheless maintains autonomy.

On the other hand, the individual's consciousness is pervaded by the process of communication in the social system. This is disorder for the individual's consciousness, which endangers its identity but is needed to produce just that identity. What goes on in communication always threatens to break up the boundaries of an individual's consciousness but also produces the resources that the consciousness needs in order to produce its identity. The individual needs statements on him- or herself communicated by other actors in order to make up his or her perception of him- or herself. Nevertheless, the autonomous consciousness does that in its own terms. What an individual knows of other people's perceptions of him- or herself is always that person's own processed perception of other's perception of him- or herself. In this way, the social system penetrates the psychic system of an individual, while the psychic system maintains its autonomy. Inasmuch as both act in this way, they interpenetrate.

Self-Reference

Thus far we have reached a point where we can introduce the master concept of Luhmann's recent version of systems theory: self-reference (Luhmann, 1984: 57–67, 593–646; Maturana and Varela, 1980). When we spoke of systems maintaining their autonomy in recording and processing the complex and contingent productions of other systems in their *environment*, this was a description of what Luhmann calls the self-reference of systems. In his earlier writings, he used the term "relative autonomy" for that property of systems, meaning that such systems are open for recording and processing the complex and contingent events in their environment according to their own laws, thus turning an external threat to their autonomy into an internal resource that contributes to that very autonomy. Luhmann calls that process "self-reference," or the Greek term, *autopoiesis*. Systems that have this ability are termed autopoietic systems. The abstract first social system that is built up by the convergence of experiencing double contingency and the convergence of actors' interests in solving that problem is a self-referential system inasmuch as everything that happens in the environment of that system—for example, in individual consciousnesses—is referred to the very problem of coping with double contingency.

Each thing that the actors experience while engaged in social interaction is recorded and processed by them according to its *connectability* with what has been happening so far and what is going to happen next, that is, with a foregoing action and a succeeding action. Connectability within a network of ongoing actions so that actors can predict and calculate their actions and reduce insecurity is the criterion of recording and processing everything that happens in the environment of the social system and pervades that system. That is, whatever happens in the environment, it will be recorded and processed according to the problem of mastering double contingency. Closing out everything new is one possible strategy, as is accommodating its meaning to what prevails in the social system. However, even unsuccessful attempts at closing out and accommodation work in the direction of self-reference: they are the necessary events that are a reminder of the problem of double contingency leading to renewed efforts to solve that problem. Nothing could break up this self-referential nature of the social system as long as actors face each other and converge in their experience of double contingency.

On the most abstract level, the social world is always an autopoietic system. This does not mean that there are no disruptions and breakdowns. However, these are part of a never-ending search for reducing complexity and contingency. On a less abstract level, there are more concrete problems that can be conceived as specifications of the abstract problem of double contingency. Events are recorded and processed not according to the abstract criterion of whether they can be connected with foregoing and succeeding events but according to criteria like the following: Do they indicate that I can trust or that I have to mistrust the other actor? Do they fit in with a commonly shared view of the world? Are they consistent with a tradition, with a rationally grounded value system, with reason? Do they conform to established norms? and so on.

These are all concretizations of the more abstract problem of double contingency. Trust and mistrust are closest to the abstract level. Both are strategies for solving the problem of double contingency and themselves become problems that have to be solved. In a self-referential way, everything that happens is recorded and processed with regard to maintaining trust or mistrust as a means of reducing complexity and contingency. In a world in which we mistrust each other, everything we do will be treated as a threat by other parties and vice versa. In this way, we can protect ourselves from unpleasant surprises and thus reduce complexity and contingency. However, the capacity of mistrust in building up interconnections of actions is limited in character. Mistrust usually leads to restraint in engaging in interaction because of the ever-present fear of becoming the victim of deceit, thus leaving us with a low extent and intensity of interaction. Trust, on the other hand, motivates us much more to take part in social interaction. When we begin with an attitude of trust, everything will be related to that attitude, and any event that conforms to it contributes to the construction of a system of mutual trust that becomes self-referential. People trust each other and because of that can act in a trustful way, which corroborates the existing trust.

Communication

Every system consists of various elements and relations between those elements. In order to identify a system, we have to know its elements and the relations between them. What are the identifying elements and relations that make up a social system? The answer that Luhmann gives to this question is communication, which becomes decomposed into action attributed to actors (Luhmann, 1984: 66–67, 191–241). When actors encounter each other, they face the problem of double contingency. This is the original situation in which actors acquire meaning for each other. What Ego does becomes most important for Alter in planning his or her action. Whatever Ego does has some meaning for Alter. The meaning of Ego's actions is a selection from a great many possibilities. It implies a fundamental difference, the difference between what actually exists and the many possibilities that could exist. There is also the difference between the identity of actualized meaning of the here and now and the difference within the many alternative possibilities, which are of a different kind. It is this fundamental and twofold difference in the recording and processing of meaning that is a moving force for communication.

Meaning is always a selection between alternatives and nevertheless refers to these alternatives, which remain present as future possibilities. The processing of meaning on the one hand sets limits by way of selection and on the other hand extends the horizon for action, because the selection of meaning also refers to what has not been selected but could have been and could yet be selected. Because of this double nature of complexity reduction and production, the processing of meaning also has constraining and extending effects on subsequent action: it limits the scope for meaningful connections with the conveyed meaning but also presents a whole range of alternatives that could be taken up in order to continue interaction.

This tension (Luhmann says "difference") between actualized and possible meaning is the force that keeps communication from ending in consensus and, instead, pushes communication forward with the endless task of reducing complexity by selecting meaning and increasing imaginable complexity by referring to what could have been and could be selected at the same time. Luhmann says that if consensus were the outcome of communication, it would stop at that moment. However, this is not possible because of the double nature of the communication of meaning in reducing and producing complexity at the same time. When a professor says to a student, "We will have a multiple choice final on the material from this semester next week," he or she not only *identifies* what they *will* be doing next week but also implicitly says what they *will not* be doing next week—but could possibly do. The professor's words identify a future action and also point to something that is different but nevertheless possible.

Taking this as communication, we have to distinguish the following features: (1) the information (message) the professor gives; (2) his or her act of conveying the message; (3) the student's attempt to understand the message and the act of conveying that message; and (4) the student's acceptance or nonacceptance of the message in his or her reaction. This is all part of the process of communication. The act of conveying the message is only a part of the whole communicative process. This is why Luhmann emphasizes that communications, and with them, actions (namely, conveying messages) make up the social system. Information, conveying a message, understanding, and acceptance/nonacceptance are the fundamental elements of any social interaction in a social system.

How do these elements come into play in a communication process? Let us continue with this question by returning to our professor-student communication. First is the information: "a multiple choice final exam next week"; second is the professor's action in conveying this message; third, the student's understanding of the information; and fourth, the student's accepting or nonaccepting reaction. The difficulties in the communication between the two begin with the act of conveying the message: Has the professor said what he or she means and intends to do? Can we trust his or her words? Does he or she nevertheless presuppose the knowledge surrounding the material from this semester? These questions emphasize the chance of a discrepancy between the act of conveying the message and the true intentions of the professor. In principle the professor cannot convey sincerity. Explicitly saying that he or she is sincere removes just that sincerity from anything else he or she says without this addition. The question then arises: Is the professor's message that he or she is sincere itself sincere without saying that his or her message of sincerity is sincere? But such a thematization of sincerity leads into an endless process of questioning sincerity.

Paradoxically, as soon as sincerity is thematized in this way, there is no way of knowing whether something has been said with sincerity or not. Sincerity has to be demonstrated in a sequence of communications where one can prove the consistency between words and actions without talking about it. However, this difference between words and actions also contributes to the continuation of communication. Any doubt about the professor's sincerity gives rise to more questions posed by the student in order to narrow the gap between conveying a message and doing something in the future. Further, there is the difference between the meaning of the message itself and everything that could have been meant and the difference between the message and everything it closes out but could have been said. And there is not only this difference between the actual message and all possible messages but also a redundancy in the communication. The professor may communicate in many words what he or she intends to do with the final exam. These redundant words repeat on the one hand what he or she was saying with the sentence, "We will have a multiple choice exam next week." However, they also give rise to further differences, because they also refer to something that is not said.

Thus, in redundant speech, the professor at the same time narrows and extends the field of communication. This means that the possibilities for understanding and misunderstanding on the part of the student increase in number. Communication becomes even more difficult. There are many points at which the student can connect his or her interpretation of meaning with the professor's words. Which interpretation should he or she take? The student's interpretation is inevitably a selection from a great many alternatives and cannot avoid implicitly referring to these alternative possibilities of interpretation. Whatever the student says, it will in many cases initiate attempts at correcting the interpretation on the professor's part. Their communication continues as a search process as long as the difference experienced in that communication is not surpassed by other differences in communications, which then attract their attention.

Communication always moves in the direction of processing and reducing the greatest differences between the actual and the potential meaning of a message. And the difficulties grow still greater when we enquire into acceptance and nonacceptance of messages. Communication itself doesn't need acceptance to be successful as communication. All it aims to do is to attain understanding. However, understanding a message still leaves open whether it will be accepted or not. This very openness also contributes to the continuation of communication. Because the professor's message implicitly refers to its alternatives, the student can make use of this in his or her reaction by taking up such an alternative, say, an essay-exam, for example, and argue for that type of final examination. Any message opens up the chance of its negation. Moreover, this negation pushes communication forward. The process that goes on in such communication is self-referential.

Whatever is said by the professor and the student will be recorded and processed as a contribution to determining the meaning of examinations, whether this process involves understanding and misunderstanding, acceptance or nonacceptance of statements.

This self-referentiality determines the type of elements and relations that can be part of the ongoing processing of the system: everything that happens is taken as the communication of meaning, which can be decomposed into the elements of the message, message conveying, understanding/ misunderstanding, and acceptance/nonacceptance. The relations that can exist between these elements are also determined as relations of meaning. These can be decomposed into relations of the consistency/nonconsistency of messages, the sincerity/nonsincerity of message conveying and intentions, the correctness/noncorrectness of interpretations, and the validity/nonvalidity of reactions. Every system also implies relations of conditioning between elements and relations. In communications, a question conditions an answer, a statement conditions a reaction of acceptance or nonacceptance, a message conditions an interpretation, and conveying a message conditions whether or not it is taken to be sincere. Thus, the number of relations between elements and other relations that really do fit together is very small in comparison to the total conceivable number of such relations. This is what conditioning as a basic strategy for reducing complexity in a system means.

System and Environment

A further strategy for reducing a system's complexity is the delineation of its boundaries and its differentiation from the environment (Luhmann, 1984: 35–37, 242–85). When the professor tells the student that casting any general doubt on the curriculum may not form part of their discussion on the final exam, he or she is trying to make such a delineation of the boundaries of their system of the examination discussion and to differentiate it from all other communication and action that may take place in the world. What else can occur in the world is moved out to become part of the environment of the system. The boundaries of social and psychic systems are meaning boundaries. That is, they underlie a continuing process of definition by the actors who take part in the communications of a system.

What is part of the exams-discussion system and what is not—where the boundary lies—is defined by the professor and the students during their actual process of communication. The student may go on and say, "The curriculum has some intolerable defects, because it is devoted to the collection of very small parcels of knowledge; however, we should not petrify this system even more by parceling the exam into multiple choice questions." This may motivate the professor to reply: "Your statement is right at the boundaries of our discussion. We can take it up and relate the statement to our question of which type of exam we should have next week." In this way the student's statement about the curriculum is meaningfully connected with the question of the right exam and thus becomes part of their exams-discussion system. Because it can be made a part of the search for the right exam, the student's statement becomes part of the system. Part of that system is every communication that can be interpreted as a search for the right kind of exam.

Whether a communication belongs to a system or not can be controlled and decided in many different ways. The professor's reaction, "This doesn't belong in our current discussion," is only one possibility, and the professor may fail and the students succeed in their attempts to extend the boundaries by thematizing the whole curriculum, including the exam. Going beyond Luhmann, we could distinguish the following levels of delineating the boundaries of a system: Some communications are simply not understood by the discussants, so they are not taken up in the discussion. They are closed out because nobody can connect them meaningfully to the topic of discussion. The discussants feel a consensus that it is their aim to find a fair way of examining their knowledge. Every contribution that violates this consensus is rejected by the whole group. There may be a chairperson who leads the course of the discussion. He or she has the power, based on attribution from the whole group, to select and to close out contributions. Finally, what is included and what is excluded also results from situational negotiations between actors.

A system exists only inasmuch and as long as its boundaries can be delineated by the participants in its processes. The boundaries can be defined in a substantial sense as outlined in the example above. It is substantially defined whether a communication and/or action can be meaningfully connected with the systemic processes or not. But there is also a temporal delineation of the boundaries of a system. When the professor says: "We cannot discuss the examination now, but we can do so in the final twenty minutes of this seminar today," he or she sets the temporal limits of the exams-discussion system. Whatever happens before and after that time does not belong to the system. That it is important for many systems to maintain their boundaries is confirmed by the many cases of supplementary discussions. For example, a student may come to the professor after discussion in class and argue for another change in the exam. The professor then may answer, "Why didn't you raise this question in class? It is now too late to decide on that, because the other students have no chance to tell us their opinion, to take part in the decision, and to be informed about the result." In this way, he or she closes out the student's statement on temporal grounds.

Without such temporal boundaries, nobody would know what belongs and what does not belong to a system. Systems of decision making, in particular, need such temporal limits. Otherwise, no decision would be binding.

However, not every system needs such temporal boundaries. For example, the systems of philosophical or scientific discussion explicitly have no such limits. In temporal terms they continue into an endless future. And many systems have temporal limits in the sense that a specific time is set for meeting, for example a seminar that meets every Wednesday from 2:00 to 4:00 P.M. during the semester.

Finally, the boundaries of a system are delineated in social terms. Who belongs to the system and in what role is the question here. The participants of our exams-discussion group are exactly determined by the students who have enrolled in the class. Any student who is not registered is not allowed to take part in the discussion. If a student cannot answer positively the question, "Have you enrolled in this class," he or she has to leave the room and the discussion group. The social delineation of the system also closes out everything that cannot be thematized in social terms relevant in this system. Only as students of the class are individuals allowed to speak. Whatever interests they have that derive from personal objectives and other roles have to be transformed into legitimate students' interests in order to be communicated within the system. Students who complain that their biorhythm will be at a low next week or that they have quarrels with their girl- or boyfriend and are thus unable to work hard cannot expect to have this taken into account, because only factors that affect every student in the same way can legitimately be considered. In this way, the exams-discussion system is differentiated from all other systems in which the students and the professor take part in other respects: their organisms, personal consciousness, and other roles, like friend, husband, wife, political activist, and so on.

In setting limits on what belongs and what does not belong to a system, the difference between system and environment acquires major importance for what goes on in the world. Everything becomes structured in this way, and the relationship between system and environment becomes a primary relationship in the world. The identity of an event is then determined by its belonging to a specific system and by how it differs from what exists in the environment of a system. From the point of view of a system, everything that happens outside its boundaries is part of the environment and, as such, is seen as a contribution to the complexity of that environment. The environment is unstructured and immensely complex. Regardless of the fact that there are other systems with their own processes of reducing complexity outside a specific system, from the point view of that system, this all represents environment with the character of high complexity. And it is this complexity that, on the one hand, threatens the system's existence yet, on the other, is needed by the system for its self-production. Therefore, what characterizes a system that is able to continue its existence in such an environment is its ability to maintain a difference in complexity between itself and its environment by reducing the environment's complexity for its own use.

Thus, a working system is always less complex than its environment; otherwise, it would dissolve in the environment. The system takes its identity from the fact that not everything that may happen in the environment may also happen within the boundaries of the system. In the individual consciousnesses of the students and the professor, many different ideas may arise that threaten the exams-discussion system but are needed for feeding the discussion with ideas as well. This problem is solved by channeling every idea into terms of what is a reliable and fair method of examination. In this way, the environment's complexity is recorded and processed according to the system's criteria; it is used and reduced for the system's needs. Maintaining this difference between higher environmental complexity and reduced systemic complexity becomes the major feature of the system's relationship to the environment.

The process of maintaining the difference between lower self-complexity and higher environmental complexity throws a new light on the older notion of a system's adaptation to its environment, which was conceived in a very passive way for a long time. In the view of the system's processing of environmental complexity, the system is seen as much more actively shaping that process of adaptation. This is adaptation by selection, which means that a system's ability to adapt to an environment increases inasmuch as it possesses the means to record and process the environment's complexity according to its own criteria. The system is then capable of existing in any environment and does not have to adapt to the environment in the sense of accommodating to it. It gains much more independence from that environment and is even capable of making use of the environment's complexity for its own self-production on its own terms. This is the achievement of an autopoietic system. Inasmuch as our exams-discussion system has this capability of self-reference, it does not have to accommodate to the interests of either the professor or the students, but is capable of making use of their individual contributions in order to find a reliable and fair method of testing the students' knowledge.

A system is a form that makes a distinction between itself and its environment. Its operations always entail self-reference and other-reference by permanently re-creating the distinction between system and environment. The system relates to the environment by observing what happens out there and translates environmental events into systemic resources in its operations oriented toward maintaining the difference between system and environment.

Systemic Differentiation and Evolution

Many strategies are available for recording and processing the environment's complexity within the boundaries of a system. There are more or less rigid strategies, like pushing everything back, assimilating everything to the prevailing opinion within a system, suppressing information, censoring communications, putting everything into the terms of the system, dominating the environment, limiting membership, closing minds, discussing everything with regard to the system's identity, and negotiating about what enters and what does not enter the system from the environment. One major device for recording and processing the environment's complexity within the boundaries of a system is the repetition of the differentiation between system and environment within the system itself. There are three types of such differentiation: segmental, hierarchical, and functional (Luhmann, 1970: 123–25, 1980, 1984: 37–39, 256–65, 551–93, 624–31). Segmental differentiation is a repetition of group-formations oriented to fulfilling the same functions: families within a primitive clan society are similar in their structure and fulfill the same function of reproducing the clan's economic, communal, political, and cultural living. Splitting a seminar into four discussion groups working on the same text is a similar segmental differentiation. Splitting the seminar increases the ability to record and process a greater number of questions from students. Thus, the seminar is capable of recording and processing a higher level of complexity than the seminar group before it was split. Then the problem that has to be solved is the coordination of the discussion groups in plenary discussions.

Hierarchical differentiation assigns different functions to different subsystems that are coordinated in a hierarchical way. For example, a bureaucracy is mostly differentiated into levels of authority. At the bottom are the offices that interact with clients. Their function is to record the environment's complexity via communications of clients in terms of the bureaucratic system. Filling out a form reduces environmental complexity into systemic complexity, which can be processed and transformed into binding decisions by the system. Then the offices at the bottom may send the information formulated in terms of the system to the department that decides about a case. This department's function is making binding decisions in routine cases. The decision is authoritatively sent back to the office at the bottom, which informs the client about the decision. A third level in the hierarchy may be concerned with nonroutine cases. These are gathered at the bottom and transmitted via the second level to the third level, which decides and sends this authoritatively back via the second and the first levels to the client. Hierarchical differentiation of this kind coordinates the different subsystems by way of hierarchically organizing authority relationships. Differentiated systems are capable of recording and processing higher complexity than undifferentiated systems. The civil servant who interacts with the client can tolerate many more claims from the client than he or she could in the event of having to decide for him- or herself. Thus, the civil servant fulfills a mediating function between the client and the decision-making department.

Functional differentiation is a differentiation that assigns different functions to different subsystems that operate on the same level without any hierarchical relationship. Such functionally differentiated subsystems produce for each other prestructured complexity that is recorded and processed within each subsystem according to its own criteria. A business firm is functionally differentiated into subsystems of research, development, production, marketing, and administration. Each fulfills a different function. Research provides new ideas, development creates new prototypes, production produces, marketing sells products, and the different subsystems of administration are concerned with recruiting, promoting and coordinating personnel, and accounting. By such differentiation the firm is much more capable of recording and processing high complexity from the world of scientific research, individual creativity, the needs of its personnel, and customers' behavior. It has different subsystems which are concerned with special parts of the environmental complexity and thus can record and process a greater part of that complexity.

Of the three types of differentiation, functional differentiation allows for the greatest amount of recorded and processed environmental complexity. However, unlike the segmental type, it will break down if any one subsystem is not working. Compared to the hierarchical type, its coordination is much more flexible but also more difficult. According to Luhmann, coordination works here inasmuch as the subsystems are differentiated and mutually record and process the complexity they produce themselves. That is, the development subsystem and the production subsystem are coordinated inasmuch as the production subsystem is capable of recording everything modeled by the development subsystem yet according to its own criteria of organizing mass production. Not every good prototype passes this test of transforming it into a product that can be produced on a mass level. Inasmuch as the production subsystem has that ability of transforming a model into a mass product, the two systems are coordinated. The converse is also true. The development system takes up every complaint from the production system but only in terms of its function of generating a consistent model. In these respects both systems are well coordinated. They interpenetrate. Thus, the functional differentiation of self-referential systems is at the same time a device for recording and processing higher environmental complexity and a device for the integration of these subsystems. There is no need for a special mechanism to integrate the systems. Functional differentiation is their means of integration.

Segmental, hierarchical, and functional differentiation are not just functionally equivalent means for recording and processing environmental complexity on a higher level; according to Luhmann, they do so with an increasing level of capability from segmental to hierarchical to functional differentiation. In his view the evolution of society proceeds exactly in this order. The mechanism that guides this evolution is the increasing capability of dealing with environmental complexity. Those systems that generate this capability are better adapted to a changing environment and to different environments.

According to the theory of evolution, they have better chances of survival. Evolution proceeds by the mechanism of variation, reproduction, and selection. Variation means that types of social systems are created by chance; they are reproduced by institutionalization and socialization and are selected according to their ability to survive in a specific environment. In Luhmann's view, human society has proceeded from segmental to hierarchical to functional differentiation because of the growing capability of these types of social organization to adapt to an increasingly complex environment.

A specific differentiation that proceeds with the evolution of society is the differentiation of levels of social systems: interaction, organization, and society. In primitive societies, these three levels of social systems are co-present, that is, present in any encounter. Father-son interaction is a system of situational interaction, a relationship within the family's organization of economic production and an authority-relationship that reflects the distribution of authority throughout society. In modern times, these three systems have been much more drawn from one another and differentiated. The interaction between father and son has nothing to do with their membership in a business firm, which is an organization, and with the distribution of authority throughout society.

Systems of interaction are situational in character and are situationally separated from what happens outside. A short encounter in the elevator, a discussion on the corner, a talk with the storekeeper, a seminar discussion, and an exchange of goods for money are systems of interaction. Organizations are much less situationally differentiated; they rely on a constituted structure, definitive roles, a registered membership, a code. Examples are business firms, bureaucracies, universities, trade unions, professional organizations, and broadcasting organizations like CBS, ABC, or NBC.

Societies are even less situationally differentiated and most enduring in character. They are less formally structured than organizations. They form the final reference point for interaction. Life in society is predominantly structured according to its segmental, hierarchical, and/or functional differentiation into subsystems. A society has a specific cultural identity, a political organization for its decision making, an economic organization for dealing with scarcity, and an associational organization of its membership via citizenship. These build cultural, political, economic, and associational subsystems that become differentiated as autopoietic systems the more societies evolve. In present times, world society has been established with a worldwide cultural system, a worldwide political system, a worldwide economy, and worldwide human association.

Whether we act on the interactional, the organizational, or the societal level makes a difference for the determination, course, and outcome of our action the more these levels have been differentiated as systems in themselves. In our father-son example in a primitive society, the different levels converge. In a modern society like ours, they diverge.

Let us look at further examples in a modern society. An interaction of a couple having a romantic dinner together in a restaurant is guided by their intimacy and the situation of being together for dinner. Everything that happens around them is channeled through this perspective and influences their interaction only through that self-referential mediation. The man may get angry with the waiter for being noisy; however, the woman reminds him, "Don't worry about it. Let's concentrate on ourselves tonight and not allow anything to disturb our dinner." In this way the waiter's noise is self-referentially turned into systemically processed complexity. What characterizes this interactional system is that it only minimally takes into account what happens outside, and particularly farther away from, the situation. And it also has only minimal repercussions for its environment. Most people do not notice the two people having dinner together. This is different when we reach the organizational level. Let us imagine that we are not observing an intimate dinner between two lovers but a business dinner of two directors of the same company. Now what they are doing is still partly determined just by the situation, the sequence of the dinner, and the sequence of their conversation; but it is determined much more by their position and their corresponding roles in their organization. Let us assume the one is director of marketing and the other director of production. Now what they are talking about, the course of their conversation, and its outcome are very much determined by the departments they represent in their roles and by the established relationship between these departments. If the production department is seen as very inflexible by the marketing department, whatever they do will lead toward thematizing this situation. And the result of their talk will have repercussions for the whole organization well beyond the boundaries of their situational interaction.

The determination and repercussions of such a dinner talk will stretch even farther if the personnel director of that company has dinner with a labor union leader. Their talk is influenced by society-wide economic problems and the society-wide industry-trade union relationship. Its course is guided by that established relationship, and its outcome has society-wide repercussions. Their interaction reaches the level of society. Certainly, this societal process involves the level of organization and that of situational interaction, but it also reaches beyond these levels and brings emergent qualities of society into motion. Societal processes always involve organizational and interactional processes. However, interactional processes do not always involve organizational and societal processes. Organizational processes always involve interactional processes but do not always involve societal processes. Though the higher processes always involve the lower ones, they cannot be completely reduced to them. They display emergent properties, that is, processes of their own that occur only on their level.

The Self-Production of Systems: Applications of the Theory

The central feature of systems is their autopoietic nature, their self-referentiality. As we have noted, this is the capacity of the systems to record and process the environmental complexity in its own terms, thus turning its threatening nature into systemic resources for self-production and reproduction. As Luhmann puts it in paradoxical terms, these systems gain openness through closedness. What he means is that the internally closed character, the clear-cut boundaries of the system, and the ability to take up everything from the environment but in terms of the system allow for maximum openness to environmental complexity. Such a system does not have to hide away from the environment or to suppress it. It is able to live with everything in the environment and maintain its identity. However, Luhmann's paradoxical formulation cannot conceal that only a relatively limited openness is at work here. An autopoietic system is open only inasmuch as this does not affect its identity. It turns everything into its own language. Many times this transformation of environmental complexity into systemic terms may distort what has originated in the environment. A client at the doors of bureaucracy may not recognize what he or she has said when he or she reads what the civil servant has recorded in terms of the bureaucracy. The philosopher who has argued for equal rights of women may not recognize what he or she said in the words of the politician who makes use of parts of the philosopher's ideas in a public speech. The philosopher's criterion is truth; the politician's criterion is maximizing votes. This openness originating from self-referential closedness is a limited openness. We have to keep that in mind much more than Luhmann does.

Self-reference can be related to three distinct levels: the code, the structure or program, and the process of a system. The code is a binary scheme, like the distinctions of true/untrue, right/wrong, and reliable/unreliable; the structure or program is a set of generalized expectations, values, norms, roles, and personal attributions. The process is the ongoing interaction involving communication and action: information, conveying a message, interpretation, reaction. In our exams-discussion system, the code is the distinction of reliability/unreliability of examinations. The structure or program involves the value that every class member can participate in the discussion on equal terms, the norm that no contradiction will be tolerated, the roles of discussants who have to speak up and to wait for their turn, and the personal attributions that expect of a person certain contributions according to his or her past behavior as shy, open, spontaneous, intelligent, hesitant, well arguing, creative, quick, slow, and so on. The process is the ongoing discussion composed of communication and action. Self-reference involves all levels. The code of reliable/unreliable examinations functions as the overall guidance of structures and processes. Everything is directed to this code. Otherwise, the system would dissolve and would not be able to reproduce itself. The structure or program regulates the form of the ongoing interaction. It does not define the system's identity as the code does; therefore, it will be maintained or changed according to its capacity to contribute to the reproduction of the code. The discussants can move from one form of turn-taking to another form; thus, they change the system's structure or program but not its code. In the process of communication and action, change is most likely from situation to situation; this is the level where the environmental complexity is recorded and processed within the existing structure or program and with regard to reproducing the code.

How does such a system learn? It learns by recording environmental complexity but only in terms prescribed by the code. Whenever the code itself changes, the system does not learn but breaks down and is replaced by a new system with a new code.

The self-production of systems places much importance on the processes engaged in that daily work. We can explain this with an example from Luhmann's early writings, which fits in very well with the new self-reference language, namely, his work on legitimation by procedure (Luhmann, 1969/1983). In this work, Luhmann (1969/1983: 11–53) points out that, under the conditions of a complex world as modernity has produced it, any attempt at legitimating decision making by deriving this from preestablished stable values or an established traditional structure of authority is bound to fail. In such a world there are many more questions that can be raised regarding the legitimacy of a decision, for example, in legislation or in courts, than can be answered by referring to certain underlying values or some traditional authority. In a world in which everything is imaginable, a decision is inevitably a selection from many alternatives that still remain present. How can one close this gap between decisions and alternatives? Luhmann's answer is that the legitimation of such decisions can no longer come from the outside and from stable values or structures but has to be produced inside the very process of decision making. This lays most emphasis on the features of that process. Let us look at his example of courtroom decision making (Luhmann, 1969/1983: 57–135).

According to Luhmann, courtroom decision making first has to be differentiated as a system that is able to establish boundaries determining what belongs and what does not belong to the system. In historical perspective, the emergence of court procedure as a differentiated system has moved from proof by referring to God, to proof based on personal reputation, to free proof. If there is nothing but free proof, decisions can no longer rely on simple grounds like a sign from God or the reputation of a witness.

The decision has to be grounded using the means of the procedure itself. Tactical matters become important. The court procedure also needs to be autonomous in temporal, substantial, and social respects. It needs time, can accept only what fits in its language, and prescribes specific roles to the participants in proceedings.

Contact systems among people who meet regularly in court make it easier to handle complex matters in a patterned way. Single decisions can be embedded in a whole set of decisions allowing for processes of negotiation between the people within the contact system.

Because everybody who participates has to take up a specific role in the system, environmental complexity can be transformed into systemic resources of decision making, because now everything can be dealt with in terms of the system, and every participant becomes involved and inevitably takes part in the process of decision making that binds everybody to the outcome at least in the sense that he or she has taken part in that decision. After such a decision, anyone who is unwilling to accept it at least becomes isolated in his or her position. This strengthens the binding character of the decision.

The participants become involved in the history of the decision-making process by way of making accounts. In this process, every account has a binding effect and narrows the scope of action for a person, but a narrowing effect is produced within the system itself. The procedure allows conflict, that is, debate between competing positions; however, it has to be conducted in the judicial terms of the system. In this way, the procedure is enabled to record as much environmental complexity as possible and to process this complexity to reproduce itself in distinguishing between legally right and legally wrong, which is its code.

We cannot assume that the process of decision making leads to a considerable change of opinions by way of learning. What it produces is much more a continuous channeling of opinions toward a binding decision with the effect of splitting and isolating protests. Because the procedure seemingly involves every question raised—however, in its own terms—protest becomes isolated as the particular dissatisfaction of single individuals. It is no longer a basis for doubts regarding the legitimacy of the decision.

Presentation of the decision-making process to the public occurs independently of the factual participation of the public or the number of people in the audience. The words spoken before the public and made accessible to public proof have to be well chosen and have specific binding effects on the parties who utter them. And the potential participation of the public also binds the public to the decision. This contributes to approaching an ultimate binding decision.

Procedural legitimation of decisions is easier when a conditional programing of that process has been established instead of a goal-oriented programing. The type designated as the conditional programing of decisions prescribes certain decisions when certain conditions are given. The type entitled goal-oriented programing prescribes only a goal for which the right means have to be found. Conditional programs allow concentration on the given facts of the situation. Coming to a decision on that leads immediately to the next decision on what has to be done: a certain punishment for a certain violation of the law.

These are the features of a court procedure that make that procedure a self-referential system capable of reproducing itself as a system that is devoted to making binding legal decisions without relying on some external stable legitimation from values or authority structures. It is the very process of decision making itself that produces binding decisions by continuously narrowing the scope for action, binding participants to certain accounts, binding the public to the decision, and splitting and isolating protest as particularistic dissatisfaction of single individuals without any claim to collective legitimacy.

This is a good example to back up systems theory's claim that systems do make a difference. The very existence of the system of court procedure channels everything that can be articulated with regard to a certain violation of the law into the code, structure, and processes of that system, which determine the fate of any action, its course, and outcome. Such a system breaks regular causality. One event does not cause another event; one cause does not result in a specific effect. The establishment of systems makes a difference: cause and effect are recorded and processed in the system, which shapes the direction of the cause and its relationship to an effect. The sequence now is: environmental complexity penetrates a system, which records and processes that complexity in self-production. This produces new complexity for other systems.

A final example may serve as a further illustration of this unique feature of systems on the level of society. On that level, the functional differentiation of society into self-referential subsystems is an outcome of societal evolution in modern times (Luhmann, 1984: 624–31). Science, moral theory, education, the political system, the legal system, and the economy are such functionally differentiated subsystems of society. Each of these systems works according to specific codes, functions, structures or programs, and processes. The code of science is the distinction between true and not true; its function is to improve knowledge; its structure is determined by the rules of scientific investigation; its processes are mediated by truth as a generalized medium of communication. The code of morality is the distinction between good and bad; its function is improving moral knowledge; its structure is determined by the rules of moral discourse; its processes are mediated by respect/disrespect as the medium of communication. The code of education is the distinction between being educated and not being educated; its function is to develop personalities; its structure is determined by the rules of school education; its processes are mediated by educational values. The code of the political system is the distinction between having power and not having power; its function is establishing collectively binding decisions; its structure is determined by the institutions of legislation and bureaucracy; its processes are mediated by power as the generalized medium of communication. The code of the legal system is the distinction between legally right and legally wrong; its function is the settling of conflicts; its structure is defined by the rules of legal procedure; its processes are mediated by the law as a medium of communication. The code of the economy is the distinction between having money and not having money; its function is handling scarcity; its structure is determined by the institutions of production, distribution, and consumption; its processes are mediated by money.

Each system is self-referential, which at the same time sustains their differentiation and integration, thus allowing society to record and process higher levels of complexity.

How do these systems relate to each other? Only in the sense of systems-environment relationships under the condition of autopoiesis. This enables society to produce as much complexity as possible internally and nevertheless to be able to record and process this internally produced complexity in order to reproduce itself on a higher level of complexity. It is a unique convergence of maximum freedom and maximum order in terms of systems theory. There is only a *structural coupling* of the moral and the political systems inasmuch as moral judgments are transformed into resources of power mobilization. However, this higher level of recording and processing complexity is attained at the cost of limiting the transactions from one system to the other according to the terms of the system that receives these transactions. In this way, political decision making can only take into account the outcomes of moral discussions; it cannot shape its decisions by these outcomes without converting them into political terms. What is morally valid can become politically effective only if it is couched in terms that increase the number of votes. A truly moral critique of political decision making remains a moral critique and cannot become a part of political decision making itself. Thus, there would be no chance of moving political decision making toward a closer correspondence with moral ideas if the political system were indeed self-referential in character. There is only a *structural coupling* of the moral and the political systems inasmuch as moral judgments are transformed into resources of power mobilization. However, one then has to raise the question of why such developments as the continuing equalization of opportunities in family law, economic law, or educational law actually occur. Luhmann would have to argue that gaining votes with such movements has occasioned that development. However, many such developments have occurred well before politicians discovered the opportunities to turn them into votes. The civil rights decision making of the Supreme Court is such an example. It is part of the legal system and has produced binding *legal* decisions that have been strongly shaped by moral reasoning. And these legal decisions are also binding for political decision making. They are not just events in the environment of the political system that may be transformed into power resources. They penetrate the empirically given political system and shape its structure basically. Here a theory of the self-referential political system fails.

Summary

1. Systems are self-referential in character, that is, they record and process environmental complexity according to their own terms.
2. Systems consist of elements and relations between elements, and they condition specific relations between elements and between relations.
3. Social systems consist of communications and actions.
4. Communications can be decomposed into information, conveying of meaning, understanding/misunderstanding meaning, and accepting/not accepting the information.
5. Meaning is a selection from a great many alternatives and refers to these alternatives, which gives rise to the complicated coordination of communication.
6. Social systems are differentiated from their environment in substantial, temporal, and social terms.
7. Social systems, like any other systems, have lower complexity than their environment.
8. The more social systems or any other systems increase their complexity without exactly replicating environmental complexity, the more they will be capable of recording and processing higher complexity.
9. The more social systems internally differentiate, the more they will be capable of recording and processing environmental complexity.
10. The more social systems move from segmental to hierarchical to functional differentiation, the higher the level of environmental complexity they are capable of recording and processing.
11. Segmentally differentiated systems are integrated by common meetings, hierarchically differentiated by authority structures, and functionally differentiated just by differentiation into self-referential systems.
12. The more interaction systems, organizational systems, and society become differentiated, the higher the environmental complexity that can be recorded and processed.
13. The more the evolution of society progresses, the more it proceeds from segmental to hierarchical to functional differentiation.
14. The more social systems are self-referential, the more they will adapt to the environment in an active way by processes of selection.

15. The more a social system differentiates code, structure, and processes, the more it will be capable of self-production by directing processes via structures according to the code and the more it will change processes and structures with a view to maximum code reproduction.
16. The more decision making in courts becomes a differentiated and autonomous procedure and can rely on contact systems, role taking, accounts, isolation of protest, allowed conflict, inclusion of the public, and conditional programs, the more it will result in binding decisions.
17. The more society is composed of functionally differentiated subsystems with codes, structures, processes, and media of communication as elements of self-referential organization, the higher the environmental complexity that can be recorded and processed.
18. The more social life is organized in social systems, the more events are not simply related in cause-effect chains but in more complex chains of environmental complexity → systemic recording and processing → environmental complexity.

Critical Assessment

In a final assessment of Luhmann's systems theory, two features stand out. First, this theory demonstrates vigorously how social life is organized beyond immediate interaction. This is an insight that is an inevitable complement to the many theories so far considered in this book that remain on the interactional level. Luhmann's systems theory demonstrates how it makes a difference for the occurrence, course, and outcome of an action if it is organized within a system. In this way Luhmann breaks with the simple cause-effect and also reason-consequence schemes for analyzing social action.

The second feature of Luhmann's systems theory is its primary emphasis on how wonderfully an order emerges from disorder, systems from world complexity, order from noise. No theory has dealt with that topic in such a sophisticated way as Luhmann does with his systems theory. He shows the unlikeliness and fragility of order, which nevertheless is encouraged by the universal danger of breaking down. This universal danger is the driving force that holds systems and order together.

However, in assessing Luhmann's solution of the problem of order, one has to ask whether there is any difference between his solution and that which was provided by Hobbes. Though Luhmann rejects Hobbes's solution, he presents a solution that is very similar to it. In Hobbes's view, it is the converging experience of disorder and the accompanying fear of everybody by everybody else that gives rise to the converging interest in preferring any order to the lack of order. We do not see any difference in Luhmann's solution to that formulated by Hobbes. Certainly, Luhmann does not argue for a resulting social contract that establishes the rule of Leviathan.

Instead, he argues for a much more situational building, breakdown, and rebuilding of order in social interaction. In this way, he shares the view of symbolic interactionism and conceives of social order as negotiated order. That is, social order is not created once and for all in a social contract but is something that proceeds in time, consumes time, and is created and re-created from situation to situation by actors' efforts to connect their actions, thereby solving the problem of double contingency. Here, Luhmann's solution of the problem of order is clearly distinct from Hobbes's solution; however, this is something that is not of prime importance in Hobbes's solution and could be changed in that solution without changing its core: the convergence of experiencing disorder as intolerable, which gives rise to the convergence of interest in preferring any order to disorder, and we have to say: independently of any substantial aspect of that order.

In this regard, Luhmann absolutely replicates Hobbes. However, we have to admit that Luhmann is much more cautious than Hobbes. He does not believe that order arises once and for all from the converging interest in solving a problem. While there is a permanent interest in solving that problem, there is also a permanent breakdown, so that social life is a continuous effort of establishing order from noise. However, here the limits of Luhmann's theory become apparent. The theory does not explain the establishment of order from noise, because no regularity becomes established at all. There is nothing but the permanent search for order and the sequence of very situational orders but no enduring patterning of social action. That means Luhmann gives up explaining order because he concentrates instead on its counterpart of disorder, which is the very essence of the continual ups and downs of successful and unsuccessful connections between communications.

In this point, Luhmann's account of the question of how order emerges and dissolves in society resembles what is currently being propagated as chaos theory or chaos research, which is an application of models elaborated in the natural sciences to explain accidental orders emerging from chaos and also dissolving into chaos (see Davies, 1988; Dendrinos, 1990; Küppers, 1987). There is nothing new in what chaos theory tells us: The more individuals are freed from primordial ties and act as autonomous individuals, the more order in their relationship is something that occurs accidentally and also dissolves accidentally. Therefore, predictions of future events are nearly impossible in this area of life; this also holds true for planning of the future. However, this is far from the whole story as far as social life is concerned, for it is a composition of features displaying very different and interrelated kinds and levels of orders. Accidental orders are only one aspect of social life, and much more complex theories are needed to cover the whole complexity of that life. The history of sociology has provided us with a whole array of such tools, which we have to combine in an integrated network of theories. Chaos theory is nothing new in this array of theories and covers only a minor part of social life.

No more than accidental order can be explained in Luhmann's terms. However, there are other features of social order: continuity and validity, closed predictability of action, and constraint. These features cannot be explained in terms of Luhmann's theory. We need theories of communicative rationality, consensus formation, and domination to explain these features of social order. Luhmann's preoccupation with the distinction between order and disorder makes him insensitive to the latter features of social life and social order. He does not realize that he always operates with a very artificial assumption: world complexity. People usually do not live in such a complex world, because they are born into a preestablished life-world of commonly shared world views and norms. Their minds are closed; they are not able to have the experience of selection from a supercomplex world as Luhmann's actors almost always do. Therefore, there is no problem of order for many instances of social life because it just exists. Because social life has been organized in this way from its very beginning, this is where the very roots of social order lie. The problem then is how can this life-world order spread into the more remote fields of social life? This, however, is a question that cannot be raised in Luhmann's terms.

There are not many alternative ideas in a modern society that can be used in processes of legitimating decisions: freedom, equality, rationality, mastery of the world. Many processes of legitimation do not face the problem of complexity but apply a small set of standards to many decisions, thus criticizing them and contributing to their change in the direction of a closer consistency to these standards. Power is the typical means of creating order in a world where everything could be different. This is the constellation of Luhmann's theory. And in a certain sense, he sees the working of systems in this way. Because any order is better than no order under this constellation, the formation of systems without any qualification moves in the direction of establishing an unreflected power over the human being. There is no way to reflect on the legitimacy of one system or the other.

The latter defect of Luhmann's theory also has consequences for his theory of society. According to his theory, social evolution moves toward functional differentiation of self-referential subsystems. However, it is just this autopoietic nature of subsystems that would not allow what we see as a major feature of the development of modern society since the Enlightenment: the contribution of criticism in the light of rational discourse to societal development itself. In Luhmann's terms this criticism remains self-contained in intellectual circles. Its transformation into political circles inevitably wipes out any rationality from that criticism: it is then nothing more than one of many attempts to gain votes. This, however, is contradicted by the fact that even political decision making is shaped by rational discourse without reference to gaining votes.

Summarizing, we can say that Luhmann's systems theory provides us with enormous insights regarding the working of systems and the difference they make for explaining the occurrence of order from noise in a sophisticated but short-lived way. However, his theory is particularly limited because of his preoccupation with only one feature of the world, complexity, which is not very common in human experience. His theory of society particularly fails to address advances resulting from rational discourse. Learning on any level cannot be a continuous and rational change of a code toward approaching higher levels of validity. It can only be a sequence of structural change within the limits of an established code, a breakdown of a system with that code, and the establishment of a new system with a new code.

In this way Luhmann is on the side of Thomas Kuhn's (1970) theory of scientific development as a sequence of normal science preoccupied with solving puzzles within the boundaries of an established paradigm, the breakdown of that paradigm in a revolution, and the establishment of a new paradigm. There is no way to assess the success of the new paradigm in rational terms, to claim that it is closer to the truth than its predecessor. Contrary to this view, Karl Popper (1963, 1972) has formulated a theory of scientific progress according to which we start with problems, we propose theories for their solution, which partly fail and pose new problems, and we replace those theories with new theories that are capable of solving those problems, and so on. We can assume in this process that subsequent theories that solve the problems their predecessors did not solve are closer to the truth. This is a position that allows us to *assess* scientific development in terms of rationality.

Why should we do without such an assessment when we look at the development of society in general? Habermas's critical theory has demonstrated a way in which we can still attain it in modern times. It is here that we have to correct Luhmann's position in terms of Habermas's (1981) critical theory in order to gain a comprehensive view of societal development. Luhmann refuses to give access to such a position, because he denies the roots of the social subsystems' codes in an all-embracing common culture. In his view, they are just binary schemes that guarantee the differentiation between systems and their environment. The political code is, for example, the distinction between having or not having power. As long as political decision making proceeds alongside this distinction, the political system will maintain its boundaries. However, making the distinction between having and not having power is a communicative act that entails an understanding of the meaning of power and also of its legitimacy. The real process of power attribution is thus rooted in the cultural idea of legitimate power. If there is no consensus on its definition, there will be no undebated and distinct code of politics in the empirical sense of a really existing political system. Such a system must be conceived as a product of the interpenetration of cultural ideas on the legitimacy of power and pure power politics as acquiring and applying power for the sake of attaining collectively bind-ing decisions. The constitution of the political system is the important medi-ating link between culture and politics. In its basic and unchangeable aspects, it is part of the code of the empirically existing political system; in its change-able aspects, it is part of its program. If we do not interpret the code of the political system as a part of the common societal culture, we do not speak of an empirically given political system but only of an analytical con-struction with no empirical reference. A firmly established constitution rooted in a society's common culture has to be conceived as part of the code of an empirically working political system. Contrary to Luhmann's claim, such a code must be a cultural phenomenon.

Surprisingly, Luhmann's explanation of the social system's constitution by the interpenetration of psychic systems gives some hints at such an approach. However, he does not continue on this line when he deals with the emergence of societal subsystems. In doing so, he would have to take much more account of the fact that modern societal subsystems are not as much a product of a linear process of differentiation as they are a product of interpenetration, which implies that they incorporate very different aspects in one system to create a new emergent quality. Thus, the political system is oriented not only toward producing binding decisions via bureaucratic authority but also toward legitimating decisions via discourse, monitoring decisions via legal review, and opening decisions via legislation.

Indeed, a feature of the development of modern societies that has become very apparent now is that more and more activities and decisions take place in areas where different systems interpenetrate (Münch, 1991). The emergence of intermediate systems within which conflicting demands from a variety of systemic references are negotiated is one of the most striking developments of our time. In the United States, nearly the whole of society is organized in this way. Courts, regulatory commissions, committees, volun-tary associations, and boards of trustees are the places where the most impor-tant decisions are negotiated. They are all multifaceted and confront a variety of systemic demands with each other. Thus, it is not true here that science produces truth and that the political system deals with that as it likes to make collective decisions binding, to take only one example. In systems like the Supreme Court or one of the many regulatory commissions, truth, the law, economic interests, political exigencies, and moral consciousness meet and are set against one another in negotiations. It is in these intermediate systems that what goes on in social life is decided.

Though this is a peculiar feature of American society, it is by no means confined to that society. Indeed, we are witnessing enormous transforma-tions in the same direction in the European societies. The call for new forms of networks to be constructed between the different spheres of social life, for example, new forms of interdisciplinary work in science and the field of ecology, is one proof of this development. On the one hand, this represents a new push by modern society on to a new level where a multitude of systems are interwoven, but, on the other hand, this is just a continuation of what is characteristic of the evolution of modern society as distinct from traditional societies: the intermingling of formerly separated systems to form qualitatively new systems on a new level of development. This is true of the formation of modern science, democracy, rational capitalism, and citizenship and of all instances in which further subsystems emerge in the zones of interpenetration between these systems. It is this feature of modern societies that is completely out of range of Luhmann's theory of functional differentiation.

According to Luhmann's theory, modern societies no longer have a center but are composed of functionally differentiated closed systems that react to each other as systems react to an over-complex environment: by processing the events in the environment according to their own laws. Yet, this view gives one societal subsystem a hidden primacy, the system of administration, because this is where decisions are made and really executed, whereas the other systems — for example, moral discourse or science — remain bound to the level of mere mind games without real consequences. Whenever people try to make political or administrative decisions in moral terms, this can be interpreted only as de-differentiation and as falling back to premodern times. However, this places the center of societal decision making in the political administration of society, because that is where the decisions are really made and executed. On the one hand, Luhmann's theory of society reveals itself as constructed from the perspective of an administrative jurist who looks at the world in terms of a functioning administration that succeeds in playing with its environment without taking seriously whatever is said outside its boundaries. On the other hand, this is not so much a continuation of sociological discourse from Comte to Parsons, providing new solutions to the classical sociological problems, as it is a continuation of the philosophical discourse from Kant to Husserl, which Habermas (1985: 426) has pointed out. He provides a new world-view that explains how the complexity of the modern world is reduced and unity is produced: Luhmann replaces the classical relationship between subject and object with the relationship between system and environment. Systems reproduce themselves as distinct from, yet with reference to, the complex environment. The world is nothing but an ongoing process of this differentiation. What survives and what does not survive is determined in the evolutionary process of variation and natural selection. There is no chance of steering this process through intersubjective rational reflection in procedures of discourse. However, Luhmann misses the point that social life is a matter not only of differentiated systems but also of discourses that span the boundaries of economics, politics, law, and science.

Luhmann's crucial failure is his refusal to make a distinction between analytical and empirical systems. In analytical terms, Luhmann is right. By definition, there is, for example, a clear distinction between morals and politics. However, this does not imply that the empirically given differentiation between moral discourse and political decision making in real society replicates this distinction. The code of political systems, in the analytical sense, is the distinction between having power and not having power. Empirically, the meaning of this distinction and its legitimacy is defined in communication that occurs within the framework of a more or less common societal culture entailing basic moral ideas. The program according to which power is acquired, transmitted, and applied is determined by morally binding ideas of good or bad politics. Otherwise, there would be no stable boundary between the system of empirical politics and its environment. Moral consensus is a necessary precondition of the autonomy of modern democratic political systems. Societies that lack this consensus do not have such autonomous political systems. In analytical terms, we could refer, with Luhmann, to the *structural coupling* of moral rules and political decision making. In empirical terms, however, the moral rules are part and parcel of the political code and program that guide political operations.

We have to distinguish three levels of politics: analytical, empirical, and subjective. They have to be characterized as follows: (1) Whatever is perceived and processed according to the political code in the analytical sense will give or take away power simply by definition. (2) The boundaries of empirically differentiated political systems are rooted in the moral consensus on the rules of the game that constitute the code and the program of the system. Autonomy is guaranteed by moral consensus. (3) Subjectively, actors may or may not perceive and act according to the political code in the analytical sense, may or may not conform to the rules of the game, may or may not apply other codes, and may or may not conform to other rules.

As a person, an employer may pay employees according to their needs and not according to their achievement. In this case, he or she may subjectively act according to a moral code and increase his or her moral respect. But the employer also makes payments and loses money and might even go bankrupt. However, his or her moral act does not change the laws of economics. The employer cannot spend money without receiving equivalent services and nevertheless maintain or even increase his or her monetary budget. This insight, however, is a logical and not an empirical truth.

In real action, all of the three levels are intermingled. An environmentalist who demonstrates against a new nuclear power plant is part of the power chain, does or does not conform to the rules of the game, and may or may not be subjectively oriented toward gaining power. Subjectively, he or she could be a moral fundamentalist who violates the rules of the game and seizes power by force. In this case, he or she contributes to breaking down the moral consensus on the rules of the game and also of the boundaries of the political system. Nevertheless, on the analytical level politics never breaks down. The environmentalist's action simply continues the chain of deconstructing and reconstructing power. This is, however, only because the analytical level is nothing but the definition of politics. In this sense, autopoiesis is maintained by definition.

Related Work

Luhmann's systems theory has inspired the work of a growing number of scholars in recent times. There is, for example, Baecker's (1988) work on the modern economy, Stichweh's (1982, 1984, 1988) work on modern science, Teubner's (1987, 1988, 1989) work on the legal system, and Willke's (1982, 1983, 1989) work on systems theory and the state. Mayntz, Rosewitz, Schimank, and Stichweh (1988) have elaborated how the process of differentiation and the development of autonomous subsystems of society result from the politics and institution building of their carriers and representatives. Gerhards and Neidhardt (1990) have pointed out the preconditions for and the working of the public sphere as a differentiated subsystem of modern society.

WE HAVE gone a long way in weaving the network of sociological theory by reworking the evolution of sociological discourse over the past one hundred forty years. In summarizing the result as briefly as possible, I present the formal structure of this network on the four levels that I distinguished in the first chapter of volume one of this series: the national, international, periodically universal, and completely universal levels.

National Networks

On the national level, we have the British network centering around traditional order versus individuality, common sense and class conflict, or, in terms of paradigms, organicism, liberalism, empiricism, and unionism. We have Spencer's evolutionism with the area of individuality as home base but with expansion into other fields with elements of organicism, empiricism, and conflict theory. We have Hume, Bentham, and Mill occupying the field of common-sense utilitarianism. The anthropologists Radcliffe-Brown and Malinowski elucidated the field of traditional order. The field of class conflict has become the preoccupation of British sociologists in this century. We see the home base of Giddens's structuration theory with its emphasis on agency and power in this area, however, with the potential to stretch into the other fields because the theory has incorporated elements of Marxism, structuralism, ethnomethodology, symbolic interactionism, and discourse theory. Most contemporary British sociologists center around this area, predominantly playing a class-power-conflict game, for example, John Rex, David Lockwood, John Goldthorpe, Ralph Miliband, Perry Anderson, and Michael Mann (figure 1).

Figure 1   The British Network of Sociological Theory

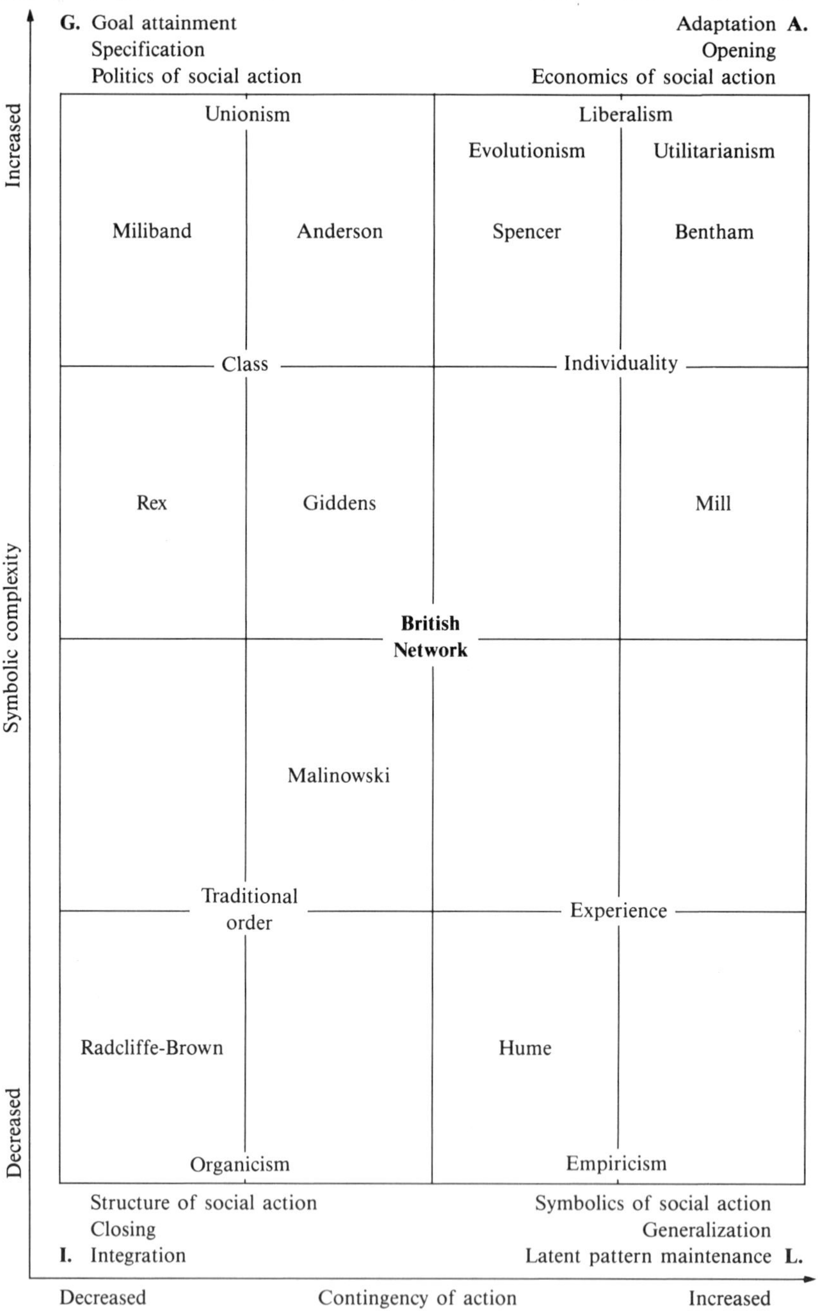

G. Goal attainment	Adaptation **A.**
Specification	Opening
Politics of social action	Economics of social action

Increased

Unionism   Liberalism

                                    Evolutionism   Utilitarianism

Miliband   Anderson   Spencer   Bentham

——— Class ———   ——— Individuality ———

Rex   Giddens   Mill

                          British Network

                    Malinowski

Traditional ——————   ——— Experience ———
order

Radcliffe-Brown   Hume

Organicism   Empiricism

Symbolic complexity

Decreased

Structure of social action	Symbolics of social action
Closing	Generalization
I. Integration	Latent pattern maintenance **L.**

Decreased   Contingency of action   Increased

308

The French network centers around power versus structure, rationality, and spontaneity; in terms of paradigms, it centers around vitalism, structuralism, rationalism, and existentialism. This area has been best illuminated in French sociology. Saint-Simon and Comte opened the game with the position of an authoritative organicist structuralism. Durkheim moved this structuralism more toward the community corner under the influence of Rousseau but reached well beyond this area by incorporating elements of British utilitarianism and evolutionism and German idealism. The French-speaking Italian scholar Vilfredo Pareto concentrated on power in the reproduction and transformation of society and is the classical opponent to Durkheim's structuralism. Marcel Mauss continued Durkheim's work while analyzing the normative structure of gift exchange. Lévi-Strauss worked on that basis while moving from studying the social structure of kinship to studying the cognitive structure of myths, claiming their impact on social structure. Foucault moved structuralism toward the field of power, studying the reproduction of power in the transformation of knowledge structures.

The French-speaking Swiss scholar Jean Piaget elaborated the development of the structure of cognition and morality in the development of the child, playing on the rationality field that had been established by Descartes's philosophy.

Bergson's vitalism in his later work and Sartre's existentialism represent the rebellion against structure, working on the fields of vitality and spontaneity. During present times, the rise of the New Philosophers has again played on this field of spontaneity against structure and rationality. This very recent movement was preceded by the movement of post-structuralists against Lévi-Strauss's structuralism. Partly learning from Lévi-Strauss, they concentrated on the production, reproduction, and transformation of structures and placed power at the core of their theories. Touraine concentrated on the dynamics of society's self-production in social movements, and Bourdieu on the reproduction and transformation of class structures as a power game played with economic, social, and cultural capital (figure 2).

The German network has always been a search for meaning, but many authors either found it in conformity to established orders or lost it in alienation, contradiction, and paradox. The philosophical foundation of this search for meaning had been laid by Kant with more emphasis on contradiction and Hegel with the expectation of attaining a dialectical synthesis from contradiction.

In terms of paradigms, the background is composed of idealism, historicism, materialism, and nihilism. Max Weber's home base is the search for meaning, exemplified in his studies on the impact of the world religions on the reproduction and transformation of large interconnected systems of societies. However, he stretched well beyond this area into the areas of conflict, contradiction and paradox, alienation, and order production, with a lead

Figure 2   The French Network of Sociological Theory

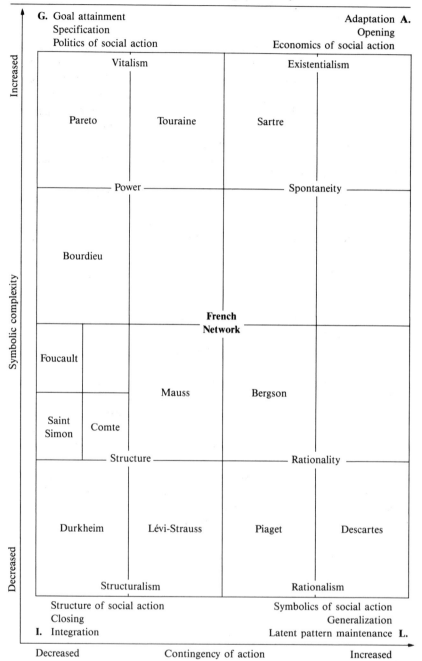

310

role taken by the meaning-contradiction-paradox-conflict axis. Simmel is Weber's counterpart who put even more emphasis on conflict, contradiction, and paradox. Dahrendorf and Elias have continued this movement and centered on conflict. Luhmann has moved in the same direction but less far toward the borders of conflict. He emphasizes the differentiation of systems with contradictory codes and sees their separation as the only way of living with the potential conflict in modern times.

Marx pushed the German network into the economic field, making alienation the key term for its analysis. Offe has contributed a theory of late capitalism that lays more stress on structural contradictions and conflict around the state-capitalism relationship. Habermas, in reworking critical theory, has reformulated Marx's alienation theory in the light of Weber's and Parsons's contributions, pushing the whole approach more toward the cultural dynamics of rationalization that initiates social rationalization, resulting in the colonization of the life-world by the systems.

The area of conformity was occupied by historicism and phenomenology, with Dilthey and Husserl concentrating on *cultural* unity, whereas Schutz and Luckmann moved toward the unity of the social life-world. Tönnies formulated the German order problematic by opposing *Gemeinschaft* (community) and *Gesellschaft* (society), thus moving between conformity and alienation (figure 3).

The American network centers around exchange, competition, consensus, and pragmatics and, in terms of paradigms, around economism, instrumentalism, voluntarism, and pragmatism. Parsons monopolized the game for a while, playing on the consensus ground. On this ground he occupied the cultural field with his emphasis on value consensus. Merton moved more toward social structure, and Berger moved toward the structure of everyday life. The theories of subculture introduced conflict, with Miller concentrating on the conformity demands of the social milieu, Cohen and Short on the conflict between subcultures and the dominating culture, Sykes and Matza on legitimation, and Yinger on the dynamics of the conflict between culture and contraculture. Garfinkel opened a game against Parsons, stressing the situationally varying features of order production in everyday life. Though Parsons did indeed have his home base in the cultural field of consensus production, the formal apparatus of his theory nevertheless expanded well beyond its boundaries into the fields of conflict, economics, and communication, albeit with a consensus bias.

A movement into the competition field was initiated by Coser, emphasizing the latent-pattern-maintenance functions of conflict. Collins plays this game with an eye on the ritualistic aspects of competition. Bacharach and Lawler have put the economic aspects into the competition network. Moore and Skocpol have introduced the power struggle between classes into the network.

Figure 3   The German Network of Sociological Theory

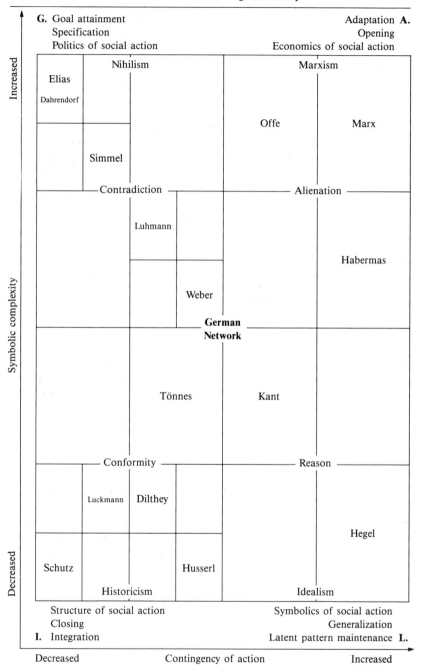

G. Goal attainment
Specification
Politics of social action

Adaptation **A.**
Opening
Economics of social action

Increased

Elias

Nihilism

Dahrendorf

Marxism

Offe

Marx

Simmel

Contradiction

Alienation

Luhmann

Habermas

Symbolic complexity

Weber

**German
Network**

Tönnes

Kant

Conformity

Reason

Luckmann

Dilthey

Hegel

Schutz

Husserl

Historicism

Idealism

Structure of social action
Closing
I. Integration

Symbolics of social action
Generalization
Latent pattern maintenance **L.**

Decreased

Decreased   Contingency of action   Increased

Homans established the exchange network, emphasizing the behavioral and economic aspects, Blau moved toward an analysis of power in exchange, and Coleman toward rational choice. The consensual foundations in exchange are examined by contractarians like Buchanan. A radical view of economics with a movement toward class conflict on a world scale has entered the scene with Wallerstein's world systems analysis.

The cultural network has its roots in pragmatism. Mead's social behaviorism occupies the symbolic part of the social field of pragmatics. Blumer built symbolic interactionism on the basis of Mead's social psychology but moved his theory toward the dynamics of communication. Strauss has laid more emphasis on the structural part of symbolic interaction. This has also been done in a much more rigorous form by Manford Kuhn. The strategic and conflict elements have been pointed out by Ralph H. Turner and by labeling theorists, with Becker leaning toward the definitorial side, Lemert toward the normative, Schur toward the dynamic, and Quinney toward the conflictual. The conflict in symbolic interaction is also at the center of Goffman's dramaturgical theory of strategic communication. A movement toward an analysis of the cognitive aspects of symbolization has been made by Kohlberg's continuation of Piaget's cognitive-developmental approach (figure 4).

The International Network

The next step is to construct the *international* network. Within that network, the British group of authors, like Hume, Bentham, Mill, Spencer, Radcliff-Brown, Malinowski, Giddens, Rex, Lockwood, Goldthorpe, Miliband, Anderson, and Mann, is pushed by the other three networks (French, German, American) toward the field of consensus. This is true even though most contemporary British sociology centers around conflict theory. However, it does this with an emphasis on the traditional features of class structure, merging power with reputation, and hierarchy with deference. This leaning of the British network toward the area of traditional order is due particularly to the more radical formulation of power and conflict, power against structure, and spontaneity against rationality by the French network, which clearly has the field of domination, conflict, power, and constraint as its home base. This also means that consensus and structure contain many elements of domination and authority, as is also the case with Durkheim's consensus structuralism.

The German network leans toward discourse, communication, meaning, and rationality, making even conflict theorists and Marxists representatives of the specifically hermeneutic approach of the German tradition. The American network leans toward markets, exchange, money, and freedom, which makes even consensus theorists like Parsons more voluntaristic

Figure 4   The American Network of Sociological Theory

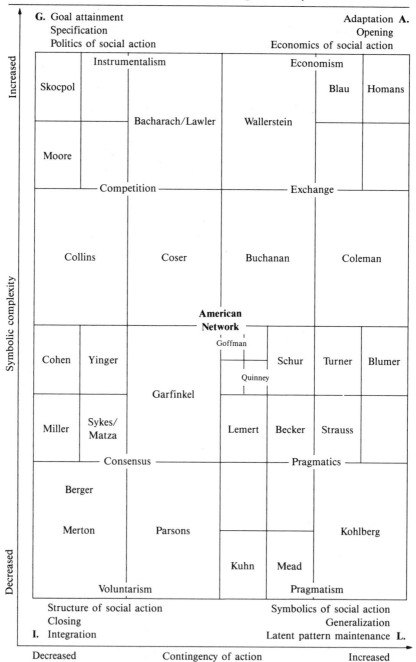

314

Figure 5 The International Network of Sociological Theory

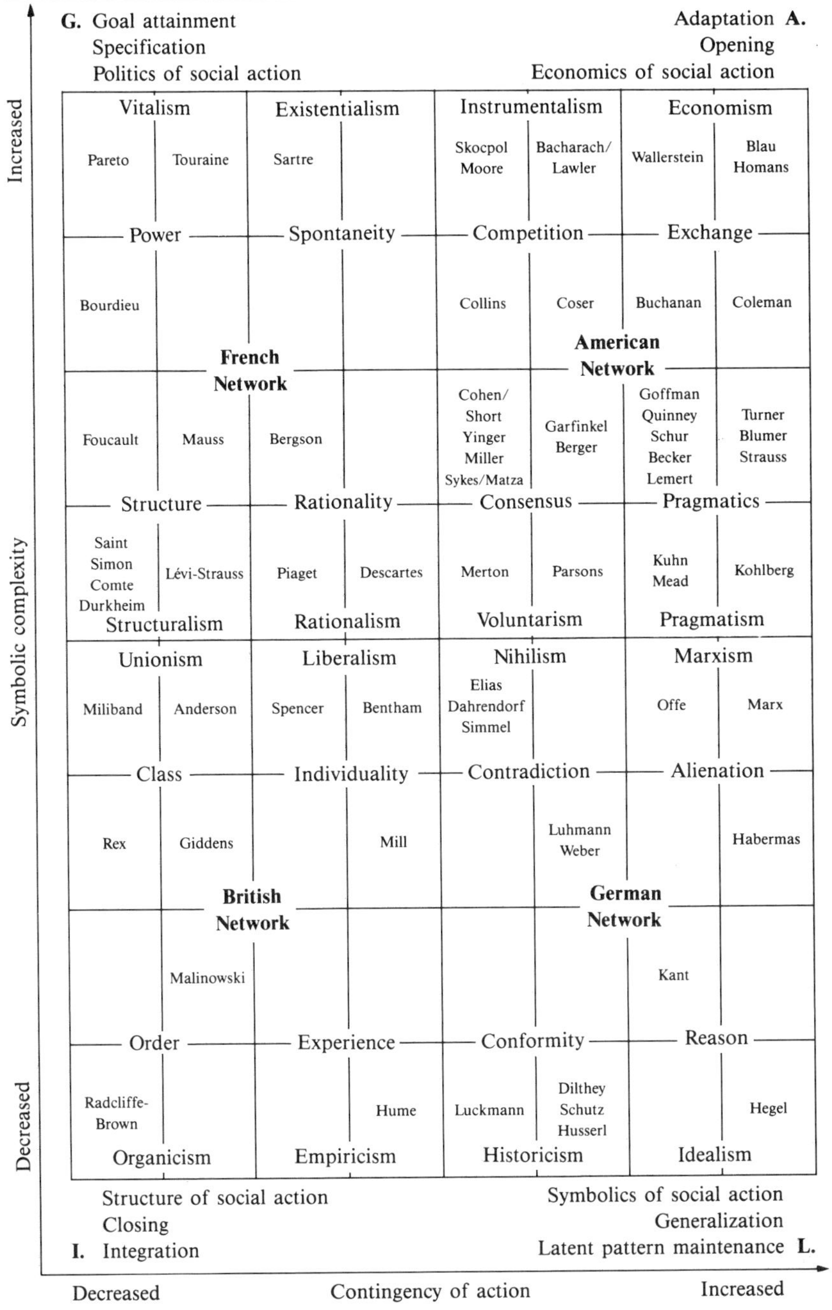

G. Goal attainment
Specification
Politics of social action
Adaptation A.
Opening
Economics of social action
Increased
Symbolic complexity
Decreased
Vitalism
Pareto
Touraine
Existentialism
Sartre
Instrumentalism
Skocpol
Moore
Bacharach/
Lawler
Economism
Wallerstein
Blau
Homans
Power
Spontaneity
Competition
Exchange
Bourdieu
Collins
Coser
Buchanan
Coleman
French
Network
American
Network
Foucault
Mauss
Bergson
Cohen/
Short
Yinger
Miller
Sykes/Matza
Garfinkel
Berger
Goffman
Quinney
Schur
Becker
Lemert
Turner
Blumer
Strauss
Structure
Rationality
Consensus
Pragmatics
Saint
Simon
Comte
Durkheim
Lévi-Strauss
Piaget
Descartes
Merton
Parsons
Kuhn
Mead
Kohlberg
Structuralism
Rationalism
Voluntarism
Pragmatism
Unionism
Liberalism
Nihilism
Marxism
Miliband
Anderson
Spencer
Bentham
Elias
Dahrendorf
Simmel
Offe
Marx
Class
Individuality
Contradiction
Alienation
Rex
Giddens
Mill
Luhmann
Weber
Habermas
British
Network
German
Network
Malinowski
Kant
Order
Experience
Conformity
Reason
Radcliffe-
Brown
Hume
Luckmann
Dilthey
Schutz
Husserl
Hegel
Organicism
Empiricism
Historicism
Idealism
Structure of social action
Closing
I. Integration
Symbolics of social action
Generalization
Latent pattern maintenance L.
Decreased
Contingency of action
Increased

than any British, French, or German approach to consensus. The American network emphasizes individualism and situational variation even outside the field of exchange theories, implanting such elements in the conflict theoretical, ethnomethodological, and symbolic interactionist approaches as well. From the standpoint of Habermas's discourse theory, Blumer's symbolic interactionism looks only slightly different from Homans's exchange theory. From the standpoint of French structuralism, Garfinkel's ethnomethodology looks like a naive children's game. From the standpoint of French conflict theory, American theories of bargaining look more like economics than politics. This is certainly also a reflection of the different political games played in these two countries (figure 5).

In summary, on the international level, we have a network comprising the British normative, the French conflict, the German hermeneutic, and the American economic networks.

The Periodical Universal Network

This picture changes, however, when we enter the level of periodical universal discourse. The classical period sees Spencer as occupying the economic field with Marx as his opponent on that field, Pareto and Simmel occupying the conflict field, and Durkheim occupying the normative field, Weber and Mead occupying the hermeneutic field as home base. Each stretched from his home base into the other fields (figure 6).

The period of consolidation and differentiation has Parsons playing from a home base in the cultural sector of the normative field, and Merton from another in its social-structural sector. The theories of subcultures concentrate on the conflictual sector in the normative field, with Cohen and Short occupying the conflict area in this sector, Miller the normative area, Sykes and Matza the symbolic area, and Yinger the dynamic area. Berger and Luckmann start from the symbolic area of the dynamic sector in the normative field; Garfinkel does so from the extreme dynamic area in this sector. Dahrendorf plays the game from the power struggle sector of the conflict field, and Coser from its latent-pattern-maintenance sector. Homans plays on the dynamic sector of the economic field and Blau on the conflict sector of the same field. Piaget occupies the symbolic sector of the hermeneutic field, Blumer the situational area, Turner the conflictual area of the variable sector of symbolic dynamics, and Goffman the conflict sector of that same field. Kuhn occupies the structured area of that field of the normative part of symbolic dynamics (figure 7).

In the discourse since the 1960s, Lévi-Strauss's structuralism and Berger and Luckmann's sociological phenomenology have replaced Parsons's analytical functionalism in the cultural sector of the *normative* field, though with strict confinement to that field and no ability to extend beyond it; within

Figure 6   The Network of Sociological Theory from the 1850s to the 1920s

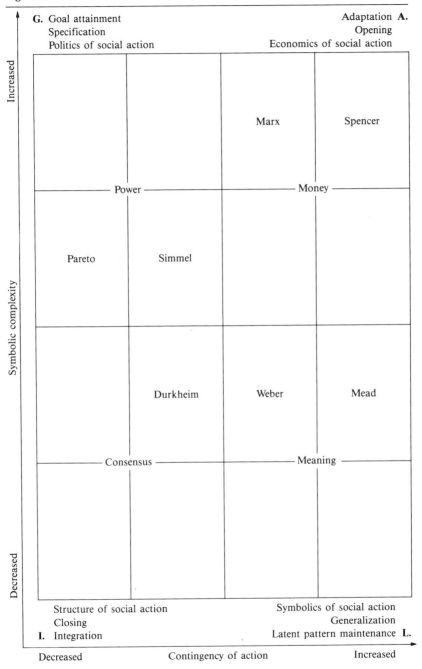

Figure 7   The Network of Sociological Theory from the 1920s to the 1960s

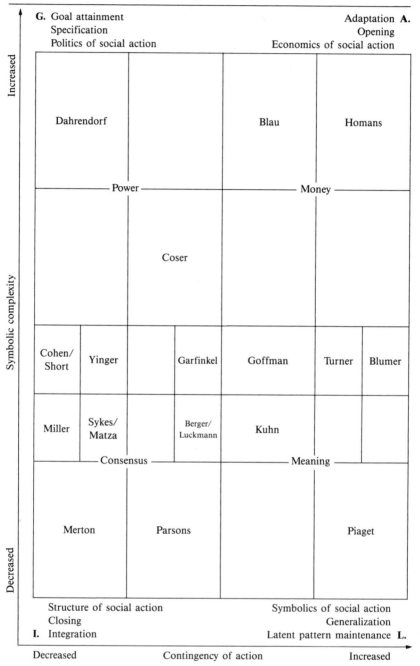

this field, Lévi-Strauss occupies the normative sector. Foucault plays in the rationality area of the power sector in this field. Coleman has replaced Homans in the dynamic sector of the *economic* field under competition from Offe occupying the conflict area of economic contradiction and from Wallerstein occupying the dynamic area of economic contradiction. On the *conflict* field, we see Bacharach and Lawler playing in the dynamic sector, Collins in the dynamic area of the consensual sector with his bargaining rituals, Bourdieu in the normative area of that sector with his theory of praxis and class habitus, and Giddens in the conflict area of the symbolic sector with his theory of power and agency of the "knowledgeable" subject. Moore and Skocpol are located in the power struggle sector of the conflict field. The hermeneutic field is filled by Habermas playing in the normative area of symbolization, Kohlberg playing in the cognitive area, Strauss in the normative structural area of the dynamic sector of symbolic dynamics, Becker in the symbolic area of the conflictual sector of symbolic dynamics, Lemert in the normative, Quinney in the power struggle, and Schur in the power dynamics areas in the same sector. Luhmann is the master of playing the communication game on the conflictual field of communication, conceiving of communication as mutual observation and internal information processing between systems in potential conflict (figure 8).

The Timeless Universal Network

The picture changes again when we construct the completely timeless universal network of sociological theory. Here we have the economic paradigm occupying the field of markets, exchange, money, and freedom. Exchange theories occupy the dynamic sector in that field, with Homans in the situational, Blau in the conflictual, and Spencer in the normative sectors. Rational choice theory, represented by Coleman, has its stronghold in the symbolic sector, and contractarians such as Buchanan, Nozick, and Rawls in the normative and Marxism in the conflictual sectors. Marx occupies the normative area of the latter with his emphasis on class struggle, Wallerstein the dynamic area, and Offe the contradiction area. The symbolic area could be filled by Lukács's theory of class consciousness.

The conflict paradigm works on the field of domination, conflict, power, and constraint. Dahrendorf, Elias, Moore, Skocpol, and Mann occupy the conflict area of the power struggle sector, Machiavelli the dynamic area with his emphasis on intelligence, Pareto the normative area with his emphasis on residues, and Simmel the symbolic area with his elaboration of the cultural dimensions of conflict. The normative sector of conflict sees Collins in the dynamic area of this part of the field, Coser in the cultural, latent-pattern-maintenance area, and Bourdieu in the normative. The cultural sector of conflict has Giddens in the conflict area.

Figure 8   The Network of Sociological Theory since the 1960s

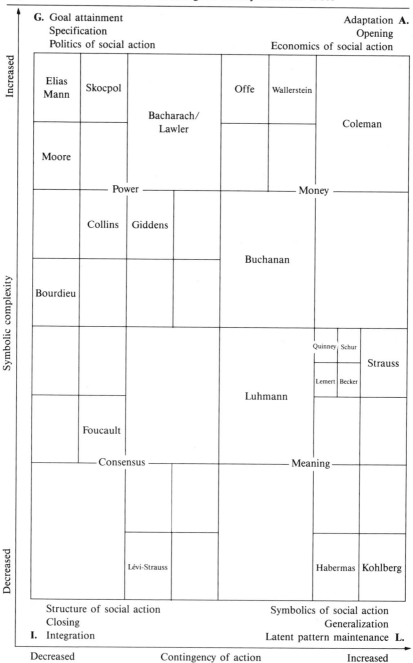

The area of structure, everyday life, consensus, and conformity is covered by the normative paradigm. Durkheim works in the community sector of that field. Lévi-Strauss works in the normative area, Schutz, Berger, and Luckmann work in the symbolic area in the cultural sector, Saint-Simon works in the normative area of the domination sector, Comte in the symbolic area and, Foucault in the power area of that sector. The dynamic sector in this field is the domain of American consensus theory, with Merton in the social-structural area, Parsons in the cultural, Garfinkel in the dynamic, Cohen and Short in the power struggle portion of the conflictual area in that sector of normative dynamics, Miller in the normative milieu portion, Yinger in the dynamic portion, and Sykes/Matza in the symbolic portion.

The symbolic paradigm works in the field of discourse, communication, meaning, and rationality. The protagonist of the cognitive ideal portion of the ideal area of the symbolic sector of that field is Kohlberg; next to him is Piaget, occupying the cognitive structural portion in this area. Habermas occupies the normative structural area of the ideal sector. Husserl occupies the normative sector of the whole field. Weber works in the cultural area of the conflictual sector, Luhmann in the administrative functional area. The dynamics of communication is the domain of interactionism, with Mead in the symbolic area, Blumer, Turner, and Strauss in the dynamic, Kuhn in the normative structural, and Becker in the symbolic portions of the conflictual area, Lemert in the normative portion of that area, Schur in the dynamic portion, and Quinney in the conflictual. Goffman goes a step further toward conflict with his dramaturgical theory of strategic communication (figure 9).

Interweaving the Network of Sociological Theory

These are the four levels of sociological discourse and the corresponding networks of sociological theory. Which one of these networks we actualize in our work—on which one we want to work—depends on our research interests. Whether we work on a specific portion, area, sector, or field or on a whole network, whether we play home, area, cross-area, or world games, also depends upon our research interests.

The different networks of sociological theory that I have elaborated are based on the work of many scholars. However, my own home base is undoubtedly the hermeneutic field. An enormous amount of accumulated knowledge is interwoven in these networks. You may go on to fill up the formal structure of those networks by putting the summary statements and evaluations of all the different theories discussed in this book into that formal structure in order to give it substance. In this perspective the formal structure is gradually filled with substantial hypotheses. However, it is also possible to concentrate on parts of a network while working with the theory

Figure 9   The Timeless Universal Network of Sociological Theory

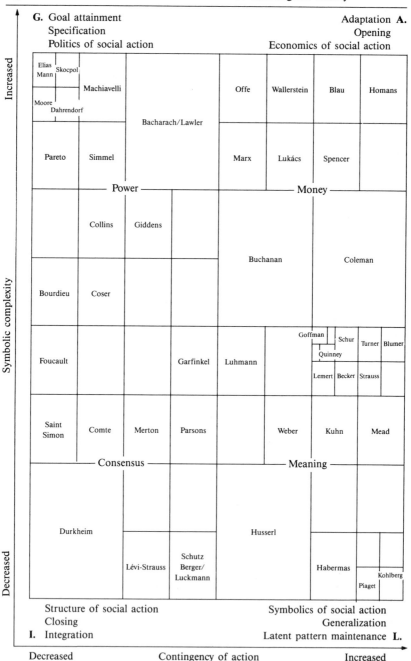

and hypotheses appropriate to that part; or one may also work on wider parts or the whole action space with hypotheses that span the whole system — of course, with less specification for any given part. The latter can be achieved by intermeshing such abstract statements with detailed hypotheses on specific parts of the whole action space. By doing this we will continue to advance the network of sociological theory into the next century.

BIBLIOGRAPHY

Abrams, Philip. 1968. *The Origins of British Sociology: 1834–1914.* Chicago: University of Chicago Press.

Abrams, Philip, Rosemary Deem, Janet Finch, and Paul Rock. 1981. *Practice and Progress: British Sociology 1950–1980.* London: Allen and Unwin.

Adorno, Theodor W. 1966/1973a. *Negative Dialektik.* In *Gesammelte Schriften,* Vol. 6. Frankfurt am Main: Suhrkamp. (Translation: 1973b. *Negative Dialectics.* New York: Seabury Press.)

Adorno, Theodor W., Hans Albert, Ralf Dahrendorf, Jürgen Habermas, Harald Pilot, and Karl R. Popper (Eds.). 1969. *Der Positivismusstreit in der deutschen Soziologie.* Neuwied and Berlin: Luchterhand.

Albert, Hans. 1980. *Traktat über die kritische Vernunft.* Tübingen: Mohr Siebeck.

Alexander, Jeffrey C., Bernhard Giesen, Richard Münch, and Neil J. Smelser (Eds.). 1987. *The Micro–Macro Link.* Berkeley and Los Angeles: University of California Press.

Althusser, Louis. 1965. *Pour Marx.* Paris: Maspero. (Translation: 1972. *For Marx.* New York: Pantheon.)

Althusser, Louis, and Etienne Balibar. 1968. *Lire le Capital.* 2 vols. Paris: Maspero. (Translation: 1970. *Reading Capital.* London: New Left Books.)

Anderson, Perry. 1974. *Passages from Antiquity to Feudalism.* London: New Left Books.

Archer, Margaret S. 1988. *Culture and Agency. The Place of Culture in Social Theory.* New York: Cambridge University Press.

Axelrod, Robert. 1984. *The Evolution of Cooperation.* New York: Basic Books.

Bacharach, Samuel, and Edward J. Lawler. 1981. *Bargaining.* San Francisco: Jossey-Bass.

Baecker, Dirk. 1988. *Information und Risiko in der Marktwirtschaft.* Frankfurt am Main: Suhrkamp.

Baran, Paul A., and Paul M. Sweezy. 1966. *Monopoly Capital.* New York: Monthly Review Press.

Barthes, Roland. 1963. *"Eléments de sémiologie."* In *Le degré zéro de l'écriture.* Paris: Gonthier. (Translation: 1964. *Elements of Semiology.* London: Jonathan Cape.)

Barthes, Roland. 1967. *Système de la mode.* Paris: Seuil. (Translation: 1983. *The Fashion System.* New York: Hill and Wang.)

Barthes, Roland. 1970a. *S/Z.* Paris: Seuil. (Translation: 1974. *S/Z.* New York: Hill and Wang.)

Barthes, Roland. 1970b. *L'Empire des signes.* Genf: Albert Skira. (Translation: 1982. *The Empire of Signs.* New York: Hill and Wang.)

Baudrillard, Jean. 1972. *Pour une critique de l'économie politique du signe.* Paris: Gallimard. (Translation: 1981. *For a Critique of the Political Economy of the Sign.* St. Louis, Mo.: Telos Press.)

Baudrillard, Jean. 1973. *Le miroir de la production: ou l'illusion critique du matérialisme historique.* Paris: Casterman. (Translation: 1975. *The Mirror of Production.* St. Louis, Mo.: Telos Press.)

Baudrillard, Jean. 1977. *L'effet beaubourg: Implosion et dissuasion.* Paris: Editions Galilée.

Baudrillard, Jean. 1979. *De la séduction: L'horizon sacré des apparences.* Paris: Denoël/Gonthier.

Baudrillard, Jean. 1983a. *Simulations.* New York: Semiotext.

Baudrillard, Jean. 1983b. *In the Shadow of the Silent Majorities.* New York: Semiotext.

Baudrillard, Jean. 1986. *Masses et postmodernité.* Quebec: Presses de l'Université Laval.

Baudrillard, Jean. 1988. *The Ecstasy of Communication.* Brooklyn, N.J.: Autonomedia.

Bauman, Zygmunt. 1987. *Legislators and Interpreters: On Modernity, Postmodernity, and the Intellectuals.* Oxford: Polity Press.

Beck, Ulrich. 1986. *Risikogesellschaft.* Frankfurt: Suhrkamp.

Becker, Gary S. 1971. *The Economics of Discrimination.* Chicago: University of Chicago Press.

Becker, Gary S. 1981. *A Treatise on the Family.* Cambridge, Mass.: Harvard University Press.

Becker, Howard S. 1963. *Outsiders: Studies in the Sociology of Deviance.* New York: Free Press.

Benjamin, Walter. 1973. *Illuminations.* London: Fontana.

Benjamin, Walter. 1974. *Gesammelte Schriften.* Edited by Rolf Tiedeman and Hermann Schweppenhäuser. Vol. 1. Frankfurt am Main: Suhrkamp.

Benoist, Jean-Marie. 1975. *Tyrannie du logos.* Paris: Minuit.

Bentham, Jeremy. 1789/1970. *An Introduction to the Principles of Morals and Legislation.* Edited by J.H. Burns and H.L.A. Hart. London: Attslone Press.

Benton, Ted. 1984. *The Rise and Fall of Structural Marxism: Althusser and His Influence.* New York: St. Martin's Press.

Berger, Johannes (Ed.). 1986. *Die Moderne—Kontinuitäten und Zäsuren. Soziale Welt.* Special vol. 4.

Berger, Joseph, David G. Wagner, and Morris Zelditch, Jr. 1985. "Theoretical and Metatheoretical Themes in Expectation States Theory." In Horst J. Helle and Shmuel N. Eisenstadt (Eds.), *Micro-Sociological Theory: Perspectives on Sociological Theory,* pp. 148–68. London: Sage.

Bergson, Henri. 1932/1959. "Les deux sources de la morale et de la religion." In *OEuvres,* vol. 2, pp. 980–1247. Paris: Presses Universitaires de France.

Bhaskar, Roy. 1979. *The Possibility of Naturalism.* Atlantic Highlands, N.J.: Humanities Press.

Blalock, Hubert, and Paul Wilken. 1979. *Intergroup Processes: A Micro-Macro Perspective.* New York: Free Press.

Blau, Peter M. 1977. *Inequality and Heterogeneity: A Primitive Theory of Social Structure.* New York: Free Press.

Bloomfield, Morton W. 1957. *Language.* London: Allen and Unwin.

Bottomore, Tom. 1984. *The Frankfurt School.* Chichester: Ellis Horwood.

Boudon, Raymond. 1977. *Effets pervers et order social.* Paris: Presses Universitaires de France.

Boudon, Raymond. 1981. *The Logic of Social Action: An Introduction to Sociological Analysis.* London: Routledge.

Bourdieu, Pierre. 1971. "Champ du pouvoir, champ intellectuel et habitus de classe." In *Scolies* I, pp. 7–26.

Bourdieu, Pierre. 1972. *Esquisse d'une théorie de la pratique, précédé de trois études d'ethnologie kabyle.* Genève: Droz. (Translation with addition: 1977. *Outline of a Theory of Practice.* Cambridge: Cambridge University Press.)

Bourdieu, Pierre. 1979. *La distinction. Critique social du jugement.* Paris: Minuit. (Translation: 1984a. *Distinction: A Social Critique of the Judgement of Taste.* Cambridge, Mass.: Harvard University Press.)

Bourdieu, Pierre. 1984b. "Espace social et genèse de 'classes.'" *Actes de la recherche en sciences sociales* (52–53): 3–15. (Translation: 1985. "The Social Space and the Genesis of Groups." *Theory and Society* 14: 723–44.)

Bourdieu, Pierre. 1986. "Three Forms of Capital." In John G. Richardson (Ed.), *Handbook of Theory and Research for the Sociology of Education,* pp. 241–58. New York: Greenwood Press.

Bourdieu, Pierre. 1987. "What Makes a Social Class? On the Theoretical and Practical Existence of Groups." *Berkeley Journal of Sociology* 32: 1–17.

Bourdieu, Pierre, and Jean Claude Passeron. 1964. *Les héritiers: Les étudiants et la culture.* Paris: Minuit. (Translation: 1979. *The Inheritors. French Students and Their Relation to Culture.* Chicago: University of Chicago Press.)

Bourdieu, Pierre, and Jean Claude Passeron. 1970. *La reproduction.* Paris: Minuit. (Translation: 1977. *Reproduction.* London and Beverly Hills: Sage.)

Boyne, Roy. 1990. "Culture and the World-System." *Theory, Culture and Society* 7: 57–62.

Buchanan, James M. 1975. *The Limits of Liberty—Between Anarchy and Leviathan.* Chicago: University of Chicago Press.

Bucher, Rue, and Leonard Schatzman. 1964. "Negotiating a Division of Labor among Professionals in the State Mental Hospital." *Psychiatry* 27: 266–77.

Burt, Ronald S. 1982. *Toward a Structural Theory of Action.* New York: Academic Press.

Burt, Ronald S. 1983. *Corporate Profits and Cooperation: Networks of Market Constraints and Directorate Ties in the American Economy.* New York: Academic Press.

Chomsky, Noam. 1957. *Syntactic Structures.* The Hague: Mouton.

Chomsky, Noam. 1964. *Current Issues in Linguistic Theory.* The Hague: Mouton.

Chomsky, Noam. 1965. *Aspects of the Theory of Syntax.* Cambridge, Mass.: MIT Press.

Chomsky, Noam. 1968. *Language and Mind.* New York: Harcourt Brace.

Clavel, Maurice. 1975. *Dieu est Dieu, nom de Dieu.* Paris: Grasset.

Coleman, James S. 1971. "Collective Decisions." In H. Turk and R.L. Simpson (Eds.), *Institutions and Social Exchange,* pp. 272–86. Indianapolis, Ind.: Bobbs-Merrill.

Coleman, James S. 1974. *Power and the Structure of Society.* New York: Norton.

Coleman, James S. 1986. *Individual Interests and Collective Action: Selected Essays.* Cambridge/Paris: Cambridge University Press/Maison des Sciences de l'Homme.

Coleman, James S. 1990. *Foundations of Social Theory.* Cambridge, Mass.: Belknap Press of Harvard University Press.

Collins, Randall. 1975. *Conflict Sociology: Toward an Explanatory Science.* New York: Academic Press.

Collins, Randall. 1988. *Theoretical Sociology.* New York: Harcourt Brace Jovanovich.

Cook, Karen S., Richard M. Emerson, Mary R. Gilmore, and Toshio Yamagishi. 1983. "The Distribution of Power in Exchange Networks." *American Journal of Sociology* 89: 275–305.

Davies, Paul C. 1988. *The Cosmic Blueprint.* New York: Simon and Schuster.

Dendrinos, Dimitrios S. 1990. *Chaos and Socio-Spatial Dynamics.* New York: Springer.

Derrida, Jacques. 1967a. *De la grammatologie.* Paris: Minuit. (Translation: 1976. *Of Grammatology.* Baltimore, Md.: Johns Hopkins University Press.)

Derrida, Jacques. 1967b. *L'écriture et la différence.* Paris: Editions du Seuil. (Translation: 1978. *Writing and Difference.* Chicago: University of Chicago Press.)

Derrida, Jacques. 1972. *Positions.* Paris: Minuit. (Translation: 1981. *Positions.* Chicago: University of Chicago Press.)

Durkheim, Emile. 1895/1973a. *Les règles de la méthode sociologique.* Paris: Presses Universitaires de France. (Translation: 1982. *The Rules of Sociological Method.* Edited by Steven Lukes. Translated by W.D. Halls. London: Macmillan.)

Durkheim, Emile. 1912/1968. *Les formes élémentaires de la vie religieuse.* Paris: Presses Universitaires de France. (Translation: 1976. *The Elementary Forms of Religious Life.* Translated by J.W. Swain. London: Allen & Unwin.)

Durkheim, Emile. 1914/1970. "Le dualism de la nature humaine et ses conditions sociales." In *La science sociale et l'action,* pp. 314–32. Edited by J.C. Filloux. Paris: Presses Universitaires de France. (Translation: 1973b. "The Dualism of Human Nature and Its Social Conditions." In *On Morality and Society,* pp. 149–63. Edited by Robert N. Bellah. Chicago: University of Chicago Press.

Durkheim, Emile. 1924/1974. *Sociologie et philosophie.* Paris: Presses Universitaires de France. (Translation: 1965. *Sociology and Philosophy.* Translated by D.F. Pocock. London: Cohen & West.)

Durkheim, Emile, and Marcel Mauss. 1901–1902. "De quelques formes primitives de classification." *L'année sociologique* 6: 1–72. (Translation: 1963. *Primitive Classification.* Chicago: University of Chicago Press.)

Eco, Umberto. 1975. *Trattato di semiotica generale.* Milan: Bompiani. (Translation: 1976. *A Theory of Semiotics.* Bloomington: Indiana University Press.)

Eder, Klaus. 1985. *Geschichte als Lernprozeß? Zur Pathogenese politischer Modernität in Deutschland.* Frankfurt am Main: Suhrkamp.

Elias, Norbert. 1939/1976. *Über den Prozß der Zivilisation.* 2 vols. Frankfurt am Main: Suhrkamp. (Translation: 1978a. *The Civilizing Process.* New York: Urizen.)

Elias, Norbert. 1969. *Die höfische Gesellschaft.* Neuwied and Berlin: Lutchterhand.

Elias, Norbert. 1970. *Was ist Soziologie?* Munich: Juventa. (Translation: 1978b. *What Is Sociology?* London: Hutchinson.)

Elias, Norbert. 1986. "Wandlungen der Machtbalance zwischen den Geschlechtern." *Kölner Zeitschrift für Soziologie und Sozialpsychologie* 38: 425–49.

Elias, Norbert. 1987. *Die Gesellschaft der Individuen.* Edited by Michael Schröter. Frankfurt am Main: Suhrkamp.

Elias, Norbert. 1990. *Studien über die Deutschen. Machtkämpfe und Habitusentwicklung im 19. und 20. Jahrhundert.* Frankfurt am Main: Suhrkamp.

Elster, Jon. 1979/1984. *Ulysses and the Sirenes: Studies in Rationality and Irrationality.* Cambridge: Cambridge University Press.

Elster, Jon. 1983. *Sour Grapes: Studies in the Subversion of Rationality.* Cambridge: Cambridge University Press.

Elster, Jon. 1985. *Making Sense of Marx.* Cambridge: Cambridge University Press.

Elster, Jon. 1989a. *The Cement of Society: A Study of Social Order.* New York: Cambridge University Press.

Elster, Jon. 1989b. *Solomonic Judgements: Studies in the Limitation of Rationality.* New York: Cambridge University Press.

Emerson, Richard M. 1972. "Exchange Theory. Part I and II." In J. Berger, M. Zelditch, Jr., and B. Anderson (Eds.), *Sociological Theories in Progress,* pp. 38–87. New York: Houghton Mifflin.

Esser, Hartmut. 1990. " 'Habits,' 'Frames,' und 'Rational Choice' — Die Reichweite von Theorien der rationalen Wahl (am Beispiel der Erklärung des Befragtenverhaltens)." *Zeitschrift für Soziologie* 19(4): 231–47.

Featherstone, Mike. 1989. "Towards a Sociology of Postmodern Culture." In Hans Haferkamp (Ed.), *Social Structure and Culture,* pp. 147–72. Berlin and New York: Walter de Gruyter.

Foucault, Michel. 1961. *Histoire de la folie.* Paris: Librairie Plon. (Translation: 1965. *Madness and Civilization.* New York: Random House.)

Foucault, Michel. 1969. *L'archéologie du savoir.* Paris: Gallimard. (Translation: 1972a. *The Archeology of Knowledge.* New York: Pantheon.)

Foucault, Michel. 1971. *L'ordre du discours.* Paris: Gallimard. (Translation: 1972b. *The Order of Discourse. The Archeology of Knowledge.* New York: Pantheon.)

Foucault, Michel. 1975. *Surveiller et punir. La naissance de la prison.* Paris: Gallimard. (Translation: 1977. *Discipline and Punish: The Birth of the Prison.* New York: Pantheon Books.)

Foucault, Michel. 1976. *Histoire de la sexualité.* Vol. 1: *La volonté de savoir.* Paris: Gallimard. (Translation: 1978. *The History of Sexuality.* New York: Pantheon Books.)

Foucault, Michel. 1984a. *Histoire de la sexualité.* Vol. 2: *L'usage des plaisirs.* Paris: Gallimard. (Translation: 1980–1986. *The History of Sexuality.* New York: Vintage Books.)

Foucault, Michel. 1984b. *Histoire de la sexualité.* Vol. 3: *Le souci de soi.* Paris: Gallimard. (Translation: 1980–1986. *The History of Sexuality.* New York: Vintage Books.)

Foucault, Michel. 1988. *Politics, Philosophy, Culture: Interviews and Other Writings, 1977–1984.* New York: Routledge.

Gadamer, Hans Georg. 1960. *Wahrheit und Methode.* Tübingen: Mohr Siebeck. (Translation: 1975. *Truth and Method.* London: Sheed and Ward.)

Gehlen, Arnold. 1950. *Der Mensch, seine Natur und seine Stellung in der Welt.* 4th rev. ed. Bonn: Athenäum-Verlag.

Gerhards, Jürgen, and Friedhelm Neidhardt. 1990. *Strukturen und Funktionen moderner Öffentlichkeit. Fragestellungen und Ansätze.* Berlin: Wissenschaftszentrum für Sozialforschung.

Giddens, Anthony. 1976. *New Rules of Sociological Method: A Positive Critique of Interpretative Sociologies.* New York: Basic Books.

Giddens, Anthony. 1979. *Central Problems in Social Theory: Action, Structure and Contradiction in Social Analysis.* Berkeley/Los Angeles: University of California Press.

Giddens, Anthony. 1981. *A Contemporary Critique of Historical Materialism.* Vol. 1: *Power, Property and the State.* Berkeley/Los Angeles: University of California Press.

Giddens, Anthony. 1982. *Profiles and Critiques in Social Theory.* London: Macmillan.

Giddens, Anthony. 1984. *The Constitution of Society: Outline of the Theory of Structuration.* Cambridge: Polity Press.

Giddens, Anthony. 1985. *A Contemporary Critique of Historical Materialism.* Vol. 2: *The Nation-State and Violence.* Cambridge: Polity Press.

Giddens, Anthony. 1987. "Structuralism, Post-Structuralism and the Production of Culture." In Anthony Giddens and Jonathan H. Turner (Eds.), *Social Theory Today,* pp. 195–223. Cambridge: Polity Press.

Giddens, Anthony. 1989. *Sociology.* Cambridge: Polity Press.

Glaser, Barney, and Anselm Strauss. 1965. *Awareness of Dying.* Chicago: Aldine.

Glaser, Barney, and Anselm Strauss. 1967. *The Discovery of Grounded Theory.* Chicago: Aldine.

Gleichmann, Peter, Johan Goudsblom, and Hermann Korte (Eds.). 1979. *Materialien zu Norbert Elias' Zivilisationstheorie.* Frankfurt am Main: Suhrkamp.

Glucksmann, André. 1977. *Les maîtres penseurs.* Paris: Grasset.

Godelier, Maurice. 1972. *Rationality and Irrationality in Economics.* London: NLB.

Goldthorpe, John. 1968. *The Affluent Worker.* London: Cambridge University Press.

Goldthorpe, John. 1980. *Social Mobility and Class Structure in Modern Britain.* Oxford: Clarendon Press.

Goudsblom, Johan, Edward L. Jones, and Stephen Mennell. 1989. *Human History and Social Process.* Exeter: University of Exeter Press.

Granovetter, Mark. 1985. "Economic Action and Social Structure: The Problem of Embeddedness." *American Journal of Sociology* 91: 481–510.

Habermas, Jürgen. 1968a. *Technik and Wissenschaft als Ideologie.* Frankfurt am Main: Suhrkamp. (Partly translated: 1970a. *Towards a Rational Society.* Translated by Jeremy J. Shapiro. Boston: Beacon Press.)

Habermas, Jürgen. 1968b. *Erkenntnis und Interesse.* Frankfurt am Main: Suhrkamp. (Translation: 1970b. *Knowledge and Human Interest.* London: Heinemann.)

Habermas, Jürgen. 1969. *Protestbewegung und Hochschulreform.* Frankfurt am Main: Suhrkamp. (Partly translated: 1970a. *Towards a Rational Society.* Translated by Jeremy J. Shapiro. Boston: Beacon Press.)

Habermas, Jürgen. 1971a. *Theorie und Praxis.* Frankfurt am Main: Suhrkamp. (Translation: 1973a. *Theory and Practice.* Boston: Beacon Press.)

Habermas, Jürgen. 1971b. "Vorbereitende Bemerkungen zu einer Theorie der kommunikativen Kompetenz." In Jürgen Habermas and Niklas Luhmann, *Theorie der Gesellschaft oder Sozialtechnologie — Was leistet die Systemforschung?* pp. 101–41. Frankfurt am Main: Suhrkamp. (Translation: 1970c. "Toward a Theory of Communicative Competence." *Inquiry* 13: 360–75.)

Habermas, Jürgen. 1973b. *Legitimationsprobleme im Spätkapitalismus.* Frankfurt am Main: Suhrkamp. (Translation: 1976a. *Legitimation Crisis.* London: Heinemann.)

Habermas, Jürgen. 1973c. "Wahrheitstheorien." In H. Fahrenbach (Ed.), *Wirklichkeit und Reflexion. Walter Schulz zum 60, Geburtstag,* pp. 211–65. Pfullingen: Neske.

Habermas, Jürgen. 1976b. *Zur Rekonstruktion des Historischen Materialismus.* Frankfurt am Main: Suhrkamp. (Translation: 1979. *Communication and the Evolution of Society.* London: Heinemann.)

Habermas, Jürgen. 1981. *Theorie des kommunikativen Handelns.* 2 vols. Frankfurt am Main: Suhrkamp. (Translation: 1984, 1987a. *The Theory of Communicative Action.* 2 vols. Boston: Beacon Press.)

Habermas, Jürgen. 1983. *Moralbewußtsein und kommunikatives Handeln.* Frankfurt am Main: Suhrkamp.

Habermas, Jürgen. 1985. *Der philosophische Diskurs der Moderne.* Frankfurt am Main: Suhrkamp. (Translation: 1987b. *The Philosophical Discourse of Modernity.* Cambridge: Polity Press.)

Halévy, Elie. 1900. *La formation du radicalisme philosophique: La révolution et la doctrine de l'utilité (1789–1815).* Paris: F. Alcan. (Translation: 1928. *The Growth of Philosophic Radicalism.* Translated by Mary Morris. New York: Macmillan.)

Harris, Zellig Sabbetai. 1951/1960. *Methods in Structural Linguistics.* (Reprint title: *Structural Linguistics.*) Chicago: University of Chicago Press.)

Hechter, Michael. 1987. *Principles of Group Solidarity.* Berkeley and London: University of California Press.

Hegel, Georg Wilhelm Friedrich. 1807/1964–1971. *Phänomenologie des Geistes.* In *Sämtliche Werke.* Edited by H. Glockner. Vol. 2, Stuttgart: Frommann Holzboog. (Translation: 1977. *Phenomenology of Spirit.* Oxford: Clarendon Press.)

Hegel, Georg Wilhelm Friedrich. 1821/1964–1971. *Grundlinien der Philosphie des Rechts.* In *Sämtliche Werke.* Edited by H. Glockner. Vol. 7. Stuttgart: Frommann Holzboog. (Translation: 1965. *Philosophy of Right.* Oxford: Clarendon Press.)

Hegel, Georg Wilhelm Friedrich. 1964–1971. *Sämtliche Werke.* Edited by H. Glockner. Stuttgart: Frommann Holzboog. (Partly translated: 1974. *The Essential Writings.* New York: Harper & Row; 1972. *Hegel's Philosophy of Mind.* Freeport, N.J.: Books for Library Press.)

Held, David. 1980. *Introduction to Critical Theory: Horkheimer to Habermas.* Berkeley and Los Angeles: University of California Press.

Hirschman, Albert O. 1970. *Exit, Voice and Loyalty: Responses to Decline in Firms, Organizations, and States.* Cambridge, Mass.: Harvard University Press.

Hobbes, Thomas. 1651/1966. *Leviathan.* In W. Molesworth (Ed.), *Collected English Works of Thomas Hobbes.* Vol. 3. Aalen, Germany: Scientia.

Honneth, Axel. 1985. *Kritik der Macht.* Frankfurt am Main: Suhrkamp.

Honneth, Axel, Thomas McCarthy, Claus Offe, and Albrecht Wellmer (Eds.). 1989. *Zwischenbetrachtungen. Im Prozeß der Aufklärung. Jürgen Habermas zum 60. Geburtstag.* Frankfurt am Main: Suhrkamp.

Hopkins, Terence K., and Immanuel Wallerstein. 1982. *World-Systems Analysis. Theory and Methodology.* Beverly Hills, Calif.: Sage.

Horkheimer, Max. 1947/1974a. *Eclipse of Reason.* New York: Seabury Press. (See also under the title: *Critique of Instrumental Reason.*)

Horkheimer, Max. 1967. *Zur Kritik der instrumentellen Vernunft.* Frankfurt am Main: S. Fischer. (Translation: 1974b. *Critique of Instrumental Reason.* New York: Seabury Press.)

Horkheimer, Max. 1968. *Kritische Theorie.* 2 vols. Frankfurt am Main: S. Fischer. (Translation: 1972. *Critical Theory: Selected Essays.* New York: Herder & Herder.)

Horkheimer, Max, and Theodor W. Adorno. 1947. *Dialektik der Aufklärung.* Amsterdam: Nijhoff. (Translation: 1972. *Dialectic of Enlightenment.* New York: Seabury Press.)

Ingham, Geoffrey K. 1984. *Capitalism Divided? The City and Industry in Britain.* London: Macmillan.

Janning, Frank. 1991. *Pierre Bourdieus Theorie der Praxis.* Opladen: Westdeutscher Verlag.

Jay, Martin. 1973. *The Dialectical Imagination.* Boston: Little, Brown.

Jay, Martin. 1984. *Marxism and Totality: The Adventures of a Concept from Lukács to Habermas.* Berkeley and Los Angeles: University of California Press.

Jay, Martin. 1986. *Permanent Essays on the Intellectual Migration from Germany to America.* New York: Columbia University Press.

Kant, Immanuel. 1781/1964a. *Kritik der reinen Vernunft.* In *Werke in sechs Bänden.* Edited by Wilhelm Weischedel. Vol. 2. Frankfurt am Main: Insel Verlag. (Translation: 1952a. *Critique of Pure Reason.* In *Great Books of the Western World* 42: *Kant,* pp. 1–250. Chicago/London: Encyclopaedia Britannica.

Kant, Immanuel. 1788/1964b. *Kritik der praktischen Vernunft.* In *Werke in sechs Bänden.* Edited by Wilhelm Weischedel. Vol. 4, pp. 103–302. Frankfurt am Main: Insel Verlag. (Translation: 1952b. *Critique of Practical Reason.* In *Great Books of the Western World* 42: *Kant,* pp. 291–361. Chicago/London: Encylopaedia Britannica.

Kant, Immanuel. 1790/1964c. *Kritik der Urteilskraft.* In *Werke in sechs Bänden.* Edited by Wilhelm Weischedel. Vol. 5. Frankfurt am Main: Insel Verlag. (Translation: 1952c: *Critique of Judgement.* In *Great Books of the Western World* 42: *Kant,* pp. 461–613. Chicago/London: Encyclopaedia Britannica.

Kant, Immanuel. 1793/1964d. "Über den Gemeinspruch: Das mag in der Theorie richtig sein, taugt aber nicht für die Praxis." In *Werke in sechs Bänden.* Edited by Wilhelm Weischedel. Vol. 6, pp. 125–72. Frankfurt am Main: Insel Verlag. (Translation: 1974. *On the Old Say: That May Be Right in Theory But It Won't Work in Practice.* Philadelphia: University of Philadelphia Press.)

Knorr-Cetina, Karin D., and Aaron V. Cicourel (Eds.). 1981. *Advances in Social Theory and Methodology: Toward an Integration of Micro-Macro-Sociologies.* London: Routledge.

Kohlberg, Lawrence. 1969. "Stage and Sequence: The Cognitive-Developmental Approach to Socialization." In D.A. Goslin (Ed.), *Handbook of Socialization Theory and Research,* pp. 347–480. Chicago: Rand McNally.

Kohlberg, Lawrence. 1975. "Moral Stages and Moralization: The Cognitive-Developmental Approach." In T. Lickona (Ed.), *Moral Development and Behavior,* pp. 31–53. New York: Holt, Rinehart & Winston.

Kohlberg, Lawrence. 1981. *The Philosophy of Moral Development.* San Francisco: Harper & Row.

Kohlberg, Lawrence. 1984. *The Psychology of Moral Development. Essays on Moral Development.* Vol. 2. San Francisco: Harper & Row.

Kohlberg, Lawrence. 1987. *Child Psychology and Childhood Education. A Cognitive-Developmental View.* New York and London: Longman.

Küppers, Bernd-Olaf. 1987. *Ordnung aus dem Chaos: Prinzipien der Selbst-organisation und Evolution des Lebens.* Munich: Piper.

Kuhn, Thomas. 1970. *The Structure of Scientific Revolutions.* Chicago: University of Chicago Press.

Kurzweil, Edith. 1980. *The Age of Structuralism: Lévi-Strauss to Foucault.* New York: Columbia University Press.

Lacan, Jacques. 1966. *Ecrits.* Paris: Editions du Seuil. (Translation: 1977. *Ecrits: A Selection.* New York: Norton.

Laumann, Edward O., and Franz U. Pappi. 1976. *Networks of Collective Action: A Perspective on Community Influence Systems.* New York: Academic Press.

Leach, Edmund. 1974. *Claude Lévi-Strauss.* New York: Penguin.

Lemert, Charles. 1979. *Sociology and the Twilight of Man: Homocentrism and Discourse in Sociological Theory.* Carbondale: Southern Illinois University Press.

Lemert, Charles (Ed.). 1981. *French Sociology: Rupture and Renewal since 1968.* New York: Columbia University Press.

Lemert, Edwin M. 1972. *Human Deviance. Social Problems and Social Control.* Englewood Cliffs, N.J.: Prentice Hall.

Lévi-Strauss, Claude. 1947. *Les structures élémentaires de la parenté.* Paris: Mouton. (Translation: 1969a. *The Elementary Structures of Kinship.* New York: Basic Books.)

Lévi-Strauss, Claude. 1962. *La pensée sauvage.* Paris: Librairie Plon. (Translation: 1966. *The Savage Mind.* Chicago: University of Chicago Press.)

Lévi-Strauss, Claude. 1964. *Mythologiques. Le cru et le cuit.* Paris: Librairie Plon. (Translation: 1969b. *The Raw and the Cooked.* New York: Harper & Row.)

Lévi-Strauss, Claude. 1967. *Mythologiques. Du miel aux cendres.* Paris: Librairie Plon. (Translation: 1973. *From Honey to Ashes.* New York: Harper & Row.)

Lévi-Strauss, Claude. 1968. *Mythologiques. L'origine des manières de table.* Paris: Librairie Plon. (Translation: 1978. *The Origin of Table Manners.* New York: Harper & Row.

Lévi-Strauss, Claude. 1971. *Mythologiques. L'homme nu.* Paris: Librairie Plon. (Translation: 1981. *The Naked Man.* New York: Harper & Row.)

Lévy, Bernard-Henri. 1977. *La Barbarie à visage humain.* Paris: Grasset.

Lindenberg, Siegwart. 1989. "Choice and Culture: The Behavioral Basis of Cultural Impact on Transactions." In Hans Haferkamp (Ed.), *Social Structure and Culture,* pp. 176–200. Berlin and New York: Walter de Gruyter.

Locke, John. 1690/1967. *Two Treatises on Government.* In *The Works.* 10 vols. Aalen, Germany: Scientia.

Lockwood, David. 1956. "Some Notes on the Social System." *British Journal of Sociology* 7: 134–46.

Lockwood, David. 1958. *The Blackcoated Worker: A Study in Class Consciousness.* London: Allen and Unwin.

Lockwood, David. 1960. "The New Working Class." *Archives Européennes de Sociologie* 1: 248–59.

Löwenthal, Leo. 1980. *Gesammelte Schriften.* Edited by Helmut Dubiel. Vol. 1. Frankfurt am Main: Suhrkamp.

Löwenthal, Leo. 1981. *Gesammelte Schriften.* Edited by Helmut Dubiel. Vol. 2. Frankfurt am Main: Suhrkamp.

Luhmann, Niklas. 1969/1983. *Legitimation durch Verfahren.* Frankfurt am Main: Suhrkamp.

Luhmann, Niklas. 1970. *Soziologische Aufklärung.* Vol. 1. Opladen: Westdeutscher Verlag. (Translation: 1982a. *The Differentiation of Society.* Translated by Stephen Holmes and Charles Larmore. New York: Columbia University Press.)

Luhmann, Niklas. 1972. *Rechtssoziologie.* 2 vols. Reinbek, Hamburg: Rowohlt. (Translation: 1985. *A Sociological Theory of Law.* London: Routledge.)

Luhmann, Niklas. 1973. *Vertrauen. Ein Mechanismus zur Reduktion sozialer Komplexität.* Stuttgart: Enke. (Translation: 1979. *Trust and Power.* New York: Wiley.)

Luhmann, Niklas. 1975. *Macht.* Stuttgart: Enke. (Translation: 1979. *Trust and Power.* New York: Wiley.)

Luhmann, Niklas. 1980. *Gesellschaftsstruktur und Semantik.* Vol. 1. Frankfurt am Main: Suhrkamp.

Luhmann, Niklas. 1982b. *Liebe als Passion: Zur Codierung von Intimität.* Frankfurt am Main: Suhrkamp. (Translation: 1982c. *Love as Passion: The Codification of Intimacy.* Cambridge, Mass.: Harvard University Press.)

Luhmann, Niklas. 1982d. "Autopoiesis, Handlung und kommunikative Verständigung." *Zeitschrift für Soziologie* 11: 366–79.

Luhmann, Niklas. 1984. *Soziale Systeme. Grundriß einer allgemeinen Theorie.* Frankfurt am Main: Suhrkamp.

Luhmann, Niklas. 1986. *Ökologische Kommunikation.* Opladen: Westdeutscher Verlag. (Translation: 1989. *Ecological Communication.* Chicago: University of Chicago Press.)

Luhmann, Niklas. 1988. *Die Wirtschaft der Gesellschaft.* Frankfurt am Main: Suhrkamp.

Lukács, Georg. 1923/1968. *Geschichte und Klassenbewußtsein.* 2 vols. Neuwied: Luchterhand (Translation: 1971. *History and Class Consciousness.* Cambridge, Mass.: MIT Press.)

Lyotard, Jean-François. 1979. *La condition postmoderne. Rapport sur le savoir.* Paris: Minuit. (Translation: 1984. *The Postmodern Condition: A Report on Knowledge.* Manchester: Manchester University Press.)

Lyotard, Jean-François. 1983. *Le différend.* Paris: Minuit.

Maffesoli, Michel. 1988. *Le temps des tribus: le déclin de l'individualisme dans les sociétés de masse.* Paris: Librairie des Meridiens Klinksieck.

Mann, Michael. 1986. *The Sources of Social Power.* Vol. 1. New York: Cambridge University Press.

Marcuse, Herbert. 1960. *Reason and Revolution.* Boston: Beacon Press.

Marcuse, Herbert. 1964. *One-Dimensional Man.* Boston: Beacon Press.

Marshall, Thomas H. 1964/1976. *Class, Citizenship, and Social Development.* Westport, Conn.: Greenwood Press.

Marx, Karl. 1844/1968. *Ökonomisch-philosophische Manuskripte aus dem Jahre 1844.* Marx-Engels Werke, Supp. vol., part 1, pp. 465–588. Berlin: Dietz. (Translation: 1971. *The Early Texts.* Edited by David McLellan. Oxford: Blackwell.)

Marx, Karl. 1845/1969. *Thesen über Feuerbach.* Marx-Engels Werke. Vol. 3, pp. 5–7. Berlin: Dietz. (Translation: 1971. *The Early Texts.* Edited by David McLellan. Oxford: Blackwell.)

Marx, Karl. 1867/1962, 1885/1963, 1894/1964. *Das Kapital.* Vols. 1–3. *Marx-Engels Werke.* Vol. 23–25. Berlin: Dietz. (Translation: 1967. *Capital.* 3 vols. New York: International Pub.)

Marx, Karl, and Friedrich Engels. 1846/1969. *Die deutsche Ideologie.* Marx-Engels Werke. Vol. 3, pp. 9–530. Berlin: Dietz. (Translation: 1947. *The German Ideology.* New York: International Pub.)

Marx, Karl, and Friedrich Engels. 1848/1959a. *Manifest der kommunistischen Partei. Marx-Engels Werke.* Vol. 4, pp. 459–93. Berlin: Dietz. (Translation: 1959b. *The Communist Manifesto.* In L. Feuer (Ed.), *Marx and Engels: Basic Writings on Politics and Philosophy.* New York: Doubleday.)

Maturana, Humberto, and Francisco J. Varela. 1980. *Autopoiesis and Cognition: The Realization of the Living.* Dordrecht: Reidel.

Mauss, Marcel. 1923–1924. "Essai sur le don. Forme archaïque de l'échange." *L'année sociologique* 1:30–186. (Translation: 1967. *The Gift.* New York: Norton.)

Mayntz, Renate, Bernd Rosewitz, Uwe Schimank, and Rudolf Stichweh. 1988. *Differenzierung und Verselbständigung. Zur Entwicklung gesellschaftlicher Teilsysteme.* Frankfurt am Main: Campus.

McCarthy, Thomas. 1982. *The Critical Theory of Jürgen Habermas.* Cambridge, Mass.: MIT Press.

Mead, George Herbert. 1934. *Mind, Self, and Society.* Edited and introduced by Charles W. Morris. Chicago: University of Chicago Press.

Mennell, Stephen. 1989. *Norbert Elias, Civilization and the Human Self-Image.* London: Basil Blackwell.

Mennell, Stephen. 1990. "The Globalization of Human Society as a Very Long-Term Social Process: Elias' Theory." *Theory, Culture and Society* 7:359–71.

Merton, Robert K. 1949/1968. *Social Theory and Social Structure.* New York: Free Press.

Miliband, Ralph. 1982. *Capitalist Democracy in Britain.* London: Oxford University Press.

Mill, John Stuart. 1861/1974. *Utilitarianism.* In *Utilitarianism; On Liberty; Essays on Bentham; Selected Writings of Jeremy Bentham and John Austin.* Edited by Mary Warnock. Hecho En Westford, Mass.: New American Library.

Miller, Max. 1986. *Kollektive Lernprozesse. Studien zur Grundlegung einer soziologischen Lerntheorie.* Frankfurt am Main: Suhrkamp.

Moore, Barrington. 1966. *Social Origins of Dictatorship and Democracy: Lord and Peasant in the Making of the Modern World.* Boston: Beacon Press.

Münch, Richard. 1982. *Theorie des Handelns. Zur Rekonstruktion der Beiträge von Talcott Parsons, Emile Durkheim und Max Weber.* Frankfurt am Main: Suhrkamp. (Translation in two parts: 1987a. *Theory of Action: Towards a New Synthesis Going Beyond Parsons.* London: Routledge; 1988. *Understanding Modernity: Towards a New Perspective Going Beyond Durkheim and Weber.* London: Routledge.)

Münch, Richard. 1984. *Die Struktur der Moderne.* Frankfurt am Main: Suhrkamp.
Münch, Richard. 1986. *Die Kultur der Moderne.* 2 vols. Vol. 1: *Ihre Grundlagen und ihre Entwicklung in England und Amerika.* Vol. 2: *Ihre Entwicklung in Frankreich und Deutschland.* Frankfurt am Main: Suhrkamp.
Münch, Richard. 1987b. "Parsonian Theory Today: In Search of a New Synthesis." In Anthony Giddens and Jonathan H. Turner (Eds.), *Social Theory Today,* pp. 116–55. Cambridge: Polity Press.
Münch, Richard. 1991. *Dialektik der Kommunikationsgesellschaft.* Frankfurt am Main: Suhrkamp.
Nietzsche, Friedrich. 1901/1961. *Der Wille zur Macht.* Stuttgart: Kröner. (Translation: 1968. *The Will to Power.* New York: Viking.)
Nozick, Robert. 1974. *Anarchy, State, and Utopia.* New York: Basic Books.
O'Connor, James. 1973. *The Fiscal Crisis of the State.* New York: St. Martin's Press.
Offe, Claus. 1972. *Strukturprobleme des kapitalistischen Staates.* Frankfurt am Main: Suhrkamp.
Offe, Claus. 1984a. *"Arbeitsgesellschaft": Strukturprobleme und Zukunftsperspektiven.* Frankfurt am Main and New York: Campus.
Offe, Claus. 1984b. *Contradictions of the Welfare State.* Edited by John Keane. London: Hutchinson.
Offe, Claus. 1984c. *Societal Preconditions of Corporatism and Some Current Dilemmas of Democratic Theory.* Notre Dame, Ind.: Helen Kellogg Institute for International Studies.
Offe, Claus. 1985. *Disorganized Capitalism. Contemporary Transformations of Work and Politics.* Cambridge: Polity Press.
Offe, Claus. 1986. "Die Utopie der Null-Option. Modernität und Modernisierung als politische Gütekriterien." In Johannes Berger (Ed.), *Die Moderne— Kontinuitäten und Zäsuren. Soziale Welt,* Sonderband 4, pp. 97–117. Göttingen: Otto Schwartz.
Offe, Claus. 1987. "Democracy Against the Welfare-State? Structural Foundations of Neoconservative Political Opportunities." *Political Theory* 15:501-37.
Offe, Claus. 1989. "Fessel und Bremse. Moralische und institutionelle Aspekte 'intelligenter Selbstbeschränkung.'" In Axel Honneth, Thomas McCarthy, Claus Offe, and Albrecht Wellmer (Eds.), *Zwischenbetrachtungen. Im Prozeß der Aufklärung. Jürgen Habermas zum 60. Geburtstag,* pp. 739-74. Frankfurt am Main: Suhrkamp.
Offe, Claus. 1990. "Die Wirtschaft der Gesellschaft." (Review of Niklas Luhmann, *Die Wirtschaft der Gesellschaft.* Frankfurt am Main: Suhrkamp, 1988). In *Soziologische Revue* 13, pp. 389-93.
Offe, Claus, and Rolf G. Heinze. 1986. "Am Arbeitsmarkt vorbei. Überlegungen zur Neubestimmung 'haushaltlicher' Wohlfahrtsproduktion in ihrem Verhältnis zu Markt und Staat." *Leviathan* 14, pp. 471-95.
Parsons, Talcott. 1937/1968. *The Structure of Social Action.* New York: Free Press.
Parsons, Talcott. 1951. *The Social System.* Glencoe, Ill.: Free Press.
Parsons, Talcott. 1967. *Sociological Theory and Modern Society.* New York: Free Press.
Parsons, Talcott. 1977. *Social Systems and the Evolution of Action Theory.* New York: Free Press.
Parsons, Talcott. 1978. *Action Theory and the Human Condition.* New York: Free Press.

Parsons, Talcott, and Gerald M. Platt. 1973. *The American University.* Cambridge, Mass.: Harvard University Press.

Popper, Karl R. 1944/1966. *The Open Society and Its Enemies.* 2 vols. Princeton, N.J.: Princeton University Press.

Popper, Karl R. 1962. "Die Logik der Sozialwissenschaften." *Kölner Zeitschrift für Soziologie und Sozialpsychologie* 14:233–48; and in: 1969. Theodor W. Adorno, Hans Albert, Ralf Dahrendorf, Jürgen Habermas, Harald Pilot and Karl R. Popper (Eds.), *Der Positivismusstreit in der deutschen Soziologie,* pp. 103–23. Neuwied and Berlin: Luchterhand.

Popper, Karl R. 1963. *Conjectures and Refutations: The Growth of Scientific Knowledge.* London: Routledge.

Popper, Karl R. 1972. *Objective Knowledge: An Evolutionary Approach.* Oxford: Clarendon Press.

Poulantzas, Nicos. 1968a. *Pouvoir politique et classes sociales de l'état capitaliste.* Paris: Maspero. (Translation: 1968b. *Political Power and Social Classes.* London: New Left Books.)

Quinney, Richard. 1970. *The Social Reality of Crime.* Boston: Little, Brown.

Quinney, Richard. 1973. "Crime Control in Capitalist Society: A Critical Philosophy of Legal Order." *Issues in Criminology* 8:75–95.

Rawls, John. 1972. *A Theory of Justice.* Oxford: Clarendon Press.

Rex, John. 1961. *Key Problems in Sociological Theory.* London: Routledge.

Rex, John. 1981. *Social Conflict: A Conceptual and Theoretical Analysis.* London: Longman.

Robertson, Roland. 1978. *Meaning and Change: Explorations in the Cultural Sociology of Modern Societies.* New York: Oxford University Press.

Robertson, Roland. 1980. "Aspects of Identity and Authority in Sociological Theory." In R. Robertson and B. Holzner (Eds.), *Identity and Authority,* pp. 218–65. Oxford: Blackwell.

Robertson, Roland. 1990. "Mapping the Global Condition: Globalization as the Central Concept." *Theory, Culture and Society* 7:15–30.

Rossi, Ino (Ed.). 1982. *Structural Sociology.* New York: Columbia University Press.

Rossi, Ino. 1983. *From the Sociology of Symbols to the Sociology of Signs: Toward a Dialectical Sociology.* New York: Columbia University Press.

Rousseau, Jean-Jacques. 1762/1964. *Du contrat social ou principes du droit politique.* In *OEuvres complètes.* Edited by B. Gagnebin and M. Raymond. Paris: Gallimard. (Translation: 1973. *The Social Contract and Discourses.* Translation and introduction by G.D.H. Cole. London: Dent.)

Sartre, Jean Paul. 1943. *L'être et le néant.* Paris: Gallimard. (Translation: 1966. *Being and Nothingness. An Essay on Phenomenological Ontology.* Edited by Hazel F. Barnes. New York: Pocket Books.)

Saussure, Ferdinand de. 1916. *Cours de linguistique générale.* Edited by Charles Bally and Charles-Albert Sechehaye. Lausanne-Paris: Payot. (Translation: 1966. *Course in General Linguistics.* New York: McGraw-Hill.)

Schur, Edwin M. 1980. *The Politics of Deviance: Stigma Contests and the Uses of Power.* Englewood Cliffs, N.J.: Prentice Hall.

Simmel, Georg. 1908. *Soziologie. Untersuchungen über die Formen der Vergesellschaftung.* Berlin: Duncker & Humblot.

Simmel, Georg. 1914/1926. *Der Konflikt der modernen Kultur.* Berlin: Duncker & Humblot. (Translation: 1968. *The Conflict of Modern Culture.* New York: Teacher College Press.)

Simon, Herbert. 1957. *Administrative Behavior.* New York: Free Press.

Skocpol, Theda. 1979. *Social Revolutions.* New York: Cambridge University Press.

Smith, Adam. 1776/1937. *The Wealth of Nations.* New York: Modern Library.

Stichweh, Rudolf. 1982. *Ausdifferenzierung der Wissenschaft—eine Analyse am deutschen Beispiel.* Bielefeld: Kleine.

Stichweh, Rudolf. 1984. *Zur Entstehung des modernen Systems wissenschaftlicher Disziplinen: Physik in Deutschland 1740–1890.* Frankfurt am Main: Suhrkamp.

Stichweh, Rudolf. 1988. "Technologie, Naturwissenschaft und die Strukturen wissenschaftlicher Gemeinschaften." *Kölner Zeitschrift für Soziologie und Sozialpsychologie* 40:684–705.

Strauss, Anselm. 1959. *Mirrors and Masks: The Search for Identity.* Glencoe, Ill.: Sociology Press.

Strauss, Anselm. 1978. *Negotiations: Varieties, Contexts, Processes and Social Order.* San Francisco: Jossey-Bass.

Strauss, Anselm, et al. 1963. "The Hospital and Its Negotiated Order." In E. Freidson (Ed.), *The Hospital in Modern Society,* pp. 147–69. New York: Free Press.

Strauss, Anselm, et al. 1964. *Psychiatric Ideologies and Institutions.* New York: Free Press.

Sykes, Gresham M., and David Matza. 1957. "Techniques of Neutralization: A Theory of Delinquency." *American Sociological Review* 22:664–670.

Tar, Zoltan. 1977. *The Frankfurt School: The Critical Theories of Max Horkheimer and Theodor W. Adorno.* London: Routledge.

Teubner, Gunther. 1987. "Hyperzyklus in Recht und Organisation. Zum Verhältnis von Selbstbeobachtung, Selbstkonstitution und Autopoiese." In Hans Haferkamp and Michael Schmid (Eds.), *Sinn, Kommunikation und soziale Differenzierung. Beiträge zu Luhmanns Theorie sozialer Systeme,* pp. 89–128. Frankfurt am Main: Suhrkamp.

Teubner, Gunther. 1988. *Autopoietic Law: A New Approach to Law and Society.* Berlin: De Gruyter.

Teubner, Gunther. 1989. *Das Recht als autopoietisches System.* Frankfurt am Main: Suhrkamp.

Touraine, Alain. 1965. *Sociologie de l'action.* Paris: Editions du Seuil.

Touraine, Alain. 1969. *La société post-industrielle.* Paris: Denoël. (Translation: 1974a. *The Post-Industrial Society. Tomorrow's Social History: Classes, Conflicts and Culture in the Programmed Society.* London: Wildwood House.)

Touraine, Alain. 1973. *Production de la société.* Paris: Editions du Seuil. (Translation: 1977. *The Self-Production of Society.* Chicago: University of Chicago Press.)

Touraine, Alain. 1974b. *Pour la sociologie.* Paris: Editions du Seuil.

Touraine, Alain. 1978. *La voix et le regard.* Paris: Editions du Seuil. (Translation: 1981. *The Voice and the Eye: An Analysis of Social Movements.* Cambridge: Cambridge University Press.)

Touraine, Alain. 1980. *La prophétie anti-nucléaire.* Paris: Editions du Seuil.

Wallerstein, Immanuel. 1974. *The Modern World System.* Vol. 1: *Capitalist Agriculture and the Origins of the European World-Economy in the Sixteenth Century.* New York: Academic Press.

Wallerstein, Immanuel. 1979. *The Capitalist World Economy.* Cambridge/New York: Cambridge University Press.

Wallerstein, Immanuel. 1980. *The Modern World System.* Vol. 2: *Mercantilism and the Consolidation of the European World-Economy 1600–1950.* New York: Academic Press.

Wallerstein, Immanuel. 1983. *Historical Capitalism.* London: Verso.

Wallerstein, Immanuel. 1984. *The Politics of the World Economy.* Cambridge: Cambridge University Press.

Wallerstein, Immanuel. 1989. *The Modern World System.* Vol. 3: *The Second Era of Great Expansion of the Capitalist World Economy, 1730–1840s.* New York: Cambridge University Press.

Wallerstein, Immanuel. 1990a. "Culture as the Ideological Battleground of the Modern World System." *Theory, Culture and Society* 7:31–55.

Wallerstein, Immanuel. 1990b. "Culture Is the World-System: A Reply to Boyne." *Theory, Culture and Society* 7:63–65.

Weber, Max. 1920–1921a/1972a. *Gesammelte Aufsätze zur Religionssoziologie.* Vol. 1. Tübingen: Mohr Siebeck. (Translation in two parts: 1976. *The Protestant Ethic and the Spirit of Capitalism.* Translated by Talcott Parsons. New York: Scribner's; 1964. *The Religion of China. Confucianism and Taoism.* Translated and edited by H.H. Gerth and D. Martindale. New York: Free Press.)

Weber, Max. 1920–1921b/1972b. *Gesammelte Aufsätze zur Religionssoziologie.* Vol. 2. Tübingen: Mohr Siebeck. (Translation: 1967. *The Religion of India: The Sociology of Hinduism and Buddhism.* Translated and edited by H.H. Gerth and D. Martindale, New York: Free Press.)

Weber, Max. 1920–1921c/1971a. *Gesammelte Aufsätze zur Religionssoziologie.* Vol. 3. Tübingen: Mohr Siebeck. (Translation: 1952. *Ancient Judaism.* Translated and edited by H.H. Gerth and D. Martindale. New York: Free Press.)

Weber, Max. 1921/1971b. *Gesammelte Politische Schriften.* Tübingen: Mohr Siebeck. (Partly translated: 1968. *Economy and Society.* 3 vols. Edited by G. Roth and C. Wittich. New York: Bedminster Press; 1974. *From Max Weber: Essays in Sociology.* Translated and edited by H.H. Gerth and C.W. Mills. New York: Oxford University Press.)

Weber, Max. 1922/1972c. *Wirtschaft und Gesellschaft.* Tübingen: Mohr Siebeck. (Translation: 1968. *Economy and Society.* 3 vols. Edited by G. Roth and C. Wittich. New York: Bedminster Press.)

Wellman, Barry. 1983. "Network Analysis: Some Basic Principles." *Sociological Theory* 1:155–200.

Wellmer, Albrecht. 1971. *Critical Theory of Society.* New York: Seabury.

Willer, David, and Bo Anderson. 1981. *Networks, Exchange and Coercion: The Elementary Theory and Its Applications.* New York: Elsevier.

Willis, Paul. 1977. *Learning to Labour.* Farnborough: Sascon House.

Willke, Helmut. 1982. *Systemtheorie: Eine Einführung in die Grundprobleme.* Stuttgart: UTB. Gustav Fischer.

Willke, Helmut. 1983. *Entzauberung des Staates. Überlegungen zu einer sozietalen Steuerungstheorie.* Königstein/Taunus: Athenäum.

Willke, Helmut. 1989. *Systemtheorie entwickelter Gesellschaften: Dynamik und Distanz moderner gesellschaftlicher Selbstorganisation.* Weinheim: Juventa.

Wippler, Reinhard, and Siegwart Lindenberg. 1987. "Collective Phenomena and Rational Choice." In J.C. Alexander, B. Giesen, R. Münch and N.J. Smelser (Eds.), *The Micro-Macro Link,* pp. 135–52. Berkeley and Los Angeles: University of California Press.

Wittgenstein, Ludwig. 1953. *Philosophical Investigations.* Oxford: Basil Blackwell.

Abrams, Philip, 175
Adorno, Theodor W., 256, 263–64
Albert, Hans, 14
Alexander, Jeffrey C., 67
Althusser, Louis, 8–9
Anderson, Bo, 78
Anderson, Perry, 199, 307–8, 313, 316
Archer, Margaret S., 196
Axelrod, Robert, 79

Bacharach, Samuel B., x, 123–38, 311, 314, 316, 319–20, 322
Baecker, Dirk, 305
Balibar, Etienne, 8
Baran, Paul A., 93
Barthes, Roland, 9
Baudrillard, Jean, x, 9, 11–12
Bauman, Zygmunt, 11
Beck, Ulrich, 269
Becker, Gary S., 77
Becker, Howard S., x, 209–11, 217, 313–14, 316, 319–22
Benjamin, Walter, 263
Benoist, Jean-Marie, 10
Bentham, Jeremy, 28, 55, 307–8, 313, 316

Benton, Ted, 8
Berger, Johannes, 11
Berger, Joseph, 80
Berger, Peter L., 311, 314–16, 318, 321–22
Bergson, Henri, 11, 309–10, 316
Bhaskar, Roy, 190
Blalock, Hubert, 67
Blau, Peter M., 10, 37, 313–16, 318–19, 322
Bloomfield, Morton W., 8
Blumer, Herbert, 219, 313–16, 318, 321–22
Bottomore, Tom, 256
Boudon, Raymond, 80
Bourdieu, Pierre, x, 15, 139–41, 143–47, 150–51, 153–55, 157, 309–10, 316, 319–20, 322
Boyne, Roy, 106
Buchanan, James M., 55, 77–78, 313–14, 316, 319–20, 322
Bucher, Rue, 222–23
Burt, Ronald S., 78–79

Chomsky, Noam, 7–8
Cicourel, Aaron V., 67
Clavel, Maurice, 10

341

Subject Index

Abortion conflict, 217
Abstraction, analytical, 198–99
Accumulation, 160
Achievement, 151, 156
Action
  communicative, 240, 241, 243,
    246, 268–69
  corporate, 46
  economically calculated, 246
  enabling resources for, 190
  goal oriented, 246
  pedagogic, 143
  strategic, 240, 242–43, 246, 248
  strategic and communicative, 241
  structures of, 41
  systems of, 48
  unacknowledged conditions and
    unintended consequences of,
    181
Action and crisis, 162
Actions, interdependence of, 203
Actor, 39
Actors, corporate, 46, 49–50
  responsibility of, 49
Affect control, 200, 202, 204
Agency, 176–77, 180–81, 183, 191, 194
  and knowledgeability, 177

Agent, 176–77, 181, 196
  knowledge of, 182
Agreement, 136–38
Alienation, 259, 262, 309
  theory of, 11
Alternative outcome, 128
  sources of, 127
Alternatives, 126, 130–32
Anthropological need for order, 277
Argument, 188
Art, 264
Association, 186
Author, 21
Authoritarian control, 53
Authoritarian rule, 197
Authoritarianism, 55
Authority, 54, 64, 76, 112
Authority relationships, 40
Authority systems, 42
Autonomy, 204, 278
Autopoiesis, 280, 296
Autopoietic system, 280, 290, 292

Bargaining, 111, 114, 123–26, 131,
  134, 137
  peaceful, 138
  theory of, 137

Marxism, 8, 82, 92, 176
Marxist conflict theory, 215
Marxist structuralism, 9, 11
Marxist theory, 81, 93, 194, 263, 268
Materialism, 309
Matthew principle, 149
Me, 196
Meaning, 9, 65, 113–14, 121, 239–40,
    258, 271, 281–82, 284, 309
  loss of, 261, 266
Meaning and history, 260
Meaning constructions, 248
Mental illness, 216
Micro-macro link, 38, 67
Middle class, 142
Mistrust, 59, 280–81
Modernity, 12–14, 16, 271
  theory of, 265
Modern society, 15–16, 49, 200, 267,
    291, 300, 302–3
Money, 171, 187–88, 265
Monopolies, 85, 90
Moral autonomy, 204–5
Moral consciousness, 237
Moral development, 231–32, 236
Moral discourse, 266–69
Moral judgment, 231–32
Moral learning, 205
Moral responsibility, 204
Moral universalism, 205
Morality, 261
  conventional, 234
  postconventional, 234
  preconventional, 232
Mythologies, 5

Nation states, 172
Nature
  mastering of, 260
  state of, 112
Negotiation, 70, 111, 114–17, 120,
    122, 171, 187, 219–23, 225,
    228–29, 239
  conversational, 117
Negotiation context, 222–23, 225–26
Negotiation paradigm, 228
Negotiation ritual, 111

Network
  American, 311
  British, 307
  French, 309
  German, 309
  international, 313
  periodical universal, 315
  timeless universal, 319
Network analysis, 77–79
Network of sociological theory, 307,
    321
Networks, national, 307
Nihilism, 309
Normative arguments, 135
Norms, 43–45, 61–62, 68–69, 276

Objectification (Verdinglichung),
    263–64
Objectivism, 175–76, 196
Oligopolies, 85, 90
Openness through closedness, 292
Options, 129–30
Order, 77, 112, 275–77, 299–300
  accidental, 300
  negotiated, 219–21, 228
  negotiation of, 220
  problem of, 276, 298, 300
  social, 71, 171, 219–20, 222, 225,
    228–29, 254, 275, 299
  traditional, 307
Order and change, 162
Order from noise, 276, 298–99
Organicism, 307
Organization, 290
Organizational level, 291

Paradox, 309
Parole, 3–4
Penal system, 24
Peripheralization, 95
Physical force, 186, 200
  monopolization of, 202
Pluralism, 14–15
Pluralist society, 16
Pluralistic society, 14
Political domination, 97
Political market, 76